GENERALS IN BLUE AND GRAY

★

Generals in Blue and Gray

VOLUME I

LINCOLN'S GENERALS

_____

Wilmer L. Jones

Westport, Connecticut
London

Library of Congress Cataloging-in-Publication Data

Jones, Wilmer L., 1931–
    Generals in Blue and Gray/Wilmer L. Jones.
        p. cm.
    Includes bibliographical references and index.
    Contents: v. 1. Lincoln's generals—v. 2. Davis's generals.
    ISBN 0-275-98322-6 (set: alk. paper)—ISBN 0-275-98323-4 (v. 1)—
ISBN 0-275-98324-2 (v. 2)
    1. Generals—United States—Biography. 2. Generals—Confederate States of
America—Biography. 3. United States. Army—Biography. 4. Confederate
States of America. Army—Biography. 5. United States—History—Civil War,
1861–1865—Campaigns. 6. Lincoln, Abraham, 1809–1865—Military
leadership. 7. Davis, Jefferson, 1808–1889—Military leadership.
8. Strategy—Case studies. 9. Command of troops—Case studies. I. Title.
E467.J795 2004
973.7'3'092—dc22
  [B]   2004052153

British Library Cataloguing in Publication Data is available.

Library of Congress Catalog Card Number: 2004052153

ISBN: 0-275-98322-6 (set)
     0-275-98323-4 (vol. I)
     0-275-98324-2 (vol. II)

First published in 2004

Praeger Publishers, 88 Post Road West, Westport, CT 06881
An imprint of Greenwood Publishing Group, Inc.
www.praeger.com

Printed in the United States of America

The paper used in this book complies with the
Permanent Paper Standard issued by the National
Information Standards Organization (Z39.48-1984).

10 9 8 7 6 5 4 3 2 1

To My Loving Family

Carol, Scott, Jolanta, Christa,
J.P., Ashleigh, Thomas, and Jordan

"You are green, it is true; but they are green, also;
    you are all green alike."

LINCOLN to General McDowell before the Battle of Manassas

"McClellan has the army with him."

LINCOLN after General Pope's defeat at the Second Battle of Manassas

"I said I would remove him if he let Lee's army get away from him,
    and I must do so. He has got the 'slows.'"

LINCOLN after removing McClellan from command

"He was the first man he had found who was willing to relieve him
    of a particle of responsibility."

LINCOLN of General Burnside after his defeat at Fredericksburg

"My God, my God, what will the country say! What will the country say!"

LINCOLN after General Hooker's defeat at Chancellorsville

"I can't spare this man; he fights."

LINCOLN of General Grant after the failure of his first campaign against Vicksburg

"Our army held the war in the hollow of their hand and would not close it."

LINCOLN after General Meade failed to follow-up his victory at Gettysburg

"Many, many thanks for your Christmas gift, the capture of Savannah."

LINCOLN in a letter to General Sherman after the capture of Savannah

Contents

Introduction

The famous Civil War historian, James M. McPherson, stated: "America prepares for war after the war has begun." Such was the case during the American Civil War. This preparation proved to be a monumental task for the two men destined to lead their countries during the war. One, Abraham Lincoln, a key character in this book, had no prior military service and had been elected without a majority of the popular vote. He, at least, had a government structure and remnants of an army in place. The other, Jefferson Davis, was a graduate of West Point and had served during the Mexican War and as secretary of war under the Pierce administration. Davis had to start from scratch to build both a governmental structure and an army.

Volume I: Lincoln's Generals is not a military history of the Civil War or a detailed description of the battles themselves. It is about Abraham Lincoln's actions as commander-in-chief and the key Union generals who served under him. To this end, the book contains twenty-one biographies of the Union generals responsible for carrying out Lincoln's strategies. Obviously, the better-known generals such as Ulysses S. Grant, William T. Sherman, George B. McClellan, and Joseph Hooker appear in the book, but other, less well-known figures such as John A. McClernand, George H. Thomas, Daniel E. Sickles, and Don Carlos Buell are included as well.

The format for *Volume I: Lincoln's Generals* is unique. This work is not a history book in the traditional sense; rather, it tells the story of the Civil War through the actions of the major participants. Though I have not neglected important events that occurred during the war, battles are discussed only to the extent necessary to understand the main course of events. In telling the story, each actor comes to life in incisive sketches. The main emphasis in each portrait is on the general's character, ability to command, personality, and family background, and on how these factors influenced his actions. The role politics, friendships, and competence played in their performance is also examined. Since the generals studied in this book served in various theaters of the war, insight can be gained on the entire war.

Each of the biographies stands on its own and can be read individually and in any order. They provide an excellent introduction to the lives of these important men. The extensive bibliography in the back of the book contains additional reading resources for those interested.

The Civil War was a long and deadly war. It lasted four years and resulted in over a million casualties. It was fought primarily to reunite the Union, secondarily to free the slaves. Repercussions from the war are still being felt today. Many heroic persons participated in this war; this book hopes to introduce a few of them to the reader.

Volume I: Lincoln's Generals is the result of my forty-five years of interest in the Civil War. It was written with the general reader and Civil War buff in mind and should appeal to a broad and general readership.

I would like to thank my two good friends, Shirley and Don Johnson, who read my manuscript and offered both encouragement and valuable suggestions and comments.

I hope you enjoy reading this book as much as I enjoyed writing it.

1　The Making of a President

On July 4, 1863, having lost a third of his men at Gettysburg, Lee's Army of Northern Virginia faced the possibility of disaster. In Washington, Abraham Lincoln was aware of this vulnerability; in his mind, he pictured the end of Lee's army and of the Confederacy. General Meade's Army of the Potomac held the outcome of the war "in the hollow of their hands."[1]

Lincoln spent ten days agonizing over what Meade would do. Nothing Lincoln could say or do could make Meade move. Lee was allowed to escape. Eleven days after Gettysburg, the president felt defeated—defeated by his own generals. Although he had been disappointed in the past, he was not prepared for this setback. "We had them within our grasp. We had only to stretch forth our hands and they were ours," he said. The tears came, and although they helped, the war would continue; many more would die. Lincoln, however, was resolute in his mission.[2]

When the Civil War began, the United States had almost no army, few good weapons, and an officer corps with little war experience. The general-in-chief of the army was the seventy-five-year-old veteran of two wars, Winfield Scott. Scott was physically incapable of commanding an army in the field, and his strategic plan for subduing the South did not meet with Lincoln's approval. As a result, the conduct of the war became the responsibility of the newly elected president, Abraham Lincoln. As commander-in-chief of all the armed forces of the nation, this burden would be his.[3]

When Lincoln took office as the sixteenth president of the United States, he came to the position with a decided lack of military experience. Compared to his counterpart in the South, Jefferson Davis, Lincoln was an amateur. Davis was a West Point graduate, a hero of the Mexican War, and a former secretary of war. The limited military experience Lincoln did have came during the 1832 Black Hawk War on the western frontier. Lincoln was almost comically unprepared for the task he faced.[4]

With no knowledge of the theory of war or technical training, Lincoln faced overwhelming odds. But meeting a challenge was not new for him. All his life he had overcome the odds, eventually rising to the highest position in America, president of the United States. Born in a log cabin in Kentucky on February 12, 1809, Abraham Lincoln was the second child of Thomas and Nancy Hanks Lincoln. The Lincolns struggled to survive in a portion of Kentucky that is referred to as Appalachia. When he was a candidate for president of the United States, Lincoln was asked about his childhood years. His answer was short: "Why, it is a great piece of folly to attempt to make anything of my early life. It can be condensed into a single sentence— The short and simple annals of the poor." It was this rough road that Lincoln traveled to greatness as president.[5]

As a youth, Lincoln did not exhibit any unusual characteristics. He enjoyed playing, hunting, and fishing. At the age of seven, his family moved to Indiana, a state free from slavery. Thomas was very much opposed to slavery for both religious and economic reasons. Small farmers like Thomas Lincoln had difficulty competing with farmers utilizing slave labor. Young Abraham shared his parents' views on slavery, remarking in 1864, "I cannot remember when I did not so think, and feel."[6]

At their new home, Abraham helped his father plant and harvest his crops. The rustic area lacked medical care, and the people were ravaged by disease. When Nancy fell ill, little could be done, and she died. Lincoln would later express his love for his mother, referring to her as "angel mother." Within a year of Nancy's death, Thomas Lincoln remarried, this time to Sarah Bush Johnston, a widow with three children. The arrival of Sarah marked a turning point in young Lincoln's life.[7]

Sarah brought orderliness to the Lincoln family, and within weeks she had taken Abraham and his sister under her wing. She loved the Lincoln children as if they were her own. Young Lincoln learned to love his stepmother just as much in return. "Abe was the best boy I ever saw or expect to see," she said later.[8] Young Lincoln enjoyed a happy childhood, with his stepmother providing the love he needed. Even though the family of seven was poor and had to live in a single room in a crude log cabin, their affection brought the family together. Lincoln received very little formal education, attending school less than one year; but Abe was an avid reader, and on his own he devoured Shakespeare, books on history, and any book he could borrow from neighbors.[9]

As much as Lincoln loved his stepmother, the opposite was true of his father. Young Lincoln resented that his father favored his stepbrother over him. The source of the difficulty between the two seemed to be Lincoln's dislike for farmwork. Lincoln once told his mother "that his father had taught him to work but never learned him to love it." Thomas Lincoln often scolded and whipped his son for reading instead of doing his chores. He was opposed to his son's obsession with learning and even went so far as to hide his books to discourage him from reading. Years later, when Lincoln had left home, Thomas Lincoln told a friend, "I suppose that Abe is still fooling himself with education. I tried to stop it, but he got that fool idea in his head, and it can't be got out. Now I hain't got no education, but I got along far better than if I had."[10]

In 1851, when Lincoln learned that his father was dying, he refused to go home to see him despite his father's request that he have the chance to say farewell. He told his stepbrother to tell his father "that if we could meet now, it is doubtful whether it would not be more painful than pleasant." When his father died shortly thereafter, Lincoln did not attend his funeral, nor did he mark his gravesite with a stone.[11]

Although Lincoln enjoyed reading and intellectual pursuits, there was another side to him. During the few months each year that he attended school, he entertained both his teacher and students with his humor and amusing stories. Because he was so much taller and stronger than his boyhood friends, he starred in all the athletic activities at school and at other community affairs. It was obvious to everyone who knew him that he had the makings of a leader.[12]

By the time Lincoln was seventeen, he had grown to his full height of six feet, four inches, weighing only 162 pounds but possessing great strength. He went to barn raisings and helped his neighbors build houses and clear fields, achieving the reputation for being the best rail-splitter in the country. Young Lincoln became well known and liked in the community.

In 1831, Lincoln left home and moved to New Salem, Illinois, where he took a job running a general store. Here he developed a reputation for spinning yarns and telling stories. "His countenance would brighten up, his eyes would sparkle, all terminating in an unrestrained laugh in which every one present, willing or unwilling, were compelled to take part," said a friend.[13]

Lincoln made quite an impression on the people of Salem. His physical strength was remarkable; it was said that he could lift a large barrel weighing several hundred pounds to eye level. More importantly, however, his intellectual curiosity left a lasting impression. The people found Lincoln anxious to learn all that he could. When a man told him that he needed a grammar book for his studies, he walked six miles to borrow one. The townspeople were also in awe of his knowledge of the Bible and his ability to quote from it, although no one ever remembered seeing him in church.[14]

Lincoln's friends convinced him to run for a seat in the Illinois state assembly. He accepted the challenge, promising, if elected, to work for the common man. Although he lost the election, he was pleased to have won 277 of the 300 votes cast in New Salem. It was the only time he would ever be beaten on a direct vote of the people.[15]

The year 1832 was also the year of the Black Hawk War. The local militia elected Lincoln as their captain; but the duration of war was short, and he served only eighty days. Lincoln jokingly said to someone who had served in the war that "if he saw any live, fighting Indians, it was more than I did."[16]

Shortly after returning from the Black Hawk War, Lincoln began his law studies. Unable to afford to study law at a college, he borrowed dozens of books on the law and read them over and over again, hoping to make himself a lawyer. In the process, he made friends with every lawyer he could. Among those was John Stuart of Springfield. With Stuart's help and tutelage, Lincoln ran for the state legislature again. This time he was successful, receiving 1,376 votes (the second-highest total), and was one of the four elected.[17]

Lincoln quickly learned the art of persuasion and the skill of winning votes, growing into an effective and popular legislator. To succeed in politics, Lincoln involved himself in every aspect of the political process. He built large networks of politicians whom he helped and in turn could call on for help later. He learned to get along with different kinds of people, many of whom did not share his view. Lincoln was flexible enough to adopt a persona to accept different opinions. It was this part of his personality that was his strongest asset when he was president.[18]

While serving in the legislature, Lincoln worked in the office of John Stuart. Lincoln was a good lawyer; his self-taught experience and hard work turned out to be just as valuable as if he had attended college. In 1844, Lincoln set up his own law office with William Herndon, who remained his partner until Lincoln left Springfield for Washington to become president.[19]

In 1839, Lincoln met Mary Todd, the twenty-two-year-old daughter of a prosperous merchant and banker of Lexington, Kentucky. Mary had been reared in luxury, attended by slaves, and educated in private schools. She was both pretty and an excellent conversationalist. Lincoln was immediately attracted to her, charmed by her quick wit and cultured manner. When Lincoln began to give her his attention, Mary began to think of him as a future husband. Despite his lack of social graces, his considerate manner more than compensated. They shared many things in common, including their political views and love of poetry. She had often said jokingly that she intended to marry a man who some day would become president of the United States.[20]

In December 1840, Lincoln and Mary Todd became engaged, but after making the commitment, he began to have second thoughts. He worried about his ability to support a wife, and he felt he could not provide Mary with the lifestyle to which she had grown accustomed. As a result of his apprehension about marriage, he decided to break off the engagement.[21]

Instead of feeling relieved, Lincoln was devastated by what he had done. He became severely depressed, and friends feared he might commit suicide. He became very critical of himself for what he had done to Mary. "My own ability to keep my resolve when they are made," he told a friend, "was once the source of pride, as the only, or at least the chief, gem of my character." Now Lincoln felt he had lost his steadfastness. Because he had made Mary unhappy, he believed it was unfair for him to be happy. "I am now the most miserable man living," he told Stuart. Rumors spread that Lincoln's depression was caused because Mary Todd had broken the engagement.[22]

When Lincoln learned that his friend Joshua Speed, who had also been reluctant about marriage, had married and was happy, he changed his mind and once more considered marrying Mary Todd. After their breakup, the two had tried to avoid each other, until a friend of Lincoln decided to intervene, inviting both to a social affair at his home. The meeting was a success, and soon the two began seeing each other again. Lincoln renewed his offer of marriage, and Mary accepted. On November 4, 1842, the two were married.[23]

The Lincolns began married life in the Globe Tavern, a two-story structure in Springfield. For $4 a week, they occupied an eight-by-fourteen-foot room and took their meals in a common dining room. Now Lincoln began working harder than ever, hoping to earn enough money to buy a house.[24] In 1843, Mary gave birth to their first son, Robert. Three years later, a second son, Edward, was born, but he died at the age of four. Both Lincoln and Mary were distraught at their loss; however, a third son, Willie, was born in 1850, helping to relieve their grief. Tad, their last child was born in 1853.[25]

Although the Lincolns loved each other, their marriage was anything but smooth. Mary was high strung and had a fiery temper. Nothing in Springfield seemed to please her. She was often crude and abusive and had difficulty getting along with Lincoln's friends and his partner, William Herndon. She was just as tempestuous at home, taking advantage of Lincoln's casual and easy-going personality to get her way with him.

Despite her disposition, Lincoln loved his wife; his letters and statements about her left no doubt as to his feelings. "My wife is as handsome as when she was a girl," he said, "and I, a poor nobody, then fell in love with her and what is more, I have never fallen out." Their married life had no more problems than that of other married couples. Mrs. Lincoln was jealous of other women who spoke to her husband and often had words with him when she caught him talking to other women. Although Mary had many faults, she was always a good mother and a faithful and loving wife.[26]

Lincoln won election to the Illinois state legislature four times, gaining friends and experience. In 1846, he ran for Congress. Lincoln's opponent was Peter Cartwright. Cartwright accused Lincoln of being irreverent because he did not belong to any church. Lincoln indicated that religion was personal and not political, stating: "When any church will inscribe over its altar, as its sole qualification for membership, the Savior's statement . . . 'Thou shalt love the Lord thy God with all thy heart, and with all thy soul, and thy neighbor as thy self,' that church will I join with all my heart and all my soul."[27]

The campaign between Cartwright and Lincoln was hard fought. There is a story that during the campaign, Lincoln attended a religious meeting conducted by Cartwright. After his sermon, Cartwright asked "all those who desire to lead a new life, to give their hearts to God, and to go to heaven" to stand. Some in the group stood. Then he asked all those who did not want to go to hell to stand. This time all the rest of the congregation stood, except for Lincoln. Cartwright seized the opportunity to attack his opponent. "May I inquire of you, Mr. Lincoln, where you are going?" Lincoln's reply was typical of his sense of humor: "If it is all the same to you—I am going to Congress."[28] On election day, Lincoln received 6,340 votes to Cartwright's 4,829. Lincoln was ready to make his first appearance in Washington.[29]

When Lincoln took his place in Congress in 1847, the Mexican War was in progress. The Southern wing of President Polk's Democratic Party had led the fight to annex and admit Texas as a slave state. Lincoln was opposed to the extension of slavery, as were many Northern abolitionists. He did not wait long to express his views on America's involvement in the war. Just two weeks after taking his seat in Congress, Lincoln spoke out against America's intervention on the behalf of Texas and accused the president of being the aggressor.[30]

The House took no action on Lincoln's resolutions, but there was immediate backlash from his constituents who accused him of not supporting the troops in Mexico and of giving aid and comfort to the enemy. Lincoln's peace position and his speeches against the war came back to haunt him and his party. Two years later, he would pay the price. Not only did he not get his party's nomination to run for a second term, but the party's candidate was badly defeated.[31]

From 1849 until 1854, Lincoln was not involved in politics. He spent these five years in personal growth and improvement, broadening his education by studying astronomy and mathematics, including Euclidian geometry.[32]

Lincoln also rode the Eighth Circuit and established himself as a good lawyer. "His knowledge of the law was acquired almost entirely by his own unaided study and by the practice of his profession," said one of his colleagues. Lincoln not only established himself as a competent lawyer but as a fair one. When he tried a case, he never intentionally misrepresented a witness's testimony or an opponent's argument.

Although generally successful in his personal and professional life, Lincoln suffered from bouts of melancholy and depression throughout his life. He deeply mourned the death of his son Edward in 1850 and the death of his beloved Willie in 1862. During the war, as casualties mounted, his depression deepened. Lincoln's depression, however, was not just limited to encounters with death or personal loss.[33]

In his earlier years, Lincoln attempted to escape the world of his parents and rise into the genteel middle class. He obtained his sense of worth from the acceptance and approval of others. In his first political platform written in 1832, he said, "I have no other [ambition] so great as that of being truly esteemed by my fellow men."[34] When Lincoln was defeated at the polls or failed to realize his ambitions and ideals, he was devastated. Although he would make light of a political defeat to cover his true feelings, he often felt rejected and depressed.[35]

Lincoln's psychological problems persisted during the war, especially during the early months as the Union army suffered a series of military defeats. Many of the best generals had joined the Confederacy, and his administration was young and its relationship with Congress uncertain. Orville Browning, one of Lincoln's old friends, noted his condition during a conversation with him during the summer of 1861: "Lincoln seemed very melancholy, admitted he was so, but said he knew of no special cause for it."[36]

Despite Lincoln's bout with depression, he was able to cope with his problem. Elton Trueblood, the theologian, noted that "Lincoln was the kind of mind which did not reach its true magnitude except in experience of sorrow and strain." Humor became a vehicle for his escape from depression.

Lincoln's use of anecdotes and humor in his speeches became his hallmark. For some, humor meant sarcasm or making someone else the butt of the joke, but not so for Lincoln. Part of the appeal of his humor was the self-deprecating nature of many of his jokes—often about his own appearance. Some found this trait offensive, especially early in his career. On November 23, 1839, the *Springfield Register* lectured Lincoln for his "assumed clownishness" and warned him that "this game of Buffoonery" would convince no one. By 1854, however, the *Register* had changed its opinion, stating that the form of humor in his speeches "will be understood by all who know him." He joked with legal clients and often repeated a story several times in the course of one day. As president, Lincoln used anecdotes to ward off angry citizens and politicians who were demanding action on specific issues.[37]

Humor seemed to vitalize Lincoln and keep his depression under control. In a way it served as a form of therapy for him, put his clients at ease, helped keep his political opponents in their places, won him friends, and eased his position as president. Humor never completely eliminated his depression, but it helped ease his radical mood changes and gave him confidence.[38]

Lincoln might have quit politics altogether had it not been for the "Peculiar Institution"—slavery. Until the Mexican War, the discussion of slavery had not been intense. The Mexican peace treaty, however, triggered a debate about the extension of slavery into the territories.

The issue of slavery and its expansion westward had been discussed in America for many years. As early as 1820, the Missouri Compromise admitted Missouri as a slave state and Maine as a free state, as well as banned slavery north of Missouri's southern boundary. After the Mexican War, the Compromise of 1850 allowed California to enter the Union as a free state in return for passage of the strong Fugitive Slave Law, which eased the pursuit of runaway slaves into free states. In 1854, Congress passed the Kansas–Nebraska Act, which favored "popular sovereignty" and allowed settlers to decide whether the territory would become a free or slave state. The act turned Kansas into a battleground; as settlers moved into Kansas, rival gangs battled each other, burning opponents' farms and staging midnight raids. Federal troops eventually restored order, but only after the death of two hundred settlers.[39]

In 1856, Lincoln addressed an audience at Bloomington, Illinois, speaking out against the expansion of slavery. This speech was his strongest against slavery to this date. "This thing of slavery is more powerful than its supporters," Lincoln said. "It debauches even our greatest men. Monstrous crimes are committed in its name." William Herndon was so impressed by Lincoln's words that he said it was the greatest speech he'd ever heard Lincoln make.[40]

In 1857, the Supreme Court handed down a decision in the Dred Scott case. Dred Scott, a slave, sued to obtain his freedom, because he had lived with his master in free territory. The Supreme Court rejected his plea, ruling that he was not a citizen and, as a black man, "had no rights which a white man was bound to respect."[41]

Lincoln continued to speak out against the spread of slavery. These speeches were directed against Stephen Douglas who supported "popular sovereignty." Lincoln insisted that this policy would increase the growth of slavery. Lincoln soon became a leading antislavery spokesman in Illinois. In the process, he switched his political allegiance from the Whig Party to the newly formed Republican Party and again sought public office. This time he challenged Stephen Douglas, former judge of the Illinois Supreme Court, congressman, and the leader of the Democratic Party, for his Senate seat.[42]

In 1858, Lincoln won his party's nomination for the Senate. He launched his campaign with his famous speech: "A house divided against itself cannot endure, permanently half slave and half free."[43]

The campaign between Lincoln and Douglas captured the attention of the entire nation. In July, Lincoln challenged Douglas to a series of debates. Douglas accepted and agreed to seven three-hour debates. There was great interest in the debates, with 12,000 people attending the first and, a week later (and despite heavy rain), more than 15,000 showing up. People came from miles away to hear the candidates, and newspapers all over the country reported what the debaters had to say.[44]

What made the debates even more interesting was the contrast in physical appearance of the two candidates. The newspapers referred to them as the "Little Giant" and "Long Abe." Douglas was five-feet, four-inches tall with massive shoulders, a booming voice, and an aggressive, self-confident manner. Lincoln was a full foot taller than his opponent, and his gangly body seemed plain in his rumpled suit.[45]

The contrast between the two men regarding their views on slavery was just as striking. Douglas defended his doctrine of popular sovereignty, believing that each state had the right to decide the question for itself. He argued that the Constitution guaranteed equality to white citizens but not to blacks, since the Supreme Court had ruled that African Americans were not citizens. "I am opposed to Negro equality," Douglas said. "I believe this government was made by the white man for the white man to be administered by the white man."[46]

Popular sovereignty, Lincoln said, was just a pretense to allow for the spread of slavery. Slavery was not just a matter of states' rights, he believed, but was a moral issue that affected the whole country. Lincoln added, "There is no reason in the world why the Negro is not entitled to all the natural rights enumerated in the Declaration of Independence, the right to life, liberty, and the pursuit of happiness. I hold that he is as much entitled to these as the white man."[47]

The Lincoln–Douglas contest became more than a race for an Illinois Senate seat; it became the focus for the national debate over slavery. At that time, senators were selected by state legislatures and not by the direct vote of the people. The election in the legislature was extremely close; but when the votes were counted, the Republicans did not have the majority necessary to send Lincoln to the Senate, and Douglas retained his seat. Lincoln was deeply disappointed by the results of the election. "I feel like the boy who stumped his toe," he said. "I am too big to cry and too badly hurt to laugh."[48]

Lincoln lost his bid for the Senate, but in doing so he irreparably destroyed Douglas's chances of becoming president. In a series of letters, Lincoln called for the "fight to go on." From 1859 until the presidential election, Lincoln worked to strengthen the Republican Party and to stress his position on slavery. His speeches seldom failed to mention that slavery was wrong.[49]

Although Lincoln lost his bid for the Senate, the debates between the two candidates brought national attention to him. He continued to speak out against slavery and by 1860 was being mentioned as a possible candidate for president or as a running mate for the front-runner in the party, William Henry Seward of New York.[50]

In May, when the Republican Party held their national convention, three leading candidates sought the nomination. Lincoln's managers were able to undermine the leaders' support through secret deals, however, and had their candidate nominated on the third ballot.[51]

Meanwhile, the Democratic Party split: the Northern Democrats nominated Stephen Douglas, while the Southern Democrats held their own convention and nominated John C. Breckinridge of Kentucky. Old-line Whigs nominated John Bell of Tennessee.

Lincoln followed the custom of the time by not campaigning on his own behalf. Americans thought it was "undignified" for a presidential candidate to campaign for himself. Lincoln remained at home in Springfield, neither making speeches nor giving interviews to the press, while his supporters carried on a spirited campaign. At Republican rallies, Lincoln was hailed as "Honest Abe," a man of the people, the rail-splitter born in a log cabin now seeking the presidency.[52]

In the meantime, Douglas ignored custom and campaigned vigorously. He accused Lincoln of being an abolitionist and played upon racial prejudice and fear. He called Lincoln a "nigger worshiper" and charged that Senator Hannibal Hamlin of Maine, Lincoln's first running mate, was a mulatto.[53]

On November 6, 1860, Abraham Lincoln was elected president of the United States. He received almost 1.9 million votes to Douglas's 1.4 million, while a total of 2.8 million votes were cast for his three opponents. Lincoln won the election though receiving less than 40 percent of the votes cast. The North elected Lincoln; in the South, his name had not even appeared on the ballot. The results of the election clearly demonstrated the political divisions that existed throughout the country at the time. In December, three months before Lincoln took the oath of office, South Carolina, fearing what position Lincoln might take on slavery, seceded from the Union.[54] Clearly, Lincoln had his work cut out for him.

2 *Abraham Lincoln*

Commander-in-Chief

When Lincoln assumed the presidency on March 4, 1861, seven states had already seceded from the Union, and there were rumblings from Fort Sumter located in Charleston's harbor. Although cordial on the surface, Lincoln stood firm on his position on secession. In his inaugural address he had clearly stated that "the Union is perpetual" and older than the Constitution; "it was his duty to hold, occupy, and possess the property of the United States," he said. "No bloodshed or violence was called for. In your hands, . . . not in mine, is the momentous issue of civil war."[1]

Lincoln was very much aware that he was not well prepared to lead the Union in military affairs. To make up for this deficiency, he borrowed books on military strategy and read extensively, teaching himself military concept just as he had in his self-study of the law. By 1862, his orders and dispatches demonstrated how completely he had mastered the principles.[2]

In addition to his military deficiencies, Lincoln had no administrative experience. Lincoln had never held any position in industry and had not been a governor, nor had he worked in any government office. Even more important, Lincoln had not been trained to command as Jefferson Davis had at West Point. In addition, he was an outsider to Washington and had no close political connections. He would have to learn on the job in the midst of the country's greatest crisis.[3] Yet Lincoln was not completely lacking in skills that might serve the nation and his office. He was a skilled politician who knew how to organize political support. The undisputed leader of the Republican Party, he became its first president. During the war, when questioned or challenged about decisions he had made, his political skills proved helpful in finding a way to explain his methods.[4]

But there was more to Lincoln's skill than his ability to maneuver various factions—there was the nature of the man himself. He was secure in his own self-worth, allowing him to work with friends and foes alike. Lincoln had an ego—as his secretary John Hay noted: "It is absurd to call him a modest man. No great man was ever modest." Although Lincoln had a strong ego, he did not have to be right all the time. When he was not, he was willing to admit it.[5]

Few men were so willing to admit their own failures and limitations as was Lincoln. He often had concerns about his appearance, his early background, his lack of formal education, and his political prospects. When asked about his life, his reply was short: "There is little of me." During the war he apologized to General McClellan, who had insulted him publicly, and offered to hold his horse if McClellan would win a victory. Lincoln's frame of mind and temperament helped to bring unity to party divisions by stressing the benefits members had received rather than the wrongs they had suffered.[6]

Just after Lincoln's inauguration, Major Robert Anderson, commander of Fort Sumter, notified him that his provisions were running low and that he was in danger of having to surrender to the Confederates. Lincoln had promised the nation to hold onto all property belonging to the federal government. Now he faced a difficult situation. If he sent supplies to Fort Sumter, the seven seceded states might resist with arms. If he failed to supply the garrison, it would appear that he did not have the courage of his convictions.[7]

Lincoln did not have to wait long to make a decision. The governor of South Carolina notified him that they would "no longer suffer the presence" of Federal troops within their border and demanded the immediate surrender of Fort Sumter. When Major Robert Anderson, commander at Sumter, refused to evacuate the fort, the batteries of Charleston opened fire.

The firing on Fort Sumter and its eventual surrender eased Lincoln's indecision. He issued a proclamation declaring that the seven seceded states had broken the laws of the land, and that he was forced to call on the states for militia troops to suppress the insurrection. The challenge against the federal authority would not be tolerated.[8] "We must settle this question now," Lincoln said, "whether in a free government the minority has the right to break up the government whenever they choose. If we fail, it will go to prove the incapability of the people to govern themselves."[9]

At the outbreak of the war, Lincoln believed that the majority of Southerners were opposed to secession but had been enticed into the Confederacy by the passion of a few. Once the federal government showed they were firm in their position and determined to restore the Union, he believed, the Southern people would regain control of their states and end their rebellion. In his July 4, 1861, message to Congress, Lincoln questioned whether there was a majority of qualified voters in South Carolina in favor of secession. Initially Lincoln labeled the conflict not a war, but a "domestic insurrection" and only called for 75,000 militia to put it down.[10]

Abraham Lincoln, around 1846. This daguerreo-
type was probably the work of N. H. Shepard, one
of the first photographers in Springfield, Illinois.
COURTESY OF THE LIBRARY OF CONGRESS

But Lincoln had underestimated the South's resolve. Both sides were convinced of the rightness and justness of their cause. For the Southern-ers, the purpose of the fight seemed clear; they believed each state had the right to secede and the federal government had no authority to interfere. For the South, the North was the aggressor; they had no choice but to respond to their aggression, if they were to keep their freedom and con-tinue their way of life. Most individuals in the North entered the struggle, not for the eradication of slavery, but to defend the Union. They believed that a minority did not have the right to break up the government at will.[11]

As commander-in-chief, Lincoln had to choose generals to manage the war. At the outset of the war, he was plagued with requests for positions of command from politicians, their friends, and officers who had spent years in the regular army in junior ranks and now hoped to get their star. Requests also poured in from former officers who wanted to return to the army after having resigned earlier to take more lucrative civilian jobs.[12]

Lincoln issued numerous commissions at the start of the war, using military patronage to help unite the North and discordant groups. Lincoln was quick to realize the importance of having a coalition of Democrats and Republicans to support and participate in the war effort. Maintaining national unity was critical at this time. He awarded civil offices primarily to Republicans but was careful to balance the number of military commissions between Republicans and Democrats. He realized it was important to issue commissions to ambitious politicians with large personal followings, especially if they were members of the opposition. Influential Democrats with no military experience, such as Nathaniel Banks, John McClernand, Daniel Sickles, and Benjamin Butler, were appointed generals. Although not all of Lincoln's appointments were competent military men, he felt the investment in national cohesion to be worth it.[13]

Lincoln did not begrudge any regular army officer his political allegiance, granting a generalship to long-time Democrats such as George McClellan. Lincoln believed it would be to his advantage to place his opponents in the army where they could give orders for him rather than give speeches against him.[14]

Lincoln was very careful in picking his cabinet. Just as he had done when selecting his generals, he made certain that all areas of the North were represented. The office of secretary of state was offered to William H. Seward of New York in recognition of his service to the Republican Party and his position in the Senate. Montgomery Blair was selected as postmaster general. Although he had campaigned vigorously for Lincoln, his appointment was seen as an appeasement to the border slave state of Maryland. The former governor and newly elected senator from Ohio, Salmon P. Chase, was selected as secretary of treasury. Representing New England, a former Democrat and editor of the influential *Hartford Evening Press*, Gideon Welles, was appointed secretary of the navy. The Missouri lawyer, Edward Bates, was picked for the post of attorney general. Caleb Smith of Indiana was Lincoln's first secretary of the interior. The first secretary of war was Senator Simon Cameron of Pennsylvania. At the beginning of 1862, evidence of corruption surfaced in the War Department. Lincoln thus eased Cameron out of the cabinet, replacing him with Edwin M. Stanton. By selecting a diverse collection of advisors, Lincoln would never enjoy a cabinet that was harmonious or completely loyal to him, but because it did help bring unity to the nation, he was content to live with the situation.[15]

Throughout most of his life, Lincoln was surrounded by men who were better educated and often considered smarter than he. A fellow lawyer analyzed Lincoln's ability to write letters, prepare cases, and make decisions.

Although slow and methodical in all these tasks, he nevertheless was accurate. Lincoln's law partner, William Herndon, was sometimes impatient with this deliberate manner in researching or arguing a case, but Herndon admitted that, although Lincoln was slow in making decisions, he "not only went to the root of the question, but dug up the root, and separated and analyzed every fiber of it." Leonard Swett, a Republican friend, observed that in legal cases Lincoln would often concede nonessential points to his opposition, lulling them into a false sense of confidence. Then, after giving away six points, he carried the seventh and won his case. "Any man who took Lincoln for a simple-minded man would wind up with his back in a ditch," he said.[16] The same underestimation of Lincoln's ability was made during the war, and he more than made up for his lack of formal education with his good, common sense.

As commander-in-chief, Lincoln believed he was responsible for the strategy of the war. It was a responsibility he guarded closely. At first, Lincoln deferred to General-in-Chief Winfield Scott, who formulated a strategy for ending the war known as the "Anaconda Plan." Scott's plan called for surrounding the Confederacy with a blockade along the coast and a fleet of gunboats, supported by troops, along the Mississippi River. This strategy, Scott believed, would shut off the Confederacy from the rest of the world and force it to terms without extensive loss of life. Lincoln approved of the plan, and it would eventually achieve its purpose. Before it did, however, there would be many other attempts to win the war.[17]

The earliest important battle of the Civil War took place at Manassas, Virginia (also referred to as the Battle of Bull Run), a battle that General Scott did not want to fight. Fearing that his ninety-day militia was not yet ready for combat, he advised Lincoln against using the troops at this time. But Northern opinion demanded immediate action; their cry was "Forward to Richmond." Lincoln wanted to bring a quick end to war and believed it would only happen with a decisive Union victory on the battlefield. Brigadier General Irvin McDowell was selected to carry out this task. McDowell protested that he needed more time to train his new recruits, but Lincoln's response was: "You are green, it is true; but they are green, also; you are all green alike."

On Sunday, July 21, 1861, General McDowell's forces engaged Confederate General P. G. T. Beauregard's troops north of the railroad junction near Manassas. His task was a difficult one. As he had predicted, the newly created Union army, consisting of recruits, was not properly prepared for a major battle. To win a significant battle was a great challenge for any general and more than McDowell was able to accomplish.

The first news of the battle was encouraging, but by early evening the arrival of reinforcements from General Joseph E. Johnston's army turned the tide in favor of the Confederates. As afternoon developed into evening, the Union army was in complete and unregimented chaos. McDowell's army had fallen apart. When Confederate President Jefferson Davis reached the scene, he met with Johnston and Beauregard, and the decision was reached not to pursue the enemy. The Confederates thus lost a golden opportunity to achieve an early end to the war. Immediately after the battle, Lincoln made a point of telling McDowell, "I have not lost a particle of confidence in you." McDowell's response was, "I don't see why you should, Mr. President."[18]

The Union defeat at Manassas awakened the North to reality and sobered Lincoln, but it did not change his resolve. Before there could be another campaign, an army had to be assembled, organized, trained, and disciplined. Lincoln did not think McDowell was the man for the job. After the defeat and criticism that followed Manassas, Lincoln was determined personally to take more decisive action from then on. Although he had earlier indicated his confidence in McDowell, he decided to replace him with Major General George McClellan.[19]

After the humiliating Union defeat at Manassas, the war's scope and strategy had to be reappraised. It was now clear that this war was going to be a long one, requiring more fighting and a much greater mobilization of resources and men than originally thought. As a result, Congress authorized the enlistment of one million three-year volunteers. By 1862, nearly 700,000 Northerners and 300,000 Southerners were under arms. Although the war was now in full swing, Lincoln's aim was still the restoration of the Union.[20]

Lincoln followed the progress of the war very closely. He checked constantly with the military telegraph bureau in the War Department for the latest information from the front and could often be found in the field visiting with the army.

Lincoln supported his generals and gave them the freedom to plan their own movements within the campaign plan. Although he set policy and planned campaigns with commanding generals, Lincoln did not interfere with their day-to-day operations. Lincoln was rarely critical of his generals and always found time to thank them for their efforts and to assure them that the country supported them. He did not hold grudges against those who insulted or spoke out against him. Lincoln was willing to do almost anything to support his generals.[21] As commander-in-chief, Lincoln was actively involved in many of the promotions of the high-ranking officers in the army; he was always eager to reward men who had demonstrated bravery. He would often send long lists of promotions, as many as twenty to thirty officers at a time, to his generals.[22]

When possible, Lincoln preferred to make recommendations rather than give orders, but recipients knew they were intended to be more than that. When Major General David Hunter was ordered to Missouri to aid Major General Fremont, Lincoln wrote, "Will you not serve the country and oblige me by taking it voluntarily."[23]

There were times when Lincoln had to be more direct with his generals. In October 1861, when Major General John Fremont issued a military order that emancipated the slaves of Confederate supporters in Missouri, Lincoln rescinded it. Lincoln believed this move would threaten his strategy of keeping the border states—Delaware, Maryland, Kentucky, and Missouri—in the Union. Eight months later, General Hunter issued a similar proclamation freeing slaves in his military district. Again Lincoln rescinded the order, stating that "no commanding general shall do such a thing, upon my responsibility, without consulting me."[24]

By January 1862, Lincoln was becoming desperate for some kind of military movement. He could not wait any longer; public opinion was sagging, national finances were limited, and there was a need to prevent the South from solidifying their separation from the Union. The time had come for immediate action.[25]

In a memo to Major General Don Carlos Buell in the Western theater, Lincoln tried to encourage him to move. He wrote, "We have the greatest numbers, and the enemy has the greatest facility of concentrating forces upon points of collision. . . . We must find some way of making our advantage an over-match for his." Lincoln believed it was important for Union forces to attack the Confederates at different points at the same time. In this way, he said, "we can safely attack, one, or both, if he makes no change, and if he weakens one to strengthen the other, forebear to attack the strengthened one, but seize, and hold the weakened one, gaining so much."[26]

When Buell ignored his suggestion to take action, Lincoln was still too insecure to play the proper role of commander-in-chief. He offered suggestions he hoped would be "respectfully considered," but Buell did not perceive them as orders. As a result, he felt free not to follow them if he wished.[27]

McClellan, too, had not moved his army by January 1862. Lincoln spoke of him as the general "with the slows." Finally, Lincoln wrote to McClellan "either to attack Richmond or give up the job." Faced with the order to attack, McClellan proposed to approach Richmond by moving his army to the Virginia peninsula and advancing on the Confederate capital from the Chesapeake Bay.[28]

During the spring of 1862, McClellan made his plans for attacking the Confederates. Lincoln was not pleased with the strategy but consented to its execution when eight of McClellan's division commanders voted in its favor. Lincoln insisted, however, that sufficient troops be left to defend the capital.[29]

On April 1, McClellan's troops landed at Fortress Monroe. Even as his army moved into position, he complained that he did not have enough men. He resented bitterly that Lincoln had held General McDowell's corps to defend Washington. Throughout the campaign, McClellan continued to complain and request more men.[30]

Confederate General Joseph Johnston was wounded during the Battle of

Seven Pines and was replaced by Robert E. Lee. When McClellan learned that Lee had replaced Johnston, he was elated. "General Lee," he assured Lincoln, "is too cautious and weak under grave responsibility . . . and is likely to be timid and irresolute in action." McClellan was confident of victory.[31]

On June 26 the Confederates launched their attack, resulting in the Battle of Seven Days. The two armies fought valiantly, but McClellan was forced to fall back and entrench his position. Ironically, it was he, not General Lee, who behaved too cautiously. Unable to defeat Lee's army, McClellan blamed his hesitation on being outnumbered and needing reinforcements. When his request for more troops was denied, McClellan anticipated defeat. In July, McClellan was ordered to withdraw from the peninsula.[32]

McClellan blamed Lincoln and his constant intervention for his failure to capture Richmond. "If I save this army now," he wrote in a dispatch to Secretary of War Stanton, "I tell you plainly that I owe no thanks to you or any other persons in Washington. You have done your best to sacrifice this army."[33]

Throughout the war, the relationship between McClellan and Lincoln was strained. Their political affiliation was partially responsible for this tension. General McClellan, a Democrat, was suspicious of President Lincoln, a Republican. When Lincoln detached a division to General John Fremont, a Republican, in western Virginia, McClellan believed Lincoln was building up a Republican's army at the expense of his army, which was poised for a decisive campaign.[34]

But Lincoln had other problems. Winfield Scott, the army's general-in-chief, was too old and infirm to command, so Lincoln had replaced him with General McClellan. Now, when McClellan began his long-awaited campaign in Virginia during the spring of 1862, Lincoln realized that McClellan could not effectively conduct a field command and administer the army in other zones of combat at the same time. Moreover, with his performance during the Peninsula Campaign, Lincoln decided that McClellan's style of warfare would never defeat the Confederacy. On July 11, 1862, he removed McClellan from supreme command, leaving him in charge of the Army of the Potomac but appointing Major General Henry W. Halleck general-in-chief in his place.[35]

Lincoln hoped Halleck would be able to conduct the war aggressively with little direction from him. Halleck was a West Point graduate with many years of experience in the regular army and had recently been victorious at Corinth, Mississippi. At first, he appeared to be a good choice.[36]

After General Pope's defeat at the Second Battle of Manassas in August 1862, however, Halleck lost confidence in himself and his generals. As a result, he was reluctant to give direct orders to his subordinates to attack the enemy. Rather, he provided only advice. "If a general is unwilling to fight, he is not likely to gain a victory," he said. Like McClellan, Halleck was a master of procrastination when he did not approve of the president's plan.[37]

Lincoln soon came to view Halleck as "little more than a first class clerk" who had to be forced to adopt a more active style. When Ulysses Grant was appointed to the position of general-in-chief in 1864, Halleck continued to serve Lincoln, but only as a conduit for communication between the president and his generals. On important matters, however, Lincoln communicated directly with his field commanders by telegraph.[38]

In the summer of 1862, Confederate General Stonewall Jackson embarrassed three Union armies in Virginia's Shenandoah Valley. Lincoln realized that Jackson's success was due in part to the disorganized nature of the forces operating in the valley. To correct this situation, he combined the armies into one, naming it the Army of Virginia under the command of Major General John Pope. Lincoln recalled McClellan's army from the peninsula to join Pope in another anticipated battle in Virginia. As usual, McClellan was slow to move.[39] Lincoln's decision to place Pope in command of the new army was a further repudiation of McClellan and additional evidence of Lincoln's desire to change the military strategy of the war. Pope made it clear that, unlike McClellan, he would not fight a "soft war." Pope, however, had many of McClellan's faults in reverse. Whereas McClellan was timid, Pope was rash. McClellan magnified dangers, but Pope tended to overlook them. Pope's shortcomings would contribute to his defeat at the Second Battle of Manassas.[40] Repeatedly Halleck ordered McClellan to move his army from the peninsula back to Washington to reinforce Pope, but McClellan was sluggish. The hope for a Union victory rested squarely on Pope's shoulders.

On August 31, when the news reached Lincoln of Pope's defeat at Manassas, he ordered the army back to Washington. The loss stunned Northerners and caused home morale to drop, but Lincoln did not falter. He issued a new call for volunteers and declared that "I expect to maintain this contest until successful, or till I die, or am conquered, or my term expires, or Congress or the country forsakes me."[41]

In a conversation with Lincoln, Pope accused officers formerly under McClellan of refusing to follow his orders. The president feared that Pope's charges would further demoralize the army. For the sake of their morale, Lincoln decided that Pope would have to be removed. Against the advice of his cabinet, he replaced him with McClellan. Although Lincoln was disturbed at McClellan's failure to reinforce Pope, he needed him to restore the army's shattered morale. "He has the army with him," Lincoln said. "We must use the tools we have. There is no man in the army who can lick these troops into shape as well as he. . . . If he can't fight for himself, he excels in making others ready to fight."[42]

When the Union army learned that McClellan was returning, the men were pleased. In a short time, he reinvigorated the troops. When Lee moved into Frederick, Maryland, McClellan moved to intercept him. On September 17, 1862, the two armies met at Antietam in the bloodiest single day of the Civil War. After forcing Lee from the field, McClellan allowed him to escape. In the weeks that followed, Lincoln tried to coax McClellan to attack Lee. "Cross the Potomac and give battle," Lincoln telegraphed McClellan, even making a personal visit to see the general at the front, hoping to press him into action. McClellan argued that he could not march and fight until he was fully equipped.[43]

Lincoln was also exasperated with General Buell, who continued to ignore directions to invade mountainous eastern Tennessee. His dissatisfaction with the general increased when two Confederate armies under Braxton Bragg and Edmund Kirby-Smith invaded Kentucky, a move timed to coincide with Lee's invasion of Maryland. His patience finally exhausted, Lincoln transferred the command of Buell's army to Major General George Thomas. By the time Thomas received the orders, however, Buell was preparing to fight the Battle of Perryville. Buell thus continued in command.[44]

As Lincoln gained more experience in military affairs, he created a command structure that was better able to evaluate the fighting qualities of his generals. Just as important, Lincoln did not neglect the western theater of the war. Although not successful as general-in-chief, Halleck did provide Lincoln with useful advice about the western front.[45]

It would take two long years before Lincoln would find a general-in-chief who understood his war plan. From Major Generals Don Carlos Buell and George B. McClellan came only excuses for not moving forward. In the West, however, Brigadier General Grant was making a name for himself and earning Lincoln's confidence. In early 1862, Grant had captured Forts Henry and Donelson in Tennessee and opened the Tennessee and Cumberland rivers into the Confederacy's heartland, but by September the Confederate counteroffensive had slowed his advances. In October, Lincoln lost his patience with Buell when he allowed the Confederates to escape to Tennessee. Lincoln replaced him with Brigadier General William S. Rosecrans. Additionally, two weeks after meeting with McClellan, McClellan still had not pursued Lee.

Many Republicans in Congress grew impatient with the progress of the war. They demanded to know what Lincoln intended to do to bring the war to a victorious conclusion. Congress appointed the Committee on the Conduct of the War, headed by Senator Benjamin Wade of Ohio. Wade was no fan of Lincoln and his administration; privately, he considered them "blundering, cowardly, and inefficient."[46]

As the war intensified and more pressure was placed on Lincoln, he began considering using free blacks and former slaves as soldiers. As early as July 1861, General Butler had considered runaway slaves as "contraband of war" and refused to send them back to bondage. Lincoln supported this position, stating that the government neither should, nor would, return runaway slaves as they came to the armies. Politicians and army commanders, however, did not believe that African Americans would make good soldiers. Lincoln's beliefs were to the contrary, however, and he cited the freed slaves used by the French in a war in Haiti as an example. Before the war was over, Lincoln's dream of having freedmen fight for the Union became a reality—over 180,000 would eventually serve in the army.[47]

Although Lincoln was opposed to slavery, his original objective for winning the war was to save the Union, not to rid the country of slavery. In a letter of August 1862, Lincoln wrote to Horace Greeley, editor of the *New York Tribune*: "If I could save the Union without freeing any slave, I would do it; and if I could save it by freeing all the slaves, I would do it; and if I could do it by freeing some and leave the others alone, I would also do that."[48]

Lincoln hoped that once the Union was restored under its legitimate government, he would be able to work out a program of gradual emancipation. Now, with the war going badly for the Union, Lincoln began to look for ways to reverse the situation. Senator Charles Sumner suggested emancipating and inducting slaves into the Union army. "You need more men," Sumner had told him.[49]

Lincoln also listened to Frederick Douglass, a former slave and abolitionist, who had argued that the "Negro is the key to the situation—the pivot upon which the whole rebellion turns. . . . Teach the rebels and traitors that the price they are to pay for the attempt to abolish this government must be the abolition of slavery." Despite numerous petitions, newspaper editorials, and visits to the White House from abolitionists urging him to free the slaves, Lincoln still hesitated. Freeing the slaves at this time would appear to be a desperate act by the government to save itself by encouraging a slave insurrection in the South. Lincoln wanted to wait for the appropriate time before acting on this issue.[50]

The right moment came in the fall of 1862. Five days after the Battle of Antietam, Lincoln issued a preliminary Emancipation Proclamation: "On January 1, 1863, all persons held as slaves in any state in rebellion against the Union would be then, thenceforward, and forever free." Lincoln was careful to craft the document to suit the moment. He did not define which parts of the Confederacy would be affected by the proclamation and wisely excluded the loyal slave states. He promised to define the included areas on January 1, allowing time for portions of the Confederacy to lay down their arms and rejoin the Union. Those that did would not be included in the proclamation.[51]

The document was not well received by some of the men in the Union army. When Lincoln visited McClellan at Antietam in October, some of the regiments were less enthusiastic in their cheering for him than they had been in the past. McClellan and his officers were opposed to the proclamation; some even ridiculed it and suggested that the army march on Washington to insist that the president rescind the order.[52]

Strangely, enlisted men were more likely to support the Emancipation Proclamation. Samuel Nichols of the 37th Massachusetts reasoned, "I think all true men of all parties see the necessity and patriotism from which this state paper emanated, even if not all men are ready for it yet." "I am glad more than ever that I enlisted since I have read the President's Proclamation because I think the fight is for freedom or slavery," said another Union private.[53]

On November 7, McClellan received an order from Lincoln relieving him from command of the Army of the Potomac and appointing Major General Ambrose E. Burnside to replace him. McClellan's war career was finished; he would never receive another command. Some members of Congress and Lincoln's cabinet were opposed to McClellan's removal, but Lincoln's explanation for his action was simple. "I said I would remove him if he let Lee's army get away from him, and I must do so. He has got the 'slows.'"[54]

Lincoln was careful with his new selections, Rosecrans and Burnside. Unlike McClellan, both were politically neutral and generally supportive of the president's policies. Whether the appointments of Burnside and Rosecrans were good military moves was another question. Many radical Republicans were dismayed at the selection of Ambrose Burnside to command the Army of the Potomac, preferring the less conservative general, Joseph Hooker.[55]

Burnside neither wanted the command nor believed he was ready for the responsibility. Within a week, however, he had reorganized the Army of the Potomac into three Grand Divisions. Any chance for a speedy restoration of the Union was lost on December 13 when General Burnside, against the warning of the president, crossed the Rappahannock into Fredericksburg. There, Burnside ordered an ill-conceived frontal attack on the well-entrenched Marye's Heights. All day long the Federals charged the almost impregnable Confederate position only to be repulsed with heavy losses. The Union suffered over 12,000 casualties compared to the Confederate losses of only 5,000.

When Lincoln learned of the results of the battle, he said, "I hope it is not so bad as all that," but it was. Now, after the failure of the Peninsula Campaign, the Fredericksburg defeat wrought overall disillusionment with Lincoln and his administration. There were demands for his resignation, and, as one senator stated, "There is no hope for the country except in the death of the President and a new administration."[56]

The Army of the Potomac was demoralized after the defeat at Fredericksburg, but Burnside gained the respect of the president when he claimed that he alone was responsible for the defeat. Lincoln, who was so accustomed to being blamed for the failure of his subordinates, told Burnside that "he was the first man he had found who was willing to relieve him of a particle of responsibility." Burnside, however, had lost the confidence of his subordinate officers and troops. Burnside, on the other hand, believed that several of his officers had been disloyal to him and requested that Lincoln replace either them or him.[57]

Despite the defeat at Fredericksburg, Lincoln officially signed the Emancipation Proclamation on New Year's Day, 1863. "If my name goes into history," Lincoln said, "it will be for this act." The proclamation, however, did not free a single slave since it only applied to the Confederate states, where it could not be enforced.[58] By January 1863, the news in the West was encouraging: Rosecrans was ready to begin a campaign to drive the Confederate forces from Tennessee. In the East, however, the defeat at Fredericksburg had Lincoln under severe attack again. "We are on the brink of destruction," he told a friend. "It appears to me the Almighty is against us and I can hardly see a ray of hope." But Lincoln was still resolved to unite the country.[59]

Although Lincoln liked Burnside and admired his honesty and humility, he had lost confidence in him to lead the army. He had to be removed to prevent a complete breakdown in the morale of the Army of the Potomac. Lincoln resisted pressure to bring back McClellan and replaced Burnside with Major General Joseph Hooker.[60]

Lincoln had his doubts about Hooker; the general had been very vocal in his criticism of Burnside, but he had performed well as a corps commander. Although Hooker boasted loudly, nobody doubted his ability; he was noted for leading from the front, encouraging his men by example. Like McClellan, "Fighting Joe" Hooker had little respect for Lincoln, calling him "a played-out imbecile." "The country," he said, "would do better under a military dictator."[61]

Soon after Hooker's remarks, Lincoln swallowed his pride and called him to the White House. After talking with Hooker, Lincoln gave him a letter and left the room: "I have heard, in such a way as to believe, of your recent saying that both the Army and the Government need a Dictator. Of course it was not for this, but in spite of it, that I have given you the command. Only those generals who gain successes, can set up dictators. What I ask of you now is military success, and I will risk the dictatorship."[62]

Hooker rose to the challenge. He revived morale, improved living conditions, and returned self-respect to the Army of the Potomac. By the summer of 1863, Lincoln had changed his view on the strategic plan for the war. He told Hooker that the best strategy was not to capture Richmond but to attack the Confederate army until it was destroyed. With the destruction of the Army of Northern Virginia, the South would be defeated. "Lee's army and not Richmond is your true objective point," Lincoln told Hooker. "Fight him when the opportunity offers."[63]

Although the Army of the Potomac numbered 135,000 men—more than double the Army of Northern Virginia—Lee had built twenty-five miles of trenches along the Rappahannock River. Hooker planned to move behind Lee, drive him out of his defenses, and engage him in the open. Lincoln agreed with the plan but had reservations about Hooker's ability to carry it out. "Fighting Joe" bragged about his army and the action he would take. "My plans are perfect," he said, "and when I start to carry them out, may God have mercy on General Lee, for I will have none." Lincoln warned Hooker of being overconfident. "The hen," he noted, "is the wisest of all the animal creations, because she never cackles until the egg is laid."[64]

Lincoln watched closely as Hooker prepared to meet Lee at Chancellorsville, hoping that Hooker would not make the same mistake that the other generals before him had made—attacking piecemeal and not engaging all of the enemy's forces at the same time. This concern was warranted.

Unfortunately, Hooker's plans did not go as he had hoped; Confederate scouts detected the Union troops' movements. Rather than wait to be hit, Lee attacked. During the Battle of Chancellorsville, which lasted from May 1 through May 4, Hooker's plan fell apart. He had expected Lee to flee in panic. When he attacked instead, Hooker lost his nerve. The result was disastrous for Hooker and the Army of the Potomac.[65] When Lincoln learned of Hooker's defeat, his face turned ash gray. Pacing back and forth across the room, he muttered, "My God! My God! What will the country say! What will the country say!"[66]

By May 7, Lincoln was trying to inspire Hooker to make another attempt. He wrote to Hooker inquiring if he had a plan to rebound from the recent defeat. On May 13, Lincoln met with Hooker in Washington and informed him that he expected him to do more than merely keep the Confederates at bay.

In early June, Lincoln invited Major General John F. Reynolds to Washington to offer him command of the Army of the Potomac. When he was not promised a free hand in directing the army, Reynolds did not accept.[67] Lincoln's hopes rose when Lee began his second invasion of the North. Now was a chance, Lincoln believed, to capture Lee's entire army. He was convinced that the Army of the Potomac would be able to beat the rebels on Union soil, but he worried that Hooker might commit the same error McClellan had made at Antietam and allow the enemy to escape.

Hooker's job was to keep his army between the enemy's forces and Washington. He moved north tracking Lee, but complained that the administration was failing to support him. In late June, Hooker and General-in-Chief Halleck disagreed over where troops should be located at Harper's Ferry. Hooker resigned, assuming that on the eve of a major battle his resignation would not be accepted and that he would have his own way. To his surprise, Lincoln accepted it. Just three days before the Battle of Gettysburg, Lincoln appointed Major General George Meade to command the Army of the Potomac.[68]

Hours later, Hooker wrote: "In conformity with orders of the War Department, dated June 27, 1863, I relinquish the command of the Army of the Potomac. It is transferred to Major General George G. Meade, a brave and accomplished soldier, who has nobly earned the confidence and esteem of this army on many a well fought field."[69]

Although Lincoln continued to change one commander after another in the East, in the West he retained Ulysses S. Grant as the commander of the Army of Tennessee. After his success at Fort Donelson, Grant had a scare at Shiloh, barely managing to win the battle. Rumors of Grant's excessive drinking surfaced, and the failure of his first campaign against Vicksburg in December 1862 fueled demands for his replacement. Despite these flaws, Lincoln saw qualities in Grant that others did not. "I can't spare this man; he fights," Lincoln said in his defense.[70]

Grant's advance on Vicksburg was hampered by the actions of another general. In October 1862, John A. McClernand, a politically appointed general, was commissioned to raise 60,000 troops as an expeditionary force to aid Grant in the capture of Vicksburg. After McClernand had completed his task, he joined Grant, expecting to operate independently. Grant believed that two generals focusing on the same target was one too many, and he requested that McClernand and his troops be placed under his command. When Lincoln supported Grant's position, McClernand complained about the unfairness of the decision. Lincoln responded: "I have too many family controversies already on my hands to voluntarily, or so long as I can avoid it, take up another. . . . Allow me to beg that for your sake, for my sake, and for the country's sake, you give your whole attention to the better work."[71]

Grant continued to have trouble with McClernand during the Vicksburg campaign. McClernand was incompetent and at times insubordinate, but Grant was reluctant to relieve the president's appointee. Finally, McClernand forced Grant's hand. McClernand reported to the newspaper that his corps had done most of the fighting and was responsible for the success of the recent campaign. When Grant saw the article, he was irate; he acted quickly, relieving McClernand from command. McClernand argued that he had been appointed by Lincoln and challenged Grant's authority to remove him.[72] Lincoln refused to intervene on McClernand's behalf. If he ruled against Grant, Grant might resign. "Better leave it where the law of the case has placed it," he advised McClernand, placing him on inactive duty until near the end of the war.[73]

McClernand and McClellan were not the only two generals with whom Lincoln had difficulty. In Tennessee, Brigadier General William S. Rosecrans continued to request more supplies while making no effort to move. To induce him to act, Halleck attempted to develop a spirit of competition between Rosecrans and Grant. Halleck sent a letter to each offering a major generalship in the regular army to the first to win an "important, decisive victory." Rosecrans was insulted by the offer and let Lincoln know it, further worsening his relationship with the president.[74]

By July 1863, Grant was ready to end his nine-month campaign to capture Vicksburg, the last Confederate stronghold on the Mississippi River. Jefferson Davis called Vicksburg the "nailhead that holds the South's two halves together." Lincoln agreed. "Vicksburg is the key," he said. "The war can never be brought to a close until that key is in our pocket."[75]

Finally, on July 4, the "key was in the Union's pocket." Lieutenant General John C. Pemberton surrendered Vicksburg and 30,000 troops to Grant. Grant sent a message to Halleck informing him that the "enemy surrendered this morning." Lincoln responded to the good news by sending Grant a gracious letter of appreciation: "I do not remember that you and I have met personally. I write this now as a grateful acknowledgment for the almost inestimable service you have done the country. . . . When you got below [Vicksburg] and took Port Gibson, Grand Gulf, and vicinity, I thought you should go down the river and join General Banks; and when you turned Northward, East of Big Black, I feared it was a mistake. I now wish to make the personal acknowledgment that you were right, and I was wrong."[76]

At the same time in the East, other events were about to change the direction of the war. On July 1, just three days after assuming command of the Army of the Potomac, General Meade engaged Lee at Gettysburg. Lincoln kept up with the action via telegrams sent to the War Department. The result of the three-day battle was a victory for the Union; also, it was the last time Lee would attempt to take his army onto enemy soil. Lincoln was elated. He placed great pressure on Meade to follow up the victory and attack Lee's army before it could retreat across the Potomac River. On July 7, when Meade showed no signs of pursuing Lee, Halleck telegraphed Meade: "Give him another [hard blow] before he can reach the Potomac." Lincoln believed that if General Meade could destroy Lee's army, the rebellion would be over. Finally, on July 12, Meade notified the president that he would attack the next day. When Lincoln received the message, he said, "They will be ready to fight a magnificent battle when there is no enemy to fight."[77]

Lincoln was right. As he anticipated, Lee's army escaped with little additional harm done to it. He was devastated by Meade's failure to destroy Lee's army. After the battle, Lincoln wrote a letter to General Meade expressing both his gratitude for his "magnificent success" at Gettysburg and his disappointment in letting the enemy escape: "My dear general, I do not believe you appreciate the magnitude of the misfortune involved in Lee's escape. He was within easy grasp. . . . Your golden opportunity is gone, and I am distressed immeasurably because of it." Then, after cooling down, he did not send the letter; he concluded that he was expecting too much of Meade.[78]

Lincoln believed that Meade was not taking advantage of his superior number of troops. Meade's plan to push Lee's army back into their entrenchments at Richmond did not please Lincoln. None of his commanders seemed to understand that their objective should be the destruction of Lee's army, not the capture of Richmond.[79]

Lincoln had not yet found the commander he needed and feared the war would never end. "What can I do with such generals as we have?" he asked. "Who among them is any better than Meade?"[80]

The Union victories at Gettysburg and Vicksburg were not only a turning point for the army but for the president as well. Unfortunately, the good news from the army was followed by bad news in New York. The proposed military draft, which would allow a man to buy his way out by hiring a substitute, resulted in a riot causing one hundred deaths. Lincoln, always willing to compromise, postponed the draft, making amendments to it so that there would be less resistance.[81]

After the Battle of Gettysburg, a citizens' committee decided to buy land on the battlefield to create a national soldiers' cemetery as a final burial place for the Union dead. The dedication ceremony was set for the third week in November. Edward Everett, a former governor of Massachusetts and an excellent speaker, was selected to deliver the main address. Lincoln received an invitation, but no one expected him to come. Lincoln, however, saw this occasion as an opportunity to honor the dead and to emphasize the message of the Emancipation Proclamation—that the Civil War was also a struggle for freedom and equality.[82]

Edward Everett's speech lasted two hours; he compared the Union dead to the heroes of ancient Greece. After Everett finished, Lincoln rose and gave his speech, reading from a handwritten sheet of paper; it contained just ten sentences totaling 271 words. The entire speech lasted only two minutes.[83]

The audience was silent; they were shocked and disappointed. They had expected the president to say more. Some members of the press labeled the Gettysburg Address as "dull, silly, and vulgar"; others, however, praised it as a work of genius. Gradually, over time, most Americans grasped the meaning of the speech and applauded its beauty and eloquence.[84]

By 1863, the desertion rate from the Union army had grown to a critical level. Many regiments had lost as many as 25 percent of their men. Although some men deserted because they no longer wanted to fight, many did not understand army rules and left to care for sick relatives at home. Deserters were supposed to be shot, but Lincoln was opposed to such harsh sentences and commuted most of them. Out of 200,000 Union deserters, only 276 were executed. Lincoln pardoned almost any soldier whose parents pleaded his case. He was especially lenient with boys under the age of eighteen who had lied about their ages to join the army.[85]

Lincoln's compassion toward deserters did not sit well with the military. They believed his policy was hindering their efforts to maintain a disciplined army. Secretary of War Stanton intervened, scolding Lincoln severely over his clemency policy and getting him to agree not to sign any more pardons. A few days later, Lincoln pardoned more soldiers who were scheduled to be executed; this time he sent a telegram so he did not have to sign the pardon papers.[86]

During the summer of 1863, General Rosecrans stockpiled supplies for an early fall advance into Tennessee. Lincoln wanted a quick advance into the state, but Rosecrans was slow to move. Halleck telegraphed him: "Your forces must move forward without delay." Finally, on August 16, Rosecrans's Army of Cumberland moved, forcing General Braxton Bragg's Army of Tennessee to retreat into Georgia.[87]

Rosecrans, however, overextended his army and was forced to consolidate it near the Chickamauga Creek, ten miles south of Chattanooga. When the Confederates attacked the Union position, Rosecrans was forced back to Chattanooga. It was only a determined stand by Major General George Thomas that saved the Army of Cumberland from complete disaster. By mid-October, Lincoln decided it was time for a change in the leadership in the West. He promoted Grant to command the armies from Tennessee westward and gave him the authority to retain or relieve Rosecrans. Grant chose to replace Rosecrans with Major General George H. Thomas and then went to Chattanooga. On November 23, Grant launched an attack on Bragg's army; by November 25, the Confederates were in full retreat, clearing the way for Sherman's move into Georgia.[88]

During the winter of 1863 through 1864, Lincoln attempted to break the military stalemate. When General Hugh Kilpatrick proposed a two-pronged cavalry raid on Richmond, simultaneously from the east and west, to free Union prisoners held in the Belle Isle Prison, Lincoln gave his approval. Unfortunately, the plan failed. Both forces were repulsed outside of Richmond, and Colonel Ulric Dahlgren, leader of one of the attacking parties, was killed. On his body, the Confederates claimed, papers were found that detailed a plan to burn the capital and to capture or kill Confederate Davis and "his hateful crew." Lincoln denied the charge and the authenticity of the document found on Dahlgren. Kilpatrick's raid did, however, indicate the steps Lincoln was willing to take to end the war.[89]

By the end of 1863, Lincoln had found the aggressive general he had been looking for since the beginning of the war. With McClellan being considered as a candidate for president on the Democratic ticket, Lincoln did not want to appoint another general-in-chief with political aspirations. When asked about his political ambitions, Grant advised the president that nothing could persuade him to become a candidate for president. After hearing that response, Lincoln promoted Grant to lieutenant general and appointed him general-in-chief, replacing Henry Halleck. Halleck remained in Washington as chief-of-staff, while Grant directed operations in the field with the Army of the Potomac.[90]

Lincoln liked and trusted Grant. Like Lincoln, Grant was not flamboyant or concerned about rank and protocol. Lincoln was impressed by the simplicity and brevity of Grant's language. Most of all, as he told a friend, "He doesn't worry and bother me. He isn't shrieking for reinforcements all the time. He takes what troops we can safely give him . . . and does the best he can with what he has got."[91]

Lincoln had solid leadership skills; while giving his generals the assurance of independence, he was often successful in reshaping their strategies. He demonstrated this skill with General Grant. Without ordering any specific strategy, Lincoln persuaded Grant to develop a plan that focused on destroying Confederate armies rather than capturing cities. Grant's plan called for a massive, simultaneous attack by all Union armies on the Confederate heartland. Lincoln had always believed this strategy was the way to fight the war, since it exercised the greatest advantage of the Union—superior numbers. When Grant presented his plan, Lincoln pretended to be surprised and said: "Oh, yes! I see that. As we say out west, if a man can't skin, he must hold a leg while somebody else does."[92]

Lincoln finally had a commander who agreed with his strategy for conducting the war. In the past, Union armies on various fronts had acted independently and not in concert with each other. This behavior had enabled the Confederates to shift troops as needed to meet the most pressing danger. Now Grant planned a campaign that would stretch over a thousand-mile front and would require a coordinated offensive. The two principal armies involved in this plan were the Army of the Potomac, commanded by General Meade in Virginia, and the Army of the Tennessee, commanded by Major General William T. Sherman in Georgia. Meade was to attack Lee wherever he went, and Sherman was to engage General Joseph Johnston whenever possible. There was no plan to capture Richmond; the objective was to inflict all the damage possible against the enemy's war resources.[93]

By the beginning of 1864, Lincoln believed his military plan and team were in place and he could now concentrate on improving national unity and planning for the peace he hoped would follow. The war, however, was more than a year from its end. On May 1, 1864, Grant engaged Lee in a Virginia forest called the Wilderness. More than 2,000 Union troops died in hand-to-hand fighting and numerous others in the fires ignited by exploding cannonballs. Grant, however, unlike his predecessors, did not fall back; rather, he continued to move south in pursuit of Lee. A week later, the two armies clashed again at Spotsylvania. This time the Union casualties exceeded 11,000. At Cold Harbor, two weeks later, 7,000 men were killed or wounded in just eight minutes. Under Grant, the Army of the Potomac had suffered over 50,000 casualties in a single month of fighting.[94]

As the wounded poured into Washington, hospitals ran short of medicines and bandages, and surgeons were overcome with fatigue. Lincoln saw the wounded as they returned from the front. "Those poor fellows," he said. "I cannot bear it. This suffering, this loss of life is dreadful."[95]

The nation had expected casualties, but these numbers were astounding. Newspapers labeled Grant the "butcher" and called for his replacement. Despite enormous pressure to replace Grant, Lincoln did not lose confidence in his general-in-chief; he would stick with Grant no matter what the consequences.[96] Lincoln directed his attention to ensuring that Grant was adequately supplied with both arms and manpower. In May 1864, the president called for an additional conscription of 300,000 men, and Congress offered special inducements for re-enlistment, such as bounties and furloughs.

Grant continued to advance south of Richmond and laid siege to Petersburg, a city defended by Lee. Meanwhile, Sherman moved into Georgia in an effort to take Atlanta. As the Union advances slowed down, again Lincoln was criticized. Lincoln continued to call up more troops to replace the casualties. By the summer of 1864, more than 300,000 Northerners had been killed. As the election drew near, some members of Lincoln's party were talking about replacing him on the Republican ticket. A Republican splinter group held its own convention and nominated General Fremont as a third-party candidate.[97]

Lincoln, however, was a politician. Using all his skill, he was able to secure the nomination at the convention in Baltimore. He dropped Hannibal Hamlin as vice president on the Republican ticket, and in his place he selected a Southerner from Tennessee, Andrew Johnson. Lincoln was hoping to create a genial atmosphere for the returning Southern states when the war ended. His Democratic opponent was General George McClellan.[98]

By the beginning of September, Union forces appeared to be at an impasse everywhere. The press praised McClellan; it seemed certain he would be the new president. A downhearted Lincoln wrote a letter to his cabinet—to be opened after the election—urging them to support the new president, McClellan.[99]

Just as Lincoln's situation seemed bleakest, the Union army and navy came to Lincoln's rescue. On August 5, Admiral David Farragut led his fleet into Mobile Bay, forcing the seaport to close. On August 21, Major General Philip H. Sheridan marched into the Shenandoah Valley with orders to torch everything in his path. On September 2, Sherman captured Atlanta. "Atlanta is ours, and fairly won!" he telegraphed Lincoln. On October 19, Sheridan won a major battle at Cedar Creek and went on to burn the valley. The Confederate "breadbasket" lay in ruins. Grant's siege at Petersburg continued.[100]

These timely victories saved Lincoln's presidency. The war was not a hopeless failure as the Democrats claimed. Victory was in reach; all the voters had to do was let Lincoln finish the job. On November 8, Lincoln won a decisive victory at the polls. The final count showed that he had received nearly 350,000 more votes than he had in 1860. This time he received 55 percent of the vote compared to 40 percent four years earlier. Contrary to what was expected, Lincoln received 86 percent of the vote from Sherman's army.[101]

With Atlanta now in Union hands, Sherman began to plan for his next campaign. Convinced that Confederate Hood's weakened Army of Tennessee in the West was no longer a threat, Sherman proposed taking the bulk of his army and marching through Georgia, leaving the rest of his troops with General Thomas to halt any invasion by Hood into Tennessee. Neither Lincoln nor Henry Halleck approved of the plan; even Grant was skeptical. Sherman persisted, however, appealing to Grant: "Instead of being on the defensive, I would be on the offensive; instead of guessing what he [Hood] means to do, he would have to guess at my plans." Grant still had reservations about the march, but his trust in Sherman's judgment outweighed his concerns. Permission was granted for the march.[102]

Leaving Atlanta in flames, Sherman, with 60,000 troops, began his devastating march to Savannah and the sea. A believer in "hard war," Sherman intended to burn everything of value to the enemy on his march. By this tactic, he hoped to keep supplies from the Confederate army and make living so difficult for Southerners that they would force their leaders to surrender.[103]

During his march, Sherman freed more slaves than any other general; many African Americans saw him as the answer to their prayers. "Marse Lincoln done remember us!" they said.[104]

By December 10, Sherman was outside of Savannah and began to lay siege to the city. On December 21, the Confederates evacuated the city. On December 22, Lincoln received a telegram from Sherman announcing his Christmas gift to the nation. Lincoln was delighted with Sherman's success. In his letter of appreciation, Lincoln said: "Many, many thanks for your Christmas gift, the capture of Savannah. When you were about leaving Atlanta for the Atlantic coast, I was anxious, if not fearful; but feeling that you were the better judge, and remembering that 'nothing risked, nothing gained,' I did not interfere. Now, the undertaking being a success, the honor is all yours; for I believe none of us went further than to acquiesce."[105] At the same time, General George Thomas checked Confederate General Hood's invasion of Tennessee at Franklin and routed him in a decisive battle at Nashville.

In December, the last two of Lincoln's politically appointed generals, Banks and Butler, were removed from their commands. After 1863, Lincoln had refused to keep political generals in field commands, if they were incompetent. During the election year of 1864, Lincoln wanted Butler removed from field command, but due to the political nature of the election, he was reluctant to act on his own. Rather, he asked Grant to take the responsibility for the act. [106] In January 1865, Sherman moved northward from Savannah, while Grant continued to hammer away at Petersburg. The plan was for Sherman to march through the Carolinas and attack Lee from the west. On February 18, Sherman took Charleston. The Confederacy was dying. Lincoln saw this occasion as an opportunity to solidify the Emancipation Proclamation. The only way to prevent Congress or another president from reversing the proclamation in later years was to pass a constitutional amendment abolishing slavery throughout the country. Regarding his landslide election as a mandate to continue his emancipation program, Lincoln placed pressure on Congress to pass such an amendment. On January 31, Congress approved the Thirteenth Amendment, prohibiting slavery in the United States.[107]

A month later, Lincoln took his oath of office a second time. The pressures of the war were evident by the appearance of his face. His features, a friend later recalled, were "haggard with care, tempest tossed, and weatherbeaten." In his second inaugural address, Lincoln said it was now time for healing and that he felt no malice or hatred toward the Southern people: "With malice toward none; with charity for all; with firmness in the right, as God gives us to see the right, let us strive on to finish the work we are in; to bind up the nation's wounds, to care for him who shall have borne the battle, and for his widow, and his orphan—to do all which may achieve and cherish a just and lasting peace among ourselves, and with all nations."[108]

On March 28, Lincoln met with his top commanders—Grant, Sherman, and Admiral David Dixon Porter, commander of the North Atlantic Blockading Squadron—to discuss final plans for ending the war. They all agreed that the Confederacy was doomed. During the meeting, Lincoln kept asking: "Must more blood be shed? Cannot this last bloody battle be avoided?"[109]

During the meeting, the future was also discussed. The kind of peace Lincoln wanted was reflective of his second inaugural address. Lincoln believed that harsh peace terms would only increase sectional hatred throughout the nation. There must be no revenge, no treason trials, and no executions. Lincoln required only that the Confederates cease fighting and turn in their weapons. "Let them once surrender and reach their homes, they won't take up arms again. Let them all go, officers and all. . . . Let them have their horses to plow with. . . . I want no one punished; treat them liberally all around. We want those people to return to their allegiance to the Union and submit to the laws."[110]

On April 2, Lee's army evacuated Petersburg. The next day, General Grant and his troops marched into the city uncontested. The streets along the riverfront were crowded with Confederate soldiers attempting to get away. Grant, following Lincoln's view, showed compassion; he could have wreaked havoc on the stragglers with his artillery, but he decided to let them escape. "I had not the heart," he explained later, "to turn the artillery upon such a mass of defeated and fleeing men. Besides I hope to capture them soon."[111]

On April 3, Richmond fell. That night, Lincoln told Admiral Porter: "Thank God I have lived to see this. It seems to me that I have been dreaming a horrid dream for four years, and now the nightmare is gone. I want to see Richmond!"[112] On the morning of April 4, Lincoln visited Richmond. His son Tad, Admiral Porter, and William Crook, a White House guard, were with him, accompanied by one dozen armed sailors. As they walked through the streets, Lincoln was met by large groups of former slaves. "God bless you, sir!" said one. "Hurrah! Hurrah! President Lincoln has come! President Lincoln has come!" rang through the streets.[113]

Five days later, Lee surrendered to Grant at Appomattox. Although Joseph Johnston's army was still at large, Lee's surrender truly ended the war. Grant's terms were those outlined by Lincoln in their recent meeting.

April 14, 1865, was also Good Friday. Many Americans solemnly observed the day with prayer, fasting, and meditation. For Lincoln it was another day of work. That evening, however, he planned to relax by attending the theater, his favorite form of entertainment. The newspapers carried the announcement that General Grant, President Lincoln, and their wives would be in attendance at Ford's Theater.[114] John Wilkes Booth was also making plans to attend Ford's Theater that evening.

3 *Winfield Scott*

"Old Fuss and Feathers"

Just before daybreak, on November 2, 1861, a carriage pulled up at the Washington railway station. Assisted by his staff, an old general climbed out of the carriage and entered the station. His bulky weight made every step an effort. A small group of friends and officials were there to see him off on the train to New York. A young general dashed into the station. He grasped the old general's hand, and they chatted for a few minutes. Then the old general got on the train, which moved off into the darkness.[1] The military career of the old general had come to an end. The next day the young general, thirty-five-year-old George B. McClellan, would succeed the man he had seen off at the station as general-in-chief of the Union army. That evening McClellan wrote to his wife: "I saw the end of the career of the first soldier of the nation; and it was a feeble old man, scarce able to walk; hardly anyone there to see him off but his successor. Should I ever become vain-glorious and ambitious, remind me of this spectacle." Ironically, in just one year, McClellan's own military career would come to an end as President Lincoln, disgusted with his slowness in advancing the Civil War, relieved him of command.[2]

The old general for whom McClellan expressed such pity was Brevet Lieutenant General Winfield Scott. Age had been unkind to General Scott. He was a mere caricature of his formal self; the brilliant commander who had led the victorious campaign against Mexico fourteen years earlier was no more. He had lost his soldierly bearing, his body now soft and fat. He could no longer ride a horse, and, at times, could hardly move at all. At seventy-five, he was plagued with vertigo, dropsy, and gout.[3]

At that time, General Scott was the only American soldier other than George Washington to have worn the rank of lieutenant general. He had served the United States for half a century and for the past twenty years had commanded the army. Scott had been America's preeminent soldier, serving under fourteen presidents—more than any other top military leader in history. He had fought on the battlefield in three nations of North America: in the United States, Canada, and Mexico. His service spanned the time from the War of 1812 to the Civil War. Today many historians consider Winfield Scott "the ablest soldier to appear in America between Washington and Sherman."[4]

Scott's modest origins offered few clues to the greatness to come. Winfield was born on June 13, 1786, near Petersburg, Virginia. Winfield's father, William Scott, owned land and slaves and made a comfortable living by farming. His father died when Winfield was only six years old. His mother, Anne Scott, did all she could do to raise her six children. At first, Scott was tutored at home by his mother, who not only taught him the basics of reading and writing but instilled in him a strong work ethic and the importance of being honest. As a young boy, he loved to read, borrowing books from a neighbor and even delving into the classics. When Winfield was twelve years old, he left home to attend boarding school; two years later he enrolled in a prestigious academy in Richmond. In both cases, Scott admitted, "I was no extra-ordinary success."[5]

In 1803, young Scott was saddened by the death of his mother. Later he wrote that his mother had provided the inspiration for his lifetime of achievement. At seventeen, he was now on his own; he was determined not to waste his time with mediocre scholastic achievement.[6]

After a year at Richmond, Scott enrolled at the College of William and Mary. This time he was more serious about his studies. While at William and Mary, Scott became interested in law and decided to become an attorney. After only a year of college, he left the rigors of the classroom and began to read law in the office of Petersburg lawyer David Robinson.[7]

After riding the circuit, serving summons, and writing briefs, Scott was not certain if he really wanted to be a lawyer. Then an incident in 1807 helped him make up his mind. When the British warship the *Leopard* attacked and boarded the U.S. frigate the *Chesapeake*, imprisoning several of her crew, the country demanded a declaration of war against Great Britain. To appease this clamor and give his embargo a chance to work, President Thomas Jefferson authorized the formation of an additional eight regiments to the army.[8]

The call for volunteers prompted Scott to offer his services. Obtaining a uniform and a horse, he joined a local unit. His imposing stature—he was six-feet, four-inches tall and weighed 230 pounds—may have contributed to his being assigned the rank of corporal.[9]

By the summer, the threats of war had subsided, and Scott returned to Petersburg to resume his practice of law. His short experience in the military aroused his interest in the army. With the help of a friend of the president,

General-in-chief of the Union armies was Winfield Scott, seventy-five-year-old veteran of the
War of 1812 and the Mexican War. By 1861, Scott
was swollen and dropsical, unable to mount a
horse. "I was three years old when the Constitution was adopted," he liked to remind his listeners. Although a Virginian, he intended to
maintain the federal Union so long as there was
strength in his ailing body.

COURTESY OF THE LIBRARY OF CONGRESS

Scott was able to get a commission as captain of light artillery in one of the
newly formed regiments. First, however, he had to recruit the men for his
company. At the same time he began reading books on military strategy
and tactics. By the fall of 1808, Scott's company was sent to New Orleans, a
possible British target should there be a war.[10]

   At New Orleans, Scott was involved in a conflict with Brigadier General
James Wilkinson, commander of the U.S. forces in the South, over treatment of his troops. The lack of discipline and the general mismanagement
that he observed were, he felt, to be blamed on Wilkinson. After Scott
openly denounced Wilkinson's leadership, Wilkinson retaliated by court-
martialing him. As a result, Scott was suspended for one year without rank
or pay.[11]

On June 18, 1812, less than a year after Scott returned to active duty, Congress declared war on Britain. Scott was promoted to lieutenant colonel and placed in charge of a newly formed artillery regiment.[12] In October, Scott, with two of his companies, joined the American forces invading Canada. The American troops were led by a politically appointed major general, Stephen van Renesseloer. On the night of October 13, van Renesseloer sent Scott and his men across the Niagara River in rowboats to capture the British fort at Queenston Heights. The piecemeal assault was unsuccessful. Scott's men were hopelessly outnumbered and outgunned, and he was forced to surrender. Scott learned an important lesson at Queenston. Van Renesseloer's actions had been incompetent, illustrating the consequences of allowing untrained men to lead troops in battle.[13]

Although Scott's first battle ended in a defeat, he had acquitted himself well, displaying bravery, skill, and initiative. In 1813, Scott was released as part of a prisoner exchange and promoted to the rank of colonel.

Scott was assigned as adjutant general to Major General Henry Dearborn, who replaced Van Renesseloer. Dearborn realized his own professional deficiencies and gave his young adjutant a free hand in organizing his command. Within a short time, Scott had Dearborn's 4,000 troops formed into an army ready for another invasion of the Niagara Peninsula. On May 27, an assault force led by Scott captured Fort George. Scott was wounded during the struggle but continued to lead the attack. The overcautious Dearborn decided not to pursue the enemy and settled for merely occupying the Canadian side of the Niagara. Soon after, President Madison replaced some of his incompetent generals. One of the replacements, promoted to brigadier general, was Winfield Scott.[14] At twenty-seven he became the youngest general in the army. Scott soon gained a reputation for commanding one of the best army brigades. Again Scott was assigned to the Niagara front commanded by Major General Jacob Brown. At the Battle of Chippewa on July 5, 1814, Scott's brigade, which was dressed in the gray of the New York militia rather than in the U.S. blue, drove the British regulars from the field. The surprised redcoats cried out, "Why, these are regulars!"[15] It was the first time American soldiers had defeated troops in an all-out battle and marked the birth of the U.S. regular army. To commemorate that victory, the gray uniforms were adopted and worn afterward by all West Point cadets. The man responsible for that birth was Brigadier General Winfield Scott.[16]

Shortly thereafter, Scott was wounded in the Battle of Lundy's Lane. A musket ball splintered his collarbone, knocking him down and leaving him unconscious. This event ended Scott's active part in the War of 1812. Scott emerged from the war a hero, second only to Andrew Jackson, the hero of New Orleans. He received lavish praise from his superiors and the press and a resolution of thanks from Congress. He was also promoted to brevet major general and retained in the peacetime army.[17]

In the months following the war, Scott's attention shifted from command duties to the pursuit of a wife. For several years he had hoped to win the hand of a Richmond belle, Maria Mayo. The Mayos were a family of considerable means, Maria traveling in the best of social circles. She was a talented musician and spoke French fluently. Because of Maria's beauty and charm, she had many suitors and offers of marriage. Scott had pursued Maria for several years, proposing marriage on three occasions, but she rejected his offer each time.[18]

Scott changed his approach by trying to gain the approval of Maria's father. When this attempt failed, Scott despaired, confiding to a friend, "I deeply regret not being in love and not having the prospect of marriage." He hoped this situation would change.[19]

In January 1817, while Scott was on furlough, his luck changed. His persistence paid off, and Maria finally consented to marry him. When someone later said, "So you married Captain Scott after all," Maria replied, "No—I refused Captain Scott to the last. I accepted the general." Maria's parents were not happy with her decision. They did not want her to marry a soldier and tried unsuccessfully to convince Scott to resign from the army.[20]

Within several weeks, they were married. The union produced seven children, four of whom died before adulthood. By marrying into the Mayo family, Scott improved his social standing, bringing him the kind of lifestyle he wanted.

In 1818, Scott was granted leave from his command so that he could devote himself fully to rewriting the army's regulations. Completing the general regulations took longer than he had anticipated. It was not until 1821 that the completed revisions were approved by the secretary of war and Congress. Despite the tedious and time-consuming nature of the project, Scott relished the job. It gave him a chance to bring about much-needed reform and allowed him to shape the army.[21]

From time to time, Scott considered leaving the army because he found it difficult to maintain the living standard that he and Maria desired. He was not dissatisfied with his job, but he had a growing desire for prestige and power. With his legal background, he believed, he was well suited for public office. From a practical standpoint, Scott also thought that he would be better able to provide for his increasing family if he left the army. After carefully considering the options and his love for the military, he decided to remain in his position, but he continued to prepare himself should the opportunity for public office present itself.

In June 1832, Scott participated in the Black Hawk War, the result of a festering problem with the Indians in Illinois. With a contingent of 1,000 men, Scott set sail for Fort Dearborn (Chicago). Scott was delayed in his arrival by an outbreak of cholera, an illness spread by contaminated water and unsanitary conditions. By the time he reached Fort Dearborn, most of the fighting was over. Scott was able to return to New York in November without having participated in any battles. During the campaign Scott revealed several aspects of his nature. He was a strict disciplinarian and a fanatic about sanitation and personal hygiene. Scott insisted on harsh punishment for those who broke the rules but showed compassion for those who became ill during the Black Hawk campaign.[22]

In 1835, Scott was again called upon to combat Native Americans; this time to remove the Seminoles from their native land in Florida. Despite the heat and the length of the trip, Scott carried an enormous amount of personal baggage. While his troops sought relief from the heat under shade trees or in tents, the general moved about in full dress uniform.[23]

Scott was known for his love of fine food and fancy uniforms and was nicknamed "Young Fuss and Feathers." As he grew older, the title changed to "Old Fuss and Feathers," indicating that his desire for high living had not lessened over the years. One soldier remembered Scott's camp during the Seminole War: "The general required a band of music, with a company of professional cooks and servants to attend them." In addition, these refinements included several large tents and three wagons of furniture. This "grand panoply of war," the soldier said, "was quite unsuitable for Indian bush fighting."[24]

During the Seminole campaign, Scott also demonstrated his inflexibility. He, however, was not alone; the entire corps had no training in guerrilla fighting, having only been trained to fight an enemy in the open. Scott was partially responsible for the army's lack of preparation in this area. Through his writings, he had influenced the tactics used in warfare. Scott's preoccupation with conventional European methods of fighting influenced his thinking and resulted in an unsuccessful outcome in Florida.[25]

Scott was appointed general-in-chief of the U.S. army in 1841. He had gained a reputation for being a good commander as well as for his diplomatic and political skills. In 1832, during the Nullification Crisis, President Andrew Jackson had sent Scott to Charleston, South Carolina, to calm the situation. Later in 1838, President Martin Van Buren made use of Scott's skills to calm hostilities aroused after pro-British Canadians burned an American ship, the *Caroline*. Scott's high visibility placed him in contact with prominent politicians, and by 1839, the Whig Party was viewing him as a possible presidential candidate. Scott, too, considered himself a worthy candidate for the White House and was ready to answer the call if it came.[26]

Scott's peacekeeping activities showed him to be a diplomat and won him the title of the "Great Pacificator." His presidential aspirations, however, were hampered by being constantly involved in controversies with other public figures and fellow officers in the army. Scott's pompous manner and vanity caused many people to dislike him, and his stylish living did little to enhance his popularity with the average voter during an age of "frontier mentality." When he was not on active duty, he lived in a mansion in Elizabethtown, New Jersey, and indulged himself with fine food and drink. Nevertheless, many Whigs regarded Scott as their best candidate for the 1848 presidential election. In 1846, however, the war with Mexico began, and Scott's services were needed elsewhere.[27]

When Congress declared war against Mexico, Scott was general-in-chief. As such, he believed he should lead the army against Mexico and that he would have a reasonable amount of time to prepare and equip his troops. He was mistaken. President James Polk wanted immediate action. When Polk learned that Scott had no immediate plans to invade Mexico, he believed Scott was dragging his feet to make the Democrats look bad in the eyes of the public. As a result, he ask Congress to authorize two new major generals for the army in the hope of taking the war to the enemy immediately.[28]

Scott was outraged when he learned of Polk's plan. In a letter to Polk he wrote: "I do not deserve to place myself in the most perilous of all positions—a fire upon my rear from Washington, and the fire, in front, from the Mexicans." Scott's letter infuriated the president, but Polk had no intention of backing down. He sent General Zachary Taylor to Mexico to command the forces in the field. When Taylor was successful in Mexico, he became a popular hero and a potential presidential candidate. Polk was concerned that Taylor, who was a Whig, might run for president in 1848. In an effort to dilute Taylor's fame, he decided to send another invading force to Mexico. On November 19, Polk ask Scott to lead the expedition. Scott agreed. He was on his way to Mexico two days later, having learned his lesson about lingering in Washington.[29]

By March 1847, Scott had built his army to 10,000 troops and was ready to attack the Mexican garrison at Veracruz. Utilizing both an amphibious operation and a naval bombardment, his command captured the 6,000-man garrison while suffering only eighty-two casualties.[30]

Early in April, Scott advanced into the interior of Mexico where he encountered 10,000 Mexicans under the command of Antonio Lopez de Santa Anna. With the help of Captain Robert E. Lee, who was able to find a path by which the enemy could be flanked, Scott's army attacked from the front, the flank, and the rear, capturing or scattering the enemy forces. Santa Anna barely escaped. Scott's casualties totaled less than five hundred.[31]

By August, Scott's army encountered Santa Anna near Mexico City. Once again, Lee, with the help of P. G. T. Beauregard, located a trail by which the Mexican army could be flanked. After a long and bloody battle, Scott's force routed the Mexican army, inflicting over 10,000 casualties. American losses were one-tenth that number. Finally on September 14, Mexico City fell. The American flag was raised in Mexico City's Grand Plaza.

Winfield Scott's victory was a classic case of superior generalship. "At no time during Scott's deep penetration of an enemy country," marveled Ulysses S. Grant, "did he have a force equal to one-half of that opposed to him; he was without a base . . . yet he won every battle, he captured the capital, and conquered the government."[32] Scott's victory was the zenith of his career. In London, the Duke of Wellington declared, "His [Scott's] campaign is unsurpassed in military annals. He is the greatest living soldier."[33]

During the Mexican campaign, Scott displayed an ability to plan and act decisively, combining daring with practicality. Not only did Scott visualize the Veracruz expedition, but he made it work. He planned the logistics, coordinated operations with the navy, fought one siege and five tough battles, and occupied Mexico City seven months after landing at Veracruz.[34]

Although Scott was an outstanding soldier, he never quite received the credit that was due him. Part of this disregard he brought on himself. Scott's overbearing personality earned him enemies in important places. His enormous ego often made him the butt of ridicule, and his lack of respect for his superiors made him insufferable. Scott's personality often led to conflict with members of his staff. In one situation, he had three of his officers arrested for their attempt to degrade him.[35] Despite the cracks in his personality, the Whigs nominated Scott as their candidate for president in the 1852 election, but, much to his dismay, he was badly beaten by Franklin Pierce. Although Scott's lack of a "common touch" had contributed to his loss, probably no Whig could have won at that time.[36]

With the inauguration of Franklin Pierce as president, Jefferson Davis was appointed secretary of war. Almost from the very beginning, Davis and Scott did not get along. Their differences began over travel expenses. Scott traveled extensively on official business and billed the War Department according to mileage. Army regulations called for travel funds to be authorized only "under written and special orders from their proper superiors." Scott did not acknowledge any superior other than the president. A more tactful individual than Jefferson Davis might not have selected such a minor issue over which to go to war with Scott. But such was not how Davis operated. Scott was infuriated when Davis upheld the decision of a War Department auditor who denied payment on one of Scott's travel bills. Later, Scott had his revenge in an equally insignificant dispute over pay and allowance. When Attorney General Cushing upheld Scott's position, Davis threatened to resign. Not until 1855 could Scott's supporters in Congress put through a bill promoting him to brevet lieutenant general.[37]

Throughout the Pierce administration, the feud between Davis and Scott continued. Clearly, Scott was not the easiest person with whom to get along. Scott would have been a nuisance under most circumstances, but Davis did little to prevent their relations from degenerating—despite Scott's service to the nation. Their feud ended, however, when James Buchanan took office as the fifteenth president.[38]

In 1857, President Buchanan called on Scott to send an expedition to the Utah Territory to put down a rebellious group of Mormons. Scott assigned Colonel Albert Sidney Johnston and a force of 2,500 to assist the new territorial governor and several federal judges assigned to protect the U.S. interest in the territory. Johnston was successful in peaceably bringing the Mormons under U.S. jurisdiction.[39]

During Scott's last two years of service on active duty, his health was poor. He had become grossly overweight, his weight having elevated to over 300 pounds. He suffered from dropsy, gout, and rheumatism, which diminished his energy and made it impossible for him to ride a horse or ascend stairs without help. His once soldierly presence, an object of admiration, now produced pity and sympathy. Age and his increasing infirmities made it impossible for him to lead troops in battle any longer.[40]

In 1860, Scott was greatly concerned about the political situation in the nation. He even fancied that he might be selected as a presidential candidate again, this time as a moderate who could keep the country unified. He had long advocated a gradual emancipation of the slaves, one that would use the sale of public lands to finance either sending them to Africa or helping assimilate them into American society. By 1860, however, emotions were running too high for the country to compromise.[41]

Abraham Lincoln's election intensified the emotions of the country and set off a series of events that would result in the secession of eleven states. In the early months of 1861, no one knew if the growing crisis would result in war or not, but Scott took steps to defend Washington against attack and to strengthen some of the federal forts in the South.[42]

When the Civil War began, some in the North feared that Scott, a Virginian, would join the Confederacy. There was no reason for doubt, however; Scott had been involved in too many battles for the United States and had supported its government for too long to support a rebellion. As early as 1849, he expressed his loyalties. In a letter, he discussed the possibility of a divided nation, saying, "I shall stand by the union, as it stands, and against new confederations formed out of its fragments."[43]

To Scott, the nation seemed to be crumbling around him; the disorder went against all he stood for. When Scott learned that Jefferson Davis had been elected president of the Confederacy, he denounced Davis as a "Judas" who, for political gain, would have "betrayed Christ and the Apostles and the whole Christian Church."[44]

When federal forts in the South were threatened, Scott knew they would be impossible to defend. Hoping to avoid open conflict, he advised Lincoln to evacuate the forts as a conciliatory gesture toward the South. Lincoln, however, could not do so, since he had promised "to hold, occupy, and possess the property of the United States" in his inaugural address. Finally, in April, when the Confederates attacked Fort Sumter, war became inevitable.[45]

While troop strength was building up in Washington, pro-Southern officers defected to the Confederacy, a trend that began with the secession of South Carolina in 1860. Many of the army's best officers felt that their first loyalty was to their home states and returned home to take up arms. In all,

313 officers—nearly one-third of the regulars—resigned to join the Confederacy. The defection that disappointed Scott the most was that of Colonel Robert E. Lee. Lee had served brilliantly under Scott in Mexico and had been described by him as "the very best soldier that I ever saw in the field." Lee was the choice of both Scott and Lincoln to lead the Union army in the field.[46]

On April 18, Lee was offered the position of field commander of U.S. forces. Lee listened politely but refused, saying that he looked upon secession as anarchy but would not take up arms against his native state. "If I owned every slave in the South, I would sacrifice them all to the Union," he said, "but how can I draw my sword upon Virginia, my native state?" He would return to his home at Arlington, he said, and "share the miseries of my people and save in defense, will draw my sword on none."[47]

After this meeting, Lee went to see Scott. "Lee," said the General, "you have made the greatest mistake of your life, but I feared it would be so."[48] When Lee refused to become the Union field commander, Irvin McDowell got the assignment of heading the army forming in Washington for the invasion of the South.

As in the Mexican War, Scott did not want to launch a campaign until the army was fully prepared. Additionally, Scott disagreed with the prevailing belief that one battle would end the war. The South, he believed, should be squeezed into submission by economic strangulation. His strategy, labeled the Anaconda Plan, called for a complete blockade of the Atlantic and Gulf ports in conjunction with a powerful force that would move down the Mississippi River—a plan that was consistent with the one he had used during the Mexican War. He hoped to limit the loss of life by "enveloping the insurgent states and bring them to terms with less bloodshed than by any other plan."[49]

But the Northern public and press clamored, "on to Richmond," and Lincoln called upon the army to comply. Against his better judgment, Scott drew up a plan in which General McDowell would attack the main Confederate army under General Beauregard, while Brigadier General Robert Patterson prevented another Confederate force commanded by General Joseph E. Johnston from joining Beauregard at Manassas. The plan almost worked, but Patterson failed to delay Johnston from reaching Manassas. As a result, what appeared at first to be a Union victory turned into a humiliating defeat.[50]

Scott blamed himself for the defeat. "I am the greatest coward in America!" he said. "I have fought the battle against my judgment. . . . I deserve removal because I did not stand up, when my army was not in a condition for fighting, and resist it to the last!"[51]

After the loss at Manassas, President Lincoln replaced McDowell with thirty-five-year-old George B. McClellan. As commander of the army in the field in the East, McClellan believed he was destined to save the Union.

One newspaper supported his belief when it wrote: "There is an indefinable air of success about him and something of the man of 'destiny.'" McClellan had no difficulty accepting the praise and adulation he received during his first few weeks in Washington. In a letter to his wife, he revealed his feelings of superiority: "By some strange operation of magic I seem to have become the power of the land."[52]

McClellan and Scott were alike in leadership style and personality, as well as having character flaws in common. During the summer of 1861, the two generals got along with each other, but that amity did not last long. McClellan wanted command of the entire Union army, and he was confident he could command it successfully without help from General Scott. McClellan and Scott were destined to clash. When Lincoln dismissed Scott's Anaconda Plan because he believed it was too timid and unrealistic, he seemed to be withdrawing his favor from Scott; it was now heaped upon a new man, George McClellan. Scott fiercely resented the way McClellan seemed to be taking his place and remaking his command.[53]

McClellan wanted his command to be officially called "the Army of the Potomac," but Scott was opposed to this change. McClellan also advocated the organization of brigades into divisions; Scott was opposed to this arrangement, too. Organization using brigades had worked well enough during the Mexican War when Scott had only 15,000 men to command at one time. Now McClellan would be commanding more than 80,000 men in an attack on Richmond; an army of that size would be impossible to control if organized only into brigades.[54]

This was the beginning of the feud between McClellan and Scott. McClellan soon realized that cooperation between them was impossible: "General Scott is the most dangerous antagonist I have—either he or I must leave here—our ideas are so widely different that it is impossible for us to work together much longer."[55]

For McClellan, Scott was an obstacle in his way. When McClellan tried to appoint men to his army, Scott refused to allow the appointment. As McClellan began to prepare his army for its 1862 offensive, he communicated directly with Lincoln, bypassing Scott completely.[56] These "outrages" must stop, Scott warned McClellan. When they did not, Scott considered a court-martial, but he wisely decided against it, realizing it would only hurt the army and aid the enemy.[57]

When Scott protested to Lincoln, McClellan complained that the "old general" was frustrating his plans to expand and prepare the army. "I am leaving nothing undone to increase our force," McClellan wrote to his wife, "but that confounded old Gen'l always comes in my way. He is a perfect incubus. He understands nothing, appreciates nothing. . . . If he cannot be taken out of my path, I will resign. . . . The people call upon me to save the country—I must save it and cannot respect anything that is in the way." Lincoln tried to mediate the differences between the two but only ended up delaying the inevitable. He finally gave in to the pressure from Republican senators and allowed Scott to retire on October 31, 1861, for health reasons.[58] Although Lincoln accepted Scott's resignation, he was beginning to have doubts about McClellan's ability to lead the army. He directed that Scott be allowed to retain his full rank and pay.[59]

The Civil War continued for another three-and-a-half years. Many of the generals who fought during the war owed much of their command style to Winfield Scott. Over one hundred Civil War generals had served under him in Mexico. Scott's execution of the Mexican campaign influenced their thinking during the war. The use of flanking movements, which Robert E. Lee used so effectively throughout the war, was learned from Scott.[60]

Scott retired to New York, where he spent most of the remainder of his life, visiting West Point often. He took time to write his *Memoirs*, which were published in 1864. He sent one copy to General Grant, who had served under him in Mexico and who proved to be his true successor. In it he inscribed, "From the oldest general to the greatest general."[61]

Just two weeks before his eightieth birthday, Scott died peacefully and was buried at West Point; there could have been no more appropriate place. This nation owes a great deal to Winfield Scott. He saved the honor of the army in the War of 1812, led it to victory in the Mexican War, and was the model for many of the generals who fought the Civil War. He was, indeed, one of America's greatest military leaders.

4   *Irvin McDowell*

Hard Luck General

When the Civil War began, Irvin McDowell was considered one of the out-standing officers in the U.S. army. He had an impressive military background and the respect and confidence of his peers and superiors. Additionally, he had powerful political backing and the support of Northern newspapers. Less than a year-and-a-half later, his career was in shambles, he found himself relieved of active command, and he had been deserted by both his political backers and the press. Fellow officers avoided him, and his own troops condemned him as a scoundrel and a traitor. Seldom has a person held in such high esteem slipped from favor in such a short time, but such was the case for Irvin McDowell.[1]

Clearly, there were flaws in McDowell's personality and limitations in his ability, but to a great degree his demise was the result of circumstances beyond his control. Throughout the war, he was thrust into impossible situations not of his own making. Some men could have overcome such adversity and won lasting approval. But the qualities necessary to do this—personal magnetism, insight, and intuitive perception—were never part of McDowell's makeup.[2]

Irvin McDowell was born in Ohio on October 14, 1818. He received his early education at the College of Troyes in France, where his family had moved. In 1834, he returned to the United States where he entered West Point at the age of sixteen. After graduating in 1838, ranked in the middle of a class of forty-five, he was assigned to the First Artillery. He served a three-year tour of duty in a garrison along the Canadian border. In 1841, he was appointed adjutant at West Point where he taught infantry tactics, not realizing that some of the Southern cadets would use his teachings against him in battle twenty years later.[3]

At the outset of the Mexican War in 1846, McDowell served as adjutant to Major General John E. Wood. Later he earned a brevet captaincy for conspicuous service at Buena Vista. When the war was over, McDowell continued to impress his superiors, holding important positions in the War Department and military bureaus in the East and South. In 1858, he was chosen to visit Europe to study military administration.[4]

In 1849, McDowell married Helen Burden, an heiress from Troy, New York. The marriage produced four children. The only troubling event during their marriage was the death of their firstborn son at an early age. McDowell took the loss of his son hard, saying that it was "a blow to which I never shall become reconciled!"[5]

McDowell had gained recognition from officials in Washington and with General-in-Chief Winfield Scott despite his reputation for being odd. Irvin McDowell was a mass of paradoxes. Nervous energy often caused his face to flush and his speech to thicken, giving the impression that he was inarticulate or drunk. He abstained from alcohol, tobacco, coffee, and tea, but he was a ravenous glutton when it came to food. Although he had won a promotion for gallantry in Mexico, his demeanor was not conducive to command. He could not remember faces or names and was a poor listener, letting his mind wander when others spoke to him. He often treated his subordinates with abrupt indifference, thus losing their respect and goodwill.[6]

Because of these idiosyncrasies, people often considered him cold and self-centered. "He was so intensely selfish," one acquaintance said, "that it stuck out all over him." A staff aid believed his frequent forgetfulness was a lack of "courtesy due even to a common soldier."[7]

Although not held in high esteem by his fellow officers, political officials and members of the press saw McDowell as a man of integrity. McDowell had brought attention to himself in early 1861 when he aided in the organization of Washington's defenses. Secretary of the Treasury Salmon Chase, a fellow Ohioan, and Secretary of War Simon Cameron hoped to see McDowell in a position of command as soon as possible. The opportunity came when Lincoln called for volunteers to expand the regular army. Such an expansion required the appointment of several new brigadiers and major generals. When the cabinet met to discuss appointments, Chase campaigned for McDowell to be named as one of the major generals. McDowell, however, was concerned that a promotion to major general would cause bad feelings among other officers who outranked him presently and would have to be passed over. McDowell said that he would be more than content to be a brigadier. On May 14, his request was honored, and McDowell was appointed a brigadier general in the regular army and placed in charge of the army forming in Washington.[8]

The new general was to have a tragic career in the war. Despite his ability, everything he tried went amiss. Grant said he was "one of those generals that got started wrong and never recovered."[9] McDowell, in fact, immediately

In June 1862, President Lincoln ordered General Irvin McDowell to attack the Confederate army at Manassas Junction. McDowell protested, arguing that his troops were "green." "You are green," the president replied, "but they are green too; you are green alike."

faced a gigantic problem. During the Mexican War, he had been a staff officer but had never led an army in the field. Now he found himself responsible for equipping, training, and preparing an army of 35,000 for the invasion of the Confederacy.[10]

McDowell needed time to prepare his army; he had no notion of fighting during the summer of 1861. There were too many difficulties to overcome in such a short time. He was the first American general to command an army of this size. His staff was small and inexperienced; his troops were volunteers with no military experience. Many had volunteered with visions of gaining glory but did not care to go through all the training required to be a soldier. As the army was forming in Washington, Colonel William T. Sherman noted: "No curse could be greater than an invasion by a volunteer army. McDowell and all of the generals tried their best. But to say he commanded the army is no such thing. They did as they pleased." In addition, McDowell's army had insufficient weapons, ammunition, and equipment.

He had no reliable maps of the terrain of northern Virginia. Although McDowell's troops had been drilling for weeks, they were still not ready for an all-out campaign.[11]

McDowell knew his army was not ready to go into battle, but Lincoln was under great pressure to move on Richmond. To cure the ills of his army, McDowell needed one thing he did not have—time: "I wanted very much a little time," he said, "an opportunity to test my machinery, to move it around and see whether it worked smoothly or not." General Winfield Scott, McDowell's superior, wanted to give him more time to prepare his army; he, too, preferred a slower, less bloody plan, one that would strangle the South by blockading its seacoast and controlling the Mississippi River rather than conduct an all-out battle.[12]

But the decision for when and how to fight the war was not Scott's to make. The Northern press and public continued to exhort Lincoln to mount a campaign. Lincoln finally ordered Scott to have McDowell attack northern Virginia; Scott reluctantly asked McDowell to draw up plans. When McDowell continued to insist that his army was not ready, Lincoln pointed out, "It is true that they are green. So are the Confederates. You are all green alike."[13]

McDowell worked long hours to plan and prepare his army. The task was made more difficult as more recruits entered Washington and the Lincoln administration continued to push for action: "A press and people demand action at all hazards."[14]

McDowell presented several plans of attack to Scott, Lincoln, and the cabinet before one was accepted. The approved plan called for a flanking movement around the Confederate right at Manassas Junction, twenty-five miles southwest of Washington and eighty miles north of Richmond. The move, he hoped, would allow him to attack Brigadier General P. G. T. Beauregard's force of 20,000 troops before General Joseph E. Johnston in the Shenandoah Valley could join him. The success of the plan relied upon Union Major General Joseph Patterson keeping Johnston busy in the valley. McDowell hoped to force the Rebels to retreat without an all-out battle that could possibly cripple his inexperienced army.[15]

On July 16, McDowell, with 35,000 troops, began his march toward Manassas Junction. He had intended to leave on Monday, July 8, but problems of supply and organization delayed him for eight days. The undisciplined soldiers stopped frequently to rest or plunder. Some began eating their rations before they had even reached the battlefield. Carrying forty pounds of gear while wearing heavy woolen uniforms in the hot July heat took its toll on the men. The march proved to be an ordeal for which McDowell's troops were not prepared.

McDowell had hoped to attack the Confederates on the 19th, but various problems again delayed it until July 21. This delay gave Beauregard two days of grace, allowing Johnston more time to reach the field of battle.

Although McDowell received information that Johnston had given Patterson the slip and had joined Beauregard, McDowell did not alter his plans. Johnston or no Johnston, the attack was set for the first light of day, Sunday morning.[16]

The original advantage of superior numbers that McDowell had counted on evaporated with the arrival of Johnston's army. The two armies would now be fighting on equal terms. The engagement would be a study on how not to fight a battle, mostly due to the inexperience and lack of discipline on both sides. The Union's shortcomings, however, proved to be greater. McDowell's delay in moving troops into action and his piecemeal deployment enabled the Confederates to mass at various points to blunt his assaults.[17]

During the early morning, Union forces enjoyed some measure of success. By mid-afternoon, McDowell's troops, operating on the Confederate left, suddenly found themselves facing heavy odds as Confederate troops were shifted from inactive areas to meet the Union assault. Having fought for several hours under a hot sun with little water or rest, they gave way when the Rebels launched a large-scale counterattack. As the Union army fell back, panic spread, and the withdrawal became a rout. Adding to the confusion were the throngs of sightseers who had come to witness the battle and now crowded the road blocking the retreat. One Maine private later described the chaos: "How we traveled! Nobody was tired now. Everyone for himself, and having a due regard for individuality, each gave a special attention to the rapid momentum of his legs."[18]

Despite the failure of the Confederates to pursue the retreating Yankees, McDowell was unable to rally his troops as they fled through Centreville, heading north. In the chaos, hundreds of troops and civilians were captured. Through the night and into the next rainy day, soldiers and civilians streamed into Washington.[19]

The battle that Lincoln wanted had ended in a defeat for the North. The news of the disaster was received in Washington with incredulity, then with fear. Throughout the night, Lincoln received news from the front and listened in silence to a description of the battle. McDowell had come close to victory; the decision might well have gone the other way. Two days after the battle, Lincoln visited McDowell and his troops at Arlington, Virginia. The president reassured McDowell that he "had not lost a particle of confidence in him." But in reality Lincoln had decided that the job was too large for him. He was beginning to have some doubts about Winfield Scott, too.[20]

In the face of the unexpected debacle at Manassas, the North sought to find a scapegoat. McDowell suffered quietly and accepted his fate. The journalist, William H. Russell, spoke with McDowell and wrote that he had conducted himself "with admirable fortitude, and complains of nothing, except the failure of his officers to obey orders, and the hard fate which condemned him to lead an army of volunteers." General Scott blamed only General Patterson who had allowed Johnston to slip past him and join Beauregard. If Beauregard had not received these reinforcements, Scott believed, McDowell's plan would have been a success. Those who realized the unfortunate position in which McDowell had been placed tried to cheer him, especially when it became obvious that Manassas was only the beginning of a long and tragic war.[21]

Six years after the battle, General William T. Sherman evaluated the disaster: "Bull Run Battle was lost by us," he said, "not from want of combination, strategy, or tactics, but because our army was green as grass." "The Rebel army was little if any better," he continued, "and the attacking force was sure to be beaten, unless its antagonist ran off. Though a source of great disgrace, it was no misfortune, for we then realized that organization and discipline were necessary."[22] Those who served closely with McDowell did not fault his generalship. Sherman claimed that Manassas "was one of the best-planned battles of the war," and McDowell planned it all on his own. The only defect in his plan was that he overlooked the strong defensive position open to the Confederates at the Henry House Hill line. McDowell could not have known this fact because of the inaccurate maps available to him. At the early stage of the war, no one knew how to fight. This would be a new kind of war, one where learning took place on the battlefield and not by past experiences. For all but a few, it was the first fight of their lives. The war would be fought at a more intense level, with more destructive weapons, and the casualties would be shockingly high.[23]

The soldiers who served under McDowell saw him in a different light. Many of them blamed him for their defeat at Manassas; others reacted to his stern discipline and his punishment of those who had violated Southern civilian property against his orders. Within days of his defeat, McDowell was replaced by Major General George B. McClellan.[24]

From the very beginning, McClellan and McDowell clashed. McClellan quietly criticized McDowell for his outdated military tactics and a lack of personal warmth. Despite his personal criticism, however, McClellan thought it politically expedient to name him commander of one of his twelve infantry divisions. Later McClellan would admit that he regretted the decision to do so. "I committed one of my greatest errors," he said. "He never appreciated my motives, and felt no gratitude for my forbearance and kindness." McClellan believed McDowell lacked the qualities necessary for field command, but others in Washington did not. Several months later, McDowell was promoted to the rank of major general of volunteers. In January 1862, the Army of the Potomac, now 100,000 strong, was divided into four corps; McDowell was given command of one of these corps.[25]

Lincoln still wanted the Army of the Potomac to move forward. Now he placed pressure on McClellan; however, it was not until the middle of March 1862 that McClellan took action. As McClellan moved toward Richmond along the Virginia peninsula, McDowell's First Corps was assigned to protect his rear. Before they had a chance to see action, however, McDowell's corps was ordered to return to Washington to protect the capital. McClellan considered the withdrawal of the First Corps as an act of betrayal, blaming both McDowell and the government.[26]

On May 24, McDowell was ordered to advance to Front Royal and Strasburg in the Shenandoah Valley, where he hoped to aid Major Generals John Fremont and Nathaniel Banks in trapping "Stonewall" Jackson. When Jackson was able to slip the trap and join Johnston on the peninsula, Lincoln decided to combine McDowell's, Fremont's, and Banks's forces into the 50,000-man Army of Virginia. The army was to operate east of the valley, protect Washington, and draw some of Johnston's troops from McClellan's front.[27]

Lincoln's first choice to lead the new army was McDowell until he was incapacitated by an accidental fall from his horse and knocked unconscious. While he convalesced, Lincoln picked Major General John Pope to command the army. When McDowell returned to active duty, Pope appointed him to command his Third Corps. Unlike McClellan, Pope welcomed McDowell and relied heavily on his leadership.[28]

In early August, General Robert E. Lee, now commanding the Confederate Army of Northern Virginia, learned that McClellan had been ordered to evacuate the peninsula and reinforce Pope. This withdrawal now left Lee free to direct his attention to the newly formed Army of Virginia. Appreciating the importance of striking Pope before he could be joined by McClellan, Lee moved with Longstreet's Corps to join "Stonewall" Jackson. Lee's combined force now totaled 55,000 men compared to Pope's 47,000 effectives.[29]

Under Pope, McDowell had to return to the field of his darkest hours in command, the Bull Run vicinity, near Manassas. By August 28, Jackson's troops were approaching Groveton, a hamlet near the Manassas battlefield. When McDowell inadvertently made contact with Jackson, Pope rushed with the rest of his army to join him. Pope believed he could defeat Jackson's smaller force in one sweep, but he ignored indications of Lee's and Longstreet's approach.[30]

On August 29, Pope attacked Jackson in a series of piecemeal and uncoordinated attacks. McDowell's corps was deployed on Pope's left and center. Unfortunately, McDowell's orders to a junior officer, Major General Fitz John Porter, were vague and easy to misinterpret. As a result, Porter's Fifth Corps failed to join the battle on Pope's left when his presence was vital. McDowell compounded his error by failing to notify Pope of Longstreet's approach. By August 30, Pope was surprised to find that his left flank had been enveloped and crushed by Longstreet.[31]

Now forced to retreat, Pope called on McDowell to protect the army's rear. McDowell did so with a tenacity that allowed Pope to escape without losing his entire army. While suffering 15,000 casualties, Pope's army was able to cross Bull Run and make their way back to Washington.[32]

Despite McDowell's outstanding efforts during the army's retreat, he soon began to receive criticism for the debacle at what became known as the Second Battle of Manassas. The fact that McDowell's line had been broken by Longstreet made him a target for a large share of the blame. Even his own soldiers blamed him. On the retreat, they openly expressed their feelings. One of his troopers recalled: "The most profane oaths were uttered in reference to his conduct, and his ears must have often caught the insulting taunts of thousands of brave and patriotic men. There was scarcely a moment during the march in which I did not hear the epithets 'villain,' 'traitor,' or 'scoundrel,' applied to his name."[33]

There were other insults and accusations registered against him. Some believed he was guilty of treason, bolstered by Confederate prisoners who sarcastically said, "McDowell is a fine general: why don't you give him the sole command?" Rumors continued to spread about him. One of the most ridiculous rumors involved a bamboo hat that McDowell wore during most of the campaign. The story related that the hat had been designed to help the enemy distinguish his corps from others during the battle, indicating the point where it would be best to attack. McDowell's reputation deteriorated to such a point that some of his own men threatened to kill him; even his own staff feared going among his men.[34]

McDowell sought to clear his name. In September, he asked Lincoln to convene a court of inquiry to investigate his conduct while serving under Pope; Lincoln agreed. On February 14, 1863, after sixty-seven days of testimony, McDowell was fully exonerated of all charges against him during the Second Battle of Manassas. But by now his name and reputation had been destroyed to such a degree that it was unlikely he would again be permitted to lead troops in the field.[35]

McDowell was not the only one to be blamed for the Union defeat at Second Manassas. Pope insisted that it was the "unsoldierly and dangerous conduct" of generals from McClellan's Army of the Potomac that caused his downfall—Major General Fitz John Porter being the main culprit. Pope charged Porter with disloyalty, disobedience, and misconduct in the face of the enemy. Porter was removed from command in November and placed under arrest. McDowell was the prosecution's chief witness at the court-martial, displaying a selected memory that tended to protect his reputation at the expense of Porter.[36]

A combination of defective maps and perjured and hearsay testimony was sufficient to warrant a guilty verdict. As a result, Porter was dismissed from the army on January 21, 1863. Porter spent the rest of his life trying to vindicate his name. In 1878, a board completely exonerated Porter from the 1862 charges.[37]

For the remainder of the Civil War, McDowell held minor administrative posts, but he never again commanded troops in the field. On July 1, 1864, he was assigned to the command of the Department of the Pacific. There he did see action against Native Americans in the Oregon and Arizona territories. Later he was transferred to head the Department of the East, during which time he was promoted to the rank of major general in the regular army. In December 1872, he replaced Major General George Meade as commander of the Division of the South. Later he returned to California to administer the Division of the Pacific. McDowell retired from the army in 1882.[38]

General McDowell died in San Francisco on May 4, 1885, and was buried at the Presidio there. He will forever be remembered as the hard luck general. Following his death, the *London Army and Navy Gazette* described him as "a man who, with a little luck, might have been a large page in the history of one of the greatest civil wars . . . the world has ever seen." Had he won the Battle of Manassas, he would have been the most popular man in America.[39]

5   *Benjamin F. Butler*

"The Beast"

No Civil War general has been more vilified and misjudged than Benjamin Butler. His military occupation of New Orleans has been a topic of controversy for many years. It was there that he earned the unenviable title the "Beast." Some historians extol his virtues as a great humanitarian, while others think of him as a brazen opportunist who would do anything to further his career or position.

Butler's appearance was impressive but not attractive. He was massive and stern, partially bald with reddish-brown hair and mustache, and he had a crossed eye that aroused suspicion. As a professional politician, he never let criticism bother him, whether it came from associates or opponents. Even earning the epithet "Beast" had little affect on him. Although he was not a capable field general, his political influence kept his position secure for most of the war.[1]

Benjamin Butler was a man of lofty intellect. He was a successful criminal lawyer and actively involved in politics before the war. As such, he learned two lessons—how to manipulate the rich and powerful and how to break the law without getting caught. During the war he drew on these lessons, enjoying the power, gaining wealth, and removing anyone who stood in his way. Some of his actions were outrageous and intended to be so. At the same time, he was amazingly enterprising and creative. Fearless, Butler was willing to champion unpopular causes or challenge authority at any level if need be. Because of these virtues and vices, Benjamin Butler was one of the most fascinating Civil War generals.[2]

Benjamin Butler was born on November 5, 1818, in Deerfield, New Hampshire. Soon after his birth, his mother, Charlotte Ellison Butler, learned that her husband, John, had succumbed to yellow fever in the

Caribbean. Left with three children under the age of seven, Mrs. Butler moved to the farm of her in-laws near Nottingham, New Hampshire.[3] By the time young Benjamin was four-years old, his mother realized he was not like other children. He remained weak, puny, and disfigured by a drooping eyelid and a severe case of strabism (cross-eye). His mother had faith in her son and, despite her Calvinistic beliefs, remained optimistic. She sent Benjamin to a school in Nottingham Square to learn to read the Bible, and, by the age of six, he was able to do so.[4]

Benjamin learned quickly, and, when he was nine, his mother had raised enough money to enroll him in Exeter Academy to prepare him for college. Because of his small size and frail body, he soon became an object of ridicule and the butt of jokes, but Benjamin learned to deal with the situation. When an older student called him "a little cock-eyed devil," he picked up a stick and hit the boy. Later he developed a better way of handling insults—by firing back at his tormentors with a wit that caught them off guard to the point that they found it difficult to respond.[5] Benjamin's stay at Exeter was short. In the winter of 1828, his family moved to Lowell, Massachusetts, where his mother operated a boardinghouse for young women employed in the local cotton mills. For the rest of his life, Lowell would serve as Butler's power base; all of his wealth, political influence, and military career would have their roots in that city.[6]

Young Benjamin was a brilliant student in all subjects, from language to science, and hoped to attend the U.S. Military Academy at West Point. When Benjamin was unable to get a congressional appointment, he had to settle for Waterville College, a Baptist theological institution in Maine. The fact that he was unable to attend West Point contributed to his everlasting disdain for the institution and its graduates. It also, however, impressed on him the importance of political influence. Despite his early disappointment, Butler did not lose his desire for a military career.[7]

At Waterville, Benjamin gained a reputation for being impudent, outspoken, and willing to challenge the faculty over their methods and beliefs. Although Waterville was a religious school, he balked at attending compulsory prayer meetings and church services. The school administrators considered expelling him but were willing to put up with his outrageous behavior out of respect for his devout mother. It was at Waterville, however, that Benjamin had the opportunity to hear the famous trial lawyer, Jeremiah Mason, argue a case. Benjamin was so impressed with Mason that he decided to become a lawyer.[8]

The study of law in the 1830s required that a candidate clerk in the office of an established lawyer for three years, or until the firm could vouch for the aspiring lawyer's fitness to be admitted to the bar. While clerking for William Smith—a practicing attorney who owned the largest library in Lowell—Butler spent the next two years diligently reading and studying the law. After two years of study, he felt he was ready to be admitted to the

In May 1862, General Benjamin F. Butler assumed command of the occupation of New Orleans. Swift to punish those with seccessionist sentiments, the military governor soon became known as the "Beast of New Orleans."

COURTESY OF THE LIBRARY OF CONGRESS

bar and applied to Judge Charles Warren for admission. Judge Warren was not accustomed to allowing anyone to become a lawyer without completing the prescribed three-year program but decided to give Butler a chance to prove himself. Warren questioned him about a case he had just decided, and Butler was able to answer all of his questions correctly. In closing, however, Butler said to Warren, "I thought Your Honor ruled incorrectly." The astonished judge inquired what was the basis for this opinion. Butler produced a book, *English Common Law Report*, which supported his belief. The next day Judge Warren recalled the parties and reversed his decision. Later, the revised verdict was upheld by the Massachusetts Supreme Court. At the age of twenty-one, Benjamin Butler was admitted to the bar of Massachusetts.[9]

Butler built his practice in Lowell by taking the cases of factory girls who complained of abuse at the hands of the factory owners. In one case, a suit was brought by a factory girl for unpaid wages. Butler selected a piece of mill property to attach, equal in value to the amount of the unpaid wages. He seized the mill's waterwheel, a piece of equipment necessary for the mill's operation. Butler's unorthodox way of winning cases frustrated his opponents, who referred to his methods as "legal chicanery." Judges respected him for his ability as a lawyer but often did not like him personally. Years later, Judge Josiah Abbott of Boston expressed the opinion of his fellow judges when he said, "In one faculty Butler was never excelled, that was keeping out and getting in of evidence."[10]

In 1840, Benjamin Butler met and fell in love with Sarah Hildreth. A radiant beauty, Sarah was cultured, intellectual, and a promising actress— the ideal wife for an enterprising lawyer. With the same determination that would become one of his lifelong traits, Butler began courting her. In April 1843, he traveled to Cincinnati where Sarah was starring in a play, and there he proposed. One year later, the two were married. To many, they seemed to be the odd couple: the brilliant but unattractive lawyer and the beautiful actress. Due to Butler's wit and constant devotion, however, the marriage was solid and happy. The couple would have four children.[11]

Butler soon ventured into criminal practice, an area in which his close attention to the fine points of the law brought him great success. In one case, he was able to get an acquittal for a client who had been charged with larceny for stealing a key. He established that, in a strict legal sense, the key was real estate and not personal property; therefore, taking the key could not be larceny. Baffled, the district attorney dropped the charge, and soon afterward the definition for larceny was expanded.[12] As his reputation grew, Butler opened a second office in Boston, commuting daily from Lowell. He represented a wide assortment of criminals, including murderers, and, over the course of time, he racked up more courtroom victories than many of the leading lawyers in New England. Although he was able to attract richer clients, Butler never refused cases from those with less money.[13]

Butler also became actively involved in Democratic Party politics, winning a seat in the Massachusetts legislature in 1852. In 1860, with the Southern promises of secession in the air, he was selected to be a delegate to the Democratic National Convention. Pledged to support Stephen A. Douglas for the presidential nomination, he shocked his constituents when he voted for Jefferson Davis of Mississippi. Back in Lowell, Butler defended his position by saying he believed Davis was the best candidate for appeasing the South and holding the Union together.[14]

When the Civil War broke out, Butler was ready to take part in the hostilities. He had been an active member of the Massachusetts militia since his law student days and now held the rank of colonel. When Lincoln called for troops, Butler was among the first to respond.[15]

Contacting his old political friend, Simon Cameron, now Lincoln's secretary of war, for help, Butler was named a brigadier general and head of the Massachusetts regiments. Although Butler had no military experience, he was given command of 6,000 militia. Rather than march to war, he was ordered to go to Annapolis, Maryland, where he set about suppressing local Confederate sympathizers who threatened to cut Washington off from the North. He vowed to arrest any state legislator who voted for secession.[16]

In April 1861, the Sixth Massachusetts Regiment was attacked by an angry crowd as it passed through Baltimore on its way to Washington. For days later, the situation in Baltimore remained very precarious. Train tracks were destroyed and telegraph wires cut, further isolating the nation's capital. Butler was sent to Baltimore with the Eighth Massachusetts and the Seventh New York regiments to bring order to the city. During the next few days, Butler was successful in restoring order. He ruled with an iron hand, doing whatever was necessary, whether legal or not, to maintain the peace. Clearly in violation of the law, Butler had Mayor Brown, other city officials, and many private citizens arrested and confined in prison because they were believed to favor secession. Although Butler's treatment of the citizens in Baltimore was harsh, it was mild compared to his later treatment of those in New Orleans.[17]

Butler's actions and proclamations scared Lincoln, who had been tiptoeing around the delicate issue of Maryland's status. If the state seceded, Washington would be trapped between Virginia and Maryland, and the federal government would be forced to move. Lincoln could not afford to risk an open rebellion in Maryland. Butler's actions threatened this delicate balance. Aware that Butler had important political connections and had been influential in mobilizing Democrats to support the war, Lincoln transferred him to Fortress Monroe, Virginia, where there would be less opportunity for him to cause diplomatic problems. In a further effort to gain Democratic support, Lincoln invited Butler to Washington and promoted him to major general. He was the first volunteer officer to advance to that level and was one of the highest ranked generals in the Union army.[18]

Butler's new post was an important one. Fortress Monroe dominated the entrance to Hampton Roads and controlled access to the James River. At Fortress Monroe, Butler's administrative rulings were just as controversial as his judgments in Baltimore. Virginia slaveholders were furious with Butler when he referred to fugitive slaves who escaped to Union lines as "contraband of war" and refused to return them to their masters. "I mean to abide by the decision of Virginia, as expressed in her ordinance of secession," Butler proclaimed. "I am under no constitutional obligation in a foreign country, which Virginia now claims to be. I shall hold them [the slaves] as contraband of war. You were using them against the government; I propose to use them in favor of it." As word of Butler's "contraband" proclamation spread, hundreds of runaway slaves made their way to the Federal lines at Fortress Monroe.[19]

Butler's experience and success as an administrator or attorney in the courtroom did not carry over to his tactics on the battlefield. He quickly demonstrated his lack of military experience and, worse, of any military skill. On June 10, 1861, weeks before the war's first major battle at Manassas, Butler's advance up the Virginia peninsula to clear the area of Confederate outposts ended in an embarrassing defeat. When his troops moved ahead at Big Bethel without sending skirmishers into forward positions, they encountered a concealed Confederate battery and suffered heavy losses. This early Confederate victory caused morale to soar in the South. Butler laid the blame for the setback on his subordinates.[20]

Butler was harshly criticized in the Northern press. Although the engagement had been only a skirmish by later standards, Butler's lack of military skill had been revealed. He had mistakenly sent his regiments against a well-entrenched enemy—a serious error that an experienced leader would not have made. The press suggested that the general return to the Massachusetts courts where he was more adept at fighting cases rather than troops.[21]

Butler soon had an opportunity to redeem himself. In August 1861, he proposed an attack against two small forts protecting the Hatteras Inlet on the North Carolina coast. With a naval force of seven warships and two transports, he set out for North Carolina. In the plan of attack, the warships would bombard the forts, while Butler's troops landed and mounted an assault from the rear. Butler's plan was successfully carried out, and both forts quickly succumbed. One of Butler's first moves after the surrender was to go to the powder magazine and have "a major general's salute fired in honor of the victory." After the gloom of Manassas, Lincoln was pleased to learn of the victory. "You have done all right," he told Butler. "You have done all right."[22]

Butler, however, felt that Lincoln had not given him full credit for his victory at the Hatteras Inlet. He wrote to the president requesting that his rank be increased from brevet to permanent major general. "Has anyone done more to deserve it?" he asked. "No one will do more. May I rely upon you as you have confidence in me to take this matter into consideration?"[23]

In the spring of 1862, one of the Union efforts was directed toward the capture of New Orleans, Louisiana. Butler proposed to the new secretary of war, Edwin Stanton, that an army "Department of the Gulf" be created to deal with all the Confederate coastal forts. No doubt he expected to be named as its head. Stanton accepted the suggestion, and Butler was given the departmental command.[24]

Butler was joined by Admiral David Farragut and his fleet during the New Orleans campaign. The victory proved to be remarkably easy. Confederate garrisons at Jackson and St. Philip fell to Butler's troops, while the fleet moved past them to reach New Orleans where Farragut demanded the city's surrender.

On May 1, 1862, Butler occupied New Orleans, the Confederacy's largest city. The citizens of the city were determined to show their Southern solidarity. Bales of cotton were burned to keep them from falling into Yankee hands. Other food supplies were destroyed to show the invaders that the residents were determined to resist them. When the mob saw the American flag flying, they were outraged. When a Union sympathizer dared to shout "Hurrah for the old flag," he was shot and his battered body thrown into the river.[25]

Butler was determined from the outset to impress the city's unruly insurrectionists with the hard reality of the occupation. When he entered the city, Butler marched unopposed through the streets to the St. Charles Hotel, where he established his headquarters as military governor of the city. The next morning, he met with the mayor and several members of the city council. Despite the ill-natured mood of the visitors, he was cordial; yet he was determined to have his orders followed.[26]

Butler told the committee that he intended to impose martial law, and he outlined the penalties for opposition to his rules. He said he would interfere as little as possible with the city's affairs as long as they behaved but would not tolerate any opposition to his authority. Butler's visitors seemed skeptical about his ability to enforce his rules. With a population of 170,000 secessionists and only 12,500 troops, it seemed unlikely that he could rule effectively.[27]

The city of New Orleans proved to be a hostile, defiant Rebel stronghold. When an unruly crowd gathered outside Butler's headquarters to protest the occupation, he posted artillery pieces facing the crowd and threatened to use them if necessary. The crowd soon dispersed.[28]

One of the city's citizens, William Mumford, tore down the American flag flying over the old U.S. Mint and ripped it into pieces. The act infuriated Butler: "I find the city under the domination of the mob. They have insulted the flag, torn it down with indignity. The outrage will be punished in such a manner as to my judgment will caution both the perpetrators and abettors of the act, so they shall fear the stripes if they do not reverence the stars of our banner."[29]

Butler believed that an example had to be made of Mumford. He had him tried before a military court; Mumford was found guilty and sentenced to be hanged. Butler signed the death sentence, but no one expected he would allow it to be carried out. An eyewitness on the day of the scheduled hanging noted that "the mob, who had assembled at the gallows, fully expected to hear a pardon read at the last moment." Butler defended his sentencing of Mumford in a letter to Stanton on June 10: "No words can give the extent of his guilt in the act for which he suffered. The lowering of the flag might, nay, ought, by every military rule, to have brought a bombardment upon the city, resulting in no one can know what destruction of property and life."[30]

The pressure on Butler to commute Mumford's sentence was enormous. Mumford's wife, with her small children, went to see Butler to plead for her husband's life. She wept bitterly, while the children clutched the general's leg. Butler expressed his sorrow for Mrs. Mumford's misfortune but refused to commute the sentence. He assured Mrs. Mumford that he would do his best to help her in the future if she called upon him.[31]

Mumford was hanged at the U.S. Mint with the American flag flying over it. With this act, Butler had effectively quieted the New Orleans mob, and he was now free to move about the city with only a single orderly at his side.

Many years later, information came to light that showed another side of Butler's personality. After the execution of her husband, the Mumford family was declared a public trust of the Confederacy, and funds were subscribed for their support. Unfortunately for the widow, the sums were in Confederate currency and soon became worthless.[32]

In 1869, Mrs. Mumford went to see Butler to seek help. She told him she had used the last of her funds to build a house. She did not have enough money to finish the job and was about to lose the house because of a lien held by the builder. Butler got in touch with the builder and instructed him to charge all costs to his account. He also obtained a position for her in the internal revenue office. Later, under the Hayes administration when positions were purged to make room for the new president's appointees, Mrs. Mumford lost her position. Once again Butler came to her aid, finding her a position in the U.S. Post Office Department.[33]

Once order was restored, Butler worked to improve conditions in the city. He assessed a tax on the wealthier citizens and companies, using the proceeds to create jobs and provide food for the poor. When merchants refused to open their doors of business, he fined them. When a storekeeper declined to sell shoes to Federal soldiers, he had his entire stock sold at auction.[34]

When Butler learned that the yellow fever season was approaching, he took steps to prevent an epidemic. Butler knew nothing about yellow fever except that, when it struck, it spread rapidly. The best defense against it, he believed, was to quarantine ships that might be carrying the infection and to make certain that the city was clean. A study showed that the areas of the city hit the worst were the dirtiest sections. As a result, he took steps to see that trash and refuse were removed from streets and canals. For the first time in memory, New Orleans was free of the scourge and was cleaner than it had ever been.[35]

Despite Butler's efforts to make the city of New Orleans a better place to live, many still resented the Yankee intrusion. The women of New Orleans found an effective way to annoy the occupying troops. When they encountered a soldier on the street, they would draw their skirts aside so as not to be contaminated by contact with a Yankee uniform. On other occasions, they would hold their handkerchief to their noses when passing a Union soldier as if there was a stench. At first the troops found it amusing, and Butler ignored the ladies' disrespect. But when one of them spit in the face of an officer attending a church service, he decided they had gone too far. What had started as a minor annoyance was now affecting morale.[36]

On May 15, 1862, Butler issued General Order No. 28, which earned him the sobriquet of "Beast" Butler throughout the South. It stated:

> As the officers and soldiers of the United States here have been sub-
> jected to repeated insults from women calling themselves ladies of
> New Orleans, in return for the most scrupulous non-interference and
> courtesy on our part, it is ordered that hereafter when any Female
> shall by word, gesture, or movement, insult or show contempt for any
> officer or soldier of the United States, shall be regarded and held liable
> to be treated as a woman of the town plying her avocation.

Butler's action was considered a gross insult to Southern women and turned his enemies absolutely livid.[37] Mary Chesnut wrote in her diary, "Thus is the measure of his iniquities filled. . . . This hideous, cross-eyed beast orders his men to treat the ladies of New Orleans as women of the town—to punish them, he says, for their insolence."[38]

Never one to avoid controversy, Butler saw to it that the black population in his command area was given full rights in the courts and was fed, housed, and as far as possible, gainfully employed. Butler's regulations established full access for them to the formerly segregated public transit system. African American soldiers were trained and equipped, all without approval from Washington.[39]

As a result of Butler's treatment of the citizens of New Orleans, Confederate President Jefferson Davis issued a proclamation declaring him an outlaw and ordering him to be hanged if captured. Probably the real source of concern and anger prompting Davis's proclamation was Butler's arming and training of free blacks to be Union soldiers. Davis declared, "African slaves have not only been incited to insurrection by every license and encouragement, but numbers of them have actually been armed for a servile war."[40]

Constant rumors of corruption damaged Butler's reputation even more. His detractors believed that he used his position as military governor to illegally profit from the war. According to rumors, Butler allowed his brother, Andrew, to issue passes and waivers for trading behind enemy lines. He and others close to him made fortunes exchanging critical items such as salt and medicine for Confederate-grown cotton and sugar.[41]

Speculators such as Andrew Butler were elated at the passage of the Confiscation Act of Congress on July 17, 1862, which allowed the confiscation of personal property belonging to Confederates in civil and military service and to others who would not take the oath of allegiance. Nowhere in the South was the confiscation law more strictly enforced. Butler seized $250,000 belonging to the Confederate government and deposited it in local banks. He confiscated private homes, money, furniture, jewelry, works of art, and clothing from private individuals. These items were sold at public auctions to benefit the U.S. government, but many of the valuables were reduced in price and sold to speculators for a fraction of their worth.[42]

One of the unexplained events during Butler's administration was the disappearance of some of his official records, including, perhaps, an incriminating "Special Permit Memorandum Book." There are gaps in Butler's own five-volume *Private and Official Correspondence*, which suggests that he may have destroyed incriminating evidence.[43]

During his administration in New Orleans, Butler paid little attention to army regulations. Because of his remoteness from Washington, he made his own rules as events dictated. Influential Southerners, who were accustomed to getting their own way, tried to use their influence to have him recalled, but with little success.[44]

Although Butler had control over the citizens of New Orleans, he did not have the same influence with foreign consuls, who made constant complaints to their respective ministers in Washington. Not only did Butler quarantine their ships, but he confiscated large sums of money from them, cash he suspected belonged to the Confederacy. At a time when Washington feared European military intervention in the Civil War, Lincoln could not afford constantly to offend these countries. He decided to remove Butler from his post, replacing him with Major General Nathaniel Banks.[45]

Before taking his leave from New Orleans, Butler learned that the wife of Confederate General Beauregard was dangerously ill at her home in New Orleans. Butler wrote to Beauregard, offering his sympathy and sending him a pass guaranteeing him safe passage to and from his home.[46]

When the citizens of New Orleans learned of Butler's recall, they were elated. A newspaper reported, "We have seen more smiling faces on the streets within a day or two past than for months before," and a visitor wrote, "His departure was certainly hailed with universal joy by the inhabitants."[47]

Upon his return to Washington, Butler went to see Lincoln and members of the cabinet. The president greeted him with great cordiality, but the general was unimpressed by the friendly reception. Butler demanded an explanation for his removal, but no one was willing to discuss the matter. Lincoln finally suggested that he might be transferred to the Mississippi River Valley, but Butler demanded nothing less than his old appointment back. Lincoln refused to honor his request, stating that it would unjustifiably disgrace General Banks. Butler stormed out of the White House and returned to Lowell.[48]

Upon Butler's return home, he was greeted as a hero. He received formal votes of thanks from the Massachusetts House of Representatives, the state legislature, and the City of New York. A grateful nation, unhappy with recent Union defeats, raised the general to new heights of popularity. Butler, however, would have to wait another year before receiving another command.[49]

Although Butler's behavior in New Orleans had been an embarrassment for Lincoln, he had become very popular with the radical Republicans who sought harsh treatment of the Rebels. Butler knew how to treat the Confederates, they said—the tougher, the better. Butler soon became a favorite at political rallies and was even spoken of as a potential presidential candidate.[50]

In October 1863, Butler consented to return to Fortress Monroe and was given command of the Army of the James, consisting of two corps. In March 1864, Ulysses S. Grant arrived in Washington as general-in-chief. As Grant began preparing for his spring campaign, he informed Butler that he was counting on his army to play a major role in it.

About the same time, Lincoln offered Butler a position on the Republican ticket to replace Vice President Hannibal Hamlin. Although Butler had not achieved great military success, his administration in New Orleans had given him name recognition in the North, making him a viable candidate. Butler, however, wasted no time in rejecting the offer. Although Butler appreciated the compliment, he would not quit the field to be vice president because of the prospect of the campaign against Lee in the near future. "Tell the President I will do everything I can to aid in his election if nominated," he said, "but in a military capacity only."[51]

In Grant's plan for the spring offensive, the Army of the Potomac was to advance on Richmond and on Lee's Army of Northern Virginia, while Major General Franz Sigel was to occupy the Shenandoah Valley. At the same time, Butler was to advance up Virginia's James River to cut off Lee's supply line and approach Richmond from the rear. Butler's assignment required his army to sail up the James to a point near Petersburg and there to land his troops.[52]

On May 12, Butler landed his troops at Bermuda Hundred, a peninsula located only twelve miles from Richmond and eight miles from Petersburg. Unfortunately, the peninsula had a narrow, four-mile-wide neck that could easily be defended by a smaller Confederate force. A swift advance by Butler's army could have cut Lee's supply line and possibly reached Richmond. Instead, Butler quarreled with his corps commanders for several days, allowing the enemy to rush reinforcements into the area. By the time Butler was ready to advance his army, the Confederates had blocked his path at the narrow part of the peninsula.[53]

After a feeble attack on Beauregard's forces, Butler was forced to withdraw due to pressure from Confederate batteries. The narrow neck of land that Butler had selected sealed off his army from the rest of Virginia, making it virtually useless. Grant described Butler's predicament: "His army was . . . as completely shut off from further operations directly against Richmond as if it had been in a bottle, strongly corked."[54]

After the Bermuda Hundred fiasco, Lincoln had sufficient justification to fire Butler, but it was an election year. Though also dissatisfied with his performance, Grant was sensitive to Butler's political influence. Rather than replace him, he decided to diminish his command. Grant gradually began to remove troops from the Army of the James to reinforce the Army of the Potomac. Finally, in July, Grant decided to replace Butler. He wrote to Chief-of-Staff Henry Halleck suggesting that Butler would be more valuable "in taking charge of a department where there are no great battles to be fought, but a dissatisfied element to control: no one could manage it better than he."[55]

Butler was relieved of his command and ordered back to Fortress Monroe. Soon complaints surfaced again about his profiteering. As one observer said, "Wherever he was in command came rumors of jobs, frauds, trading with rebels through the lines, and the putting of unfit persons in responsible positions."[56]

Butler tried one more time to restore his damaged reputation as a general. This time he proposed capturing Fort Fisher, North Carolina, the only port still open to Confederate blockade runners.

To capture the heavily fortified fort, Butler would need assistance from the navy and Admiral David Porter's squadron. Butler's plan was to send a steamer loaded with three hundred tons of powder directly into the fort, causing a powerful explosion. Once the fort was reduced, Butler would attack and overwhelm the startled Confederate troops.[57]

The steamer loaded with explosives ran aground and exploded far from the walls of the fort, barely disturbing the sleeping defenders of Fort Fisher. At midmorning, Porter began a heavy bombardment that lasted all day, but Butler's troops did not come until late afternoon, and then only part of his force arrived. Butler landed with his troops. When they were repulsed, Butler fled the scene, while his men were stranded on the beach.[58]

After the Fort Fisher embarrassment, Grant's patience was exhausted. Grant wrote to Stanton calling for his removal: "I do this with reluctance, but the good of the service requires it. . . . [T]here is a lack of confidence felt in his military ability, making him an unsafe commander for a large army."[59]

After the election of 1864, Lincoln no longer needed Butler's political support and, on January 7, 1865, relieved him of command. Butler appealed his case before the Joint Committee on the Conduct of the War, claiming that Porter was responsible for his defeat at Fort Fisher. Grant sent a second force under Major General Alfred Terry to Fort Fisher; this time the fort fell.[60]

Although Butler's military career was over, his political career flourished—now as a radical Republican. After the war, when President Andrew Johnson attempted to follow Lincoln's policy of leniency toward the South, Butler supported him only until it became clear that the president was not going to appoint him military governor of one of the Confederate states. After resigning his commission in the army, Butler ran for Congress in 1866, pledging to impeach Johnson. He won easily.[61]

When Congress impeached Johnson, Butler presented the impeachment case against him in the Senate. With a four-hour opening speech, he demonstrated his legal skill. His effort failed, however, by a single vote. Unwilling to accept the decision, Butler singled out seven senators and placed great pressure on them to change their vote in a second session. The final vote remained the same.[62] By the time Grant became president, Butler wielded considerable power in Congress. Although he did not like Grant or hold him in high regard, Butler did not let that opinion interfere with their working relationship. "I can say without fear of contradiction, that few men possessed a greater share of his confidence, or had more personal influence with General Grant under public question than I had," he said.[63]

Butler became Grant's man in the House, helping him pass legislation that he proposed. In return for his help and influence, Butler got what he wanted from the president, becoming the "patronage chief" for federal government appointments. Butler took good care of his friends, recommending many of them to the president. The most corrupt of Grant's appointments were at Butler's suggestion. In fact, much of the corruption during the Grant administration could be attributed to Butler's friends. One editor wrote, "The failure of Reconstruction is due almost entirely to Butler." By the end of Grant's second term, Butler was being blamed for the administration's scandals, and, in 1874, he lost his seat in Congress.[64]

Butler rebounded in 1878, switching party allegiance and winning election to Congress as a Democrat. In 1882, he was elected governor of Massachusetts. As governor, he fought for election reform, women's suffrage, and better protection for working women and children. He also named the first African American to judicial office in Massachusetts's history.[65]

Defeated for reelection as governor, Butler turned his attention to presidential politics. He opposed the nomination of Grover Cleveland as the Democratic candidate for president and formed a third party, hoping to draw votes away from Cleveland. As the torchbearer for the new party in the presidential election of 1884, he received very few votes in the November balloting, failing to block Cleveland's election as he had hoped to.[66]

Butler's fall from power came swiftly. At the age of sixty-six, he had little hope of becoming a candidate in either the Democratic or Republican party. Now he devoted his full attention to the practice of law.

In January 1893, Butler caught a bad cold, but, because of his busy schedule, he continued to work. The cold grew worse, and on January 11, he died, succumbing to a severe case of pneumonia.[67]

Butler was honored by members of the Grand Army of the Republic and by the citizens of his home city of Lowell. Butler went to his final rest in the Old Hildreth Burying Ground next to his beloved wife. His family erected a monument, on which the inscription reads: "Benjamin Frank Butler, jurist, soldier, and statesman. His talents were devoted to the service of his country and the advancement of his fellow men."[68]

Butler's military and tactical skills were lacking and could not match his ability as a politician and administrator. His treatment of secessionists and Southern citizens endeared him to the radical Republicans but drew the wrath of Confederates. Butler's seven months as commander of the Department of the Gulf were controversial, even scandalous. He offended Southern sensibilities and inflamed foreign opinion, earning him the title of the "Beast of New Orleans."[69]

Although Butler was no saint, he had his virtues. In New Orleans, he improved sanitation, helping to eradicate the dreaded yellow fever, and stabilized the city's economy. He championed the poor, especially African Americans, many of whom would have starved had he not fed and employed them. Despite these efforts, he was an embarrassment to the Lincoln administration.[70]

Controversy still rages today concerning Major General Benjamin Butler's career both as a soldier and politician. To some he was a humanitarian; to others he was an opportunist; to none was he a competent general.

6   *George B. McClellan*

The General with the "Slows"

In the weeks following the Battle of Antietam, Lincoln wanted to know what General McClellan's plans were for his army's future. The president had been disappointed that Lee's army had not been destroyed during the Maryland campaign. Lincoln urged McClellan to advance promptly into Virginia, but the general refused to move his troops until he felt they were ready. He needed more men and equipment, he declared.

Ten days after the battle, McClellan still had not moved his army. Lincoln decided to visit with McClellan in the field to press him into action, saying it was necessary for him to strike a blow and chiding him for his "overcautiousness." McClellan said he would move at the earliest opportunity. Lincoln knew McClellan well enough to know he could not rely on any assurance from the general that he would advance at an early date. With McClellan, it might mean weeks from now or never.

While visiting with McClellan, Lincoln took the opportunity to visit hospitals, review troops, and tour the battlefield. The two continued to speak about advancing the army into Virginia, but McClellan still insisted that his army was not ready to move. Later, while looking at the army from a nearby hill, Lincoln asked a friend what he saw. The man responded that it was the Army of the Potomac. "So it is called, but that is a mistake," Lincoln said. "It is only McClellan's bodyguard."[1]

Not until late October, over a month after Lincoln's meeting with him, did McClellan move his army into Virginia. McClellan's march was anything but rapid, advancing at a rate of six or seven miles a day, allowing Lee ample time to block him. Lincoln had seen enough. On November 7, 1862, he removed McClellan from command of the Army of the Potomac.

George Brinton McClellan had been the man Lincoln picked to lead the

Union armies; now he was forced to fire him. No Civil War general would inspire as much passion and controversy. After McClellan's early victory in western Virginia, Lincoln believed he had found the man to lead the army to victory. He named him commander of the Army of the Potomac and general-in-chief of the entire Union army. As the war progressed, it was clear to Lincoln that he had made a serious mistake. Few Civil War commanders had shown such promise and delivered so little as George McClellan.

McClellan's early life and military career gave no indication of the controversies that would plague him later. George McClellan was born on December 3, 1826, to Dr. George and Elizabeth McClellan. George's father was a part of Philadelphia society and many notables were numbered as his acquaintances; his mother was also from one of the leading families in Philadelphia. Together the couple had five children. Elizabeth was a woman of culture and refinement and saw to it that her children had the best education Philadelphia could offer. In 1838, George enrolled at a preparatory academy of the University of Pennsylvania. Two years later, at the age of thirteen, he entered the university.[2]

George's sister, Frederica, remembered him as "the brightest, merriest most unselfish of boys, . . . fond of books and study . . . and always the soul of honor." George had early success with his studies; he was gifted, bordering on genius. In 1842 at the age of fifteen, he entered the U.S. Military Academy at West Point.[3]

George was actually too young to enter West Point, but due to his outstanding academic record, the board waived the age requirements for him. Despite his youth, he had already passed two years at the University of Pennsylvania, where he had mastered language, the classics, and modern literature as well as courses in mathematics. From the age of ten, George had dreamed of going to West Point and becoming a soldier. In a letter to his sister, Frederica, he wrote, "I feel in high spirits. . . . I know I can do as well as anyone in both my studies and my military duties. If this state of mind continues, I will be able to stay here for four years."[4]

As one of the best and brightest in his class, McClellan became an engineer. When he directed his military campaigns, he utilized his engineering skills in almost everything he did. McClellan, like others in his class, was greatly influenced by the military legacy of Napoleon. McClellan soon came to see himself as a young Napoleon, although he did not call himself such. He did not, however, discourage others when they made that comparison.

As a cadet, McClellan sometimes worked only as hard as was necessary. Years later, fellow student Charles Stewart would say, "He was well educated, and, when he chose to be, brilliant." The competition between McClellan and Stewart was intense. McClellan felt he deserved first place in the class of 1846, but he had to settle for second behind Stewart. As was typical of McClellan, he did not accept the verdict gracefully. "I must confess

General and Mrs. Ellen McClellan in early 1862 during the time he was general-in-chief of the Union army.

COURTESY OF THE LIBRARY OF CONGRESS

that I have malice enough to want to show them that if I did not graduate head of my class, I can nevertheless do something," he wrote his family.[5]

Years later, McClellan would look back at his accomplishments at West Point with satisfaction. The Class of 1846 was an outstanding one. Forty-four of the fifty-eight classmates would fight in the Civil War and, of these, six would serve under him as generals in the Army of the Potomac and four others against him in the Army of Northern Virginia. Two of the Confederates were destined for military greatness: Thomas Jackson, seventeenth in class rank, would be known as "Stonewall" Jackson; George Pickett, who finished last, was remembered for his famous charge at Gettysburg.[6]

William Gardner, one of McClellan's classmates, later said that he was thought to be "the ablest man in the class. . . . We expected him to make a great record in the army, and if opportunity presented, we predicted real military fame for him."[7]

The Mexican War broke out in 1846, the year George McClellan graduated from West Point. When he heard the news, he was elated; graduation had come at the most opportune time. "Hip! Hip! Hurrah!" he wrote home. "War at last, sure enough! Ain't it glorious!" McClellan had his heart set on graduating and going directly to Mexico.[8]

McClellan and his classmates were delighted with the government's plans to double the size of the army to meet the needs of the war. This meant quick promotions. In the peacetime army, one could expect to remain a brevet lieutenant until a second lieutenant was promoted, resigned, or died. In wartime, promotions were much more rapid. The war promised advancement and was very popular at West Point.[9]

McClellan did not go to Mexico immediately after graduation as he had hoped. He was ordered instead to a newly formed engineer outfit where he was to assist in soldier training. Four months later, he sailed from New York City for Mexico, arriving at Brazos de Santiago in fourteen days.

In Mexico, McClellan quickly made use of his training in engineering and mapmaking. His combat responsibilities were limited, but McClellan did see some action. At the battle of Conteras, he had a narrow escape. In the course of battle he lost two horses and was knocked to the ground by enemy artillery fire. His commander, Brigadier General Persifor Smith, noted that "nothing seemed to [McClellan] too bold to be undertaken or too difficult to be executed." McClellan was commended and promoted to brevet first lieutenant "for gallant and meritorious conduct."[10]

McClellan wrote to his brother John telling him of his accomplishments: "I feel so glad and proud that I have got safely through the battles of this war. . . . Thank God! our name has not suffered, so far, at my hands." He had reason to be proud. He had demonstrated his courage at Vera Cruz, Cerro Gordo, Mexico City, and Chapultepec and would earn a second brevet promotion to captain before returning home.[11]

After the war, McClellan was assigned to duty in the West. It was during his western tour of duty that McClellan met Mary Ellen Marcy, the eighteen-year-old daughter of Captain Randolph B. Marcy, his commanding officer. Soon George was courting her. Ellen Marcy was an attractive, vivacious young woman who was the apple of her father's eye. Captain Marcy was happy to see George show interest in his daughter, believing him to be "one of the most brilliant men of his rank" and from a good family. McClellan was a good catch, he said, "that any young lady might justly be proud of."[12] Unfortunately, Ellen had other plans about whom she wanted to marry. One morning in June, McClellan declared his love for her and proposed marriage. To his dismay, she rejected him. He was furious with himself for being foolish and acting too quickly. He would bide his time and hope for a change of heart.[13]

Ellen continued to put off McClellan's offers of marriage. Perhaps it was the sheer number of suitors attracted to her. Before she was twenty-five,

Ellen had received at least nine proposals of marriage. But McClellan did not give up, continuing to write to her.

McClellan quickly earned a reputation as one of the army's brightest military minds. As a result, he was chosen to be a member of a team of army officers to observe and collect information about the war in the Crimea where both France and England were involved. The fact that McClellan was sent to Europe with a group of senior officers is some indication of his standing in the army. His star was on the rise.[14]

McClellan later put to use some of the things he had learned while abroad. He developed a saddle, which he adapted from those he had seen in Europe. He introduced the shelter tent, which later became known as the pup tent. The bayonet manual and drill that the army adopted were the result of translations and modifications McClellan made from a French text.[15]

Promotion was a slow process during peacetime. Early in 1857, McClellan resigned his commission to become chief engineer for the Illinois Central Railroad. He welcomed the new freedom and authority of this position and enjoyed the luxury of being able to make decisions on his own without first referring to the adjutant general or the secretary of war. "I feel already as if a heavy load was removed from my shoulders," he said. His salary was $3000 a year, more than twice his army pay. Two years later he rose to the position of vice president, and by 1860, he moved to Cincinnati as president of the eastern division of the Ohio and Mississippi Railroad.[16]

McClellan continued to write to Ellen after he left the army. In his letters, he hoped to win her sympathy for his bachelor's existence. He "dreaded to think of the future," he said. "It seems so blank—no goal to reach, no objective to strive for!" Despite his efforts, Ellen continued to see other men.[17]

One suitor in whom she showed an interest was McClellan's friend from West Point, Ambrose Powell Hill. Hill quickly fell in love with Ellen and proposed; she accepted. When the Marcys became aware of the situation, they reacted with anything but joy and urged Ellen to wait at least six months before marrying. Ellen's father painted a harsh picture of life on the frontier as an army officer's wife; additionally, "Hill's means were limited," he said. To marry him was to resign herself to "a life of exile, deprivation, and poverty." He also pointed out differences in their backgrounds. They were Northerners, and he was a Southerner, brought up in a slave environment. Because her father wanted better for her, he forbade her to see Hill again. Ellen's mother preferred McClellan, writing to her: "How very kind he [McClellan] is. . . . Such a treasure you have lost forever. . . . The time is coming sooner or later . . . when you will regret if ever a woman did—mark my words."[18]

Mrs. Marcy took action to prevent the union. She began to circulate stories about Hill's medical problems, the most embarrassing of which involved a sexual disease. When McClellan learned what she had done, he took the honorable approach and wrote to Mrs. Marcy to defend his friend's honor: "You have been unjust to him, and you have said unpleasant and bitter things . . . about one of my oldest and dearest friends."[19]

The damage had been done, however, and in July Ellen told her parents that the affair was over and that she had returned the engagement ring to Hill. Hill wrote to McClellan to express his concern that people might have a false impression of his affair with Ellen. At the expense of his own reputation, he admitted to McClellan that it was she, not he, that had broken the engagement. The two continued to be good friends despite the fact that they loved the same woman. Finally, Ellen accepted McClellan's offer of marriage, and they were married on May 22, 1860. Hill was a groomsman in the wedding.

During the war, McClellan's army was often attacked by Hill's division. McClellan's troops believed that Hill's fierce assaults were an effort to get revenge on his rival for Ellen's hand. After one of these attacks, a Union veteran exclaimed, "My God Nelly [Ellen], why didn't you marry him [Hill]!" When McClellan heard the story, he smiled and said, "Fiction no doubt, but surely no one could have married a more gallant soldier than A. P. Hill."[20]

George and Ellen were devoted to each other. "My whole existence is wrapped up in you," he told her. During their engagement, he began his lifelong habit of writing to her at least once every day when they were apart. About that time, McClellan underwent a religious rebirth and began to follow the teachings of the Presbyterian Church. He believed that his marriage had been predestined, an example of God's will acting on those He favored. Later, when war began and he was called to lead the Union army, he believed this appointment, too, was God's will.[21]

Soon after his wedding, McClellan accepted the before-mentioned position with the Ohio and Mississippi Railroad. His salary was $10,000, double his Illinois Central salary.[22]

In 1860, with the threat of war hanging over the nation, there was no doubt that George McClellan would play a major role in the federal army. Because of his past experiences, he was considered one of the military intellectuals of the prewar army. In addition, his four years as railroad executive had provided him with valuable training in the area of military logistics. After the firing on Fort Sumter, McClellan became the most sought after former officer in the North. At the age of thirty-four, he reentered the army at the rank of major general, outranked only by the general-in-chief, Winfield Scott.[23]

McClellan was assigned to command the Ohio volunteers. In his first campaign, his responsibility was to clear western Virginia of Confederate influence. With a force of men, McClellan marched on Grafton. When the Confederates retreated southward to the village of Philippi, McClellan occupied Grafton without a single shot being fired. On June 3, the Confederate force at Philippi was routed, freeing the western part of the state of Confederate troops. Eight days later, delegates from Virginia's western counties met in convention and set up their own provisional state government. For McClellan it was an excellent way to begin his return to the army, becoming the first Yankee hero of the war. The *New York Times* wrote of his accomplishment: "We feel proud of our wise and brave young major general. There is a future behind him."[24]

On July 21, 1861, in the first major battle of the war, the Union experienced a disastrous defeat at Manassas. The rout and panic that followed the battle had a demoralizing impact on the people of Washington and on President Lincoln. Washington was threatened, danger was near, and someone was needed to bring order out of chaos. Lincoln turned to the Union hero of the war—George B. McClellan. On July 22, he informed McClellan that he was to take command of the Army of the Potomac. Showing little modesty, McClellan wrote to Ellen, "I find myself in a new and strange position here—President, cabinet, General [Winfield] Scott . . . all deferring to me. By some strange operation of magic, I seem to have become the power of the land."[25]

McClellan might have been a better general when he took over the command of the Army of the Potomac had he been tested in his first battle in western Virginia. His triumph had come too easily, and he was convinced that he was destined to lead the Union to victory. The public was eager for a hero, and he felt he was it. He looked and acted as a soldier and hero should act. His military presence and magnetic personality allowed him quickly to establish rapport with his troops. Admirers said he was the only general who, by simply riding up to them, could convince men to stop what they were doing and follow him. Standing only five-feet, eight-inches tall, he possessed tremendous shoulders and chest. Courteous and sometimes boyish in manner, he was like other Americans of the time, including smoking and chewing tobacco. The press referred to him as the young Napoleon and photographed him in a typical Napoleonic pose. Wherever he went, he was recognized. He began to believe that people looked at him as their savior, the one who could protect them from danger and lead them to victory. Later, when he became general-in-chief, he wrote to his wife, "I was called to do it; my previous life seems to have been unwittingly directed to this great end."[26]

McClellan was an excellent organizer and trainer of troops. His men, sensing that he cared for them, idolized him. In preparing for battle, he was confident and energetic, but when it came time for battle, he was slow and timid. He had a tendency to exaggerate every obstacle, particularly the size of the opposing army. In battle, he hesitated to throw his entire force at the enemy at the critical time, and he withdrew when a strong attack was made against him.[27]

Few generals were more popular with their troops than George McClellan.

The men were attracted by his cheerful personality and confident smile and affectionately called him "Little Mac." On an inspection trip, Lincoln was impressed with the enthusiasm of the soldiers for McClellan, especially when they cheered for him.

At first, Lincoln felt confident with his choice of McClellan to lead the Army of the Potomac. Later, he realized that there were some serious flaws in McClellan's character. He seemed to have a dual personality. At times, McClellan could be rude, petty, vain, and vindictive, especially when dealing with Lincoln, Stanton, and some fellow officers. His display of these personality flaws contributed to the difficulty he had with those whose support he needed the most. But this picture did not encompass the entire man; his public persona was that of a charming and engaging person who possessed the ability to remember the names of every junior officer. He was loved and held in high esteem by the men in the ranks; he worked hard to sustain their morale, pride, and self-respect. He looked after their physical needs and showed great concern over heavy casualties on the battlefield. Throughout his time as commander of the Army of the Potomac, McClellan retained the loyalty and respect of his troops.[28]

Although McClellan related well to his men, the opposite was true for his dealings with Secretary of War Stanton. Their relationship was neither friendly nor cordial. McClellan was not, however, alone in his feelings about Stanton. Virtually all the commanders who had to report to Stanton disliked him intensely.[29]

At the beginning of the war, few realized the extent of McClellan's egotism, but he was soon at odds with General Scott. When Lincoln realized that General Scott was no longer effective as a military leader, he retired him with honors and tributes. In his place he assigned McClellan. On November 1, 1861, at the age of thirty-four, George McClellan assumed the nation's highest military position.[30]

McClellan now faced the difficult task of restoring confidence in his army after their defeat at Manassas. He began by requesting and receiving the best for his troops. McClellan made every man under his command, from officer to private, believe that he cared about them, and indeed he did. In the end, it might be that he cared too much for his soldiers.[31]

McClellan set about to train his men, drilling them constantly; camps circled the entire city of Washington. As a result of his efforts, the Army of the Potomac gained confidence and began to see themselves as part of a coordinated military machine. Their sense of accomplishment and pride contributed to the feelings the army had for McClellan. In a letter to Ellen, he bragged of his success: "I have restored order very completely. . . . You have no idea how the men brighten up now when I go among them. I can see every eye glisten. Yesterday they nearly pulled me to pieces in one regiment. You never heard such yelling."[32]

As leader of the Army of the Potomac, McClellan felt that this army was his. He would refer to it as such almost to the day he died. Although McClellan was skilled in creating and training an army, he was reluctant to send it into battle. He wanted his army to be the best that ever took the field, but at the same time he wanted no harm to come to it. Throughout the summer and fall of 1861, McClellan continued to prepare his men, but they still remained outside of Washington. Pressure increased for him to take action. Winter, however, provided the perfect excuse for not moving his army. During that time, he did nothing but stay in camp and build his troops.[33]

Lincoln put pressure on McClellan to move, but he refused to do so. His response was, "So soon as I feel that my army is well organized and well disciplined and strong enough, I will advance and force the Rebels to a battle on a field of my own selection. A long time must elapse before I can do that."[34]

In addition to the disagreement about when he would move his army, McClellan had philosophical problems that strained his relations with the president. He was far more conservative in his war aims than was Lincoln. As a Democrat, McClellan believed strongly in preserving the Union but was opposed to freeing the slaves. He did not get along with Lincoln and his administration and showed little respect for them. "The President is an idiot! I only wish to save my country and find the incapables around me will not permit it," he said.[35]

McClellan's contempt for Lincoln grew to the point of insubordination. One evening Lincoln went to McClellan's house only to find that he was not at home. Lincoln decided to wait; when McClellan returned, he went directly to his room. Lincoln asked a servant to tell him he wanted to see him. McClellan sent word back, "Tell him I have gone to bed." When Lincoln's friends asked why he put up with such insubordination, he replied humbly, "I would hold McClellan's horse if it would help win the war."[36]

At the beginning of 1862, McClellan had still not moved his army. More and more often, Lincoln spoke of McClellan as the general "with the slows." Finally he ordered McClellan to either attack Richmond or give up his command of the Army of the Potomac. McClellan decided to attack the Confederate capital by moving his army to the Virginia peninsula and advancing from there. The Peninsula Campaign began in March. McClellan, with an army of 120,000 men, landed on the Virginia peninsula and moved to Yorktown, where he laid siege to the Confederate line. Commanding the army on the other side was General Joseph E. Johnston, a man similar to McClellan in leadership style. Both were brave men but feared the responsibility for leading an army and risking defeat. Although McClellan's army moved steadily up the peninsula with very little resistance, he still insisted that he needed more troops.[37]

Lincoln soon realized that the dual responsibility of commanding the Army of the Potomac and being general-in-chief of the army was too much for one man, even McClellan. He waited until McClellan was involved in the Peninsula Campaign before issuing the order relieving him as general-in-chief. McClellan accepted the demotion without grumbling, even though it was a setback to his public image.[38]

In the Battle of Seven Pines in late May, Confederate Johnston was wounded and replaced by Robert E. Lee. When McClellan learned that Johnston was being replaced by Lee, he was pleased. He assured President Lincoln that Lee was "too cautious and weak under grave responsibility—personally brave and energetic to a fault, he yet is wanting in moral firmness when pressed by heavy responsibility and is likely to be timid and irresolute in action." When finally they met in the Battle of Seven Days outside of Richmond two months later, McClellan quickly found he had misjudged his opponent. Ironically, he had precisely predicted his own, not Lee's, response to the pressure of command. At the time, each general was seen by its respective army as a great leader. Lee was eventually recognized as one of the best generals America ever produced, while McClellan is now thought of, in the words of one historian, as "merely an attractive, but vain and unstable man, with considerable military knowledge, who set on a horse well and wanted to be president."[39]

When McClellan was unable to defeat Lee's army, he blamed the failure on the fact that he was outnumbered and needed reinforcements. On June 25, he reported: "The Rebel force is stated at 200,000. I shall have to contend against vastly superior odds if these reports be true. I regret my inferiority in numbers, but I feel that I am in no way responsible for it." Confederate strength was actually 80,000. McClellan's request for more troops was denied. In July, McClellan was ordered to withdraw from his position on the peninsula.[40]

General McClellan blamed his failure during the Peninsula Campaign on Lincoln and his administration. Those responsible for the defeat, he said, were the "heartless villains" in Washington who "have done their best to sacrifice as noble an army as ever marched to battle." From the very beginning, he said, "Stanton and his cohorts had wanted him defeated and overthrown, so that disunion would prevail and they could be free to rule unhampered in the North." McClellan believed that Stanton saw him as his enemy; one who must be destroyed. "They are aware that I have seen through their villainous schemes and that if I succeed my foot will be on their necks," McClellan said.[41]

McClellan continued to rationalize his defeat, believing that what had happened to him on the peninsula was God's will. Because God had dictated the outcome of the campaign, McClellan believed his defeat was actually a blessing in disguise. "I think I begin to see His wise purpose in all this," McClellan told his wife. "If I had succeeded in taking Richmond now, the fanatics of the North might have been too powerful and reunion impossible."[42]

After the failure on the peninsula, Lincoln placed McClellan's army under the command of General John Pope and ordered him to assist in the Second Battle of Manassas. Only two of McClellan's corps arrived at the battlefield in time to join Pope's army in the fight. As a result, the Union army suffered another crushing defeat. Pope's army and the rest of McClellan's army now crowded together in Washington. For Lincoln, this major setback was a nightmare. Despite his frustrations with McClellan's cautiousness, he had no one else to whom he could turn.[43]

On September 1, Lincoln restored McClellan to his former position as the head of the Army of the Potomac. His decision was contrary to the wishes of the majority of his cabinet, which was about to present him with a petition calling for McClellan's dismissal. Lincoln was faced with little choice despite his earlier statement that "McClellan can be trusted to act on the defensive, but having the 'slows' he is good for nothing for an onward movement."[44]

Despite strong protests from certain members of his cabinet, Lincoln stood firm. He insisted that McClellan "had beyond any officer the confidence of the army. Though deficient in the positive qualities which are necessary for an energetic commander, his organizing powers could be made temporarily available till the troops were rallied." Secretary of the Treasury Salmon Chase later wrote: "I could not but feel that giving the command to him [McClellan] was equivalent to giving Washington to the Rebels." Stanton was equally angry at Lincoln's renewed confidence in McClellan and felt so disgusted that for a while he considered resigning as secretary of war. But Lincoln did not change his mind. In fact, he came to the defense of McClellan: "There is no man in the army who can lick these troops of ours into shape half as well as he." "McClellan has the army with him," he also said.[45]

When the men of the Army of the Potomac learned that McClellan was returning, they broke into cheers. Despite the failure of the Peninsula Campaign, they retained their faith in him. Again McClellan was at his best, doing the job he knew best—rebuilding the army's confidence and preparing them for their next campaign. In a short time, McClellan had the army organized and ready to fight. Meanwhile, Lee moved into western Maryland hoping to draw McClellan out of Washington and into the open.[46]

The strategy worked, and McClellan's army began moving towards Frederick, Maryland, to intercept Lee. Then on September 13, McClellan experienced one of his most extraordinary pieces of luck; two soldiers found a copy of a Confederate dispatch relating that Lee had divided his army. Lee's army was already smaller than McClellan's. To divide it, particularly in enemy territory, was a very dangerous move. One part of Lee's army, under Stonewall Jackson, had been sent to Harper's Ferry, while the remaining part was deployed around Hagerstown to the north. "Here is a paper," McClellan said, "with which if I cannot whip Bobbie Lee I will be willing to go home."[47]

McClellan set his troops in motion, but with his customary caution. Not until late on September 16 did he bring his 70,000-man army into position to attack the Confederates. By that time, Jackson had captured Harper's Ferry, and Lee had regrouped all of his army except A. P. Hill's division, which was still at Harper's Ferry. Lee took up a position behind Antietam Creek with less than 40,000 men when the battle began. A. P. Hill's division returned just in time to prevent the destruction of Lee's army.[48]

McClellan believed that the Antietam campaign had secured his military reputation in history. "Perhaps one day," he wrote, "history will, I trust, do me justice in deciding that it was not my fault that the campaign of the Peninsula was not successful. . . . I have shown that I can fight battles and win them!" He based his claim of triumph on the tradition that the victory goes to whichever army holds the battlefield. In that day's struggle the Confederate line had been pressed back, but it never broke. When Lee left the field, it was not a rout.[49]

Antietam was the only campaign George McClellan ever directed from start to finish. On it rests, in a large measure, his reputation as a battlefield commander and tactician. Antietam was the bloodiest single day of the Civil War. One out of every four men who marched into the battle was killed, wounded, or missing—about 23,000 total casualties. The Confederate losses were 10,300; the Union deaths, 12,400. The campaign as a whole cost the Federals 27,000 men, including those captured at Harper's Ferry. McClellan's official report more than doubled the Confederate losses—to 30,000. The fact that the Confederate army had been repulsed from Union soil and that Maryland and Pennsylvania were now safer from invasion was a more realistic reason for claiming victory.[50]

McClellan had been tentative in his battle approach at Antietam, fighting less to win than to prevent his own defeat. He could have defeated Lee and probably ended the war had he advanced his entire army simultaneously in an assault on the Confederates and prevented Hill's division from joining Lee. Moreover, he held an additional 24,000 fresh troops in reserve that he never used. McClellan allowed two more excellent opportunities to win a decisive victory slip away when he failed to renew the battle on September 18 and when he did not pursue the Confederates as they retreated across the Potomac on the 19th.[51]

President Lincoln was grateful for what he labeled a victory at Antietam. He took the opportunity to issue the preliminary Emancipation Proclamation. Two days later, he suspended habeas corpus, a legal protection for those who might oppose governmental policies. McClellan was opposed to Lincoln's position on slavery and was bitter in his condemnation of those in Washington who were trying to create a social revolution. McClellan called on his troops to repudiate the Emancipation Proclamation. When there was little reaction from his troops, it became obvious that he was out of step with both his army and the political officials in Washington.[52]

McClellan realized that the issue of slavery had to be faced when the war was over. "When the day of adjustment comes," he told his wife, "I will . . . throw my sword into the scale to force an improvement in the condition of those poor blacks." Although he would never speak out for abolition, McClellan supported any gradual emancipation that would guarantee equal rights for slaves.[53]

Lincoln was very disappointed that Lee's army had not been destroyed at Antietam. He urged McClellan to advance promptly into Virginia, but McClellan refused to move his troops until he felt they were ready. Lincoln visited McClellan in the field to spur him on to pursue Lee, but after a month he still had not move.

Finally, in October, McClellan advanced his army into Virginia. His plan was to move rapidly down the east side of the Blue Ridge Mountains and capture Richmond before Lee's army in the Shenandoah Valley could intercept him. But McClellan's march was slow, allowing Lee time to block his advance.

Lincoln lost his patience with McClellan and, on November 7, relieved him of his command. Twice McClellan had taken over the army after a defeat, but Lincoln did not think he was the man to lead the Union to victory. McClellan's shortcomings at and after the Battle of Antietam obscured his overall accomplishments during his time as commander of the Army of the Potomac. In less than three weeks after resuming command, McClellan had brought order to the army such that it was able to fight a highly contested battle and force Lee to withdraw from Maryland. Between the Peninsula Campaign and the end of the Antietam Campaign, McClellan inflicted over 47,000 casualties on Lee's army. These losses would later prove the undoing of the Army of Northern Virginia.[54]

Other than McClellan not being aggressive enough, Lincoln had political reasons for relieving him. The general had become the most prominent opponent of the administration and its policies. He publicly accused Secretary Stanton of leading a traitorous conspiracy to destroy him and his army on the peninsula. McClellan did not try to control his supporters when they attacked Lincoln and his administration; in some cases, he even encouraged them. There was fear in Washington that McClellan might use his army to take over the government, especially a government in the midst of a civil war. Lincoln's patience with McClellan's inaction in the field and his insubordination finally ran out. McClellan's military career was over.[55]

Throughout his life, McClellan regarded Antietam as a great victory. He told his wife: "Those in whose judgment I rely tell me that I fought the battle splendidly and that it was a masterpiece of art." Unfortunately, there are many who do not support McClellan's analysis of the battle.

On November 9, General McClellan began the painful process of saying farewell to his army. He received the officers on his staff in his tent, expressing his dismay at being removed and saying it was unexpected: "We have only to obey orders." Then he offered a toast: "To the Army of the Potomac, and bless the day when I shall return to it."[56]

The next morning McClellan's troops assembled for a review in his honor and to hear his parting words: "In parting from you I can not express the love and gratitude I bear to you. As an army you have grown up under my care. . . . The battles you have fought under my command will proudly live in our Nation's history . . . [and] unite us still by an indissoluble tie. Farewell!" McClellan was deeply moved by the final display of affection from his men. "I did not know before how much they loved me nor how dear they were to me," he wrote Ellen. "The scenes of today repay me for all that I have endured." It was the last time his army, as he always called it, would see him.[57]

There was no available administrative post for an officer of McClellan's rank in Washington. In any event, the capital was the last place Lincoln wanted him. Stanton ordered McClellan to Trenton, New Jersey, apparently for no better reason than its nearness to the Marcy's home where Ellen was staying.[58]

At Trenton, McClellan was given a hero's welcome. In a brief speech he urged his listeners to be sure the war was conducted "for the preservation of the Union and the Constitution, for your nationality and rights as citizens." This scene would be repeated wherever he went during the next few months.

McClellan soon moved to New York City. The city was the largest Democrat stronghold in the North, and his greeting there was tumultuous. When McClellan attended the opera one evening, the orchestra struck up the then famous march, "National Airs," and the audience cheered when he entered.

McClellan was replaced with Major General Ambrose Burnside. Soon afterward, on December 13, 1862, the Army of the Potomac suffered a crushing defeat at Fredericksburg, Virginia. The six weeks following the Union defeat were a time of crisis for the army, remembered ever after as the Valley Forge of its existence. Soldiers died senselessly in unsanitary hospitals and filthy camps. The food was so bad that some even died from scurvy. After McClellan's departure, the army's care and morale suffered; he was popular with his men because he was always careful to look after their welfare.[59]

After Fredericksburg, McClellan's mark on the officers who had served under him became noticeable. His critics called it "McClellanism," describing its symptoms as bad blood and general paralysis. Burnside believed that his authority was being challenged by those generals loyal to McClellan. Because the army had lost confidence in Burnside, Lincoln had no other choice but to replace him. He appointed "Fighting Joe" Hooker in his place and reassigned some of McClellan's strongest supporters. Lincoln made it clear that loyalty to the commander of the Army of the Potomac was a higher duty than loyalty to McClellan.[60]

With no official duties, McClellan devoted most of his time during the early months of 1863 to reporting on his fifteen months as commander of the Army of the Potomac. In his report, McClellan was careful to rationalize his "reasons for delays" and the "enemy's positions and numbers," including important intelligence estimates of troop size on which he had relied. After Hooker's defeat at Chancellorsville in May 1863, pressure began to mount on Lincoln to return McClellan to his command of the Army of the Potomac. The *Pennsylvania Herald*, one of the nation's most prominent newspapers, demanded that Stanton and Halleck be dismissed and McClellan be reinstated.[61]

But it was General George Meade who replaced Hooker, not McClellan. After Meade's victory at Gettysburg, McClellan wrote, "most of the army thought at Gettysburg that they were fighting under my command. . . . I have been told by many officers that 'McClellan's ghost' won the battle because the men would not have fought as they did, had they not supposed that I was in command."[62]

McClellan realized he had no chance for a command while Lincoln was still in office. He resigned his commission and returned to private life. It was not long before McClellan was in the spotlight again. This time his name was being mentioned as a possible Democratic candidate for president in the 1864 election. Because of his military career, Democrats believed he would be a viable candidate to oppose President Lincoln. His failure during the Peninsula Campaign, they believed, was due to lack of support from the administration. This ineffectiveness, as McClellan had claimed, was the result of a deliberate, treasonous intent to destroy him and further the radical Republican cause.

In July 1864, when General Grant met with Lincoln to discuss the command responsibilities for the Eastern theater, McClellan's name came up. The two agreed that, if McClellan dropped out of the election, he would be invited to return to the army, but McClellan refused. McClellan said it was his greatest wish to command the Army of the Potomac in one more great campaign but that he was not willing to trade a presidential nomination for the possibility.[63]

McClellan's views on the war had not changed since 1862. He still opposed emancipation but favored restoration of the Union by military victory. The peace wing of the Democratic Party opposed this position, favoring a cease fire followed by negotiations. Peace Democrats launched a last-minute effort to nominate Governor Horatio Seymour of New York, but when the fall came, they decided to accept McClellan.[64]

The convention tried to bridge the gap between the two wings of the party, and McClellan was nominated on the first ballot. They adopted a "peace" platform, which denounced "arbitrary military arrest, suppression of freedom of speech and of the press, and the disregard of state rights." The key plank declared that, after "four years of failure to restore the Union by the experiment of war, . . . [we] demand immediate cessation of hostilities" so that peace may be restored on the basis of the federal Union of the states.[65]

In the summer of 1864, McClellan accepted the Democratic nomination at the party's national convention. Although he had not sought out the presidency, McClellan believed the result was in God's hands. Earlier he had told his mother that he was not interested in running for the presidency, but in March he wrote her: "I know that all things will prove in the end to have been arranged for the best and am quite willing to accept what I cannot avoid."[66]

When McClellan became the Democratic candidate, his political enemies made a number of allegations about his war performance. The most sensational of these was that he had met with General Lee at Antietam, where the two agreed that the Confederate army would withdraw across the Potomac without interference, clearing the way for a compromise peace settlement that would preserve slavery. A Joint Committee on the Conduct of the War investigated the allegations and found them to be false.[67]

In one of his few public appearances during the election year, McClellan was invited to West Point to deliver a speech dedicating the site of a monument to honor the Civil War dead. In his address, he stressed what he believed to be the appropriate goal of the war. The war was being fought for a cause "just and righteous, so long as its purpose is to crush rebellion and save our nation from the infinite evils of dismemberment. The Civil War should be a war for Union and Constitution and no other object."[68]

As McClellan campaigned, Secretary Stanton's animosity toward him grew. Former members of McClellan's staff found it difficult to obtain commissions in other commands. When members of the Army of the Potomac attempted to raise money for a presentation sword to honor McClellan, the effort was halted by Stanton's order. After McClellan's West Point address, Stanton dismissed or transferred the three-member West Point committee, including the superintendent, who had invited him to speak.[69]

McClellan was embarrassed by the antiwar platform of his party and repudiated it in his letter accepting the Democratic presidential nomination. A retired West Pointer, he had fought the Confederates as Lincoln's commanding field general. Now he was running against him on what looked like a peace-at-any-price platform. McClellan tried to counteract the peace platform by stating: "I could not look into the face of my gallant comrades of the army and navy who had survived so many bloody battles and tell them that their labors . . . were in vain; that we have abandoned the Union for which we have so often paroled our lives."[70]

On the main issues of the day, Lincoln and McClellan were not completely at odds. They both were opposed to secession and agreed that the war was a righteous one. Essentially, they agreed on Reconstruction. The differences were more a matter of shading than of glaring contrasts.

Most Democrats were loyal citizens who favored the vigorous prosecution of the war, but McClellan also had the support of a small, but noisy, antiwar faction.[71] By the end of the summer, it looked as though McClellan would win the election unless the tide of the war changed. On September 2, it did—Atlanta fell. Sherman telegraphed the good news to Washington: "Atlanta is ours, and fairly won." The North was elated by the news. At Petersburg, the Army of the Potomac fired a hundred-gun salute. This was the news Lincoln had hoped for, and it came just before the election.[72]

The outcome of the election surprised both McClellan and Lincoln. Lincoln defeated his opponent by a ten-to-one margin in the electoral race. McClellan had counted on the army's vote, but after three years of fighting, they knew the road to peace lay with Lincoln. McClellan told a friend that he was relieved not to be president: "For my country's sake I deplore the result—but the people have decided with their eyes wide open and I feel that a great weight is removed from my mind."[73]

McClellan took comfort from his conclusion that he was not responsible for the outcome of the election. In an address to his supporters he said, "As I look back upon it, it seems to me a subject replete with dignity. . . . I think we have well played our parts. The mistakes made were not of our making. . . . I trust that we will see that these apparent mistakes were a part of the grand plan of the Almighty."[74]

After the election, McClellan traveled in Europe in a kind of self-imposed exile and did not return to the United States until after the 1868 election. Initially there was interest among Democrats in nominating McClellan for the presidency again in 1868, but his support dwindled after the Republicans nominated General Grant. A newspaper wrote that the party would ensure a Republican victory "by running the man who didn't take Richmond against the man who did."[75]

In 1873, McClellan returned to Europe where he began to write his memoirs. He returned to the political arena in 1876, campaigning for Samuel J. Tilden against Rutherford B. Hayes. Although McClellan's position on African Americans remained the same as it was in 1861, he was forced to acknowledge that slavery was dead and that, legally at least, blacks were citizens and could vote. "Sectional harmony was paramount," he said, "and states' rights must prevail in all social and racial questions."[76]

In 1878, McClellan was elected governor of New Jersey. He served for three years but declined to run for a second term. In the election of 1884, he campaigned vigorously for Grover Cleveland. When Cleveland won, McClellan expected to be rewarded with a cabinet position, and he was disappointed when it did not happen.

McClellan loved to speak to veteran organizations and to visit the battlefields made famous by his army. He sensed that the bond he had forged with Union soldiers was still strong, and, indeed, it was.

Early in October 1885, at the age of fifty-eight, he suffered a severe attack of angina pectoris. Under his doctor's care, McClellan seemed to make a complete recovery, but on the evening of October 28, his chest pains returned, and his condition deteriorated rapidly. At three o'clock the next morning, he murmured, "I feel easy now. Thank you." Then he died.[77]

Messages of condolence arrived by the hundreds, from the president, from generals who had fought with and against him, and from men who had served in the ranks of the Army of the Potomac. "His death," Fitz John Porter said, "is crushing to me." Beauregard described the great esteem he felt for McClellan as a man and soldier, and Joseph Johnston mourned "a dear friend whom I have so long loved and admired."[78]

There were many obituaries throughout the country, each recounting and examining the events in McClellan's life. One of these, in the *New York World*, evaluated his military service: "No general who fought in the war from its outbreak to its close was ever actuated by nobler sentiments and purer and more patriotic motives. Yet no soldier was ever more unjustly dealt with or more harshly, cruelly and unfairly criticized."[79]

Funeral services were held on November 2 at the Madison Square Presbyterian Church in New York. The honorary pallbearers included old business and political friends as well as comrades from the army years. Burial was in the McClellan and Marcy family plot in Riverview Cemetery in Trenton.

In many ways, McClellan was the most brilliant strategist to defend the Union. Even General Lee admitted that McClellan was his brightest adversary, yet some historians have not been kind to him. They view him as overly cautious, vindictive, vain, and generally a detriment to his cause.[80]

McClellan was a complex man. The love and admiration McClellan's troops had for him remains almost unparalleled in American history. In turn, he respected and loved his troops and experienced real sadness when men were killed in battle. To some, he was a military genius crippled by his own insecurity, a master of planning who lacked boldness in executing his own plans. McClellan's actions might best be described as Lincoln put it; he was "the general with the slows."

7   *Don Carlos Buell*

"The McClellan of the West"

The American Civil War was a political war. As such, major military decisions were often made with political, as well as military, considerations in mind. Generals who understood this nuance, like Ulysses S. Grant and William T. Sherman, and planned their strategies with it in mind, thrived. Generals who disregarded the political aspect of their positions usually fell by the wayside and were passed over for promotion. One general who failed to play the "political game," and suffered the consequences, was Major General Don Carlos Buell.[1]

Buell was a self-absorbed, distant, and private man. He had neither the style of George McClellan nor the brilliance of Henry Halleck, and he lacked the instincts of Grant. As the commander of the Army of the Ohio, he did not fraternize with the enlisted men. As a result, they never came to know him. The army he created and led resembled himself: a machine that was disciplined but lacked emotion. Buell was a complete professional, but he did not have the ability to motivate his army and establish esprit de corps. Although he was personally brave, he hesitated to take risks with his army. Eventually, his temperament, caution, lethargy, and unwillingness to allow politics to affect his military decisions threatened to end his career. But it was his failure to defeat Confederate General Braxton Bragg at Perryville and pursue him after the battle that led to his final demise.[2]

Don Carlos was the first of nine children born to Salmon and Elizabeth Buell. He was born on March 23, 1818, in Lowell, Ohio. As a young boy growing up on the banks of the Muskingum River, Carlos seemed at home working on his father's farm. The daily responsibilities and discipline that came from working on a farm instilled in him the value of land. The family placed a high priority on morals and religion, attending the Catholic Church on a regular basis.[3]

In the summer of 1823, Carlos's father contracted cholera and died. It was a devastating loss to the family, especially to young Carlos. His mother tried to make the best of the tragedy, and the family was able to survive. When Carlos was eight years old, however, he went to live with his uncle, George Buell, who lived in Lawrenceburg, Indiana. George Buell was successful in his pork-trading business and a devoted husband. His uncle was a good choice to rear the young Carlos, and he helped his nephew develop into a man of high moral character.[4]

The transition for Carlos from a large family setting to one in which he was the only child appeared to have an effect on the development of his personality. At first he was self-absorbed, introverted, and shy and had difficulty making friends with other children in the town, who often looked upon him with suspicion. When Carlos was challenged to a fight by the town bully, he demonstrated his courage and fighting prowess by beating the boy. From then on, he gained both self-confidence and respect from his peers. He also learned that strong resolve, determination, and a good defense could make up for a lack of physical size. He developed a rigid view of right and wrong, justice and injustice. After he made up his mind on an issue, he clung to that belief tenaciously, a trait he would display during the Civil War.[5]

Soon after moving in with his uncle, Carlos began attending a Presbyterian school. The school stressed the importance of high moral character, equality, and patriotism. These lessons, along with a firm belief in God, set for him the goals he should strive for in life.[6]

Carlos attended the high school in Lawrenceburg until he was sixteen. He demonstrated intellectual ability and was especially good in mathematics. Because of his uncle's prominence in the community, he was able to secure an appointment for Carlos at the U.S. Military Academy at West Point. When he graduated in 1841, he finished thirty-second out of a class of fifty-two. His mediocre grades and poor discipline record earned him the reputation as a non-conformist. Although years later Buell would become nostalgic for West Point, at the time he considered it one of the most unpleasant experiences of his life. Buell did not accept discipline easily, but he never forgot its value. If he disagreed with his superiors, he did not hesitate to let them know; however, with time he became a disciplined soldier. Like most graduates of West Point, Buell believed he was a superior being, created to lead.[7]

In the fall of 1841, Buell entered the army as a second lieutenant and was assigned to Florida, where the Second Seminole War had been in progress for five years. As a member of the Third Infantry Regiment, he scouted the swamps in search of bands of marauding Indians, but he participated in no major engagement and received none of the glory others received.[8]

Major General Don Carlos Buell was a complete professional, but he did not have the ability to motivate his army and establish espirit de corps. Eventually his career was threatened when he was unwilling to allow politics to affect his military decisions.

COURTESY OF THE LIBRARY OF CONGRESS

In the spring of 1843, the Third Infantry Regiment moved to St. Louis. It was here that Buell experienced his first problem with an enlisted man in his command, and his reputation for strict discipline took a more violent turn. In an effort to chastise an insulting private, he lost his temper, and, in a moment of rage, drew his sword and repeatedly slashed the man across his head. "You will repent this, sir!" shouted the injured private. "Silence, you son-of-a-bitch!" Buell responded. As a result of this act, he was arrested and ordered to stand trial on charges of "unofficial-like conduct." At the trial, Buell expressed his regret for his conduct as an officer. After deliberation, the court found no criminality in his actions and found him not guilty.[9]

There was wide criticism of the court's decision. Those who disagreed with it included General Winfield Scott, who was so disgusted that he asked Secretary of War John Porter to reconvene the court. Porter responded by ordering another trial, but when the court reassembled, it refused to retry the case. As the legal battle continued, Buell returned to duty. Finally, President John Tyler put the case to rest, claiming emphatically, "I can see no good to the service in again requiring the Court to pass upon the case. . . . Let all further proceedings, therefore, against Lieutenant Buell, for the offense with which he is charged, cease." From then on, Buell's reputation for violence preceded him wherever he went.[10]

When the Mexican government declared war on the United States on October 23, 1846, the Third Infantry was ready. In the first two days of the war at Palo Alto and Resaca de la Palma, the Americans won decisively. In his report, General Taylor commended the Third Infantry Regiment for its gallantry. Although wounded, Buell's actions in the battle earned him commendation for gallantry and a promotion to first lieutenant.[11]

In July, Buell was assigned to General David Twiggs's staff as acting assistant adjutant general for the First Division. At Monterrey, Buell caught Twiggs's eye for his "valuable and meritorious services." Shortly thereafter, he was brevetted to the rank of captain. Although seriously wounded during the Battle of Churubusco, Buell continued to carry out his responsibility to reconnoiter the enemy's position. His action so impressed a fellow lieutenant that he declared, "I have never known but one man whom I thought was absolutely ignorant of what it was to be afraid. That person was Buell, who I am certain, was the bravest man it was ever my fortune to know." For his action that day, Buell became known as the "bravest of the brave." The Mexican War was a defining point in Buell's military career. For his boldness at Churubusco, he received a major's brevet and emerged from the war a skillful combat soldier who had earned the respect of his fellow soldiers.[12]

In the fall of 1851, Buell married Margaret (Maggie) Hunter Mason, a Southern belle and the widow of Brigadier General Richard B. Mason. Maggie had two daughters who became very attached to their stepfather, and he, in turn, loved them dearly. The marriage proved to be a happy one. Her inheritance and his salary enabled them to live a comfortable life.[13]

After the Mexican War, Buell was transferred from the Third Infantry Regiment to the adjutant general's department in Washington and worked there creditably for thirteen years, rising to the rank of lieutenant colonel. While serving in the peacetime army, Buell would come in contact and serve with many future Civil War leaders. Among them were George McClellan, Winfield Scott Hancock, Albert Sidney Johnston, and William T. Sherman.

The winter of 1860 to 1861 was one of the gloomiest in Buell's career. As he read the daily dispatches coming in from the South, he was well aware of the threats to the unity of the nation. Although at the center of the military decisions made in the War Department, Buell did not agree with the government's position on the abolition of slavery. While living in Washington, however, he and his wife felt obliged to dispose of their slaves. Although Buell no longer had slaves, he did not change his views on slavery. His marriage to a Southerner and his long service in the South had helped him accept slavery. This position was not very different from that of many of the officers with whom he served. Buell's close adherence to rules and military regulations led him to develop a conservative viewpoint and a strict view of the Constitution. He considered disunion a greater evil than slavery.[14]

When the Confederates fired on Fort Sumter, just a month after Lincoln's inauguration, Buell hoped to be offered a high rank in the army. Despite his excellent military record, he was overshadowed by his good friend George McClellan. While McClellan became the most sought-after officer in the North, Buell was assigned as far away from Washington as possible and ordered to report to the Department of the Pacific to serve as assistant adjutant general. Although many of his friends, and even his brother-in-law, left the ranks to side with the Confederacy, Buell remained loyal to the Union.

After the Confederate victory at Manassas on July 21, General Irvin McDowell became the first Union commander to be dismissed. Dissatisfied with his performance, the Lincoln administration replaced him with Major General George McClellan. McClellan, now commander of the Army of the Potomac, became an overnight hero. In August 1861, Buell was ordered back to Washington and promoted to brigadier general. Because of his reputation with this fellow officers, he soon became one of the most sought-after officers in the army. Brigadier General Robert Anderson, commander of the Military Department of Kentucky, requested that he be assigned to his staff. At the same time, McClellan made a similar request. Because of the imminent Confederate threat to Washington and McClellan's influence, Buell was assigned to the Army of the Potomac. On September 11, he reported to McClellan.[15]

As a division commander, Buell soon lived up to his reputation. Cautious and deliberate by nature, he maintained a professional distance from officers and enlisted men alike. Buell was just what the division needed at this time—someone with experience who could discipline and organize it into a fighting unit. On his first meeting with the division, he inspected and drilled them for three hours in the hot sun. It was the longest drill session they had experienced, and the intensity of it caused some of the men to fall out of the ranks. Although many of the men cursed him at the time, they would ultimately come to respect him.[16]

When General Scott retired, Lincoln appointed McClellan to replace him as general-in-chief of the army. When the Western commands needed attention, McClellan organized the territory into two departments. To one department he recommended Henry Halleck; for the other, he selected Don Carlos Buell. McClellan picked Halleck because he had to give something to the man who had been his chief rival for command of the army; he selected Buell because he believed he would be one of the best generals of the war.[17]

Lincoln had high hopes for Buell to be successful in Tennessee. The people in eastern Tennessee had voted against secession, and nothing disturbed the president more than having a Union stronghold in Confederate hands. "My distress," he wrote, "is that our friends in East Tennessee are being hanged and driven to despair, and even more, I fear, are thinking of taking Rebel arms for the sake of personal protection." In addition, Lincoln saw a strategic advantage in advancing through the Cumberland Gap and taking Knoxville. This action, Lincoln believed, would cut the Confederates' northernmost east-west railroad and separate them from what he called their "hog and hominy."[18]

Buell's instructions from McClellan were to hold Kentucky and to prepare his army for a move into eastern Tennessee. Meanwhile, Buell was to impress on the people of the area that the army's purpose was the restoration of the Union, not the abolition of slavery.[19]

When Buell arrived in Louisville in November, he found the new Army of the Ohio in chaos. Although McClellan was anxious for him to move his army, Buell believed that the organization of the Army of the Ohio had to be accomplished first. Like McClellan, Buell was a perfectionist, only without McClellan's charm or glamour. He immediately began to make changes in the army's organization and firmly impressed the importance of discipline on his troops. Buell considered discipline central to a soldier's survival in combat and made great demands on his army. Because he lived the same life that he expected from his troops, the men came to respect him.[20]

By the end of November, Buell had still not advanced. McClellan was concerned about his inaction and began to prod him to move. In Washington, Buell had believed he could move into eastern Tennessee through the Cumberland Gap and then attack Knoxville; but after arriving at Louisville, he realized he could not take east Tennessee by attacking from the north. Since there were no railroads from his base at Louisville, he would have to move his supplies a long distance in wagons over poor roads. The problem of logistics was such that, even if Buell could capture Knoxville, it was doubtful he could hold it.[21]

Buell developed another plan that he believed was more realistic. He proposed simultaneous movements by his Army of the Ohio and Halleck's army. This concerted action, Buell believed, would force the Confederates to split their forces and make it easier to force them out of Kentucky and Tennessee. In the process, he would attack the Tennessee capital at Nashville, a manufacturing center. The route to Nashville was through a land rich with supplies, no natural fortresses, and a railroad. Once Nashville was taken, the Confederates defending east Tennessee would be outflanked, forcing them to fall back. Then Buell could move in unopposed.[22]

What Buell did not realize, however, was that Lincoln was receiving persistent political pressure for the immediate relief of east Tennessee. Despite the requests from his military superiors and the president, Buell considered the safety of his army more important than clearing east Tennessee of Confederates. As to the Unionists, who were waiting for his advance into the mountains, Buell believed that their "constancy could sustain them until the hour of deliverance." By the end of 1861, Buell had still not moved his army.[23]

By early 1862, McClellan was being pressured not only to move his own army but to move Buell's as well. In a letter to Buell, McClellan wrote, "You have no idea of the pressure brought to bear here upon the Government for a forward movement. It is so strong that it seems absolutely necessary to make the advance on Eastern Tennessee at once."[24]

Lincoln also expressed his desire for Buell to take action and even suggested the strategy for him to use:

> I state my general idea of this war to be that we have greater numbers, and the enemy has the greater facility of concentrating forces upon points of collision; that we must fail, unless we can find some way of making our advantage an over-match of his; and this can be done by menacing him with superior forces at different points, at the same time; so that we can safely attack, one, or both, if he makes no change.[25]

Finally, by the end of January, Buell began his advance on eastern Tennessee. After defeating a Confederate force at Mill Springs, Kentucky, however, his advance stalled because of miry roads.

In the meantime, Halleck ordered Grant to advance on Fort Henry on the Tennessee River, but Grant did not tell Buell until he was underway. When Grant ran into trouble, Halleck asked Buell to divert some of the Confederate forces away from Grant's army. Buell, who had suggested the Tennessee movement earlier and who had asked Halleck to assist him, now found reasons not to come to his aid. When Buell finally moved, he marched toward Nashville and not toward Fort Henry. As late as one month after Lincoln had ordered the two departmental commanders to cooperate with each other, they had not found a way to comply.[26]

On February 6, Grant captured Fort Henry. By February 16, Fort Donelson, with 12,000 prisoners, had also surrendered to Grant. On February 22, McClellan gave Buell permission to march on Nashville but reminded him, "We must not lose sight of Eastern Tennessee." McClellan also pressed

Halleck to support Buell. Begrudgingly, Halleck did. On February 25, 1862, Nashville fell to Buell's Army of the Ohio.[27] Immediately thereafter, Halleck withdrew his support.

Buell hoped to convince Southerners that his army did not represent a wicked Northern society, and he carefully developed principles for the occupation of Nashville to demonstrate this fact. Citizens who remained peaceable were not to be molested "in their persons or property," and "any wrongs to either" would be promptly corrected and the offenders punished. When service or the use of private property was required, fair compensation would be offered. There was to be no appropriation of private property or arrests made without the authority of the commanding general.[28]

On March 4, Lincoln appointed Andrew Johnson, the only Southern senator who had remained loyal to the Union, military governor of Tennessee. Johnson was angry about the situation in his home state, believing Buell could have captured east Tennessee just as easily as he had Nashville. Buell's unwillingness to do so left the most loyal part of the state in Confederate hands.[29]

In March, Buell was promoted to major general for his capture of Nashville, despite subverting the wishes of the president and others in Washington. During the same month, much to Buell's dismay, Halleck was named commander of the Department of the Mississippi, making Buell subordinate to him. Although Halleck assured Buell that the new arrangement of the department would not interfere with his command, it was also clear that Buell would have to accept Halleck's strategy of combining forces. Buell received more bad news when he learned that McClellan had been relieved of his position as general-in-chief. This meant that Buell could no longer count on support from his friend, McClellan. Halleck could now deal directly with Lincoln and Stanton. In addition, Buell now had Andrew Johnson to deal with. He felt he was caught in the middle of a war of egos and politics. Buell was not prepared to deal with either.[30]

On March 15, Buell's army began the march to join Grant at Savannah, Tennessee. On April 5, he arrived, only to find Grant nine miles upstream at Pittsburg Landing. Grant's Army of the Tennessee had set up camp there but had failed to develop a defensive line. In the early morning of April 6, Confederate forces attacked Grant, catching his army completely by surprise. The fighting on the first day favored the South, and by nightfall the enemy was threatening to drive Grant's army into the Tennessee River. When one of Grant's staff officers asked him if the prospects did not appear "gloomy," he replied, "not at all," and added, "they can't force our lines around those batteries tonight. It is too late. Delay counts for everything with us. Tomorrow we shall attack them with fresh troops and drive them, of course."[31]

The fresh troops Grant was referring to were those of Buell's Army of the Ohio, 20,000 strong. Grant's orders in the morning to his generals were to "advance and recapture our original camp." By noon, Buell's troops had cleared the peach orchard on the left, and Grant's troops were nearing Shiloh Chapel on the right. At the end of the day, Confederate General Beauregard ordered his troops to withdraw from the field. Although Grant could claim a victory at Shiloh, the cost had been heavy.[32]

The battle at Shiloh gave the Union its first taste of all-out war in the West. Buell was hailed as the "savior of Shiloh." When he passed by his command, the soldiers cheered and raised their hats. During the battle, he had remained in the front line, shouting out commands, leading by example, and "exposing himself freely."[33]

After the battle, it did not take long for the press to draw its own conclusions about what happened at Shiloh. The blame for the first day's embarrassment fell on Grant. Even his own men criticized him for being unprepared. Although Buell was not negligent in the handling of his army, he nevertheless received his share of criticism as well. The editor of *Frank Leslie's Illustrated* claimed that Buell knew of Grant's position and "dawdled through Tennessee." This criticism of Buell and the Army of the Ohio was unfair. Their arrival and attack on the second day ensured a Union victory. The discipline and order Buell had instilled in his men paid off handsomely in the battle.[34]

After Shiloh, Buell missed a great opportunity to win over the full support of his army. He and his men had shared a humbling experience, yet he remained the distant leader. He failed to personalize his praise, commending their actions and appearance rather than the men themselves.[35]

Buell continued to have a difference of opinion with Andrew Johnson over the deployment of his troops. Johnson insisted that Buell not withdraw more of his troops from Nashville, fearing their removal would invite the Rebel element in the city to act up. Halleck disagreed. He came to Buell's aid, stating that his troops were needed for the drive to Corinth, Mississippi, and leaving their disposition to Buell.[36]

During the advance to Corinth, however, the friction between Halleck and Buell flared up again when Halleck reprimanded him for his slowness in moving his troops. The cautious Buell lashed back at Halleck saying that he intended to carry out his orders, "but where they have not been specific, I have supposed that you expect me to exercise my own judgment." Halleck's remarks hurt Buell's pride and did little to help their relationship.[37]

Although the march from Shiloh to Corinth was only fifteen miles, it consumed the entire month of May. By the time Halleck arrived, the outnumbered Confederates had abandoned Corinth and retreated south to Tupelo, Mississippi. Halleck now decided to send Buell eastward. A rapid march would claim east Tennessee and its railroad network and prevent the Confederates at Tupelo and Chattanooga from joining forces. But Buell's march bogged down when he had to take time out to repair the railroad and rebuild a bridge that had been burned. The damage made supplying his troops more difficult and required him to place the army on half rations. Another commander would have simply taken what he needed from the countryside, but Buell believed in traditional warfare that protected citizens as much as possible from harm and looting.[38]

Buell did not hesitate to punish those who disobeyed his orders about harming citizens. He court-martialed Colonel John B. Turchin and several others for plundering and looting. Turchin was dismissed from the army, but, in the process, Buell won few friends among superiors or subordinates for his action. Colonel John Beatty, who served on the court-martial court of Turchin, later expressed his feelings about Buell's policy: "Turchin's policy is bad enough. It may indeed be the policy of the devil; but Buell's policy is that of the amiable idiot."[39] Lincoln was not pleased either. After hearing a plea from Turchin's wife, Lincoln not only reinstated Turchin but promoted him to brigadier general.[40]

In mid-July, General Halleck was appointed general-in-chief and summoned to Washington. The Department of the West was split into several commands with General Grant commanding the largest force, about 67,000 men. Buell, meanwhile, continued to command the Army of the Ohio and was ordered to continue his advance to Chattanooga and the clearing of east Tennessee. Again, Buell's movement was slower than expected, and by the time his army reached Chattanooga, the Confederates, now commanded by General Braxton Bragg, had left and were heading north.[41]

Lincoln and Stanton had lost faith in Buell, and his summer campaign did nothing to improve their opinion of him. When reprimanded for his slowness in reaching Chattanooga, Buell responded, "The advance on Chattanooga must be made in force. Otherwise it will either fail or prove a profitless and transient prize."[42] By mid-August, the Army of the Ohio was completely demoralized. From the outset of the campaign, their advance had been slow, with the average march beginning at dawn and ending before noon. Buell's policy of "watch and wait" was frustrating and debilitating for his troops. The men passed their free time searching for food and water, abusing slaves, writing letters home, and getting into trouble. Buell's strict punishment for violating his rules added to the men's misery.[43]

Buell blundered in the Chattanooga campaign when he allowed a smaller Confederate army, half his size, to escape without a fight. General Bragg now turned north into Kentucky. When Buell discovered this move, he turned his attention to Louisville, hoping to arrive there before Bragg. Buell notified Halleck of his plans, but by this time Halleck's patience had worn thin. "March where you please," he responded, "provided you will find the enemy and fight." The move toward Louisville encouraged his troops; now they were marching toward food rather than away from it.[44]

On September 25, the Army of the Ohio entered Louisville. On his march to Louisville, Buell passed up the opportunity to engage Bragg's army at Munfordville, believing that the Confederate numerically superior army was entrenched. Again Buell had failed to fight. The fact that the men wanted to fight rather than march was revealed in the diary of a disgruntled Kentucky soldier: "That old poke-easy general of ours [Buell] has allowed the thieving rebels to overrun the best position of the state and they are now in full possession of our homes." "It was the desire of the army to get into an engagement . . . to relieve the monotony of constant marching," wrote a soldier in the Tenth Indiana.[45]

After Buell arrived in Louisville, Governors Oliver P. Morton of Indiana, David Tod of Ohio, and Richard Yates of Illinois demanded to know why Buell had not attacked Bragg at Munfordville when he had had the opportunity. They petitioned the president to remove him from command. Lincoln abided by their request, replacing Buell with Major General George H. Thomas. When Thomas received his orders, he went to see Buell and told him he was going to refuse the command. Buell encouraged him to accept, but Thomas remained firm and continued to refuse. Although there were those in Washington strongly opposed to Buell, he still had the support of the majority of his division and brigade commanders. As a result, Buell continued in command.[46]

On October 1, the Army of the Ohio, now grown to 77,000 men, marched out of Louisville. Buell sent two divisions to feign an attack on Frankfort, Kentucky, while he took the remainder of his army after Bragg. On the march to Perryville, Buell's horse reared up and fell over backward on top of him. He was cut and bruised and lucky to have survived the accident; for days afterward he had to be transported in an ambulance wagon. He refused to let his doctor wash his wounds as long as the water was scarce for his men.[47]

On October 7, the stage was set for a clash of the two armies at Perryville. There was a question about who would launch a major assault first. Buell's officers were wagering that it would not be the Union army. They considered Buell too slow in both making decisions and in action. That evening, unknown to Buell, a group of his officers met behind closed doors. The result of the meeting was to prepare a dispatch to President Lincoln, asking him to relieve Buell from command of the army because they had lost confidence in him. The petition was signed by all of the officers present but was never sent.[48] It is well that Buell did not know about the meeting; he had enough problems that night without the burden of knowing his officers were asking for his removal. Even though he was still suffering from his accident, he intended to attack Bragg in the morning.[49]

Buell's deployment of the diversionary column had confused Bragg, as he had hoped it would. He did not know the main part of Buell's army was at Perryville and had a muddled picture of the enemy's strength and location, but Buell's intelligence was not much better. The Battle of Perryville actually began before Buell realized it. Although he had heard the sound of distant artillery throughout the morning, it was not until the afternoon that he became aware that his left was under attack. A natural phenomenon known as "acoustic shadow," which muffled sounds from the field of fire, was responsible for his lack of awareness. Once informed of the Confederate assault, Buell tried desperately to bring his whole army into action. At first, the Confederates were successful in driving Buell's left flank back, but when they attacked his center, they were turned back with heavy losses. The Rebel's advance eventually stalled, and, by evening, General Bragg realized he was outnumbered.[50]

The moon was bright that night, and many of Buell's officers urged another attack; but Buell, convinced that he faced Bragg's entire army, decided to wait until morning. By then, it was too late, for Bragg had ordered a hasty retreat that evening. The battle had been a costly one for both sides; Buell had suffered casualties of 4,200, while Confederate losses were just under 3,400. In the end, no one was the victor.[51]

Although some Northern newspapers credited Buell with a victory, since Bragg had departed from the field, many others were critical of his deployment of his troops. Although he had 57,000 men in the area, only a third were actually engaged, causing some of his own troops to accuse him of disloyalty. An Indiana artillerist wrote, "I left Perryville with the idea that the sooner Buell was relieved of Command of the Army of the Ohio, the better for all concerned."[52]

To Lincoln's despair, Buell failed to pursue Bragg despite his numerical advantage. Buell informed Washington that he would not follow the Confederates because the roads were too rough and the country too barren, continuing to insist that the preferable route to eastern Tennessee was from the south. Buell said he would regroup his army at Nashville and attack Bragg at Chattanooga.[53]

Halleck ordered Buell to "drive the enemy from Kentucky and East Tennessee." "If we cannot do it now," he said, "we need never to hope for it." The president, Halleck wrote, "does not understand why we cannot march as the enemy marches, live as he lives, and fight as he fights, unless we admit the inferiority of our troops and of our generals."[54]

Lincoln thought the problem lay with Buell and not with the troops. On October 30, 1862, Buell again received orders removing him from command and replacing him with Major General William S. Rosecrans. Buell was accused of dilatory tactics and an investigation was held by a military commission, but it made no recommendations. Despite the inconclusive opinion of the commission, Buell felt he had earned a personal victory—he had not compromised his principles in waging war. For more than a year he waited for new orders, but none came. In May 1864, he was dismissed from the volunteer service, and, on June 1, he resigned his regular army commission.[55] In a letter to his brother, William Sherman expressed his opinion of the actions by the politicians in Washington: "You have driven off McClellan, and is Burnside any better? Buell is displaced. Is Rosecrans any better?"[56]

After leaving the army, Buell turned to business, operating an ironworks and coal mine in Kentucky. He continued to suffer publicly from a damaged self-image after the war. When his wife died in 1881, he was devastated and grieved for months. Unlike many other veterans of the war, he did not write his memoirs but did write several articles defending his role at Shiloh.

Buell's last years were not happy ones; he spent them in seclusion, poverty, and obscurity. By 1898, he was completely disabled. On November 19, 1898, Don Carlos Buell passed away. He was buried in Bellefontaine Cemetery, St. Louis.

Buell's problems as a commander were closely related to his military philosophy and conservative view of the Civil War. Although he was aware that the war was shaped by political policies, he remained steadfast in his beliefs, refusing to subordinate military operations to political pressure. He waged war not to change Southern society by freeing slaves but rather to suppress the rebellion and unite the nation.[57]

McClellan and Buell were often compared. They were both conservative Democrats who fought a limited war for limited objectives and repeatedly ignored Lincoln's insistence on a more aggressive war. To many, Buell was the "McClellan of the West."

8   William S. Rosecrans

"Old Rosy"

Before the Civil War began, William Rosecrans was believed to have a great future with the army. He was, in some respects, President Lincoln's ablest general. He could easily have become the Union's greatest soldier; he nearly became commander of the Army of the Potomac. Before the Battle of Chickamauga, he had been the Union's most consistently successful general. Yet, in his own words, "in the midst of congratulations from all Union men, and professions of kindness from all sides, without warning or notice, or complaint, or hint of explanation," he was removed from his command and "put before the nation in disgrace."[1]

Although forced from his command, Rosecrans always retained the respect and admiration of his soldiers. Referred to affectionately as "Old Rosy" by his troops, he was often cheered when he rode among their ranks. His six-foot frame, heavily bearded face, and powerful build immediately commanded their attention and respect. Always careful to provide the best in food and equipment for his men, Rosecrans became one of the most popular officers in the Union army. According to Ohio journalist Whitelaw Reid, few officers "have inspired more confidence in the rank and file."[2]

As a soldier, Rosecrans received praise for his ability as a strategist and tactician from those who served with and against him. Even Southern newspapers acclaimed his ability. An Atlanta newspaper reported that he was "a wily strategist and brave and prudent leader." The Confederate Lieutenant General D. H. Hill praised his "fine practical sense" and "tough, tenacious fiber."[3]

Why, then, did such a gifted commander finish out the war on the inactive list? Whether or not Rosecrans realized it, his lack of deference to his military and civil superiors cost him his military career. His failure to develop a good relationship with General-in-Chief Ulysses S. Grant, Chief-of-Staff Henry Halleck, and Secretary of War Edwin Stanton led to Rosecrans's dismissal as commander of the Army of the Cumberland after forty-five months of creditable service.[4]

Although excelling in leadership and personal relationships with his men, Rosecrans did have some faults. He made enemies unwisely and needlessly. A perfectionist, he was often critical and impatient of the careless and slovenly performances of others. He had difficulty compromising and a short temper. Generally he was kind and courteous to those who served under him but abrupt with his superiors. When he thought he was being wronged, he spoke out. When his superiors erred, he had no difficulty telling them so.[5] Rosecrans was his own man—and a fiercely independent one.

Rosecrans developed an independent bent at an early age. He was born in Little Taylor Run, Delaware County, Ohio, on September 6, 1819, to Crandall and Jemima Hopkins Rosecrans. When William was a baby, the family moved to a small town nearby where his father opened a tavern and store. There they prospered well enough to purchase a farm and an additional house. Although not affiliated with any particular church, the family was deeply religious. Their religiosity manifested itself in a stern moral code, which Rosecrans would adhere to for the rest of his life.[6]

William's parents helped shape him into the man he would become. From his father, he inherited the family's patriotism and love of history. From Jemima, he learned to speak the truth, regardless of cost or pain. As a small boy, William was described as quiet, thoughtful, sensitive, and studious, with a remarkable memory. William had very little classroom education, but once he learned to read, books took the place of more formal schooling, and the future general read everything he could get his hands on. When his father died, William shouldered the burden and helped his mother make a living for the family.[7]

When the family could not afford the expense of college for young Rosecrans, he found another way to gain an education—he would attend West Point. To gain admission, however, he needed a congressional appointment. To acquire this, William trudged fifty miles to be interviewed by Congressman Alexander Harper. Harper had planned to give the appointment to his son, but after talking with Rosecrans, he was convinced to nominate him instead. With just a little more than a year of schooling, Rosecrans entered West Point, one of 112 admitted to the class of 1842.[8]

It was at the Academy that Rosecrans was given his nickname, "Old Rosy." In the class of 1842, there were such future celebrities as James Longstreet, Don Carlos Buell, and John Pope. Other cadets at West Point who Rosecrans would encounter again later included George Thomas, William T. Sherman, and Ulysses S. Grant. Because students were assigned to classes according to their ability, Rosecrans was placed in the superior

After the Battle of Chickamauga, Major General
William S. Rosecrans was removed from his command and "put before the nation in disgrace."
Although forced from his command, he was
always respected and admired by his soldiers.

COURTESY OF THE LIBRARY OF CONGRESS

group, proving "brilliant" in mathematics and finding French "tolerably
easy." By June 1841, he stood fifth in his class and received a rank of cadet
lieutenant, a high achievement. At graduation, Rosecrans ranked fifth in
the fifty-six-man class of 1842, gaining him a commission to the prestigious
Corps of Engineers. Of those graduating, twenty-nine would become generals, eighteen in the Union army and eleven in the Confederate ranks.
When the cadets speculated who would be the most successful in the class
of 1842, Rosecrans's name was the one most frequently mentioned. They
agreed he was "good at everything, his studies, his military duties, his
deportment," and that he was the "brilliant Rosy Rosecrans."[9]

While at West Point, the Ohio cadet became a Catholic, remaining devout
throughout his life. He always carried a crucifix and rosary in his uniform

pocket. His piety did not keep him from drinking or using rough language, but he was careful never to be blasphemous.[10]

Rosecrans's first assignment as a second lieutenant was at Fortress Monroe at Old Point Comfort, Virginia. In April 1843, he was commissioned first lieutenant, the only promotion he received in the eleven years of service before the Civil War. Shortly after his promotion, he married Anna Elizabeth Hegeman. The couple raised eight children. Rosecrans taught for a time at West Point and later supervised military constructions in New England, thus missing the Mexican War.[11]

In 1853, disheartened by the low pay and slow rate of promotion, Rosecrans elected to resign from the army to take a position in the private sector. He worked as an engineer and superintendent of a canal river coal company and as the president of a water navigation company in western Virginia. Just before the Civil War, he and two partners built a kerosene refinery in Cincinnati. Late in 1859, he was badly burned about the face when a safety lamp exploded and set the refinery on fire. After putting out the fire, Rosecrans walked almost two miles to his home. It took eighteen months for him to recover from his burns, but the scars that remained left the impression that he had a "smirk" on his face. To hide the scars, he grew a beard.[12]

Just after the Confederate bombardment of Fort Sumter, Rosecrans returned to the army as colonel of engineers on the staff of Major General George B. McClellan. Less than two months later, he assumed a position as commander of the Twenty-Third Ohio Volunteers with the rank of brigadier general in the regular U.S. Army.

A few months later, he was placed in command of a brigade in the army of occupation in western Virginia, and shortly afterward he led his troops in a fight on Rich Mountain. The newspapers hailed the battle as a great Union victory, but, although Rosecrans's troops had performed well, gave most of the credit to McClellan. Although it was not McClellan's fault, Rosecrans felt he had been denied his proper recognition, and from then on his relationship with McClellan was less than cordial.[13]

In his official report, however, McClellan did refer to the "great, difficult and almost superhuman effort of Rosecrans and his men" and also gave him credit for "the very handsome manner in which he planned and directed his attack upon the rebels." Before the end of July, western Virginia was in Union hands, where it remained throughout the war. Their minor success in Virginia brought recognition to both McClellan and Rosecrans in Washington, and both men were quickly rewarded. After the Union defeat at the first battle at Manassas, McClellan was called to Washington to assume command of the Army of the Potomac. On July 23, Rosecrans took command of the Army of the Ohio, which included western Virginia, Ohio, Indiana, Michigan, and Illinois.[14]

During Rosecrans's eight months as commander of the Army of the Ohio, his forces were engaged in several small actions at Carnifax Ferry and Gauley Bridge. These actions helped secure western Virginia for the Union and brought Rosecrans the acclaim that he believed he had deserved earlier. Rosecrans had been more successful than any other Union general during 1861.

Rosecrans's new fame, however, did not bring him reward or gratitude from his superiors in Washington. Rather, on March 11, 1862, his command was merged with Major General John C. Fremont's Mountain Department. Angry about his treatment, Rosecrans traveled to Washington to meet with the new secretary of war, Edwin Stanton, to learn why he had been demoted. The meeting of the two strong-willed men was more cordial than expected. Stanton praised Rosecrans for his accomplishments and promised to find him a new and larger command. In the meantime, he was to escort Brigadier General Louis Blenker's division to Fremont's headquarters. En route he met Major General Nathaniel Banks, whose corps had been detached from McClellan's army and was now also assigned to Fremont. During the meeting, Rosecrans proposed a plan by which troops under Fremont, Banks, Blenker, Major General Irvin McDowell, and Brigadier General Robert Milroy would be combined to operate against Confederate Major General "Stonewall" Jackson, now operating in the Shenandoah Valley. In the discussion, Rosecrans gave the impression he had received authorization from Stanton to carry out the plan. When Stanton learned what had happened, he was furious.[15]

Stanton recalled Rosecrans to Washington; this time there were no smiles, no flattery, and no promises of promotion. Instead, in a stormy meeting, Stanton shouted at Rosecrans, "You mind your business and I'll mind mine," and accused him of misrepresenting his authority. Rosecrans took no man's abuse quietly. His reply was just as caustic, commenting about the government's inability to deal with Jackson's small command. Stanton's strategy for fighting Jackson had been unsuccessful, and he resented Rosecrans for reminding him of that fact. Rosecrans had made a new and powerful enemy.[16]

In May 1862, Rosecrans was transferred to the West to join the armies under Major General Henry Halleck near Corinth, Mississippi. He was assigned to command the right wing of two divisions of Major General John Pope's Army of the Mississippi. A month later, when Halleck was moved to Washington as general-in-chief, Grant was selected to replace him. On July 15, Grant placed Rosecrans directly under himself, a situation that would later lead to ill feelings between the two. Two weeks later, when Pope was transferred East, Rosecrans was appointed commander of the Army of the Mississippi. This army sometimes operated closely with Grant and, at other times, independently.[17]

On September 17, 1862, when Rosecrans was ordered to advance on Iuka, Mississippi, he welcomed the opportunity to engage the enemy and was confident of victory. He planned a three-column assault on the Confederate army. While a part of his corps attacked Major General Sterling Price's command, the main body would smash the Confederate flank, cutting off his escape route. Then a part of Grant's army under Major General E. O. C. Ord would attack from the northwest. The plan looked good on paper; however, when it came time to carry it out, events did not go as planned.[18]

By the night of the 18th, Ord had moved into position and was to wait to begin his attack until he heard that Rosecrans was engaged. Due to an atmospheric phenomenon known as "acoustic shadow," Ord was unable to hear the sound of the fighting and did not know that Rosecrans had begun his attack. The problem was further compounded when Rosecrans discovered that the ground over which his troops had to pass was too broken for a coordinated movement. Keeping his army together as well as he could, he advanced, only to be attacked by Price. Rosecrans's men fought valiantly, with savage fighting taking place all day long. That evening Price withdrew from Iuka, escaping virtually unscathed.[19]

The next morning Grant came to Iuka to find out what had gone wrong and why Price's army had escaped. Rosecrans's explanation did not satisfy him. Later, Major General William Sherman reported that Grant was "much offended" by Rosecrans's failure. From then on, Grant placed less faith in Rosecrans's tactical and strategic ability, and their relationship continued to chill.[20]

After the battle at Iuka, Grant wrote two reports. In his first, dated September 20, he complimented Rosecrans saying, "I cannot speak too highly of the energy and skill displayed by General Rosecrans in the attack, and of the endurance of the troops under him."[21]

The second, dated October 22, came after a Cincinnati newspaper had praised Rosecrans but had been critical of Grant. In this report, Grant withheld all compliments about Rosecrans. This report remained "buried" for over a year, and Rosecrans did not have a chance to see or answer it.[22]

On September 24, Grant divided the troops in his department into three groups, forming a triangle, and moved his headquarters north to Jackson, Tennessee. In this plan, Major General Stephen Hurlbut remained at Bolivar and General Sherman at Memphis, while Rosecrans took up his position at Corinth. This deployment isolated the Corinth garrison and made it the focal point of a future Confederate attack. As an engineer, Rosecrans realized the value of strong fortifications. In anticipation of a Confederate attack, he had his men construct a series of intricate works containing heavy batteries. On October 2, Rosecrans sent a brigade ten miles ahead to observe and meet any Confederate assault coming his way. Early on October 3, the Confederates attacked his outpost, forcing it to fall back to the main body at Corinth. Later that day and into the next, the Confederates continued their attack but made no significant headway. By the end of the day, Rosecrans's defenders were still secure within their fortifications. Only a poor performance by Brigadier

General Charles Hamilton on the Union right prevented Rosecrans from taking the initiative.[23]

When Rosecrans failed to pursue the enemy, Grant expressed his dissatisfaction. Rosecrans was quick to defend his actions. After forty-eight hours of marching and fighting, he said, his men were exhausted, injured, and out of ammunition, water, and rations. It would have been physically impossible for them to have pursued the enemy, he claimed. On October 5th, Rosecrans set off after the Confederates but moved too slowly to satisfy Grant. Grant made no effort to conceal his disappointment and anger.[24]

Despite Rosecrans's failure to catch and destroy the Confederate army, the importance of his victory was well understood by both the North and South. From then on, the Confederate army was on the defensive, and the Union army steadily advanced.

Before the Battle of Iuka, Rosecrans had been promoted to major general of volunteers. When he learned that his date of appointment had been back-dated only to September 17, 1862, rather than the spring of 1862, he was upset. This meant all those with an earlier back-date would outrank him. In a letter to Halleck, he expressed his dissatisfaction that others who "had not rendered a tithe of service nor had a tithe of the success" had been granted greater seniority. This slight bothered Rosecrans for years. In 1865, referring to his rank of brigadier, he said, "I served in this grade long after colonels had been promoted to major generals for camp service." Lincoln later back-dated Rosecrans's promotion to March 21, 1862.[25]

On October 23, 1862, despite his poor relations with those in high command, Rosecrans was selected to replace Major General Don Carlos Buell as commander of the Department of the Cumberland. Lincoln wanted a leader who would fight, and he believed Rosecrans would do just that. Both Grant and Rosecrans were pleased with the move, but for different reasons. Later Grant wrote, "I found that I could not make him do as I wished and had determined to relieve him from duty that very day."[26] After assuming command of the Army of the Cumberland, Rosecrans set about to improve morale, streamline his administration, and bulk up its cavalry and artillery. As quickly as he could, he pushed his army toward Nashville where they could be resupplied, reaching the city on the morning of November 7.

When Rosecrans learned that Major General George Thomas was aggrieved at being passed over for the position that Rosecrans now held, he went to see him. "My command came to me unsought," Rosecrans said. "Had the government so willed, I would gladly have served under you. Anticipating the question of rank, the War Department antedated my commission. The best interests of the country demand your service with this army." Rosecrans offered him the choice of executive officer or an independent corps command. Thomas chose the latter.[27]

Much to Lincoln's dismay, by the end of November, Rosecrans had not moved his army. For a while, the president feared he would not be any better than his predecessor. Rosecrans was preparing to advance, but he could not do so until he straightened out his supply difficulties. In early December, Halleck wrote Rosecrans that the president was growing impatient at his failure to move and had twice asked him to name a new commander. "If you remain one more week at Nashville," said Halleck, "I cannot prevent your removal." Rosecrans was determined not to move until he was ready and said so, writing to Halleck that he could not be affected by threats of removal.[28]

Late in December, Rosecrans did move. At the same time, Confederate General Braxton Bragg's army moved out from his lines. The two armies met at Stone's River. The Confederates attacked Rosecrans's right wing but could not break it. That evening Rosecrans met with his corps commanders to decide on the next day's strategy.

Fortified by his generals' willingness to stay and fight, he elected to hold his position until forced to abandon it. "We move tomorrow, gentlemen! . . . Press them hard! Drive them out of their nests! Make them fight or run! Fight them! Fight them! Fight, I say!"[29]

On January 2, 1863, when Bragg launched a heavy assault against the Union left, Rosecrans and his army rose to the occasion. Under deadly fire, Rosecrans fearlessly rode along the lines, encouraging and steadying his men. Even when his close friend and chief-of-staff, Major Julius Garesche, was decapitated by a cannonball only a few feet away, spattering him with blood, Rosecrans did not abandon his efforts. As a result, the Confederates were repulsed, and Bragg withdrew from the field, retreating to his original position.[30]

When Rosecrans reported the battle to Washington as a victory, Lincoln telegraphed his thanks to him, saying: "God bless you and all with you." After Burnside's defeat at Fredericksburg just a few weeks earlier, Lincoln needed some good news. So did the country. The victory at Stone's River raised the nation's morale and brought Rosecrans the thanks of Congress and a brevet major generalship in the regular army. Although Rosecrans was a little slow, Lincoln said, he was not as slow as Buell or McClellan, and he would fight.[31]

Union casualties at Stone's River were the heaviest of any major battle of the war—almost one out of every four soldiers engaged. Rosecrans had very skillfully deployed his forces so that he could have maximum engagement. He had utilized an important military maxim to gain his victory—avoid piecemeal engagement and get the whole army into the fight at the same time. Troops held in reserve do not win battles.[32]

In addition to demonstrating his ability as a general, Rosecrans had exhibited great personal courage during the battle. Brigadier General John Palmer later wrote that "Rosecrans, whose courage upon a battlefield was always magnificent, exposed himself at many points to rally the forces, and exhibited the greatest personal bravery. If I were to fight a battle for dominion of the universe, I would give Rosecrans the command of as many men as he could see and who could see him." Grant, however, sent no congratulations.[33]

Rosecrans's victory did not lessen the tension between him and his superiors. Before the Battle of Stone's River, Halleck had demanded that he speed up his advance against Bragg or he would be replaced. To this threat, Rosecrans had replied: "I need no more stimulus to make me do my duty than the knowledge of what it is. To threats of removal or the like, I must be permitted to say that I am insensible."[34]

Soon after Stone's River, Charles A. Dana, the assistant secretary of war, was attached to Rosecrans's headquarters; his purpose was to keep Stanton informed of Rosecrans's actions. At the same time, Brigadier General James Garfield was assigned to replace Julius Garesche. Garfield became Rosecrans's chief-of-staff and confidant.[35]

Early in May 1863, Grant crossed the Mississippi to capture Vicksburg. When his assault failed, he decided to besiege the town instead. Concerned that Bragg might try to reinforce the besieged troops at Vicksburg, Grant requested that Rosecrans attack Bragg. By the end of May, Rosecrans still had not moved, claiming that his troops needed time to recover from their last action. Lincoln's concern grew, and he telegraphed Rosecrans, "I am very anxious that you do your utmost, short of rashness, to keep Bragg from getting off to help Johnston against Grant." "I will attend to it," Rosecrans replied.[36] It was not until the last week in June that Rosecrans's Army of the Cumberland moved southeastward to engage Bragg.

Although slow to move, Rosecrans was able to accomplish his mission. In doing so, he sent five columns to threaten all parts of Bragg's position. The advance confused the Confederates, forcing them to retreat below the Tennessee River, where they were no threat to Grant. Although Rosecrans had conducted the campaign with skill and small loss of men, he received very little recognition. Unfortunately for him, Meade's victory at Gettysburg and Grant's capture of Vicksburg completely overshadowed his efforts at Tullahoma.[37]

Bragg withdrew to Chattanooga, reaching it the day after Vicksburg surrendered. Rosecrans remained at Tullahoma for eight more weeks and again allowed Bragg's weakened army to escape. Finally, with more prodding from Halleck and Stanton, Rosecrans set his army in motion. His goal was to take east Tennessee and return it to the local Unionists in the state. In his plan, Major General Ambrose Burnside, now with the Army of the Ohio, would move through the Cumberland Gap to seize Knoxville, while he hoped to secure the southeast corner of the state, driving Bragg from Chattanooga.[38]

Rosecrans began a campaign of brilliant maneuvers that forced the Confederates from their position and into the fortified railroad center of Chattanooga. Then, via a skillful feint up the Tennessee, he was able to drive the Confederates out of the town without firing a single shot. Since the outset of the war, Lincoln had wanted to liberate east Tennessee; now Rosecrans had achieved that task.[39]

Occupying the city with a portion of his command, Rosecrans, now confident, went after Bragg. Because Bragg was retreating, he concluded that the enemy was beaten and that all he had to do was to pursue him and force a battle. Rosecrans forgot that he had not beaten Bragg in the field, and what he did not know was that the Confederate army had been reinforced and now outnumbered his Army of the Cumberland. Rashly he plunged southward. Bragg had withdrawn only to find a better place to fight and await reinforcements. Now, Bragg was ready for Rosecrans.[40]

On September 19, 1863, Bragg encountered Rosecrans west of Chickamauga Creek, Georgia, hoping to turn the Union left flank and cut off Rosecrans's supply line from Chattanooga. The fighting on the first day settled nothing. Bragg was holding his ground until Lieutenant General James Longstreet, detached from Lee's army, could arrive.[41]

The following day, Bragg attacked the Union's left flank, held by Major General George Thomas's Fourteenth Corps. For two hours, the Federals held off the enemy, and then Rosecrans made a serious error. He mistakenly moved Brigadier General Thomas J. Wood's corps to fill a gap he thought existed, only to create a real one. Seeing this hole, Longstreet quickly took advantage and charged through the void in the Union line. Once Rosecrans saw his error, he sent reinforcements, but it was too late.[42]

Longstreet's assault cut the Union army in half, and by afternoon much of it was streaming back toward Chattanooga. Later, Charles Dana recalled, "The first thing I saw was General Rosecrans crossing himself. 'Hello,' I said to myself. 'If the general is crossing himself, we are in a desperate situation.'" Rosecrans and his chief-of-staff, James Garfield, were swept along in the rout. The *Cincinnati Gazette* reported the retreat: "Men, animals, vehicles became a massive struggling, cursing, shouting, frightened mob."[43]

Rosecrans was spared from pursuit by the Confederates. George Thomas's corps held its position until the rest of the exhausted Union army could return to the safety of Chattanooga. Because Thomas had saved the Union army from a complete disaster, he became known as the "Rock of Chickamauga." More than 1,600 Union dead littered the Chickamauga battlefield, and another 10,000 Federal soldiers suffered wounds. Both sides suffered heavy losses in the bloodiest two-day battle of the entire war.[44]

As soon as Washington learned of the details of the battle from Dana, Grant was ordered to Chattanooga. With authorization from Stanton and Halleck, he replaced Rosecrans with Thomas. Rosecrans would have been devastated had he known that his chief-of-staff, Garfield, had contributed to his downfall. He did not learn of Garfield's part in his removal until years later. Earlier, Garfield had written to Salmon P. Chase, secretary of treasury, criticizing Rosecrans's lack of movement: "I cannot conceal from you the fact that I have been greatly tried and dissatisfied with the slow progress that we have made in this department since the battle of Stone's River. . . . But for many weeks prior to our late movement, I could not but feel that there was not that live and earnest determination to fling the great weight of this army."

Although these criticisms did not hurt Rosecrans at the time, after Chickamauga, Chase showed the letter to Lincoln.[45] There is evidence that Garfield had impugned Rosecrans's competency to Stanton and Lincoln on other occasions while all the time pretending to be his friend.

The time had finally come for Rosecrans's removal. Stanton, Halleck, and Grant, who all had difficulty with Rosecrans, now had an excuse to relieve him from command, something they had been considering for some time. The demise of Rosecrans's military career was not the result of his crushing defeat at Chickamauga but rather of his difficult, uncompromising personality and the scorn he had aroused in his superiors. Even the usual "thick-skinned" Lincoln was glad to see him go. The president believed he had outlived his usefulness, stating that since Chickamauga, Rosecrans had lost his nerve and acted "confused and stunned like a duck hit on the head."[46]

On October 19, Rosecrans received the dispatch from Washington advising him that he had been relieved of duty and was to be replaced by Thomas. Rosecrans sent for Thomas and announced to his staff that he would be leaving the next morning. When Thomas read the dispatch, he turned pale, but Rosecrans immediately put him at ease, saying: "George, we are in the face of the enemy. No one but you can safely take my place now; and for our country's sake, you must do it. Don't fear; no cloud will ever come into my mind as to your fidelity to friendship and honor."[47]

"I can't bear to meet my troops," Rosecrans told Thomas. "I want to leave before the announcement is made, and I will start early in the morning." Early the next morning a few of Rosecrans's men saw him off. Some wept openly, but Rosecrans tried to put on a cheerful face. He had a kind word for everyone and spoke highly of Thomas's appointment.[48]

Rosecrans's farewell message was circulated among his men. In it he expressed his support for Thomas: "In taking leave of you he congratulates you that your commander comes to you not as he did, a stranger. To his known prudence, dauntless courage, and true patriotism, you may look with confidence that under God he will lead you to victory."[49]

Rosecrans bore up well under the ordeal of being replaced. Major General Phil Sheridan noted that he "modestly left us without fuss or demonstration. . . . When his departure became known, deep and almost universal regret was expressed."[50]

When Rosecrans returned to Cincinnati, he received a hero's welcome. The *Cincinnati Times* wrote of Rosecrans's departure: "There is wailing and weeping in the Army of the Cumberland today." The next day the *Times* editorial said of Rosecrans: "No history of the rebellion will ever be written in which his name will not occupy a leading place. . . . There is but one living military man who has accomplished more, and that is Grant." These feelings, however, were not shared by all. Two of Rosecrans's generals, McCook and Crittenden, brought charges against him. They claimed he had fled from the battle at Chickamauga, that he had considered the battle lost, that he had disobeyed orders in advancing beyond Chattanooga, and that he had mismanaged the battle.[51]

Rosecrans's removal was greeted with elation by some in the South. On October 26, *The Richmond Examiner* wrote: "Lincoln is helping us. He has removed from command the most dangerous man in the army. Rosecrans thus retired is unquestionably the greatest captain the Yankee nation has yet produced."[52]

In January 1864, Rosecrans returned to the field as head of the Department of Missouri, a very challenging assignment. With less than 17,000 troops, he was responsible for maintaining order over an area of 69,000 square miles of territory that bordered the Confederacy, required to battle guerrillas, hostile Indians, and subversive organizations within his region. In October, he attempted to engage Major General Sterling Price's Confederate raiders when they invaded Missouri. With a limited number of troops, Rosecrans had difficulty containing Price. When he was finally able to clear Missouri of the raiders, he received no commendations from the War Department. Rather, Halleck complained to Sherman: "Rosecrans has made very bad work of it in Missouri, allowing Price with a small force to overrun the State and destroy millions of [dollars] of property." Grant, now general-in-chief, was also critical of Rosecrans's efforts to contain Price, stating: "The impunity with which Price was enabled to roam . . . shows to how little purpose a superior force may be used. There is no reason why General Rosecrans should not have concentrated his forces and beaten and driven Price before the latter reached Pilot Knob."[53]

On October 20, Grant wired Halleck: "Has Rosecrans yet come upon Price? If not he should be removed at once. Anybody will be better than Rosecrans." On December 2, Stanton agreed to remove Rosecrans and asked Grant where to assign him. "Rosecrans will do no less harm," Grant replied, "doing nothing than on duty. I know no department or army command deserving such punishment as the infliction of Rosecrans on them." On December 9, Rosecrans received orders relieving him of duty and assigning Major General Grenville Dodge as commander of the Department of the Missouri.[54]

Rosecrans was surprised when he was relieved. In his own words his removal had been "without warning, notice, or complaint, or hint of explanation." Rosecrans remained in Cincinnati, without an assignment, until the end of the war, and, on December 1865, he resigned from the army.[55]

Despite the unfortunate end to his military career, Rosecrans was still respected and courted to run for public office. During the 1860s and 1870s, his unwillingness to run for office earned him the title of "The Great Decliner." In 1868, President Andrew Johnson appointed him minister to

Mexico, a position he held for five months until Grant was elected president; Grant quickly removed him.[56]

In 1880, Rosecrans moved to San Rafael, California, where he promoted railroads, ranched, and speculated in real estate. Finally, during that year, he ran for Congress as a Democrat and was elected. After winning a second term, he became chairman of the House Military Affairs Committee; as such, he sought revenge on Grant by attempting to prevent him from receiving back-dated retirement pay. Again, Grant prevailed.[57]

Rosecrans was blessed with close family relationships. Although he was often apart from his family, the letters he wrote and received from them were rich in affection. In 1876, his oldest son, Louis, who had become a Catholic priest, died suddenly. Within a year, his daughter Mary, a Catholic nun, died of tuberculosis. The family's tears for Mary had scarcely dried when Rosecrans's brother, Sylvester, a Catholic bishop, died. Next, his beloved wife Annie died. He did not often speak of her or of his deceased family members; the pain was too deep.[58]

Rosecrans's friendship with General Thomas remained strong after the war. When Thomas was asked about the Battle of Chickamauga, he responded: "Chickamauga was a battle in which I received great credit at the expense of a better soldier, General Rosecrans." When Thomas died in 1870, Rosecrans was a pallbearer.[59]

It was not until 1877, when the *New York Sun* ran an editorial by Charles Dana, that Rosecrans learned of Garfield's letter of criticism during the Chickamauga campaign. When Garfield ran for president on the Republican ticket, Rosecrans ran for Congress as a Democrat. During the campaign, Garfield exaggerated his military exploits at Rosecrans's expense. Both men were elected. Rosecrans attempted to make friends with the president, but the breach was never healed.[60]

Throughout the years, Rosecrans's name was mentioned as a possible Democratic candidate for president. When Grover Cleveland was elected president in 1884, Rosecrans was appointed registrar of the treasury, where he continued to serve under President Harrison's term. Later, he was elected a regent of the University of California and, in 1889, was awarded an honorary Doctor of Laws degree.[61]

By 1892, Rosecrans's health began to fail. In the summer of 1897, Rosecrans grew seriously ill. He recovered for a short time, but on March 11, 1898, he succumbed. The *Los Angeles Times* reported his death: "Last great general of the Civil War goes to the bivouac with the boys in blue in the silent camping ground. Rosecrans is dead."[62]

Rosecrans lay in state at the Los Angeles City Hall and was later moved to Washington, where he was buried in Arlington Cemetery. To his men, Rosecrans remained both commander and friend. "Old Rosy" was able to inspire his men by word and deed.

9   John Pope

The "Miscreant"

In June 1862, Union General George McClellan's Army of the Potomac was bivouacked within seven miles of Richmond. In Virginia's Shenandoah Valley, the outnumbered Confederate army of "Stonewall" Jackson had outfoxed portions of three Union commanders and then slipped past them to join Lee around Richmond. Lincoln recognized that Jackson's success in the valley was due, in part, to the fragmented nature of the armies operating in the area. He corrected the problem by creating a unified command, naming it the Army of Virginia.[1]

As commander, Lincoln selected forty-year-old Major General John Pope. Much was expected of him. Several recent events had left the North both frustrated and depressed: the fiasco a year earlier at Manassas, "Stonewall" Jackson's victories in the Shenandoah Valley, and now McClellan's stalemate on the peninsula. The Northern newspapers declared not only disappointment in the Union army but spoke of its defeat. Lincoln hoped Pope would quiet the skeptics.[2]

Pope seemed to have the qualifications to do just that. A Kentuckian, John Pope had led the Army of the Mississippi during the spring of 1862, when he had been successful in breaking the Confederate hold on the upper Mississippi River. After being promoted to major general, Pope was ordered to come east to command the Army of Virginia.[3]

Unfortunately, John Pope was his own worst enemy. He was abrasive, conceited, and outspoken. When he reported to Virginia to take command, he immediately alienated his subordinates as well as the common soldiers. Brigadier General Samuel D. Sturgis, upon receipt of an order from Pope, expressed his lack of respect for him: "I don't care for John Pope, one pinch of owl dung."[4]

Pope had the same effect on the men in the ranks. He greeted them with an insulting proclamation they would not forget and that immediately raised their anger. "I have come to you from the West," he announced, "where we have always seen the backs of our enemies. . . . Dismiss from your minds certain phrases which I am sorry to find so much in vogue amongst you. I hear constantly of 'taking strong positions and holding them,' of 'lines of retreat,' and of 'bases of supplies.' Let us discard such ideas. . . . Let us look before and not behind. Success and glory are in the advance; disaster and shame lurk in the rear."[5]

Severe reaction to Pope's proclamation came from McClellan and the men of the Army of the Potomac. There was no question that the address was intended as a criticism of them. Terms such as "base of supply" and "lines of retreat" were used by McClellan during his advance and subsequent withdrawal. McClellan bristled when he heard about it. One of McClellan's chief supporters, Major General Fitz John Porter, wrote to a friend, "I regret to see that General Pope has not improved since his youth and has now written himself down as what the military world has long known, an ass. His address to his troops will make him ridiculous in the eyes of military men abroad as well as at home."[6]

The person most surprised by the angry reaction to his statements was Pope himself. His purpose in issuing it, he said, was to create "a feeling of confidence and cheerful spirit which were sadly wanting" in the army. Because of his lack of sensitivity to others' feelings, Pope never understood why the effect of his address was to make him the object of ridicule and dislike. Despite Pope's brashness and his tendency to alienate people with his remarks, he had a great zest for fighting. He was the kind of leader Lincoln wanted to command his armies.[7]

John Pope was born on March 16, 1822, in Louisville, Kentucky, and raised in Kaskaskia, Illinois. His parents, Nathaniel and Lucretia Pope, were both well educated and came from socially prominent families. John inherited many of his father's traits: a love of learning, the quality of pompousness, and a tendency toward being overweight. He also shared his father's Republican views, particularly his dislike of slavery.[8]

John had prepared for college; but, when the time came to go, his father's land speculations had wiped out the family's savings and there was no money for tuition. Hoping to use his political influence, Nathaniel traveled to Washington to seek a favor from one of his friends, Ninian Edwards, a U.S. senator. With Edwards's help, John was able to get an appointment to the military academy at West Point. On March 20, 1838, at the age of sixteen, John was accepted into the class of 1842.[9]

Young Pope was under great pressure from his father, who expected him to finish first in his class and would settle for nothing less. His words of advice to John were to always do his work first and then play. At first Pope found the going tough. Cadets from the northeastern and mid-Atlantic

Brigader General John Pope, officer of the Federal army (major general after March 21, 1861).

COURTESY OF THE LIBRARY OF CONGRESS

states arrived at the Academy better prepared academically than those from the West. As a result, cadets like John often washed out in disproportionate numbers, but young Pope was determined not to let that happen to him. At graduation, Pope stood first in his class in horsemanship and was described by fellow classmate James Longstreet as "a handsome, dashing fellow, a splendid cavalryman." Overall, his ranking was seventeenth in a class of fifty-six.[10]

Upon graduation, Pope was assigned as brevet second lieutenant to the engineer corps and ordered to active duty at Palatha, Florida. His commanding officer was Captain Joseph E. Johnston. After a year of boredom and conflict with his superiors, Pope went to Washington to lobby for a better assignment. This behavior was the first of numerous acts of insubordination and poor judgment during his career. It contributed to the poor standing he had with many of his fellow officers.[11]

Pope was no more satisfied with his next assignment, which was in the southern part of Savannah, than with his first; again he stepped outside normal military channels to request a transfer. On October 23, 1844, he got his wish and was transferred to Maine.[12] With the outbreak of the war with Mexico, Pope was assigned to field duty with General Zachary Taylor's army. He distinguished himself at the bloody American victory at Monterrey. In his report to Taylor, Major General Joseph Mansfield wrote, "Lieutenant Pope executed his duties with great coolness and self-possession and deserves my highest praise." Lieutenant Colonel John Garland, whose division Mansfield's engineers had assisted, reported that Pope "deported himself as a gallant soldier under the heaviest fire of the enemy." For his effort he was brevetted captain.[13]

Throughout his career, Pope was regarded by influential local politicians as a "favorite son of Illinois destined for a grand career." Although considered a man of action, both courageous and energetic, his personal behavior was less than desirable. He was impetuous and egotistical. Despite these personal deficiencies, Pope had an inside track with Lincoln. Lincoln knew Pope's father, a federal judge in Illinois, in whose court he had practiced law.[14]

After the war in Mexico, Pope served dutifully in the engineer corps in the West. In 1853 he was promoted to first lieutenant and, three years later, to captain. In the fall of 1859, Captain Pope was reassigned to Cincinnati, his first permanent duty away from the frontier in seventeen years. Duty in Cincinnati brought him in close contact with the political elite of Illinois and gave him an opportunity to marry. On September 15, 1859, he married Clara Pomeroy Horton, the daughter of a congressman. Clara was twenty-four years old, well educated, and as stubborn as Pope. Her family was as distinguished as his and a great deal wealthier.[15]

During the winter of 1860 to 1861, when the nation seemed to be coming apart, Pope pondered its fate and his own. In a seven-page letter to President-elect Lincoln, dated January 27, 1861, Pope advised him on how he should treat secession. He cautioned Lincoln not to presume that all officers were loyal; some might be secessionists themselves. "The fact whether we have a government, and whether it has the right to enforce its laws and protect its officers, must be brought to a speedy issue," he wrote. All secessionists, he believed, were law breakers for whom no punishment was too severe.[16] Lincoln apparently took no offense at Pope's impudent letter; in fact, he invited Pope to accompany him from Springfield to Washington for his inauguration.[17]

On the trip to Washington with Lincoln, Pope took the opportunity to speak out publicly against President James Buchanan and his policy of inaction. Pope's comments were reported in the *Cincinnati Gazette* and circulated in pamphlet form. Upon Pope's arrival in Washington, he was served with a special order summoning him before a general court-martial;

he had been charged with violating the Fifth Article of War that prohibited officers from making derogatory remarks about the president. Luckily, President Buchanan did not take Pope's remarks very seriously, countermanding the order and stating that they "would not in any manner affect [me] injuriously."[18]

When the Confederates fired on Fort Sumter in April, Pope volunteered his services to Governor Richard Yates of Illinois and was appointed brigadier general of volunteers to serve under Major General John Fremont in Missouri. In early 1862, he was placed in command of the Army of the Mississippi and participated in Major General Henry Halleck's campaign to open up the Mississippi River. Pope captured New Madrid, Missouri, and then moved downriver, capturing Island Number Ten and opening up the entire upper half of the Mississippi. In the process, he captured thousands of prisoners, equipment, and ammunition at a cost of only a few hundred Union casualties.[19]

Pope's action in the West resulted in a promotion to the rank of major general. Part of the reputation he had won in the West was the result of his own boasting and exaggerations about his accomplishments to the press. But he was a successful campaigner, something that so many of Lincoln's generals were not. Pope's efforts in the West soon brought him to the attention of the president.[20]

In the latter part of June, Secretary of War Stanton asked Pope to come to Washington. Halleck, Pope's superior in the West, did not want to lose him and objected to the request, but Stanton insisted that he come. Pope was offered the command of the newly formed Army of Virginia, which would unite the forces of McDowell, Banks, and Fremont. The object of the army was to operate east of the valley and draw away troops from the Confederate army facing McClellan at Richmond.[21]

Pope was not happy with his new assignment. "It became apparent to me at once," he later wrote, "that the duty to be assigned to me was in the nature of a forlorn hope, and my position was still further embarrassed by the fact that I was called from another army and a different field of duty to command an army in which the corps commanders were all my seniors in rank."[22]

Pope told Lincoln that the plan had little chance of working and requested to be allowed to return to the West, but Lincoln persuaded him to accept the assignment as a matter of duty. "I entered that command with great reluctance and serious foreboding," he said. Fremont, who accused Pope of plotting against him to get the position, refused to serve under him, resigned from the army, and was replaced by Major General Franz Sigel.[23]

On June 27, Pope assumed command in Washington but did not join his army in the field for over a month, leaving it disorganized and greatly in need of inspired leadership. While his army remained in the field, Pope spent his time trying to impress both the citizens and politicians in Washington. Pope made an impressive figure in uniform. He was tall in stature, with long, dark hair complemented by a long beard that spread down to his chest. What Pope did best was talk, speaking about topics that would please Lincoln and other government officials.[24]

Pope made frequent trips to the White House, often making disparaging remarks about McClellan to the president. McClellan, a Democrat, and Pope, a Republican, were divided by more than their political beliefs. Unlike McClellan, Pope favored abolition of slavery and the vigorous prosecution of all disloyal Southerners, making him an instant favorite of the radical Republicans. With their encouragement, he issued a series of orders directed at civilians in occupied territory. He stated that, while his army was in Virginia, it would be living off the land. In addition, all citizens in occupied territory would be held responsible for damage done to Federal supplies or troops by guerrilla forces, and all those aiding them would be shot. Any person refusing to take the loyalty oath would be sent beyond the lines, with the condition that they would be shot as spies if they returned.[25]

With this change in policy came a raging debate and a deep schism. When McClellan learned of these orders he wrote his wife, "I will issue tomorrow an order giving my comments on Mr. John Pope. I will strike square in the teeth of his infamous orders, and give directly the reverse instructions to my army." McClellan's closest confidant, Fitz John Porter, who disliked Pope, predicted that, if his policy was put into practice, "you may look for disaster." Although Pope's orders were not carried out, they earned for him the undying hatred of many Southerners.[26]

Later, Pope announced that any man or woman who corresponded with anyone in the Confederate army, even a parent writing to a son, would be subject to execution. When Lee learned of Pope's directive, he labeled him the "Miscreant General" and told "Stonewall" Jackson, "I want Pope to be suppressed."[27]

Finally, over a month after taking command of the Army of Virginia, Pope joined his army in the field. Pope may have impressed officials in Washington, but he was not welcomed by his army with open arms. Probably no general got off to a worse start with their command than did Pope. The men in his command remembered his earlier address in which he bragged about coming from the West from an army that always saw the backs of its enemies, implying that the opposite was true of the Eastern armies. The remark did nothing to help him establish rapport with his men, and the Army of Virginia showed its dislike for Pope by ridiculing him at every opportunity.[28]

One story circulated that Pope wrote all his orders under the heading: "Headquarters in the Saddle." It started as a joke, but soon the men began to believe it. "It became a by-word throughout the army," one of his soldiers said, "and a good deal of fun we had out of it."[29]

When McClellan's drive on Richmond stalled, the military strategy proposed by Lincoln changed. When Lincoln suggested that the Army of

Virginia move south and attack Lee's army, while McClellan attacked his flank, Pope objected strongly. Finally, Lincoln decided to withdraw the Army of the Potomac from the peninsula to unite it with Pope's Army of Virginia. Who would command the combined force was not clear, but the main reason given for the move was the protection of Washington.[30]

Now Pope was faced with a problem and placed in the unenviable position of not knowing what his responsibilities were, other than protecting Washington. Pope communicated with General-in-Chief Henry Halleck for clarification of his duties. "What is to be my command?" he wrote. "Am I to act independently against the enemy?" In addition, units from the Army of the Potomac were returning in dribbles, commanded by officers who were loyal to McClellan and who resented leaving him. "The troops arriving here came in fragments," Pope complained. Halleck urged McClellan to speed up the movement of his troops; however, he reacted slowly, as usual, and continued to protest their recall.[31]

McClellan was in no hurry to send his army to join Pope; he had no confidence in Pope's ability to command the army. "I think . . . that Pope will be badly thrashed," McClellan said, "and that they will be glad to turn over the redemption of their affairs to me." McClellan not only believed Pope would fail but seemed to hope he would.

Lee watched the situation closely. When he realized that McClellan was withdrawing from the peninsula, he rushed Major General James Longstreet's four divisions to join Jackson's troops, hoping to attack Pope before he could get reinforcements from McClellan. Lee's plan worked; he won the race to get his troops in position to attack Pope before the major portion of the Army of the Potomac could arrive.[32]

Lee's plan was a bold one. Facing an enemy that could outnumber him within a few days, he split his army, sending Jackson's division around Pope's right flank to destroy his supply base at Manassas Junction and cut communications with Washington.[33]

When Pope was informed of Jackson's movements, he replied calmly, "There is no danger." When Jackson changed positions, Pope mistakenly thought he was retreating. As a result, he left his left flank exposed for an attack from Longstreet. On August 30, Longstreet attacked Pope, catching him completely off guard. "General Pope," Longstreet wrote, "was not careful enough to keep himself informed about the movements of his enemy."[34]

Pope had made a fatal mistake: underestimating his opponent. Forced to withdraw during the night, his troops made an orderly retreat, destroying the bridges over Bull Run as they went. During the Second Battle of Manassas, Pope's Army of Virginia suffered a decisive defeat with almost 14,000 casualties. The Confederates lost only 8,000 men.

By the morning of August 31, the news reached the president that Pope had been defeated. When Lincoln saw his secretary, John Hay, he said, "Well, John, we are whipped again, I am afraid." Pope telegraphed Halleck that his army was intact, but recommending that it return to Washington. Later that night, Halleck turned to McClellan for assistance. McClellan eagerly replied that he would help, recommending to Halleck that Pope fall back to the capital defenses.[35]

Blame for the defeat fell on John Pope, who had promised much but delivered nothing. Pope accused George McClellan of treachery by withholding assistance from him in time of need. McClellan undeniably disliked Pope and saw him as a rival who threatened to replace him as Union commander in the East, but his slowness in moving his troops was probably due more from his inclination to be cautious than his desire to see Pope fail.[36]

Pope also claimed that certain officers had conspired against him and failed properly to carry out their duties. Among them was Major General Fitz John Porter. On November 12, 1862, a court-martial found him guilty as charged, and he was cashiered from the army. Fifteen years later, Porter was exonerated of all charges.[37]

Lincoln reacted quickly to restore confidence in the army by relieving Pope. The Armies of the Potomac and Virginia were consolidated into one army, and McClellan was appointed its commander. When the army heard that McClellan was returning, they responded with thunderous roars. Lincoln conceded that McClellan had "acted badly in the matter, but we must use what tools we have. . . . He is too useful now just to sacrifice."[38]

Although the president had no criticism of Pope's ability as a general, he knew he could not serve under McClellan. The bad feelings between the two had gone too far. While Pope's reputation may have been ruined in the East, he still remained a popular figure in the West. Under Lincoln's direction, Halleck told Pope that, during the present crisis, careers had to be sacrificed for the good of the army. Pope was ordered back to the West, where he held minor commands for the rest of the war. Although Pope consented to the demotion, he thought he had been treated unfairly.[39]

When William Sherman heard of the treatment Pope had received, he was outraged. "I see the people have made a clear sacrifice of Pope and McDowell," he said, "and are now content with having killed two of their own generals. This is a glorious war!"[40]

Pope went West, not to fight the Civil War, but to quell a Sioux Indian uprising in Minnesota. The War Department created a Department of the Northwest and placed Pope in command. He directed several expeditions against the Indians to protect the interests of gold seekers and emigrants. His operations against the Sioux earned him a reputation for efficient administration and an awareness of Native American problems. Under the new general-in-chief, Ulysses S. Grant, the Western command was reorganized, creating the Division of Missouri, with Pope as its sole head.[41]

With his new command, Pope planned a series of expeditions against the Great Plains Indians. At the end of the Civil War, the armies were reduced in size, which greatly inhibited his campaigns in the West. He remained a top frontier commander until his retirement in 1886.[42]

After his retirement, Pope began writing for the *National Tribune*, located in Washington, D.C. At first his articles dealt with his war experiences, but later they were expanded to include biographical sketches of other Union commanders and articles describing the plight of Native Americans. These pieces were followed with the writing of his memoirs and recollections. A spirit of goodwill and conciliation pervaded his writings, and there was none of the angry settling of scores included in the memoirs written by others after the war. Pope even spoke of McClellan in civil terms.[43]

On the evening of September 23, 1892, Pope passed away in his sleep. He was buried, beside his wife, in the Bellefontaine Cemetery in St. Louis, with full military honors. "Military critics may dispute as to General Pope's capacity as a general in command of armies in the field," the editors of the *Army and Navy Journal* wrote. "None, however, can deny that he was a faithful servant of his country, a patriot, and a scholar, deserving the fullest commendation, and a place in the hearts of his countrymen with those whose ultimate success made them foremost of the leaders of their time."[44]

10 *John A. McClernand*

The Congressman General

When the Civil War began, the U.S. Regular Army numbered only 15,000 enlisted men and 1,100 officers. By the end of the war, over 2.5 million men had served in the military. Because there was a desperate need for men to lead this army, President Lincoln looked not only to professional soldiers but to civilians as well, particularly politicians. In the early stages of the war, the selection of one of a state's favored sons to be a general could go a long way to ensure the loyalty of that state to the Union. Among those chosen to lead, appointed to the rank of brigadier general, was John Alexander McClernand, congressman from Illinois and friend of Abraham Lincoln. Unfortunately, he would be at the center of controversy in the West as the war progressed.[1]

John McClernand, the only child of Dr. John and Fatima McClernand, was born May 30, 1812, in the backwoods near Hardinsburg, Kentucky. When John was still a child, his family moved across the Ohio River to Shawneetown, Illinois. A few years later John's father died, leaving Fatima to care for her son on her own. By the time John was sixteen, he had completed all the formal education available to him. His education would have ended there were it not for William Gatewood, an Illinois state senator, who saw great potential in the young man and began to tutor him in French and Latin. Young John studied law on his own, and in 1832, he was admitted to the bar, going into practice with Albert Caldwell.[2]

In April 1832, trouble began on the western border of Illinois with Black Hawk, leader of the Sac and Fox tribes. Before practicing law on his own, John served as a private in the Black Hawk War. Soldiering alongside Captain Abraham Lincoln, McClernand made a valuable contact, which would prove helpful later in his career. It was not until 1835 that he was able to return to the practice of law after founding the first Democratic newspaper in Shawneetown.[3]

At the age of twenty-four, McClernand entered politics and promptly won a seat in the state legislature. In 1840, after a two-year absence, he, along with Lincoln, was elected to the Illinois legislature. During the 1840 to 1841 session, the two clashed over the issue of voter fraud. While both agreed that reform was long overdue, the question of how to do so became an issue. Lincoln proposed the problem be solved by a committee with a Whig majority, while McClernand favored a committee with a majority from his party. McClernand prevailed because the Democrats held a majority in the assembly at this time. The two continued to be political rivals throughout their lives.[4]

In 1843, John McClernand married Sarah Dunlap from Jacksonville, Illinois. She was a friend of Mary Todd, who, in 1842, had married Lincoln. Sarah was an attractive young lady who had been courted by Stephen A. Douglas since she arrived in Illinois in 1833. It was McClernand, however, who won her hand.[5]

After four years in the state legislature, McClernand was elected to the U.S. House of Representatives as a Jacksonian Democrat. In Congress he made a reputation for himself as a moderate on slavery and aligned himself with the party faction led by Stephen Douglas. As such, he was reelected four times.[6]

In 1846, Lincoln and McClernand again found themselves on the opposite sides of issues—this time in Congress. Whether slavery should be extended to the territories had become a significant political issue. McClernand was a staunch expansionist, declaring that "extension and expansion is the condition of our political existence." To hinder the expansion by placing arbitrary boundaries on it, he believed, would be like "caging the eagle in its upward flight." McClernand was not opposed to the continuation of slavery in the slave-holding states because he believed that slavery was a local matter. In the territories, however, he believed the federal government had jurisdiction over whether or not to allow slavery.[7] In 1848, McClernand considered running for the U.S. Senate, allowing his name to be placed on the ballot. When he finished third in the voting, he decided it would be the last time he would attempt to run for the Senate.

Throughout the debates over slavery in Congress, McClernand played the role of compromiser. Although he was opposed to the existence of slavery, he believed that the Constitution recognized slavery and that the issue had to be settled on the basis of that document.[8]

By 1852, McClernand had left his seat in Congress to resume his law practice. Still active in politics, he supported James Buchanan for president in the election of 1856, hoping to receive an appointment as minister to Russia. Although Buchanan won the election, he did not appoint

Major General John A. McClernand, officer of
the Federal army.

COURTESY OF THE LIBRARY OF CONGRESS

McClernand to the position; therefore, McClernand remained in the practice of law.[9]

In 1858, McClernand regained his seat in Congress by a landslide by
claiming his Republican opponent, John Palmer, was an abolitionist who
supported John Brown's raid on Harper's Ferry. During the election of
1860, he stumped the state in support of Stephen Douglas. In November,
McClernand was elected to Congress for a sixth term, and Lincoln won the
presidency. With Lincoln's election, the threat of disunion loomed. Preservation of the Union was foremost in McClernand's mind, as he still hoped
for a compromise to avoid war.[10]

As the Civil War approached, McClernand dropped his middle-of-the-
road position. Still not favoring the complete abolition of slavery, he was

strongly opposed to secession. As a result, the newly elected Lincoln regarded him as a valuable ally in winning the support of midwestern Democrats for the Union. When the war began, McClernand continued to travel around Illinois on behalf of the war effort; his impassioned appeal to patriotism induced many men to enlist for three years.[11]

The spring and summer of 1861 were difficult for McClernand. His wife's poor health and complications during the delivery of her sixth child led to her death on May 8. Mary Lincoln, Sarah's long-time friend, wrote, "I was grieved to hear of Mrs. McClernand's death. Her friends and orphaned children will never cease to miss her." In July, her newborn baby also died. Of his children, McClernand outlived all but one.[12]

In July, McClernand resumed his seat in Congress. McClernand urged Lincoln to appoint a number of constituents, including Ulysses S. Grant, as brigadier general of volunteers. Lincoln followed his advice and nominated McClernand as well. McClernand was one of 187 other appointed Civil War generals with little or no military experience. Having considered a military position for some time, McClernand was pleased with his appointment. He believed his natural ability would make him an outstanding military commander and could think of no better way of serving the Union than on the battlefield.[13] Lincoln appointed McClernand to the rank of general because of intense lobbying by members of the Illinois congressional delegation. He was also aware of the influence McClernand had on the state Democrats, hoping he could win their support for the war effort. Having served with him in the Black Hawk War, Lincoln believed he was a man others would be willing to follow in battle.[14]

McClernand went to work immediately, recruiting a brigade of four infantry regiments, including units of cavalry and artillery. By August, his efforts had paid off; his ranks were full. On November 7, when Grant led McClernand's brigade down the Mississippi, McClernand received his baptism by fire. Grant attacked five Confederate regiments under General Gideon Pillow outside Belmont but was repulsed. To save the day, Grant sent in McClernand with three of his regiments. He was able to turn the tide, forcing Pillow to withdraw and allowing Grant to capture Pillow's camp and burn his supplies.[15]

McClernand's first taste of combat was not entirely successful, however. Instead of following up their victory, McClernand's poorly disciplined troops broke ranks and looted the camp, allowing time for Pillow to regroup and swing around to attack Grant's flank. Grant and McClernand were able to fight through the closing circle and escape in time to avert disaster. Although the Union troops were forced to retreat, they had fought well under McClernand. In the thick of the battle, McClernand's uniform and saddle were perforated by enemy bullets. The newspapers reported the episode, giving him credit for his actions. Lincoln also acknowledged McClernand and his troops' heroic efforts: "[You] have done honor to yourselves and the flag and service to the country. Most gratefully do I thank you and them."[16]

In January of 1862, Grant named McClernand commander of the First Division. His next performance, near Fort Henry, was not as distinguished. When the Confederates withdrew to the fort, McClernand was ordered to cut off their line of retreat. His movements, however, were tentative, and the Confederates slipped past him, much to Grant's displeasure.[17]

During a meeting after the battle, McClernand read Grant a long lecture he had written on strategy. Given his inexperience, this act was as pretentious as it was inappropriate, and Grant struggled to hold back his anger. This episode was the beginning of a clash between the two that would break into the open very shortly.[18]

In February, Grant moved against Fort Donelson with a force of 27,000 men. During the attack, McClernand made an ill-advised assault on the enemy without orders from Grant. When the attack failed, Grant was livid. Although Grant was successful in capturing the fort, he began to have serious doubts about McClernand's ability to command.[19]

After Fort Donelson, Grant's distrust of McClernand grew. The day after the fort's surrender, McClernand issued a congratulatory order to his division. The memo was meant to praise and inspire his men, but it was worded in such a way that it also brought honor to him. The next day, he sent a copy of the order to Lincoln with a letter that cast doubt on the efforts of other officers at Fort Donelson and offered advice to the president about how future campaigns should be conducted. In his official report to Grant, McClernand claimed that his division had borne "the brunt and burden of the battle" and had suffered the highest losses, implying that his division alone was responsible for the victory.[20]

Shortly after his victory at Fort Donelson, Grant was promoted to major general. After the victory and his promotion, Grant was willing to let his differences with McClernand rest. When McClernand was elevated to major general, Grant did not contest the promotion.[21]

At Shiloh, McClernand fought well. He anticipated an enemy attack, urging Grant to move downriver and consolidate his forces, but Grant failed to heed the suggestion. As a result, Grant almost destroyed his army as well as his career. When Confederate Generals Albert S. Johnston and Beauregard struck the Union lines, pushing back Sherman's division and threatening the Union right, McClernand came to his aid and helped to stem the tide. By mid-day, his division had to give way along with the others, but by that time Grant was able to order up more support. The Confederate forces were never able to regain momentum and later had to withdraw toward Corinth. Grant's army had been saved, but at a high cost.[22]

The press praised McClernand's action, but Grant did not. Sherman's report, however, cited McClernand's efforts and how he "promptly and energetically responded" and "struggled most determinedly."[23] Feeling slighted for his part in the victory at Shiloh, McClernand wrote to President Lincoln bragging about his accomplishments during the battle: "My division, as usual, has borne or shared in bearing the brunt. I have lost in killed and wounded about every third man of my command. Within a radius of 200 yards of my headquarters some 150 dead bodies were left on the field." The letter only increased the ill feeling between himself and Grant.[24]

In September 1862, McClernand went to Washington to secure a command of his own and to present a plan of operation to the president. McClernand requested permission to go to Illinois and raise an army. With this army he hoped to move down the Mississippi and capture Vicksburg. "The war can never be brought to a close until that key is in our pocket!" Lincoln had said. The key he was referring to was Vicksburg. McClernand's plan was quicker and more decisive than the one proposed by Grant and Halleck.[25]

McClernand's plan and his confidence impressed Lincoln and Stanton. Without consulting either Grant or Halleck, they approved McClernand's plan. By the end of October, McClernand returned home to begin his recruitment of volunteers and to marry Minerva Dunlap, sister of his deceased wife. Although McClernand had won a political victory, he had had also earned the enmity of both Halleck and Grant, the superiors he had bypassed in going to Lincoln with his plan.[26]

McClernand was successful in his quest for volunteers. With the aid of state officials, he raised fourteen infantry regiments and a six-gun battery within two weeks. Three weeks later, the total volunteers recruited had risen to 40,000, a strong testimony to McClernand's popularity and influence. When Halleck learned what was happening, he immediately contacted Grant, who was shocked by the news. Grant was appalled by the idea of entrusting a critical campaign to a citizen-soldier, especially one such as McClernand.[27]

Allowing McClernand to organize a command on his own was a terrible mistake. The president and secretary of war had planned an important operation, raised an army to execute it, and named a commander to lead it without consulting, or even telling, the general-in-chief and department commander. When the order was issued, it was not clear whether McClernand was to be under Grant's command or was to operate independently. McClernand believed he had been given an independent command, but the order could be interpreted to mean that he was subject to Grant's control. The issue was sure to cause a dispute between the two generals.[28]

When Grant learned what McClernand was planning, he took immediate action to move against Vicksburg. In December, in McClernand's absence, Grant ordered Sherman and 30,000 of his troops to join him in his attack on Vicksburg. When McClernand finally reached Tennessee, he was furious to learn what Grant and Sherman were planning to do. Hurrying to Sherman's headquarters, McClernand proclaimed his authority and named himself commander of the "Army of the Mississippi" and prepared for his campaign against Vicksburg.[29]

Grant complained to Halleck about the problem of the command created by the order. Four days later, a compromise was reached. The War Department informed Grant that his army, including the troops that McClernand had recruited, should be organized into four corps, one of which was to be commanded by McClernand. McClernand was to lead the advance on Vicksburg but would remain under Grant's command. This was the president's wish, Halleck said. Both Grant and McClernand were disappointed—Grant because he wanted to get rid of McClernand, and McClernand because he believed he had earned the right to have an independent command.[30]

The Army of the Mississippi was dissolved and combined with Grant's Army of the Tennessee. For the first time in months, Grant felt he was able to control McClernand's ambitions. When Grant's attempt to capture Vicksburg stalled during the winter of 1862 to 1863, McClernand criticized him. In a letter to his political friends and supporters, he described Grant as unfit for command. Grant was aware of McClernand's criticism but told other subordinates, "I can't afford to quarrel with a man whom I have to command."[31]

Throughout the Vicksburg campaign, the Grant and McClernand feud continued. Although McClernand claimed credit for various victories, Grant was unimpressed and unwilling to give him the credit McClernand believed he deserved. Despite their differences and McClernand's insubordination, Grant was reluctant to remove a man with such strong political backing.

By May 19, 1863, Grant's army was in place outside of Vicksburg. When Sherman's corps attacked the Confederate fortifications, they suffered heavy losses despite able support from McClernand. Grant tried again on May 22, this time with McClernand's corps bearing the brunt of the assault. On his own, McClernand's corps was able to make surprising headway against the Rebel fortifications. When McClernand's assault stalled, he requested help from Grant. Grant complied, sending Sherman's and McPherson's corps. After heavy fighting, the Federal troops were forced to withdraw and relinquish McClernand's hard-won gains.[32]

When McClernand filed his report about breaching the Confederate line, Grant refused to believe it, despite reports from several other officers who verified it. Grant felt McClernand had exaggerated his success and was responsible for the losses suffered by the other two corps that had supported him. In his report, Grant unfairly blamed McClernand for the failure of the attack, castigating him as "entirely unfit for the position of corps commander, both on the march and on the field. Looking after his corps gives me more labor, and infinitely more uneasiness, than all the remainder in my department." From Grant's point of view, the attack had accomplished nothing and had increased his army's casualty list.[33]

Years later, when Sherman evaluated the failure of the assault on May 22, he still believed that McClernand had not reported the situation accurately but came to the conclusion that the attack "had failed by reason of the great strength of the position and the determined fighting of the garrison." In his postwar memoirs, Lieutenant Colonel James Wilson observed that "McClernand's conduct [at Vicksburg] was no more blameworthy upon the occasion than Sherman's or McPherson's. The fact is that neither corps commander made the proper provision for the contingency of success in the attack."[34]

McClernand fumed with anger when he read Grant's report. He vented his emotions a few days later when Wilson delivered a dispatch to him from Grant. Rather than accept it he snapped: "I'll be God damned if I'll do it! I am tired of being dictated to! I won't stand for it any longer, and you can go back and tell General Grant!" Wilson did just that.[35]

When Wilson reported the incident to Grant, the latter said, "I'll get rid of McClernand the first chance I get." In mid-June, Grant's chance came. A story appeared in the Memphis *Evening Bulletin* that quoted a congratulatory order McClernand had distributed to his troops following the assault of May 22. In the order, McClernand took full credit for their success on that day and implied that his corps could have carried the day had it not been for the failure of McPherson and Sherman to provide adequate support.[36]

McPherson and Sherman were outraged. They felt McClernand had finally gone too far. Not only had he offended his fellow officers, but he had allowed an official order to be published without his commanding officer's permission, a violation of army regulations.[37] Grant dismissed McClernand, subject to the approval of the president. He had tolerated McClernand, Grant argued, in an effort to carry on without interfering with Lincoln's plan. Now Grant had the support of McPherson and Sherman in his appeal to the president to remove McClernand. "It was only when almost the entire army under my command moved to demand it, that he was relieved," Grant told Lincoln.[38]

When McClernand received the order that he was being relieved of command, he made a final effort of defiance: "Well, sir! I am relieved! By God, sir, we are both relieved!" He was replaced by Major General Edward Ord.[39]

On June 23, when McClernand arrived in Cairo, Illinois, he spoke out in his defense. In a telegram to Lincoln he said, "I have been relieved for an omission of my adjutant. Hear me." At the same time he sent a seven-page letter reporting his operations. In the report he stated that his adjutant, not he, was responsible for not providing Grant with a copy of his congratulatory order; however, he made no mention of how his order got into the hands of the press. In his view the facts in the order were true and respectful. Grant's motives, he wrote, were personal and hostile toward him because

Lincoln had assigned him to an independent command and because of his success in the field in contrast to Grant's "previous failure and disasters."[40]

Back home, McClernand was welcomed with enthusiasm. From there he bombarded Lincoln with demands that he be restored to his command, continuing to claim that Grant had been motivated by personal hostility, jealousy, and West Point-type prejudice. Although Lincoln sympathized with McClernand's feelings, he had no intention of intervening. Lincoln concluded that McClernand's effect on the morale of the general staff was a detriment to the army. "Better leave it where the law of the case has placed it," he told McClernand.[41]

In February 1864, McClernand was given command of the Eighth Corps, a part of Major General Nathaniel Banks's Army of the Gulf. McClernand hoped for an opportunity to redeem himself, but his service was limited to inspection duties along the Rio Grande. In April, McClernand contracted malaria and was sent home to recuperate.[42]

On November 23, 1864, Major General John McClernand resigned from the army, stating that he could do more for the war effort as a civilian. Lincoln and others were relieved by his decision. The president's secretary, John Hay, was delighted that McClernand was out of the picture. In his opinion he was "a vain, irritable, overbearing, exacting man."[43]

After the war, McClernand returned to his law practice. He supported President Andrew Johnson and believed he should continue Lincoln's moderate reconstruction policies. In the election of 1868, the Republican-leaning *Daily State Journal* supported Grant. It accused McClernand of being "guilty of shameful inconsistency" when he campaigned against Grant. Despite the *Journal's* opposition, McClernand remained popular with Democrats.[44]

In 1875, when Sherman's memoirs were published, the feud between Sherman and McClernand was reopened. The memoirs only reinforced McClernand's belief that Sherman had conspired to remove him from command. Their feud continued when McClernand disputed Sherman's continuing claim that he was not surprised at Shiloh. Through the years, McClernand's opinion of Grant remained the same, and he continued to speak out against him.[45]

In later years, McClernand served as a circuit court judge, president of the 1876 Democratic National Convention, and chairman of the commission that admitted Utah to the Union in 1896.[46] During the last few years of his life, McClernand suffered from ill health. On September 20, 1900, the old soldier died. Attired in his military uniform, he lay in state in his home. On the afternoon of September 23, he was laid to rest in Oak Ridge Cemetery, not far from the tomb of Abraham Lincoln.[47]

"Lawyer, Legislature, Soldier, Judge, Patriot" is the inscription on John McClernand's tombstone. Few men could claim a more varied life; few men could have served their country in more ways. As a patriot, he had few equals.

11 *Henry Wagner Halleck*

"Old Brains"

When General Meade failed to follow up his victory at Gettysburg, allowing Robert E. Lee's crippled Army of Northern Virginia to slip back into Virginia, Major General Henry Halleck, the Union's general-in-chief, received most of the criticism. Lincoln was not the only dissatisfied Northern official, but he was one of the few to blame Meade rather than Halleck. Lincoln told Secretary of the Navy Gideon Welles that he had not interfered with the campaign because "Halleck knows better than I what to do. . . . It is better that I, who am not a military man, should defer to him, rather than he to me." Welles, who usually respected Lincoln's judgment, was less kind in his evaluation of Halleck: "I have been unable to see, hear, or obtain evidence of power, or will, or talent, or originality on the part of General Halleck. He originates nothing, anticipates nothing to assist others; takes no responsibility, plans nothing, suggests nothing, is good for nothing."[1]

Other officials in the North were dissatisfied with Halleck's leadership, too. Later, when a rumor circulated that he might be leaving Washington to assume a field position, a congressman remarked: "Put Halleck in command of 20,000 men, and he will not scare three setting geese from their nests."[2]

Halleck did not attempt to answer his critics. He told one general that he tried not to notice the abuse he received in the newspapers. "Taking arms against the sea of troubles would neither improve my position nor strengthen Lincoln's," he said. In a letter to Grant he expressed his frustration: "I sincerely wish I was with you again in the West. I am utterly sick of this political hell."[3]

Probably no man was better prepared for the Civil War than Henry Halleck. General Grant said of him: "He is a man of gigantic intellect and well studied in the profession of arms." To Grant's dismay, Halleck would become one of the most vilified generals of the Civil War.[4]

Born January 16, 1815, in the Mohawk Valley of New York to Joseph and Catherine Wagner Halleck, Henry was the first of thirteen children. Henry worked on his father's farm until he was sixteen years old. Then in 1831, he rebelled against the monotony and drudgery of farming and went to live with his grandfather, Henry Wagner. His grandfather sent him to Fairfield Academy in Hudson, New York, and later to Union College in Schenectady. At the age of twenty, young Halleck became a cadet at West Point. There he excelled, graduating third in the class of 1839. At West Point Halleck adopted the military strategy and tactics of the famous Swiss military historian Baron Henri Jomini. It consisted of doing the "greatest damage to your opponent by the least exposure of your troops to those of the enemy." Jomini believed in the concentration of forces and maneuvering into a position where the enemy could be attacked in parts. Jomini never advised an attack be made en masse against a concentrated enemy (a tactic unfortunately repeated frequently during the war).[5]

After graduation, Halleck stayed at West Point to teach French for one year. In 1840, he left the Academy to work on the fortifications of New York City. General Winfield Scott rewarded Halleck for his outstanding work there by sending him to France to study European military science. After six months, he returned and wrote *Elements of Military Art and Science,* closely modeled after Jomini's writings.

During the Mexican War in 1846, Halleck was considered one of the army's leading experts on fortifications. The War Department ordered him to California to construct and inspect fortifications in the area. His duties in California were interrupted when Colonel H. S. Burton of the Third Artillery enlisted his services in combat duty in Baja, California, along the northwest coast of Mexico. When Burton's forces were successful in capturing the Mexican seaport of Mazatlan, Halleck was installed as lieutenant governor and promoted to the rank of brevet captain for his gallantry.[6]

In 1848, Halleck returned to California as its secretary of state, a difficult assignment. California was a foreign territory occupied by American military forces. Congress had not provided for its civil government, and much of the territory had been divided into large Spanish and Mexican ranches; disputes over titles to the land were frequent and often violent. Halleck was determined to bring order out of chaos by publishing reports on land titles and on Spanish and Mexican law.[7]

Halleck played an important role in the successful admission of California to the Union as a free state in 1850. Although he was well suited to run for governor of California or the U.S. Congress, Halleck was no politician and elected not to run. His experience as secretary of state, however, provided him with knowledge and experience in the law, and at the end of 1849, he formed a partnership with two San Francisco lawyers. The firm

Major General Henry W. Halleck, general-in-
chief of the armies of the United States, July 1862.

COURTESY OF THE LIBRARY OF CONGRESS

of Halleck, Peachy, and Billings opened for business in 1850 and soon was
a thriving enterprise.[8]

In 1854, Halleck resigned from the army. On a trip to New York a year
later, he married Elizabeth Hamilton, granddaughter of Alexander Hamilton. The couple had one child, a son. By 1861, they had amassed a fortune
of more than $500,000.

In 1861, when the clouds of war arose, Halleck's sympathies were with
the Union, and when, in August, General-in-Chief Winfield Scott and President Lincoln asked him to return to the army, he gladly accepted. On
October 1, Halleck and his wife boarded a steamer in San Francisco and
headed for Washington.[9]

In November, Halleck returned to the army as a major general and took
command of the Department of the Missouri. Halleck was far from the
image of a dashing commanding officer; his appearance, however, belied
his true ability. At five-feet, nine-inches tall and 190 pounds, he looked more
like a college professor than a wartime general. He was aloof; his speech and
movements were slow and deliberate. His gigantic intellect earned him the

title of "Old Brains." William T. Sherman praised him as a man of "great capacity." Halleck's success as a soldier and businessman were due more to his intellect and energy than to any qualities of charm or warmth. Lincoln once said that he was Halleck's friend because nobody else was.[10]

On November 2, when Major General John Frémont was relieved of command, the Western Department was split into two parts. The Department of Kansas went to Major General David Hunter, while the Department of Missouri was assigned to Halleck. At the same time, Brigadier General Don Carlos Buell replaced Sherman as commander of the Army of the Ohio. Both Halleck and Buell were concerned about the splitting of Frémont's command, and each wanted it restored to its original condition with himself as its head.[11]

After assuming command of the Army of Missouri, Halleck turned his attention to correcting the corruption and chaos he found in the department. One of the problems Halleck faced was the disrespect shown by Southern sympathizers in the St. Louis area. The women of the city wore red rosettes to show their contempt for the Union soldiers stationed there. Although he could be harsh at times, Halleck chose to solve the problem by the use of humor. He purchased a large quantity of rosettes and had them handed out to prostitutes in the city. When the ladies saw the streetwalkers wearing the flowers, they quickly disposed of theirs, and the issue was over.[12]

Lincoln expected Halleck and Buell to work in concert with each other, but neither was willing to do so. Each wanted to continue building, arming, and training his own army. As a result, the affairs in the West came to a standstill. Buell wanted to advance on Nashville, asking Halleck to aid him by moving up the Tennessee and Cumberland rivers. Halleck refused, using as an excuse the fact that he did not have enough men. When, by the end of December, neither army had moved, Lincoln ordered both generals to communicate with each other at once and to act in concert. The two exchanged some letters, making a feeble attempt to comply with Lincoln's request, but were unable to agree with each other on anything.[13]

On January 20, 1862, Halleck advised General-in-Chief McClellan of a plan he had for attacking Fort Henry, Tennessee. While waiting for McClellan's reply, Halleck made preparations for the attack. By the end of January, he directed Brigadier General Ulysses S. Grant to move on Fort Henry. Hoping to get a jump on Buell, Halleck did not notify him of his plans until he was well under way. It was not until he learned that Confederate General P. G. T. Beauregard, with 15,000 men, was en route to Tennessee that he requested help from Buell.[14]

Grant captured Fort Henry and moved against Fort Donelson on the Cumberland, and in a short time it too fell to his army. The double victory broke the center of the Confederate line in Kentucky. Although Grant had been the person mainly responsible for the victories, Halleck tried to take the credit. Halleck had directed the offensive from his desk in St. Louis and had not been on the front line with Grant. Nevertheless, he telegraphed McClellan demanding to be given command in the West. "I ask this in return for Forts Henry and Donelson," he said. When McClellan refused, Halleck went over his commander's head and made the same request to the new secretary of war, Edwin Stanton. Stanton also refused.[15]

After the fall of Fort Donelson, the Union forces kept the heat on the Confederates, driving them south from Columbus, Bowling Green, and Nashville, and finally out of Kentucky. On April 7, Major General John Pope's forces captured an island called Number Ten, acquiring over 6,000 prisoners, numerous supplies, and ammunition—all without a single Union casualty. Halleck was elated.[16]

Early on the morning of April 6, three of Albert S. Johnston's Confederate corps attacked Grant's army at Pittsburg Landing, catching him completely by surprise. The Union losses were heavy on that first day, but after the initial shock, Grant was able to recover. Early in the battle, General Johnston was killed; he was replaced by Beauregard. During the night, Buell's army crossed the river and came to Grant's aid. The next morning, with Buell's reinforcements, Grant was able to drive Beauregard from the field.[17]

The Battle of Shiloh, named for a small church nearby, was the first great bloody battle of the war. The casualty list for the Union was large, and charges were made that Grant was responsible either by his incompetence, neglect, or drunkenness. Publicly, Halleck refused to blame Grant for the heavy losses, saying, "The sad casualties were due in part to the conduct of the officers who were utterly unfit for their places, and in part to the numbers and bravery of the enemy." The unfit officers, Halleck believed, were volunteers, not those from West Point. Privately, however, Halleck was very critical of Grant. "Brave and able on the field, he had no idea of how to regulate and organize his forces before a battle or how to conduct the operations of a campaign," Halleck wrote.[18]

On April 11, Halleck arrived at Pittsburg Landing to take charge of the troops. He removed Grant from field command and appointed him to a new position: second-in-command of the armies in the West. Humiliated by the apparent demotion, Grant considered resigning from the army but was persuaded not to. Halleck began to prepare for an attack on Corinth but waited until he received sufficient reinforcements. When Halleck's army arrived at the outskirts of Corinth on May 28, it was clear to Beauregard that he was outnumbered and that defeat was inevitable if he remained to fight. In an effort to escape with his army intact, he used a clever deception. He had locomotives move in and out of town, announcing their arrival by having his troops cheer. The cheering was designed to convince Halleck that he was receiving massive reinforcements. It was not until Halleck heard the Confederate rear guard blowing up their supplies that he realized that the enemy had slipped away. On May 30, Halleck entered Corinth unopposed.[19]

In the spring of 1862, McClellan began his campaign on the Virginia peninsula. Because it was difficult to direct the army in the field and at the same time give attention to the war in the West, Lincoln removed McClellan as general-in-chief. Lincoln meant the move to be only temporary, planning to restore McClellan in the position after he captured Richmond.[20]

In July, Lincoln called Halleck to Washington to serve as general-in-chief. Since removing McClellan in April, Lincoln had exercised all the functions of that position. Now he wanted a military man in Washington to advise him about military matters. At this time, because of his success in the West, Halleck was considered the most successful Northern general. Who better than Halleck? Lincoln thought. Although the western victories were won on the field by Grant and other generals, they were credited to Halleck as departmental commander. "Old Brains" would hold the office until early in 1864, longer than any other general.[21]

Halleck was not excited about the promotion. He informed his friends that he was sorry to leave his current assignment because he had "studied out and [could] finish the war in the West," and would have difficulty dealing with politics in the East. Moreover, he did not want to get involved in the bickering between Stanton and McClellan. Although Halleck was flattered by his selection, he believed he could serve the country better in the West.[22]

Arriving in Washington on July 23, Halleck's first decision upon assuming the position of general-in-chief was to try to make an improvement in the Army of the Potomac, now stalled on the Virginia peninsula. When Halleck visited him, McClellan asked him for reinforcements and another chance to attack Richmond. McClellan continued to insist that Lee had an army of 200,000 opposing him. Halleck concluded that no feasible amount of reinforcements would satisfy McClellan to the point that he would be moved to take Richmond. On July 30, Halleck returned to Washington and, after consulting with Stanton, ordered McClellan to begin shifting the Army of the Potomac back to northern Virginia.[23]

Halleck's decision to discard the huge investment the Union had committed to McClellan's Peninsula Campaign required courage on his part, but it was probably not a wise move. With the newly formed Army of Virginia under the command of Major General John Pope, it would have been possible to attack Lee on two fronts near Richmond. Moreover, the transfer of the Army of Potomac from the peninsula exposed Pope's army to grave peril. Once Lee realized that the pressure on the peninsula had been reduced, he would be free to attack Pope's relatively small army of 56,000 men before McClellan could return with his army.[24]

Halleck was quick to realize the potential danger to Pope's army and ordered McClellan to bring his army back from Virginia with the greatest possible speed. McClellan, however, proceeded with inexcusable slowness. Despite some sharp dispatches from Halleck, McClellan continued to move slowly. Perhaps he delayed somewhat in the hope that Halleck would rescind his order to withdraw.[25]

In August, Lee moved to engage Pope. When Pope realized he was facing a larger enemy force, he fell back to the safety of the Rappahannock, hoping that McClellan would arrive with reinforcements before he had to fight Lee. Halleck continued to request McClellan to speed up his withdrawal and reinforce Pope, but McClellan received the news of Pope's danger with indifference.[26]

Three days before the Second Battle of Manassas, Pope continued to complain to Halleck that he was being kept in the dark about the whereabouts of McClellan's army. Halleck seemed to show little regard for Pope's concern, replying, "just think of the immense amount of telegraphing I have to do and then say whether I can be expected to give you any details as to the movements of others, even when I know them." The note offended Pope, and he requested that Halleck come out and take charge of the army. Halleck refused, saying that it was impossible for him to leave Washington. On another occasion, when Pope requested additional artillerymen for the defense of Washington, Halleck again put him off: "If you are deficient in anything for the defense of the forts, make your requisitions on the proper office. . . . I have no time for these details and don't come to me until you exhaust other resources."[27]

Lee's opportunity to crush Pope before McClellan's troops could join him came at the end of August at Manassas Junction, site of the first major battle of the war. By August 30, Pope's army was in full retreat back to Washington, having suffered heavy losses. Although General Pope took most of the criticism for the defeat at the Second Battle of Manassas, Halleck deserves at least some of the blame. As general-in-chief, he had the authority to coordinate the activities of McClellan and Pope. This he did not do well. On September 2, Halleck relieved Pope, and Lincoln personally asked McClellan to command the defense of Washington and the combined troops of the Army of the Potomac and the Army of Virginia.[28]

Halleck's job was to advise the president on technical matters and to translate his civilian terms into military language for the generals in the field. Throughout the war, however, Lincoln often used him as a shield against unfavorable decisions he, himself, had made. When Lincoln wanted to remove a general, he had Halleck sign the order, thus giving the impression that it was Halleck's decision. When asked about his military moves, Lincoln would respond, "I wish not to control. That I now leave to General Halleck," or "You must call on General Halleck, who commands." This is not to say that Halleck was always a pawn in Lincoln's hands. Many of Halleck's theories on war strategy became the guiding principles of the Union armies.[29]

Although Lincoln learned a great deal from Halleck as general-in-chief, he did not always give him the credit he deserved. Part of this was due to Halleck's personal demeanor. Halleck had a reputation for being the most unpopular man in Washington. He had no restraints about insulting people, including governmental officials. He disliked politicians and let them know it. Halleck was an easy man to hate.[30]

In September, Lee crossed the Potomac in force and moved into Maryland. Halleck ordered McClellan to move his troops immediately to meet the challenge. By September 13, Lee had his whole army north of the Potomac. McClellan had an incredible piece of luck when his soldiers found one of Lee's communiqués detailing his orders. McClellan thus found out that Lee had divided his forces, and he decided to send one of his corps into the gap between the two groups. At the same time, McClellan moved the rest of his army in the general direction of the Confederate army in Maryland, forcing Lee to take up a defensive position near the Potomac on Antietam Creek. Lee, however, was able to reassemble his entire army before McClellan could mount his attack on September 17. Although the battle was indecisive, McClellan claimed a complete victory.

Halleck tried to reinforce McClellan, hoping he would repeat his victory, but, after several days, McClellan had made no effort to pursue Lee. McClellan continued to claim he needed more men. Lincoln tried to get McClellan to move by visiting him in the field but was unable to do so. In a letter to his wife, Halleck expressed his concern about McClellan's inactivity: "He has lain still twenty days since the battle of Antietam, and I cannot persuade him to advance an inch. It puts me all out of patience."[31]

Meanwhile, in the West, Major General Don Carlos Buell was having difficulties with the governors of three states who wished to dictate military policy for his army. Despite their complaints to Lincoln, Buell continued to run his army as he saw fit. In Washington, Treasury Secretary Salmon Chase also expressed concern about Buell: "For months and months the country has witnessed with pain and indignation the waste of opportunities and sluggishness of movement which has characterized the action of Buell." Halleck warned Buell that neither the country nor the government could stand repeated delays in his movement. Buell was not impressed and did not advance as Lincoln and Halleck had requested. The country could not afford to wait for Buell. On October 23, Halleck prepared orders relieving Buell of command and replacing him with Major General William Rosecrans.[32]

Buell refused to let politicians dictate his military movements and had paid the price. Halleck was aware of the part politics played in conducting a war. "The time has come," he said, "when we must apply the sterner rules of war, whenever such applications become necessary to support our armies and move them rapidly upon the enemy. . . . Neither the country nor the government will much longer put up with the inactivity of some of our armies and generals."[33]

McClellan continued to make excuses for not advancing his army. Forty days after the Battle of Antietam, McClellan finally began to move. Three days later, he was still going slowly. Lincoln had passed the point where he would accept further excuses from McClellan; on November 5, he issued an order to Halleck to remove McClellan and replace him with Major General Ambrose Burnside. Halleck acted quickly; McClellan's career as a soldier had ended.[34]

The replacement of McClellan and Buell with Burnside and Rosecrans would prove to be no great improvement. Lincoln's relationship with Halleck had not changed; he still hoped to give the impression that it was Halleck, not he, who had made the decision to remove McClellan. McClellan believed that Halleck was responsible for his removal, and in his memoirs he took the opportunity to express his feelings about him: "Of all the men whom I encountered in high positions, Halleck was the most hopelessly stupid. . . . I do not think he ever had a correct military idea from the beginning to end."[35]

Halleck adjusted quickly to his new role as general-in-chief, playing the "political game" when necessary. He used the same approach with each general regardless of his ability. Whenever possible he would offer his opinion and advice but avoided giving exact instructions; rather, he would leave the final execution of the plan to the general's own judgment.[36]

Burnside took immediate action to draw up a plan to go on the offensive, but Halleck did not like the plan. "Old Brains" urged the general against crossing the Rappahannock River at Fredericksburg and then attacking Richmond, but Burnside stubbornly insisted on doing so. When Halleck informed the president of Burnside's plan to go to Fredericksburg, the latter was not enthusiastic about the move either, but finally consented. It will only succeed, Lincoln told Burnside, if you move quickly.[37]

Lincoln's analysis of the plan was correct. Burnside's only chance for success was to cross the Rappahannock and to advance toward Richmond before Lee could shift his army to confront him. The timing of the move was vital. Unfortunately, the pontoons Burnside needed to cross the river were late in arriving. As a result, Lee beat him to Fredericksburg and forced Burnside to attack him on ground that favored the Confederates. On December 13, Burnside's army fought the bloody Battle of Fredericksburg. Burnside attacked the enemy in a piecemeal fashion and was repulsed, suffering heavy losses. By the end of the day, the Army of the Potomac had suffered over 12,000 casualties with nothing to show for it.[38]

Burnside blamed his defeat at Fredericksburg on the delay in the arrival of the pontoons. Halleck refuted the charge, claiming that Burnside did not carry out the plan that had been approved. Although Halleck tried to make Burnside the scapegoat for the fiasco at Fredericksburg, the *New York World* did not let him off so easily: "The hour has struck when we must have an immediate change of measures, and of men. . . . The country has had enough of the blundering pretension. If the General-in-Chief and the Secretary of War are not promptly replaced by competent men, the country is irretrievably ruined."[39]

For five weeks after the Battle of Fredericksburg, Burnside did nothing. His army was torn by dissension, with some of his corps commanders openly criticizing his generalship. On January 24, Burnside traveled to Washington to meet with Lincoln. He had prepared two letters: one ordering the dismissal of the two generals—Joseph Hooker and William Franklin— who had been openly critical of him; the other was his resignation. He asked Lincoln to take one or the other. Lincoln decided to relieve Burnside of his command and replaced him with Major General Joseph Hooker; however, he refused to accept his resignation.[40]

By the fall of 1862, the change of command in the West was showing no noticeable difference in results. During the first two months after Rosecrans replaced Buell, he, too, gave no indication of moving. Halleck tried to light a fire under Rosecrans and finally did. On January 2, 1863, Rosecrans defeated a Confederate force under General Braxton Bragg at Stone's River.

In December 1862, Halleck was involved in a dispute between Generals Grant and McClernand. Halleck settled the issue by siding with Grant. McClernand fought back, charging Halleck with "willful contempt of superior authority and utter incompetence." Lincoln did not come to Halleck's aid by rebuking McClernand for contempt of his superior. Instead, he tried to pacify McClernand by appealing to his sense of duty to the country. Later, however, McClernand would be relieved of independent command, leaving Grant free to direct his full attention to the capture of Vicksburg.[41]

Lincoln appointed "Fighting Joe" Hooker to command the Army of the Potomac without consulting Stanton, Halleck, or members of the cabinet. The new leader of the army had known Halleck earlier in California where he had borrowed money from him and never repaid it. Halleck's opinion of Hooker was colored by that episode, and it had not improved over the years. Hooker, likewise, did not like Halleck and made no secret of his opinion. He told Lincoln that he could not command the army efficiently if he had to deal personally with Halleck. Halleck was his enemy, he said, and did not want him to be successful. Desperate for a general who could lead the Army of the Potomac to victory, Lincoln consented to his request. During his tenure of command, Hooker was permitted to report directly to Lincoln for all of his instructions. Halleck was partially to blame for Lincoln's decision to allow Hooker to bypass the chain of command. Since the Second Battle of Manassas, Halleck had increasingly refused to exercise the full function of his office and had disappointed Lincoln.[42]

During February and March, Hooker reorganized the army. When Halleck sent suggestions to Hooker, he completely ignored them and did not even have the courtesy to reply to the general-in-chief. Hooker was determined not to make the same mistake that Burnside had. Lee's army held an elaborate network of trenches along the Rappahannock River near Fredericksburg. Hooker had no intention of assaulting these trenches; rather, he planned to maneuver his army to force Lee into the open for a showdown fight. Hooker was so confident of victory he reportedly said: "May God have mercy on General Lee, for I will have none."[43]

"Fighting Joe's" plan, however, did not work the way he had hoped. Guessing correctly that the main threat from Union troops was at Chancellorsville, Lee left a small force under Major General Jubal Early to hold the Fredericksburg defenses, while he marched with the rest of the army westward to the Wilderness. Although outnumbered two to one, Lee decided to attack Hooker's exposed right flank. Stonewall Jackson, with 30,000 infantry and artillery, marched to attack the Union flank, while Lee remained with only 15,000 men to face Hooker's main force.[44]

In the late afternoon of May 2, Jackson attacked Hooker from the west on a front two miles wide. By dusk, Jackson had penetrated the Union right, inflicting heavy casualties on the enemy. After Jackson's crushing blow on an unsuspecting corps, Hooker withdrew, and the victory was Lee's. On the evening of May 4, against the advice of his corps commanders, Hooker decided to retreat across the Rappahannock River.[45]

After Chancellorsville, Lee began his invasion of the North and again threw the capital into an uproar. Hooker proposed taking his army south to capture the undefended Richmond while Lee was away. The president rejected the proposal and asked Halleck for his opinion. "Old Brains" agreed fully with Lincoln.[46]

Finally, a plan was agreed upon, the primary objective of which was the destruction of Lee's army, not the capture of Richmond. By late June, Lee was roaming at will through Pennsylvania. If Hooker had intentionally wanted to anger Lincoln, he could have chosen no more effective way than to ask for more troops and, at the same time, refuse to move until he received them. When reinforcements were not forthcoming, Hooker asked Halleck for permission to remove the troops from Harper's Ferry so they could join his army. When Halleck refused, Hooker asked to be relieved. He believed Lincoln would not replace him at this time, and thus he could force his will on Halleck; but on June 28, 1863, to his surprise, the president relieved him and appointed Major General George Meade to command the army.

Lincoln and Stanton made the selection of Meade to command the army without consulting Halleck. Although hurt by the slight, Halleck told Meade that he would not be "hampered by any minute instructions" from him and that he was free to act as he saw fit with his army, except that he would be expected to fight if Lee moved toward Washington or Baltimore. When Meade assumed command, the Confederate army was spread over a wide area in Pennsylvania. He moved to concentrate his forces west of the Susquehanna River, hoping to draw Lee into a battle. The two armies converged on Gettysburg at the same time, and on July 1 to 3 the two armies engaged in one of the greatest battles of the war.[47]

On the afternoon of July 2, Meade wired Halleck that he was waiting for Lee to attack. After the Confederate assaults had been repulsed, Meade decided to remain in his present position. On July 3, Lee elected to attack Meade with a massive assault, hoping to break the Union line. The attack failed, and Lee was forced to withdraw.

Like McClellan at Antietam, Meade allowed the enemy to withdraw without following up his victory. After Lee crossed the Potomac, Halleck ordered Meade to pursue the Confederate army, keeping between the enemy and Washington. Although Halleck was blamed for Meade's reluctance to move as directed, "Old Brains" did not attempt to challenge his accusers. Finally on July 29, Halleck told Meade to discontinue a pursuit that he had never really mounted.[48]

On July 7, Lincoln received more good news from the West—Vicksburg had fallen. All during June, Grant had laid siege to the town, and demands were made on Lincoln to remove him because the capture of Vicksburg was taking too long. But the president had refused to yield to the pressure. After Vicksburg, Lincoln said, "Grant is my man, and I am his the rest of the war."[49]

While Grant's actions pleased Lincoln, Rosecrans was as inactive as General Buell had been. The president, Halleck told Rosecrans, had promised relief to the citizens of east Tennessee. In September, Rosecrans moved after Bragg, and in a series of maneuvers, he gained control of Chattanooga without a battle. Because Bragg was retreating, Rosecrans believed he could achieve a complete victory if he pursued him. Bragg, however, had retired only to take up a better position from which to engage Rosecrans. On September 19, Bragg attacked Rosecrans south of Chattanooga near Chickamauga Creek. The fighting in the dense woods at Chickamauga was fierce and bloody. In a short time Bragg swept the Union forces from the field, forcing Rosecrans to retreat back to Chattanooga. Halleck and Lincoln decided that the city had to be held, and reinforcements were sent. At the same time, Lincoln decided to make a change in the Western command structure. All the departments of the army in the West, including Rosecrans's, were placed under Grant.[50]

Grant did not disappoint Lincoln. After taking control of the operations at Chattanooga, he attacked Bragg, driving his army into Georgia. In March 1864, after Grant was promoted to lieutenant general in the regular army, Halleck requested that Grant be appointed general-in-chief. Halleck willingly accepted the demotion in favor of a new position as chief-of-staff. The change in title meant little real change in Halleck's responsibilities. After receiving the news of his appointment as general-in-chief, Grant stopped at Washington only long enough to shake Lincoln's hand before leaving for the field and Meade's army, where he stayed to the end of the war. Halleck continued to advise Lincoln and Stanton, carrying out the same functions as he had for the previous two years. The new arrangement suited the strengths of both Halleck and Grant.[51]

As chief-of-staff, Halleck distributed reinforcements to the armies, coached field generals, directed the flow of supplies, and tried to raise the professional level of the army. He also assumed a new role: acting as a liaison between Lincoln and Grant and between the departmental commanders.[52]

Grant began his tenure as general-in-chief with plans for a double thrust into the Confederate line. Sherman would move south from Chattanooga against Atlanta, while he would attack Lee to keep him from reinforcing Joseph Johnston in Georgia. Halleck tried to anticipate Grant and Sherman's needs, keeping both armies fully supplied. This arrangement worked well. Halleck was now in his element, doing what he did best: administering armies in the field.

When he felt it necessary, Halleck worked to remove politically appointed officers from important command positions. One such general was Nathaniel Banks, whom Lincoln had appointed as a major general of volunteers. Banks was defeated in several major engagements, including one with Stonewall Jackson during his celebrated Shenandoah Valley campaign in 1862. When Halleck proposed combining Banks's Department of the Gulf with Major General Frederick Steele's Department of the Arkansas, Lincoln vetoed the merger. Later, with the support of Grant, Halleck was able to convince Lincoln to remove Banks. On May 7, Halleck informed Major General Edward Canby that he was now in command of the Departments of the Gulf and Arkansas.[53]

During the summer of 1864, Confederate Lieutenant General Jubal Early was active in the Shenandoah Valley. The valley provided a direct route for Confederate advances toward Washington and the North. It also provided a protective cover for the movement of troops and contained an ample food supply. Grant sent one of his best subordinates, Major General Philip Sheridan, to clear the valley of Confederate troops. "Give the enemy no rest," Grant instructed Sheridan. "Do all the damage to railroads and crops you can. Carry off stock of all descriptions, and Negroes, so as to prevent further planting. If the war is to last another year, we want the Shenandoah Valley to remain a barren waste." Halleck agreed with Grant's proposal to destroy the valley, giving Sheridan his approval. This plan of destruction was a major change of policy from what Lincoln had originally envisioned.[54]

While Grant continued his war of attrition with Lee in Virginia, Sherman was making his way toward Atlanta. Although he was sending supplies and reinforcements to Sherman, Halleck made no attempt to influence the general's moves. By December 1864, Sherman had taken Savannah.

In that month, Grant sent a dispatch to Stanton recommending that Major General George Thomas be relieved and replaced by Major General

John Schofield. When Halleck learned of Grant's recommendation, he did all he could to delay the action, allowing Thomas time to move. Halleck's inaction proved beneficial to the Union cause. Several days later, Thomas was victorious at Nashville.[55]

By March 1865, Sherman marched steadily northward, opposed only by a small force under General Joseph Johnston. At the same time, Grant was exerting pressure on Lee at Petersburg. Finally, on April 9, Lee surrendered at Appomattox Court House. Less than two weeks later, Johnston surrendered to Sherman at Bennett's farm.

After the war, Halleck served out his days in the army, commanding the Military Division of the James. Later, he commanded the Department of the Pacific in San Francisco and finally the Division of the South, with headquarters in Louisville, Kentucky.[56]

Halleck died in Louisville in January 1872, just a few days before his fifty-seventh birthday. His passing was noted with little fanfare in papers in San Francisco and New York. He was buried in Green-Wood Cemetery, Brooklyn, New York.

Henry Halleck was not a great field general like Sherman or Grant. He did not win the admiration and respect of the army he served. But a nation waging a total war required a businessman-soldier to manage the army. "Old Brains" did this well, serving his nation in time of need.

12 Ambrose E. Burnside

Reluctant Commander

In the midst of a blinding snowstorm, a courier from the War Department arrived at the headquarters of Major General Ambrose Burnside, commander of the Ninth Corps of the Union army. He carried a dispatch appointing Burnside commander of the Army of the Potomac in place of Major General George B. McClellan. Surprised at the news, Burnside protested vigorously that he had not sought the command and did not want it. He had rejected the offer twice before when it was made, but this time his staff convinced him that this was not an offer, but an order. Thus, Burnside was thrust into a position he did not want and was not capable of handling.[1]

Burnside was liked by his men because of his concern for them. He was a trusting man with an optimistic outlook on life and found it difficult to believe another person could wish him harm until it was so obvious he could not ignore it. When his plans fell short, he tended to take the blame himself. At difficult moments in his life, he accepted responsibility and tried to solve his problems on his own. Ambrose was six feet tall with a deep chest and broad shoulders and sported a bushy pair of whiskers that met his mustache on both sides, henceforth called sideburns in his memory. Despite his intimidating size, his smile and good humor drew people to him.[2]

Although Burnside was popular with his men, many of the officers in the Army of the Potomac had their doubts and concerns about his appointment. To them, Burnside had not demonstrated the qualities necessary successfully to command a large army. After the Battle of Antietam in September 1862, his friend McClellan criticized him for slowness in moving his troops and for "confusion in action." McClellan believed he was "not fit to command more than a regiment."[3]

If Burnside had heard these criticisms of his leadership potential, he would have agreed. "The responsibility is so great that at times I tremble at the thought of assuming so large a command," he wrote to a friend. In a letter to his wife concerning Burnside's appointment, Major General George Meade wrote: "Burnside, it is said, wept like a child, and is the most distressed man in the army, openly saying he is not fit for the job."[4]

Although Burnside may have been unhappy and fearful of his new assignment, he tried not to show it. He came from honest, independent stock. Born on May 27, 1824, in Liberty, Indiana, he was the fourth of nine children of Edghill and Pamelia Brown Burnside. Although Ambrose's father served on the bench of the circuit court as an associate justice and in the state legislature, his income and economic condition were considered moderate for the times. Young Ambrose attended a one-room school run by a gentle Quaker named William Haughton. It was here, and at home, that he developed the strict honesty and kindness for which he became well known.[5]

Although Ambrose was a bright boy, his intelligence alone was not enough to ensure that he would be successful on the Indiana frontier. The family's financial situation did not allow for Ambrose to further his education beyond the rudiments of language and arithmetic. Continued education was a luxury the family could not afford. In 1840, Ambrose became an apprentice to a tailor in a nearby town, and, when his mother died, he returned home to Liberty to open a tailor shop of his own. In a short time, he realized he would not be content with a life as a tailor.[6]

Ambrose's father was able to use his influence with the governor and two U.S. senators to obtain an appointment to West Point for his son. In 1843, Burnside entered West Point. His accomplishments during his first two years at the Academy were mediocre at best. During the summer after his second year, Burnside went on furlough, returning home to Indiana. This reintroduction to the drudgery of farm work quickly reminded him of the consequences of being dismissed from the Academy. By the end of the summer, his attitude toward school had changed, and he returned to West Point motivated to improve his class standing. In 1847, he graduated eighteenth in a small class of thirty-eight and was commissioned a second lieutenant in the Third U.S. Artillery.[7]

The Mexican War was in progress when Burnside graduated, and his first assignment was at Vera Cruz. Unfortunately for his military career, the war ended before he arrived. After returning to the states, Burnside spent several uneventful years soldiering in the West and fighting the Apache Indians in New Mexico. In one encounter, he came away from the fight with an arrow in his neck and a gem of an idea. Burnside noted that the only weapons his men were able to use while in mounted combat were sabers. Revolvers were not yet in general issue, and it was awkward and time consuming for a mounted soldier to reload a muzzle-loading weapon

Portrait of Major General Ambrose E. Burnside, officer of the Federal army.

COURTESY OF THE LIBRARY OF CONGRESS

in the midst of a battle. While recovering from his wound, he began thinking about a light, breech-loading carbine that would replace the ones currently in use.[8]

During the winter of 1850 to 1851, Burnside took an extended furlough, returning home to Liberty. It was during this time that he courted and prepared to marry Charlotte Moon. As a local legend insists, Burnside proposed to Charlotte, and a date was set for their marriage. All went well until the wedding day when the minister asked Charlotte if she would take Burnside for her husband. She supposedly replied, "No siree, Bob, I won't," and walked out. As the tale goes, Charlotte later agreed to marry an Ohio lawyer. When the time came for the vows to be exchanged, the Ohio lawyer took his pistol out of its holster and announced that there would either be a "wedding tonight or a funeral tomorrow."[9]

Burnside was determined to find a wife. In 1851, shortly after being promoted to first lieutenant, he married Mary Richmond, a twenty-three-year-old woman whom he had met in his first assignment in Rhode

Island. They set up housekeeping at Fort Adams, New Mexico, his current station.[10]

In October 1853, Burnside resigned from the army, hoping to enhance his financial position. Having improved the design of his breech-loading rifle, he borrowed money and started a business known as the Bristol Rifle Works. At first, sales were slow but adequate to cover expenses. When it appeared he was about to receive a lucrative contract for the purchase of carbines for the U.S. Cavalry, Burnside borrowed more money and increased production. When the contract was not forthcoming as expected, Burnside had to file for bankruptcy. He assigned all of his possessions, including his uniform, sword, and firearm patent, to the investors in his company. His wife moved in with relatives while he moved West, hoping to earn enough to repay his debt.[11]

Burnside turned to his former schoolmate and friend, George McClellan, for help. McClellan had also left the army and was serving as an engineer and vice president of the Illinois Central Railroad at this time. With the help of his friend, Burnside was able to land a job with the railroad, later becoming treasurer of the company. For two years, Burnside remained in Chicago, paying off his debt and living with the McClellans. By 1860, with his debt paid off, he and his wife were able to afford their own accommodations.[12]

After the firing on Fort Sumter, Burnside was preparing to offer his services to the army when he received a telegram from the governor of Rhode Island, asking if he would command a regiment from the state. The next morning Burnside arrived in Providence, where he was commissioned colonel in the Rhode Island militia.[13]

Burnside's first action came during the summer of 1861 at Manassas Junction, Virginia. Assigned to David Hunter's division, Burnside now commanded a brigade consisting of two Rhode Island regiments, the Second New Hampshire and the Seventy-First New York militia. On July 16, the men collected their marching rations, salt pork, and hardtack and prepared for their first battle. A festive atmosphere existed as they made their way to Manassas, stopping to eat their rations, picking berries, and, in general, enjoying themselves.[14]

The soldiers were not the only ones enjoying themselves. Hundreds of civilians had ridden out in buggies, bringing picnic baskets and blankets to spread on the hillside near the battlefield to watch the battle. The fact that citizens from Washington had created a festive atmosphere before the battle indicated that the nation expected the war to come to a quick conclusion, perhaps as a result of this battle. In just a few hours, their thoughts on the war would quickly change.[15]

By the time Major General Irvin McDowell's untrained army reached the battlefield, they were exhausted, having marched for two days over narrow roads through heat and dust. Covered with sweat and dirt and having eaten all their rations, the troops were in no shape to fight.[16] The relaxed attitude and fatigue of the Union army gave the Confederates time to prepare for the attack. As Burnside's brigade approached the field of battle, the men could hear the fighting up ahead; the atmosphere quickly turned more serious.

On the evening of July 19, McDowell selected Hunter's division to lead the main flanking attack in the morning. Moving out in the darkness of night and slowed by fallen trees that blocked the road, the division took more than seven hours to advance just three miles.[17] When the troops did finally reach the battlefield, they engaged the enemy in a piecemeal fashion. Burnside's brigade was the vanguard of the assault on Matthews Hill, and, although novices to combat, they held their own. For almost two hours a fierce battle raged, but the badly outnumbered Confederates held on. Then, for some unknown reason, between noon and two o'clock in the afternoon, McDowell stopped fighting, giving the Confederates time to reinforce their position. This delay helped turn the tide of battle. McDowell, well behind the lines, could not see the Confederate reinforcements arriving. Had he been aware of this, he might have pushed harder.[18]

Slowly the Confederates retreated from Matthews Hill to nearby Henry House Hill. Still outnumbered, they were reinforced by Brigadier General Thomas Jonathan Jackson. It was here that the Union advance was halted and the legend of "Stonewall" Jackson was born. Jackson's volley devastated the Federal lines and stopped the attack.[19]

Now the tide of battle changed. As Union troops fell by the hundreds in uncoordinated attacks, more Confederate reinforcements arrived. By four o'clock in the afternoon, the Yankees began to fall back from Henry House Hill, first in an orderly retreat and then as a rout.[20]

As the Union army fled the field, the retreating troops came upon the civilians who had come out to watch the battle. The picnickers were now blocking the Federals' line of retreat. Before they could remove their buggies from the road, the army, canons, wagons, and ambulances piled into them, causing a gigantic traffic jam, only adding to the confusion and chaos. Men dropped their knapsacks and weapons and ran for their lives. Burnside's retreat was orderly at first, until a direct hit on a bridge overturned a wagon in the middle of the span, causing even more of a bottleneck. Soon Burnside's brigade was part of the flight, and it was every man for himself.[21]

The retreat continued into the night and the next morning. A large fragment of what had been Burnside's brigade gathered at the site of their pre-battle camp to rest. That evening, what was left of his brigade staggered into Washington. Burnside's brigade disbanded, and Burnside was released from the militia.[22]

On July 21, 1861, Burnside's friend, Major General George McClellan, assumed command of the Army of the Potomac. Burnside was pleased with

McClellan's appointment, but he was even more elated to learn that he had been commissioned as brigadier general in the Federal army.

In the fall of 1861, Burnside's first assignment as a brigadier general was the training of recruits for McClellan's army. In October, he presented a plan to McClellan for forming a coastal division with which to invade and occupy land areas and inland waterways along the North Carolina coast. With McClellan's approval, he began training troops, procuring ships, and preparing for the expedition. By the middle of December, Burnside had assembled 15,000 men and a fleet of various kinds of steamers, barges, ferryboats, and tugs to transport his troops. On January 9, 1862, he sailed for Fort Monroe, Virginia. There the "Burnside Expedition," as it was labeled, met with its supply ships and headed for Cape Hatteras. Storms, cold weather, and navigation problems slowed the division's movements, and it was not until February 7 that the first wave was ready for a landing on the shore of Roanoke Island.[23]

The Confederates did not seriously contest the landing. Fire from Union gunboats forced them to withdraw, allowing Burnside to land his troops with a minimum of casualties. Burnside's pursuit was rapid, and, by mid-April, Roanoke Island was under Union control. Although the Battle of Roanoke was an insignificant affair compared to future engagements, Burnside had handled the expedition very well, having worked out all the details of the landing and the land campaign. He had proven himself a capable leader, one whose star was rising. In recognition of his bold, aggressive campaign in North Carolina, Burnside was promoted to the rank of major general and recalled to reinforce McClellan's army, which had stalled on the Virginia peninsula.[24]

Shortly after Burnside returned to Virginia, he was invited to meet with Secretary of War Stanton and the president. To his surprise and discomfort, Lincoln asked if he would be willing to replace McClellan as head of the Army of the Potomac. Burnside explained that McClellan was the better general and needed more time to prove it. Lincoln was surprised at Burnside's response and reason for refusing; he was not accustomed to officers who freely admitted their limitations. For the time being, McClellan would remain in command, and Burnside had left a good impression with the president.[25]

McClellan, with his army stalled on the peninsula, continued to appeal to Lincoln for still more troops. In frustration, the president ordered the Army of the Potomac back to Washington to support Major General John Pope's newly formed Army of Virginia. When McClellan's army began its withdrawal from the peninsula, General Robert E. Lee, now commander of the Army of Northern Virginia, moved to engage Pope's army. As a result, Burnside's troops were ordered to return to northern Virginia. By August 4, he arrived at Fredericksburg where he provided a shield for both Pope's left flank and Washington. Burnside was urged to send all the troops he could spare from his Ninth Corps to Pope. On August 12, he dispatched two of his divisions, while he remained behind to hold the Union line at the Rappahannock River. Although Pope's Army of Virginia suffered a disastrous defeat at the Second Battle of Manassas, Burnside's divisions distinguished themselves. After the battle, they were returned to him, and he was now placed in command of two corps, the Ninth and the Twelfth.[26]

Fresh from his victory at Manassas, Lee took the offensive. Early in September, he crossed the Potomac River at Leesburg and invaded Maryland, hoping to take advantage of the demoralized Army of the Potomac. The president sent for Burnside and again offered him command of the army. For the second time, Burnside declined the offer and urged Lincoln to retain McClellan in command. After agonizing over the situation, Lincoln decided to stick with McClellan, replacing John Pope. When asked why he was planning to continue with McClellan, he said, "We must use the tools we have. There is no man in the army who can man the fortification and lick these troops into shape half as well as he." Lincoln went to see McClellan and told him of his decision: "General, you will take command of the forces in the field."[27]

Using his organizational talents, McClellan merged General Pope's Army of Virginia into the Army of the Potomac in a matter of days. He restructured the army, dividing it into eight corps, assigning Burnside to command the Ninth Corps. On September 5, McClellan began marching the bulk of his army northwest into Maryland. Taking six of his corps, about 84,000 troops, with him, he left two corps behind to defend Washington.[28]

On September 7, the last of Lee's columns crossed the Potomac and joined the main body of the Confederate army. McClellan followed Lee into Maryland by a parallel route. As he approached the enemy, McClellan had a wonderful piece of luck. He came in possession of a Confederate document indicating the disposition of Lee's army. From it he learned that the army was not concentrated but, rather, widely separated. McClellan was exultant when he read the order. To one of his generals, he said: "Here is a paper with which if I cannot whip 'Bobbie Lee,' I will be willing to go home."[29]

With the information McClellan had about the disposition of Lee's army, he should have been able to defeat it piece-by-piece. Even so, such good fortune did not spur McClellan into speedy action. When Lee realized McClellan was planning to attack him, he hastily began to concentrate his forces. At Antietam Creek, Lee decided to make his stand. Although McClellan had missed his opportunity to destroy the Confederate army in parts, he still outnumbered Lee.[30]

The two armies met on September 17, 1862, at Antietam Creek near the town of Sharpsburg. McClellan's plan called for Burnside's Ninth Corps to attack the Confederate right flank, while Major General Joseph Hooker launched the main attack on the left flank. To reach their objective, Burnside's corps had to cross a bridge spanning the Antietam. Residents called it the Rohrbach's Bridge after the family that lived nearby, but after the battle the bridge would forever bear the name of the Union commander who made it famous, Ambrose Burnside.[31]

Early in the morning, Burnside moved his four divisions to the hill overlooking the approaches to the bridge and waited for McClellan's order to move. At 10 a.m. it came, but only after Hooker's First Corps had been repulsed on the Confederate's left. The ever-cautious McClellan did not give Burnside the order to move until Major General William Franklin's Sixth Corps arrived as his backup. Burnside read the orders, still operating under the impression that his corps was to act as a diversion for Hooker's attack.[32]

A few hundred Confederate sharpshooters were positioned on the heights on the opposite side of the bridge and were able to keep Burnside's troops at bay. McClellan had ordered Burnside to cross the creek and gain a foothold on the opposite bank. Although his men could have waded across the shallow creek at several points, Burnside was determined to cross on the bridge. Time and again his clustered troops tried to cross at this point, only to be repulsed. To motivate the men, Burnside offered a ration of whiskey if they were able to secure the position on the opposite bank.[33]

After finally crossing the creek, Burnside moved his men forward. As he did, his corps was met by Major General A. P. Hill's light division. Seeing Hill, McClellan believed he was the first wave of Confederate reinforcements joining the battle. Rather than press the attack, McClellan decided to stop and hold his ground. The battle was over.[34]

The battle had been a costly one for both sides, producing nearly 23,000 casualties, the largest in a single day in American history. While McClellan congratulated himself on what he believed was a victory, Lee slipped back across the Potomac into Virginia. McClellan failed to pursue Lee, missing a golden opportunity to destroy the Confederate army. By September 19, the Confederate army had completely escaped. McClellan telegraphed Washington, telling Lincoln that he had won a great victory, but, to some extent, he knew this was a half-truth. Over time, the American people would know it, too. McClellan chose to sacrifice his friend Burnside in an effort to save his place in history. He charged that Burnside had hesitated to attack the Confederates at Burnside's Bridge and, to a degree, this hesitation had contributed to the limited success by his army. Burnside refused to answer McClellan's accusations, leaving the final judgment to history.[35]

Nearly two months after the battle at Antietam, McClellan still had not pursued Lee. Lincoln was frustrated by his unwillingness to take action. Although McClellan eventually crossed the Potomac and began marching south, Lincoln had had enough of McClellan's excuses and stalling. It was time for a change in command. In his place, he appointed Burnside. Burnside had declined the position two times before, believing he was not competent enough to direct a large army and that McClellan was better qualified for the position. Burnside did not like Joseph Hooker, and it was only after he learned that the position would go to him if he did not accept that he agreed to take command.[36]

McClellan advised Burnside to take the position and said he would furnish him with all the information he had about the condition of the army. With McClellan's blessing, Burnside took command of the Army of the Potomac, now 130,000 strong, on November 7, 1862. At the time, the army was spread out over the twenty miles between Manassas and Waterloo, Virginia.

Ambrose Burnside was well liked by his army. He had a charming personality and possessed a winning way, casting a spell over most people when they first met him. His imposing size and striking figure were difficult not to notice. He was looked on as a dashing fellow, which he certainly was, but, above all else, he was an honest and humble man. While a good subordinate general, he was not suited to command a large army. He had been correct when he twice before refused the command of the Army of the Potomac. Burnside had a good record, but Lincoln did not know that the general lacked the competence for such a command.[37]

Burnside reorganized the army into three grand divisions. The right wing was commanded by Major General Edwin Sumner; the center, by Major General Joseph Hooker; the left wing, by Major General William Franklin. Although it was customary for armies not to campaign during the winter, Lincoln made it clear to Burnside that he did not want him to wait until spring before moving against Lee. Lincoln was impressed when Burnside quickly moved his army south. To get to Richmond, Burnside decided to cross the Rappahannock at Fredericksburg.[38]

To cross the Rappahannock, Burnside would need pontoon boats. He planned to march quickly to Falmouth, Virginia, on the north bank of the Rappahannock, where pontoon boats would be waiting, and cross to Fredericksburg before he could be opposed by Lee. Once at Fredericksburg, he would move quickly toward Richmond. If all went according to plan, Burnside believed he could steal a march on Lee, whose army would still be in winter quarters west of Fredericksburg. The plan was a good one but relied heavily on precise coordination with the War Department and General-in-Chief Henry Halleck, who would have to make certain that the pontoon boats arrived on time.[39]

When Burnside arrived at the north bank of the Rappahannock, the pontoon boats were not there, forcing him to wait ten days before they arrived. Lee had been surprised at first by Burnside's swift movement, but because of the delay, he had an opportunity to mass his troops in front of the Union army on the opposite shore. The delay cost Burnside's army the jump they were counting on, and they could no longer enter Fredericksburg uncontested.[40]

Burnside's movement was delayed even more while he considered other possible river crossings. In the meantime, Lee continued to reinforce his army, deploying them on the high ground on the opposite side of the river. When Burnside finally decided he was ready to cross the river, he proposed that it be in full view of the enemy.[41]

The men of General Sumner's grand division were appalled by Burnside's plan for attacking General Lee. When Burnside learned of the grumbling among the troops, he assembled the general officers of his command to discuss the plan. Colonel Rush Hawkins spoke out against the plan: "If you make the attack as contemplated, it will be the greatest slaughter of the war; there isn't infantry enough in our whole army to carry the heights if they are defended." Colonel J. H. Taylor was even more direct: "The carrying out of your plan will be murder, not warfare." Despite the concern expressed at the meeting, Burnside did not change his plan.[42]

Burnside must have been the only person who thought the plan would work. Later, Colonel Edward Cross of the Fifth New Hampshire recalled: "As God is my witness, it seemed to my heart that it was to be a failure. I had the sense we were marching to disaster."[43]

The Confederate army held a strong position on the heights outside of Fredericksburg. Lee did little to prevent the Union army from crossing the river, content to let Burnside attack him on the high ground he had chosen. By December 10, Lee had amassed a force of 72,000 men; opposing him was Burnside's Army of the Potomac, 116,000 strong.[44]

Burnside ordered a bombardment of Fredericksburg to rid the town of Confederate sharpshooters. One Union soldier later wrote: "The bombardment was terrific and seemed ridiculously disproportionate to the enemy therein. Like an elephant attacking a mosquito." After chasing the Confederates out of town, the Yankees began to plunder it, destroying everything they could not use. Some commanders tried to stop the looting but were unable to do so. For a night, the Union troops drank, sang, and forgot about the seriousness of what they had to face the next day.[45]

Lee watched the destruction of Fredericksburg with sadness and anger, but the Union's delay in attacking him only allowed the Confederates time to strengthen their position. Burnside's generals recognized the danger. Major General William Smith wrote, "Burnside persisted in crossing the river after all hope of surprise had faded away. And now we must fight against great disadvantage." The Army of the Potomac would soon pay for Burnside's delay.[46]

Although most of Burnside's generals thought that the Confederate position on the high ground was difficult, if not impossible, to penetrate, Burnside still insisted on a frontal attack. The stronger part of Lee's line was on the left and held by Lieutenant General James Longstreet's corps. Here the terrain was more favorable for defense with an elongated steep elevation known as "Marye's Heights." Moreover, Longstreet's artillery was carefully placed and, as artillerist E. Porter Alexander stated, "the ground in front of them was so well covered that a chicken could not live on the field when we open on it!"[47]

"Stonewall" Jackson's corps was deployed on the Confederate right along a low, but heavily wooded ridge. Burnside decided that the main attack would be against the Confederate right. His orders were somewhat vague, leading to misinterpretation by General Franklin. Instead of using his entire division to attack in full force, Franklin held the bulk of it in reserve. In the morning, fog had set in, making it difficult for the Confederates to detect the Union advance. They were able to make headway for a time, but when the fog lifted, the Confederates were able to repel the Union advance.[48]

At the other end of the field, General Sumner's men and then Hooker's reserves hopelessly stormed Marye's Heights time and time again as the slaughter continued into late afternoon. As one Confederate prepared to fire on the onrushing Union infantry, he expressed his feelings: "Ye Gods! It is no longer a battle, it is butchery." Confederate rifle fire cut down more than 8,000 Yankee soldiers, and none of the Federals ever reached the fieldstone wall in front of the heights. Thomas Galwey of the Eighth Ohio Volunteers recalled: "Line after line of our men advanced in magnificent order. Poor glorious fellows shaking good-bye to us with their hats. They reached a point within a stone's throw of the wall, no farther. They tried to go beyond, but were slaughtered. Nothing could advance farther and live."[49]

Frustrated by Jackson on the left and mauled by Longstreet on the right, the Army of the Potomac came to a halt, but Burnside was not ready to quit. He ordered the attack on Jackson to be renewed and called on Hooker to bring up his reserves. Hooker was convinced that another attack would be a "useless waste of life," but Burnside insisted on another attack. Hooker sent in his Third Division, but they too were driven back. At nightfall, he discontinued the fighting, saying that he "had lost as many men as his orders required."[50]

The Army of the Potomac had displayed incredible courage, but their officers had used poor judgment. On one point both sides agreed: there had been useless loss of life. Longstreet described the action at Marye's Heights thus: "The Federals had fallen like the steady dripping of rain from the eaves of a house." A Union general said, "It was a great slaughter pen. . . . They might as well have tried to take Hell."[51]

Mercifully, darkness put an end to the slaughter. Officers and men who were able stayed on the field during the night since no order to withdraw had been given. One officer later wrote: "The writhing concord was broken by cries for help, pierced by shrieks. . . . Some begged for a drop of water. Some called God for pity, and some on friendly hands to finish what the enemy had so horribly begun. Some with delirious, dreaming voices murmured loved names."[52]

The cost in lives was heavy; almost 13,000 Federals and a little over 5,300 Confederates were casualties. Viewing the slaughter and carnage from the heights, Lee commented to the officers near him, "It is well war is so terrible, else we should grow too fond of it." Burnside considered renewing the fighting the next day, but his generals persuaded him to withdraw to the north bank of the Rappahannock.[53]

After the Battle of Fredericksburg, the Army of the Potomac was in desperate shape. Demoralized soldiers were deserting in droves, and thousands of others were ill with dysentery, typhoid, and diphtheria. As for Burnside, he had lost the confidence and loyalty of his men. A group of his high-ranking officers campaigned to bring McClellan back again, arguing that "no human intelligence can mend matters here till that is done." At the same time, General Hooker was campaigning to become the next commander of the army, casting aspersions on Burnside's character and praising his own talents.[54]

Despite the grumbling that infested his army, Burnside was determined to cross the Rappahannock again. He sent a letter to Lincoln telling him of his plan to cross the river eight miles north of Fredericksburg and attack Lee's left with the bulk of the army. In the meantime, General Sumner's division would feint a crossing in front of Fredericksburg. The massed Union troops on Lee's left would then force the Confederates out of position and into an open battle.[55]

In his letter to the president, Burnside was forthright, advising him that his subordinates were "almost unanimously opposed to his plan" and offering to resign if he wanted to appoint a new commander. Lincoln declined to accept the resignation and approved Burnside's plan.[56]

On the morning of January 20, 1863, Burnside's troops began their march. Good progress was made at first; the sun was shining, and the roads were dry and firm. Unfortunately, that evening it began to storm. What had passed for roads now became beds of muck, and the men were forced to pitch their tents in the icy rain. When morning came, the rain grew heavier. As the men tried to move through the mud, big globs stuck to their boots, and the pontoon trains and wagons became mired hub-deep in mud. Dozens of animals dropped dead from exhaustion, while all the time the rain continued to pour down in torrents.[57]

January 22 dawned with rain still pouring in torrents, and the army stalled. With the troops' morale low, Burnside decided to comfort his men by issuing a whiskey ration for them. To one brigade, the amounts distributed were too generous, and, on empty stomachs, the result was an inebriated brigade. The whiskey fueled rage, and soon fighting broke out.[58]

By noon, Burnside had had enough; he gave the order for the army to turn around and go back. The "Mud March" was over, and so was Burnside's career as commander of the Army of Potomac. Hooker and several other generals who had openly criticized him were calling for his replacement. On January 26, they got their wish. Burnside was relieved of command, and Major General Joseph Hooker was appointed in his place. Burnside offered to resign from the army, but Lincoln would not hear of it. He said, "General, I cannot accept your resignation; we need you." Lincoln liked Burnside and respected his honesty. He undoubtedly regretted that he had to relieve him, but he did so to prevent a breakdown in administration of the Army of the Potomac.[59]

On the morning of January 26, Burnside sent for Hooker and turned the army over to him. Later in the morning he invited numerous officers to visit his headquarters, asking them to give Hooker all their confidence and cooperation. The next day, he boarded a train for home. On a stopover in New York, Burnside was greeted by a cheering crowd of well-wishers; public opinion did not coincide with that of the army.[60]

In March 1863, Burnside was assigned to command the Army of the Ohio. In his new assignment, he encountered new kinds of problems. Among these were the military difficulties of securing Kentucky against guerrilla forces and the steady pressure to invade east Tennessee. An even greater problem for Burnside came from the civilian population. The draft law had infuriated many citizens and helped to gain support for the local "Copperhead" Democrats who favored peace. These peace Democrats were more numerous in the Midwest, a region that traditionally distrusted the Northeast where the Republican Party dominated.[61]

By taking swift action against spies and malcontents, Burnside hoped to discourage Southern sympathizers and Copperheads from joining the Confederate army, committing acts of sabotage, and harboring escaped prisoners. When ex-Congressman Clement L. Vallandigham, a Democrat, spoke out against the war, Burnside had him arrested. Despite his determination to crush the seditious elements in the state, Burnside did not lose his sense of justice. Although Vallandigham had been stirring up rebellion against the federal government, Burnside protected him from harassment, to the extent of housing him in the Burnet House Hotel while he awaited trial. A military court found him guilty as charged and sentenced him to confinement for the duration of the war. Later, President Lincoln intervened in Vallandigham's behalf, sending him South into the Confederacy.[62]

Burnside shared Lincoln's concern for the well-being of the pro-Union population of east Tennessee. Since the outset of the war, a large number of loyalists in the region had suffered the loss of property and life at the hands of the Confederates. During the fall of 1863, Burnside moved his army through the Cumberland Gap, liberating the area and occupying Knoxville. Despite attacks from Confederate forces, he was successful in defending Knoxville. Burnside's success in the Knoxville campaign helped to ease the sting of his defeat at Fredericksburg.[63]

In September, Major General William Rosecrans's army was defeated at Chickamauga and forced to retreat to Chattanooga. Lincoln was anxious for Rosecrans to hold Chattanooga because of its strategic importance and took immediate steps to strengthen his position. On September 22, Rosecrans telegraphed Lincoln that the fate of the army was in God's hand.

Before the battle at Chickamauga, Burnside had been ordered to stand ready to support Rosecrans if needed. After the capture of Chattanooga, Rosecrans had informed Burnside that Confederate General Bragg was in full retreat. Burnside took this statement to mean that he would not be needed to reinforce Rosecrans. As a result, he moved his army toward Jonesboro in a direction away from Chattanooga. When Lincoln learned where Burnside was, he was horrified. "Damn Jonesboro," he said, and immediately sent orders for Burnside to join Rosecrans. When Burnside tried to explain his reason for advancing toward Jonesboro, Lincoln was in no mood to understand. He responded by writing a nasty letter to Burnside. His letter opened with, "Yours of the 23rd is just received and makes me doubt whether I am awake or dreaming." After writing the letter, he decided not to send it, thinking it would hurt Burnside and accomplish no good purpose.[64] As things turned out, Burnside was too far away to help Rosecrans, and Lincoln decided it was better for Burnside to hold the territory he had occupied.[65]

In the spring of 1864, Burnside's old Ninth Corps was recruited to full strength and returned to the Eastern theater with Burnside as its commander. As an independent unit, the Ninth Corps supported the Army of the Potomac and was assigned to guard the supply line for Meade's army.[66]

During the Battle of the Wilderness, Burnside's corps helped repel Lee's final attack, their action bringing praise from General Grant, now general-in-chief. On May 24, Grant reassigned Burnside and the Ninth Corps to the Army of the Potomac under Meade's command.

When Grant struck Lee at Cold Harbor on June 3, the Ninth Corps was posted on the army's extreme right flank, away from the main assault. As a result, they escaped the butchery the Union forces experienced in the battle. Burnside's corps continued to take part in the Virginia campaign, which culminated in the siege of Petersburg. Early in the siege of Petersburg, an officer in Burnside's corps, Colonel Edward Pleasants, developed a plan for breaking through the enemy's fortifications. It consisted of tunneling under the Confederate earthworks and blowing a huge hole in their defenses through which the Union army would be able to get at the enemy. Although Grant and Meade were reluctant to approve the plan, Burnside was able to convince them to let him try it. While the tunnel was being dug, Burnside trained his Fourth Division, which was all black, to lead the attack. Just hours before the planned attack, Grant and Meade changed the plan to lead with the Fourth Division.[67] They feared that, if the attack failed, radical Republicans in Congress would think "we were shoving these people ahead to get killed because we did not care anything about them." Burnside vehemently protested the last-minute change, but to no avail.

When detonated, the explosion blew a large hole in the Confederate line, but the untrained troops leading the attack were unable to exploit the situation. Slow in advancing and lacking ladders to scale the steep trench created by the blast, the Union troops were repelled. The result was a colossal failure, with the loss of more than 4,000 of Burnside's troops.[68]

Burnside was incensed. He blamed Meade for not sending reinforcements when he asked for them. He believed that support had been withheld at the most critical time, and, when he saw Meade, he told him so in no uncertain terms. Meade charged Burnside with insubordination, and a court of inquiry was selected to investigate the disaster at the crater. The court found Burnside and his corps responsible for the failure. By the time the court presented its findings, Burnside had gone home on furlough.[69]

When, by January 1865, Burnside had still not been reassigned, he went to see the president. Lincoln promised a command "forthwith," but by spring, he still had not secured an assignment. On March 23, he wired Secretary Stanton: "If I can be of any service to General Grant or General Sherman as a subordinate commander or aide-de-camp, or as a bearer of dispatches from you to either of them, I am quite ready." Stanton did not acknowledge Burnside's telegram. On the last afternoon of Lincoln's life, Burnside mailed a letter of resignation and a note congratulating Stanton for his part in the victory.[70]

The years that followed the war were better for Burnside than those during the war. He continued to enjoy the confidence of his civilian friends, holding numerous railroad and industrial directorships. In 1866 and again in 1867 and 1868, he was elected governor of Rhode Island. In 1874, he was elected to the U.S. Senate and served until his death in 1881.[71]

Burnside died suddenly of a heart attack on September 13, 1881. A memorial service was held for him at St. Michael's Church in Bristol, Rhode Island, and his body was carried to Providence to lie in state at City Hall. He was buried in Swan Point Cemetery in Providence.[72]

Ambrose Burnside is best remembered as the general who lost the Battle of Fredericksburg. But, as Augustus Woodbury eulogized at his funeral, "He should be remembered for his thoroughly unselfish nature." At Fredericksburg, when he could have made excuses and defended his reputation, he refused to embroil the army in a greater controversy. "I have simply to do my duty," he said. Woodbury ended his eulogy by alluding to Burnside's greatest strength as well as his greatest flaw: his trust in the essential goodness and honesty of men. Such was Ambrose Burnside—soldier, patriot, and statesman.[73]

13   Ulysses S. Grant

"Unconditional Surrender Grant"

On the morning of February 15, 1862, the fighting was fierce outside of Fort Donelson, a Confederate fort located in Tennessee along the Cumberland River. Rather than throw his raw recruits at the fortifications, Brigadier General Ulysses S. Grant had earlier elected to lay siege to the fort. Taking the Union forces by surprise that morning, the Confederates had successfully attacked Grant's right flank and established a defensive position there. When Grant received the news, he galloped over to his right flank. After hearing from his generals, his face grew red; then he spoke: "Gentlemen, the position on the right must be retaken."[1]

During the lull in the fighting, Grant rode forward. It became apparent to him that the Confederates were trying to break out and escape from Fort Donelson. Reasoning that the Confederates had concentrated their forces for an attack on his right, Grant assumed that the strength of opposing troops on his left had been reduced. Immediately, he ordered an attack on the Confederate right. Unable to take advantage of their earlier gains on Grant's right, the confused Confederate forces slowly pulled back. Grant returned to his headquarters to await the renewal of the battle. After giving instructions to his generals to attack in the morning, Grant went to bed.[2]

Grant did not have long to sleep; at three in the morning he was awakened when a Confederate courier arrived with a white flag of truce and a dispatch for him. General Simon Buckner, commander of the garrison at the fort, was requesting an armistice until noon and asking what terms Grant would offer for the surrender of Fort Donelson. Grant turned to Brigadier General Charles Smith and asked, "What answer shall I send to the general?" Without hesitation Smith responded: "No terms to the damn Rebels!"[3]

In just a few moments, Grant had penned his response: "Sir: Yours of this date proposing an Armistice, and appointment of commissioners, to settle terms of capitulation is just received. No terms except unconditional and immediate surrender can be accepted. I propose to move immediately against your works."[4]

There was no need for further bloodshed. Buckner notified Grant that he would "accept the ungenerous and unchivalrous terms" he had proposed. Fort Donelson had fallen, and with it Grant had earned the moniker "Unconditional Surrender" Grant.[5]

Grant was five-feet eight-inches tall, weighed only 135 pounds, and had light brown hair and beard and clear blue eyes. Until the Civil War, he had failed in every enterprise he had attempted. As a young man working in his father's leather-tanning business, Ulysses had been given the name "Useless" by the townspeople. In 1854, as a lieutenant, he had to resign from the army to avoid a court-martial. No one could possibly have predicted that he would one day become the savior of the Union and the eighteenth president of the United States.[6]

One of Grant's closest friends, William Tecumseh Sherman, said of him: "I knew him as a cadet at West Point, as a lieutenant of the Fourth Infantry, as a citizen of St. Louis, and as a growing general all through the bloody Civil War. Yet to me he is a mystery, and I believe he is a mystery to himself." As a young man, Grant showed little interest in pursuing a military career. Later, he said, "The truth is I am more a farmer than a soldier. I take little or no interest in military affairs. I never went into the army without regret and never retired without pleasure."[7]

He was born Hiram Ulysses Grant on April 27, 1822, in the village of Point Pleasant, Ohio. His father, Jesse, was an enterprising tanner who had left Kentucky at the age of twenty-one because, as he put it, "I would not own slaves and I would not live where there were slaves." Grant's mother was a farmer's daughter, quietly strong and direct. Grant later said, "I never saw my mother cry." In 1832, the Grants moved to Georgetown, Ohio, where Ulysses was to spend his boyhood. One of six children, his early life was free of both hardship and luxury. Young Grant farmed, hauled wood, helped his father at the tannery, and gained a reputation for being able to ride and break horses.[8]

Grant did not favor his father, who was outgoing and aggressive. Ulysses was more like his mother—quiet and determined. His determination played an important part in his success during the Civil War. He loved horses, a passion he held all his life: "I love to train young colts. When old age comes on, I expect to derive my chief pleasure from holding a colt's leading line in my hand and watching him run around the training horse ring."[9]

Ulysses's father believed that his son had little potential, and nothing Ulysses did, or would ever do, seemed to please him. Events in Ulysses's early life helped his father form this opinion. When Ulysses was eight, Jesse

Major General Ulysses Simpson Grant, U.S.A., in
the fall of 1863.

COURTESY OF THE LIBRARY OF CONGRESS

sent him to a neighbor with instructions on how to bargain for a colt he
wanted to purchase. Young Grant wanted the colt so badly he went up to
the man and blurted: "Papa said I may offer you twenty dollars, but if you
won't take that, I am to offer twenty-two-and-a-half, and if you won't take
that, to give you twenty-five." The story quickly spread around Georgetown,
and many people had a good laugh at young Grant's expense.[10]

At age eighteen, Ulysses went away to boarding school at Maysville, Kentucky. Upon his return, his father encouraged him to go to the U.S. Military Academy at West Point. His father believed the Academy would provide
his son with a solid education in engineering, after which he could resign
his commission and go to work in the private sector. At first, Ulysses rejected his father's plan, but in a short time he gave in and entered West
Point in 1839.[11]

When he arrived at the Academy, Grant found that the congressman who had signed his appointment papers had submitted his name as Ulysses S. Grant. Grant informed the adjutant that his name was incorrectly listed on the roster, but he was told that, as the appointment was in the name of Ulysses S. Grant, it would have to remain that way, at least as long as he was in the army. Hiram Ulysses Grant thus became Ulysses Simpson Grant, Simpson being his mother's maiden name.[12]

At first, Grant had a fear of failing and bringing disgrace to his family; but, as time progressed, he soon realized he could cope with West Point, and his fear subsided. It was at the Academy that his classmates saddled him with the nickname "Uncle Sam"—from his initials. Soon it became just plain Sam Grant.[13]

As a cadet, Grant received numerous demerits for slovenly dress, unsoldierly bearing, and tardiness. When promoted to sergeant in his third year, he confessed that the higher rank was "too much" for him and that he was willing to serve his senior year as a private. At first, Grant had no interest in being a soldier: "A military life had no charm for me, and I had not the faintest idea of staying in the army." Soon his attitude changed. He learned to admire the Academy as the "most beautiful place I have ever seen," and he saw it as providing for his future security. "If a man graduates here, he is safe for life, let him go where he will."[14]

Grant graduated in 1843, finishing twenty-first in a class of thirty-nine. His modest showing made him ineligible for both the engineering corps and the artillery. His attempt at joining the cavalry failed, and he was assigned as a second lieutenant in the Fourth U.S. Infantry Regiment.[15]

While on a leave of absence, Grant experienced an embarrassing incident involving his uniform. When traveling to his home in Bethel, Ohio, he encountered a young boy on the street who gaped at him and jeered, "Soldier! Will you work? No sur-eee; I'll sell my shirt first." To add further insult to injury, when he reached Bethel, a local resident marched around the village streets dressed in a homemade caricature of Grant's uniform. Later Grant wrote that "the joke was a high one in the mind of many people, and was much enjoyed by them; but I did not appreciate it so highly." After that point, he had a distaste for military uniforms; even when he became general-in-chief of all the Federal armies, he wore a private's blouse with his rank insignia stitched on it.[16]

By 1840, the question of slavery was dominating political discussion. Grant saw slavery for the evil it was, but, because of his shyness, he seldom engaged in conversation about the topic. In fact, Grant never argued with anyone, viewing all argument as a waste of time and a means of creating bad feelings. "He never had a personal controversy with man or boy in his life," said his father, who always seemed to be involved in one himself.[17]

In 1843, Grant was assigned to Jefferson Barracks outside of St. Louis, Missouri. During this time he met and courted seventeen-year-old Julia Dent. Five years later, on August 22, 1848, Grant married Julia. Their union was a strong one and gave both a solid base upon which to build their lives. Although not a beautiful woman, Julia had enduring qualities that made her an excellent match for Grant. She gave him a sense of stability he had never known from his own family. The marriage produced four children; the oldest, Fred, maintained close ties with his father. When he was eleven, Fred accompanied his father through several Civil War campaigns and later followed his example and attended West Point.[18]

In May 1846, the war with Mexico began. Although Grant was opposed to the war, he felt he had no choice but to do his duty. "With a soldier, the flag is paramount," he explained years later. "I know the struggle I had with my conscience during the Mexican War. I have never altogether forgiven myself for going into that. I had very strong opinions on the subject. I don't think there was ever a more wicked war. . . . I had not moral courage enough to resign. . . . I considered my supreme duty was to my flag."[19]

On March 1847, an American force under Major General Winfield Scott launched an attack against Veracruz, capturing it and then moving against Mexico City. Grant's Fourth Infantry went with Scott, and he participated in the final battle for the Mexican capital. With a small party of men, he dragged a howitzer into a church belfry and fired on Mexicans defending the San Cosme city gate. His daring affected the outcome of the battle, and Grant was given recognition for his efforts and mentioned in Scott's dispatches.[20]

Grant's opposition to the Mexican War and his sympathy for the ragged and starving Mexicans show a side of him that few knew. Despite his Civil War title of "Butcher," he was opposed to the cruelty of hunting, and he found bullfights "sickening." He also did not like to view the blood of men killed or wounded in battle. "I never went into battle willingly or with enthusiasm," he would later state.[21]

In 1852, Grant's regiment was transferred to the Pacific coast. The boredom and loneliness of peacetime garrison life depressed him, and he began to drink. In April 1854, Grant, then a commissioned captain, was discovered drunk in public by his commanding officer. He demanded that Grant either resign or stand trial. Fearing a scandal and the heartbreak a trial would bring to Julia, Grant chose to resign.[22]

He returned to his family and tried to support them by working in a variety of jobs but was unsuccessful in each endeavor. He failed as a real estate agent and collector of overdue accounts. He tried farming, working mainly by himself. When he had to resort to outside help, he worked in the fields beside the workers, preferring to use freedmen to slaves. It was upsetting to his neighbors that he paid his help more than the current rate for black farmhands. Although Julia owned four slaves, Grant made it clear to her and her family that he was opposed to slavery and planned to give his wife's slaves their freedom as soon as he was able.[23]

Grant continued to have financial problems and was forced to appeal to his father for help. Jesse Grant helped by setting Ulysses up in his leather business, where Grant was able to eke out a living. What saved him from monotony, as with so many other men of his generation, was the outbreak of the Civil War.[24]

When President Lincoln issued his call for 75,000 Union volunteers, Grant promptly offered to drill a company of Galena, Illinois, volunteers. In June 1861, he was appointed a colonel to lead the Twenty-first Illinois Volunteers. By August, he was promoted to the rank of brigadier general, in charge of troops in southern Illinois and southeastern Missouri. Early in 1862, Grant's fortunes changed drastically. He captured Confederate-held Fort Henry on the Tennessee River, then Fort Donelson on the Cumberland River, pushing the enemy back into Tennessee. As mentioned earlier, it was here that Grant earned the new nickname "Unconditional Surrender" Grant. President Lincoln was jubilant and showed his appreciation by naming Grant a major general.[25]

The capture of Fort Donelson was the first important Union victory of the war. News reports informed the public that Grant smoked cigars, so well-wishers mailed him crate-loads. The report, however, was erroneous; Grant smoked a pipe, but he switched over to cigars after finding himself swamped with them.[26]

Two months later, Grant's reputation suffered a setback. In April 1862, Grant's troops were camped at Pittsburg Landing on the Tennessee River near a little church known as Shiloh. In the early morning, he was surprised by a Confederate attack. Grant was on the verge of losing his entire army when he ordered a counterattack. Cries from the wounded filled the air, and for two days the intense battle raged on. Grant managed to halt the Confederate assault, but the price was high. The heavy casualties horrified both the North and South, and Grant gained a new reputation and nickname—"Butcher." Many who had praised Grant a few weeks earlier now wanted him to be removed.[27]

Ever since he had resigned from the army in 1854, rumors had followed Grant. He drank, people said, and not for conviviality but to get drunk. Grant suffered from migraine headaches and was often forced to take time away from his duties to rest. His headaches were believed by some to be caused by heavy drinking. Before Shiloh, the newspapers had not reported the stories, but now they blamed the heavy Union losses on Grant's drinking. President Lincoln, however, could see beyond the losses and rumors. "I can't spare this man," Lincoln said. "He fights." Grant felt badly about the losses and even considered resigning, but his friend General Sherman talked him out of it.[28]

Grant continued his tenacious drive and siege against the Confederate stronghold on the Mississippi River at Vicksburg. During the campaign, Grant moved ahead of his own supply and communication lines as he fought through a large part of Mississippi, something unheard of in military strategy. His army was able to live off the surroundings, an approach used by Sherman a year later marching through Georgia.[29]

For nine weeks, Grant looked for a way to position his troops for an advance on Vicksburg. Finally, he was in a position to attack the enemy's left flank. Grant believed this chance would be his last to capture Vicksburg and thus remain in command. Newspaper reports indicated that his men were dying of disease contracted in the wetlands west of the city, and rumors were circulating that Grant was off drinking again. John McClernand, one of Lincoln's politically appointed generals, was doing all he could to regain the command he believed should be his. If this attempt at victory failed, McClernand might well get his wish.[30]

Finally, after a five-week siege and the loss of over 5,000 men, the garrison at Vicksburg surrendered. On the morning of July 3, under the cover of a flag of truce, a Confederate courier brought a message from Lieutenant General John Pemberton requesting an armistice and a meeting. When the two met, Grant again insisted on an unconditional surrender of the city and the garrison. On July 4, Grant took Vicksburg, the greatest triumph to date by a Union general. Vicksburg was now in Union hands; five days later, Port Hudson fell, and with it, the Mississippi River. When the president learned of Grant's victory, he was elated. Lincoln acclaimed the campaign as "one of the most brilliant in the world." In a letter to Grant, Lincoln thanked him for "the almost inestimable service you have done the country."[31]

In a battle at Chattanooga in late November, Grant drove the Confederate forces out of Tennessee and opened the road to Georgia. Lincoln was happy to find a general who would fight and who was not afraid to make sacrifices to reach his objectives. In March 1864, Lincoln promoted Grant to lieutenant general and placed him in charge of all Union armies. As general-in-chief, Grant made his headquarters in the field with Major General George Meade's Army of the Potomac. Grant soon met the greatest challenge of his military career by opposing one of the best generals of the Confederacy, Robert E. Lee.[32]

Grant's strategy for winning the war was to fight the enemy on two fronts. He decided he would pursue Lee in an attempt to destroy the Army of Northern Virginia, while Sherman, who now commanded the armies of the West, would attempt to eliminate Joseph Johnston's army, which was defending Atlanta. This plan was a major change in the Union's strategy. Previous campaigns had aimed at the capture of strategic geographical points, but now the main objective was the pursuit and destruction of the enemy's armies.[33]

Grant planned to cross the Rapidan River and attack Lee. He hoped to move his troops quickly through a dense wooded area known as the Wilderness and strike Lee's flank. After the battle began, dozens of small fires were started by sparks dropping from the barrels of muskets. Soon the men fighting on both sides were engulfed in smoke and fire, and many of the wounded were burned to death or suffocated before they could be carried from the inferno.[34]

When the battle started to go against Grant, one of his officers, on the verge of panic, informed him that he thought he knew what Lee was going to do. When Grant heard this, his patience snapped: "I am heartily tired of hearing about what Lee is going to do. . . . Go back to your command and try to think what we are going to do ourselves."[35]

Grant continued to suffer heavy losses, but he quickly demonstrated how different he was from his predecessors. Earlier, commanders of the Army of the Potomac had retreated to their Potomac River base after suffering losses like those sustained by Grant. But Grant stated that he "propose[d] to fight it out on this line if it takes all summer."[36]

The Army of the Potomac suffered heavy losses during the spring campaign of 1864. From the Wilderness to Spotsylvania to Cold Harbor, Grant continued to attack Lee. At Cold Harbor, Grant made an unsuccessful assault, then followed up with another attack, one he would regret for the rest of his life. Many of the Union troops had some idea of what awaited them. Before the attack, they pinned their names on their uniforms so that their bodies could be identified later. Their sense of impending death was well founded, for they made their second charge against tremendous odds. This charge was nearly as disastrous as was Pickett's charge at Gettysburg, with Union forces suffering nearly 7,000 casualties against only 1,500 for the Confederates. Both armies agreed to a brief suspension of hostilities after the charge so they could gather their wounded and dead.[37]

After Cold Harbor, Grant's reputation as the "Butcher" returned. This epithet has been repeated and exaggerated over the years, but it is undeserved. In the three years prior to 1864, the Union armies in Virginia suffered more than 100,000 casualties, with no results. In the six months after Grant took command, he removed Lee from the war by containing him at Petersburg and placing the city under siege. Although Grant's 60,000 casualties were high, he had something to show for his losses. The battle between Lee and Grant had developed into a war of attrition, but Grant had more men and could better sustain the losses. It was simply a matter of time before Grant would find a vulnerable spot in Lee's defenses.[38]

Although Grant was disappointed by his setback at Cold Harbor, the defeat did not destroy his confidence, and he continued to press forward. On July 21, he received an unanticipated visitor, Abraham Lincoln. The president had decided to see the situation for himself and to show his continued support for Grant and his army. Just a week earlier, he had wired encouragement to Grant: "You will succeed. God Bless you all." Grant had promised to fight as long as it took to achieve victory; however, Lincoln knew that many might not be willing to wait that long. Lincoln hoped that victory would come before the fall election.[39]

Grant was sitting outside his tent with his staff when the president arrived. "I don't expect I can do much good, and in fact I'm afraid I may do some harm," Lincoln said, "but I'll just put myself under your orders and if you find anything wrong just send me away." Grant reassured Lincoln that all was going well. After visiting with some of the troops, Lincoln was impressed with what he saw, remarking: "When Grant once gets possession of a place, he holds on to it as if he had inherited it." Nevertheless, Lincoln still had concerns. "I cannot pretend to advise, but I do sincerely hope that all may be accomplished with as little bloodshed as possible," he said.[40]

By April 1865, Grant's strategy to keep moving south and applying continuous pressure on Lee had worked. Grant was about to take Petersburg; Sherman had burned his way to Atlanta; and Philip Sheridan had laid waste to the Shenandoah Valley, the Confederate breadbasket. The Confederacy lay in shambles.[41]

On April 2, Lee's army evacuated Petersburg and Richmond. They converged at Amelia Court House on the Richmond-Danville Railroad, hoping to find supplies and food. What they found, however, was Sheridan's cavalry blocking the route. Lee had no choice but to move his army westward, hoping to join Joseph Johnston's army further south. When his efforts to move south were blocked, Lee continued west toward Appomattox Court House.[42] On the evening of April 7, when Grant reached Farmville, he wrote a note to Lee advising him of the hopelessness of further resistance. After dinner, as Grant stood on a hotel porch smoking and talking with his aides, dozens of regiments marched passed the hotel where he was staying. When they saw him on the porch, they broke into cheers, the cheers continuing until all the regiments had passed. Suffering from a headache, Grant went to bed, hoping to relieve the throbbing in his head.[43]

General Lee responded to Grant's note: "Genl: I have read your note this date. Though not entertaining the opinion you expressed of the hopelessness of further resistance on the part of the Army of Northern Virginia— I reciprocate your desire to avoid useless effusion of blood, and therefore before considering your proposition, ask the terms you will offer on the condition of its surrender."[44]

On April 8, a courier carried Grant's response to Lee's inquiry. Grant's only condition was "that the men and officers surrendered shall be disqualified from taking up arms against the government of the United States until properly exchanged." Lee had not expected such a generous offer from a man known for his "unconditional surrender" policy.[45]

That evening Grant still had not heard from Lee. He rode into that night's makeshift headquarters and greeted General Meade with a friendly "Old Fellow." Still suffering from his headache, Grant was laying down to rest when a dispatch arrived from Lee. Grant got up to read the message. "I did not intend to propose the surrender of the Army of Northern Virginia," Lee wrote. "To be frank I do not think the emergency has arisen to call for the surrender of this army." Lee asked to meet with Grant the next morning, not to surrender his army, but to see what effect Grant's proposal would have on his army. Again disappointed by Lee's response, Grant lay down again, hoping to relieve his throbbing headache.[46]

On April 9, Grant rose early to what was to be the greatest day of his life. Grant did not plan to meet with Lee until Lee was ready to surrender his army. Rather, he decided to take a ride on his horse, hoping the morning air might relieve the throbbing in his head. Later that morning, when Grant received a message from General Lee that he wished to discuss "the surrender of his army," he was elated. "I was still suffering with a sick headache, but the moment I saw the note I was cured," Grant recalled.[47]

That afternoon, Grant and Lee met in the village of Appomattox Court House, in the home of Wilmer McLean. It was the beginning of the nation's reconciliation. The meeting of the two leaders was charged with emotion and was a study in contrasts. Their dress was as different as their backgrounds. Lee, manor born, was well dressed in a brand-new uniform with a red sash, shining boots, and magnificent sword in a golden scabbard. Grant, the son of a tanner, arrived in boots muddied from two days in the saddle and wearing a private's blouse with lieutenant general's stars. Before the war, Lee had been successful in all his endeavors; Grant had experienced many failures and embarrassments. Now the situation was reversed. It was Grant who held the upper hand, and Lee who was compelled to rely on his mercy. Yet, it was Grant who said he was self-conscious, fearing Lee might be insulted by his appearance.[48]

Lee was accompanied by Colonel Charles Marshall. Grant brought with him Generals Ord and Sheridan, and then invited several more Union officers into the crowded parlor. Grant wanted to lessen the ordeal for Lee as much as possible. He later wrote about their meeting: "As a man of much dignity with an impassable face, it was impossible to say whether he felt inwardly glad that the end had finally come, or felt sad over the result, and was too manly to show it. Whatever his feelings, they were entirely concealed from my observation."[49]

It was at Appomattox that Grant demonstrated his humanity. He was in a position to humiliate his enemies, but he did not. He recalled, "I felt like anything rather than rejoicing at the downfall of a foe who had fought so long and valiantly and had suffered so much for a cause, though that cause was, I believe, one of the worst for which a people ever fought."[50]

In the past, Grant's terms for surrender had been unconditional. At Appomattox he gave Lee very generous terms, allowing Confederate officers to keep their sidearms and all who owned their horses to take them for spring planting. Grant also shared his army's rations with the starving enemy troops. He allowed Lee to leave Appomattox with his dignity and his sword. In the terms of the surrender, he had written that officers and men were to sign paroles and then go home, "not to be disturbed by the United States authority so long as they observe their paroles and the laws in force where they reside."[51]

Realizing that the war would soon be over, Grant believed it was time to begin working on the peace. The war had aroused much hatred and bitterness, even among those who had done no fighting. He knew that certain men in Washington were talking angrily of treason and wanted leading Confederates jailed or hanged. Grant's terms made that revenge difficult. He pledged his word at Appomattox, and he would see that the agreement was carried out. There would be no jailings or hangings.[52]

After the meeting at Appomattox, Grant informed Lincoln of Lee's surrender. He scribbled a short telegram to Stanton: "Gen. Lee surrendered the Army of Northern Virginia this afternoon."[53]

The manner in which Grant handled the surrender at Appomattox helped ease the pain for the defeated South. By their actions, Lee and Grant set the example for the nation's reunification. No matter how much fault might later be found with Grant for his presidency, people could look back and be restored by this example of his undoubted greatness—his finest hour.[54]

Victory over Lee propelled Grant into the limelight and made him a national hero. Grant received great honor for his military accomplishments, which propelled him into political realms that he should not have entered. Grant was a soldier; he was not prepared to be a politician.

Grant had his share of quirks and eccentricities. He detested the sight of blood, and when he ate red meat it had to be well done, almost burnt to a crisp. He was completely tone-deaf and found the sound of music little more than an irritant. He had difficulty telling one tune from another and once remarked that he knew exactly two songs: one was "Yankee Doodle"; the other was not. He had a sense of humor and enjoyed hearing a good story, but he took most things seriously.[55]

Grant tended to be lonely; he needed the reassuring presence of his family. He also needed the company of men who respected him and with whom he felt at ease. Whenever possible during the Civil War, he liked to have his wife, Julia, live with him in camp. His personal staff was Midwesterners who shared his common background and outlook.[56]

Grant did not openly display his religious belief, and some observers thought him to be an atheist or an agnostic. Actually he was a Methodist and had been raised in a strict religious atmosphere. As an adult, however, he was not a regular churchgoer until he became president. Some of his letters to his family indicate that he believed in God and the hereafter.[57] Some believed Grant to be a prude. He always bathed in a closed tent, with all flaps tied, whereas his associates often stood in front of their tents naked and had their orderlies pour buckets of water on them. Grant very rarely swore, abstained from obscenities, and did not contribute to the off-color stories usually told at the evening campfire, although he did not object when others did so.[58]

Grant greatly prized loyalty, and it became a part of his personal code.

He was loyal to those above him and those below him. During the war, Grant was loyal to General Halleck even when he received unfair treatment from him. He supported subordinates, even when he suspected them of working to undercut him, as long as they appeared to be devoted to the common cause of winning the war. This loyalty to his appointees, in fact, was what led to the corruption and scandal during his presidential administration. Grant had great admiration for Sheridan. Ten years after the war he told Senator George Hoar that he believed Sheridan to have "no superior as a general, either living or dead, and perhaps not an equal." He made it clear that, compared with other generals, Sheridan had no equal, not even Robert E. Lee.[59]

Although Grant did drink occasionally, the stories about his drinking have been greatly exaggerated. His drinking was usually quite moderate; only on occasion did he become intoxicated. In the years after his death, a few accounts appeared that confirmed stories of his occasional intoxication. In 1887, Sherman wrote a friend regarding some of these reports: "We all knew at the time that General Grant would occasionally drink too much." From a military standpoint, however, Grant's drinking never adversely influenced his professional judgment. He probably did not drink at times when major decisions had to be made.[60]

After Appomattox, Grant became an instant national hero, second only to Lincoln. Even the South hailed Grant for his considerate and generous terms at Appomattox. Wherever the general went, he was mobbed by crowds. When Grant returned to Washington, Lincoln welcomed him with open arms, inviting the Grants to join him and Mrs. Lincoln at Ford's Theater. They accepted the invitation, but at the last moment changed their minds and did not attend. It was a fateful decision because Grant's name was also on the assassin's list. When Grant learned of Lincoln's assassination, he was distressed. "It would be impossible for me," he wrote, "to describe the feeling that overcame me at the news."[61]

When Vice President Andrew Johnson became president, he appeared certain to impose a harsh peace on the defeated South. Blaming the rich and powerful Southerners for the Civil War, Johnson intended to hang those who had served as general officers in the Confederacy, starting with Robert E. Lee. Grant would not permit this treatment. Under the agreement he had made at Appomattox, those officers who had sworn oath to the United States and been paroled were exempt from punishment. "When can these men be tried?" asked Johnson. "Never," Grant said, "so long as they do not violate their paroles." Grant threatened to resign if Johnson tried to carry out his plan. "I will not stay in the army if they break the pledges I made," he said. Johnson realized that, if Grant resigned, his administration would be in serious trouble, so the president backed down, making several gestures to appease Grant. These included giving his son Fred an appointment to West Point and making Jesse Grant postmaster of

Covington, Kentucky. He also gave Grant a fourth star and the title "General of the Army." [62]

As time progressed, Johnson's feelings toward the South changed. He showed sympathy for the Southern people and instituted a surprisingly mild policy of Reconstruction. This change in policy soon brought Johnson into conflict with the Republican-controlled Congress. Grant found himself caught in the middle. At first, he supported Johnson, but as time went by he became more reluctant to back him in his battles with Congress. When Congress passed severe Reconstruction policies, Johnson opposed them, taking the issue to the people with speeches and using war heroes to bolster his presence and bring out the crowd. Johnson's actions disturbed Grant. Writing to Julie, he said: "I have never been so tired of anything before as I have been with political speeches of Mr. Johnson."[63]

In the 1866 congressional election, the radical Republicans strengthened their position and were able to pass several bills restricting presidential power. Johnson decided to test Congress's authority to control his actions. He suspended Secretary of War Stanton and asked Grant to serve as interim secretary of war, hoping that Grant's great popularity would help him win the coming political battle with Congress. Grant reluctantly agreed.[64]

Grant's support for Johnson soon faded—perhaps because he himself was being considered a candidate for president, and he needed Republican support. In January 1868, when he learned that the Senate had refused to confirm Stanton's dismissal, he resigned the position. Johnson was furious, feeling he had been betrayed by Grant. The president attempted to portray Grant as a vacillating liar who had committed a breach of faith. Grant responded that he would not defy the will of the Senate and had never promised Johnson that he would.[65]

In 1868, Grant ran for president, a move that seemed at odds with his personality. His decision to run was based on his damaged relationship with Andrew Johnson and his desire to see the results of the war secured. Grant further believed that a Democratic presidency would appease the South in a way that would make a mockery of the Union's sacrifice. His Democratic opponent was Horatio Seymour. Grant easily won the election.[66]

"The office," said Grant in his inaugural address, "has come to me unsought; I commence its duties untrammeled. . . . I shall on all subjects have a policy to recommend, but none to enforce against the will of the people." He advocated prompt payment of the nation's war debt of $400,000,000, sounder national credit, a fairer treatment of American Indians, and a continuation of Reconstruction.[67]

The Fifteenth Amendment, which was being considered in Congress when Grant became president, would give African Americans the right to vote. On March 30, 1870, he signed the amendment into law. In his message to Congress, he called the amendment "the most important event that had occurred since the nation came into life."[68]

President Grant led the nation at the beginning of an era of growth and optimism, creativity and shame. In Grant, the movers of American society had just the man they wanted to preside over their pursuit of wealth. Grant was easy prey for their intentions. They governed the nation through control of patronage and federal disbursements. When Grant named his cabinet appointments, most of whom were his personal friends, the hope that his administration would provide an inspired, reforming government died. The American people expected a great deal from Grant, but, unfortunately, his style of leadership, which had been so effective during the war, proved a failure in politics.[69]

Grant's presidency was plagued with corruption and scandal, for he did not have the requisite abilities to be president. He had a poor grasp of politics and frequently demonstrated almost no real understanding of the American constitutional system. He saw his job as one of administration rather than true executive leadership. Grant behaved as if he were still a general who needed only to give orders.[70]

During Grant's administration, Secretary of Treasury Benjamin Bristow uncovered a fraud involving a large group of distillers who were in collusion with government agents. These agents were permitting the sale of untaxed liquor. The scandal involved Grant's chief secretary, General Orville Babcock, who had been taking bribes. When Grant first heard of the conspiracy, he said: "Let no guilty man escape." When Babcock was prosecuted, Grant came to his aid, acting as a character witness. His voluntary testimony was so favorable that the jury did not convict him.[71]

Although Grant was not directly involved in the scandals, many Republicans opposed the direction his administration was taking. By the election of 1872, the opposition to Grant had become so strong that his chief critics left the party and created their own organization. Despite the split in the party, Grant was still able to win reelection to a second term, defeating Horace Greeley.[72]

Grant did not display good judgment in the selection of his chief advisers, often old army cronies who had no more political savvy than he. They indulged in bribe taking, influence peddling, and other forms of corruption. Grant removed them only when public pressure was so great that he had no other choice. Although Grant himself was never accused of wrongdoing, by 1876 the country had had enough of him; he left office after two terms.[73]

After leaving the presidency, Grant and his wife embarked on a two-year tour of the world. They were welcomed everywhere; everyone wanted to see the great American hero. They met and dined with Queen Victoria at Windsor Castle and with Otto von Bismarck, the Prussian chancellor. Wherever the Grants went, dignitaries and large crowds turned out to meet them.[74]

When Grant returned to the United States, he took up residence in New York. A fund of $100,000, raised by twenty friends (including A. J. Drexel and J. P. Morgan), allowed him to buy a mansion there. William H. Vanderbilt lent Grant $150,000 to found a brokerage firm. In mid-1884, the firm failed, and Grant was left penniless and humiliated. Although Vanderbilt would gladly have written off the debt, the proud Grants turned all their property over to him.[75]

Grant continued to have financial problems, along with a serious health issue. He had begun to experience stabbing pains in his throat, which was diagnosed as terminal cancer. Congress restored to him the rank and full pay of a general, but this income was not sufficient to pay his mounting bills. An admirer of his, Mark Twain, offered to help him publish his memoirs and receive a lucrative advance.[76]

Throughout the autumn and winter of 1884 and the spring of 1885, Grant worked on his memoirs. As his illness grew worse and he became tired more easily, he dictated to a stenographer. Eventually the cancer advanced to the point that it choked off his voice, and he had to go back to writing the manuscript himself. His doctor prescribed cocaine and morphine to help relieve his pain, but the medication clouded his mind, making his task all the more difficult.[77]

When the book was completed, it filled 1,200 printed pages in two volumes and covered Grant's life from his childhood in Ohio to the end of the Civil War; however, it did not cover the eight years of his presidency. In the process of writing, he survived at least one crisis when his physicians thought he would die, but he rallied and pressed forward to finish his task. His family's future welfare depended on it.[78]

On July 16, 1885, Grant completed his 295,000-word *Personal Memoirs of U. S. Grant*, which would earn $450,000 for Julia and her family. The two-volume edition sold 300,000 copies in its first printing, making it one of the most successful books of the nineteenth century. Grant's memoirs were much like Grant himself: simple and unpretentious, yet brilliant in its own way. Grant closed his memoirs with the statement: "I feel that we are on the eve of a new era when there is to be a great harmony between the Federal and the Confederate. . . . Let us have peace."[79]

Just seven days after completing his memoirs, on July 23, with his family, physicians, and trusted servant by his bedside, Grant died. It was 8:08 in the morning. To commemorate the moment, Fred Grant stopped the parlor clock.

With his memoirs complete, Grant surrendered to death with courage and grace. Grant was buried on New York's Riverside Drive in a funeral that rivaled the tribute to Lincoln. Four words are engraved on his tomb: "Let us have peace." As Lincoln's favorite general, Grant had won peace for a nation. Now he had earned it for himself.[80]

Throughout his life, Grant had faced adversity. Sometimes it came on the battlefield, sometimes in his personal life, sometimes from politicians and friends he trusted. Through his many struggles, however, Grant prevailed.

14 Daniel E. Sickles

A Man of Controversy

One of the artifacts on display in the Armed Forces Medical Museum in Washington, D.C., is the shattered remnant of a human tibia, the shin bone. At first glance it may seem to be a morbid memento of interest only to physicians and pathologists. The bone, preserved and clinically displayed, belonged to Major General Daniel E. Sickles. It may be the only part of Sickles that was totally white or clean.[1]

Few Civil War participants were more controversial, flamboyant, and charismatic than Daniel Sickles. Most public figures try to avoid controversy; a select few embrace it. Such was Daniel Sickles: Union commander, Tammany Hall politician, diplomat, friend of presidents, and one-time presidential aspirant. From his midthirties until his death at the age of ninety-four, Dan Sickles was involved in some sort of crisis, whether financial, legislative, sexual, or homicidal. These situations invariably drew him into action—action that was not always the wisest course.[2]

Sickles earned most of his notoriety while serving in the Union army. Although a politically appointed general, Sickles was an energetic recruiter and a courageous fighter. But he was unwilling to take orders from superiors he did not like. He lacked prudence and humility and was always ready to fight to settle an argument. He was often indiscreet and flamboyant; his lifestyle was ostentatious. His critics and detractors spoke of him as a "hero without a heroic deed." A cavalry captain called him "the disgrace and bane of this army." To an infantry officer he was "a man after show and notoriety, and newspaper fame, and the adulation of the mob!" Despite such opinions, Sickles remained popular not only with his troops in the Third Corps of the Army of the Potomac but with many private citizens.[3] Sickles was a remarkable individual and a fascinating mixture of both positive and negative characteristics.

Sickles was born on October 20, 1819, in New York City, to well-to-do parents. His father, George Garrett Sickles, was a shrewd patent lawyer, politician, and opportunist. He could trace his family tree back six generations to the time when the Sickles family, then named Van Sicklen, left Holland for New Amsterdam. Daniel's mother, Susan Marsh Sickles, was a devout Episcopalian who was described as gentle and warm.[4]

Daniel was a problem to his parents from the start. Handsome and head-strong, he was not afraid to express himself freely. His parents were pleased by his quick wit but appalled by his willfulness. From an early age, Sickles showed an independent, strong-willed streak, frequently running away from home when things did not go his way. His parents tried to discipline their son, but Daniel proved to be uncontrollable. When he was fifteen, they tried putting him in other hands, sending him to the academy at Glens Falls, New York, a school dedicated to turning immature boys into finished young men. The experience lasted only a short time. When one of the teachers reprimanded him, Daniel snapped back at him and left school in a rage.[5]

Daniel's abrupt departure from school was a disappointment to his parents, and they feared that, without any authority over him, he would get into trouble. For a while, Daniel stayed at home, but after a bitter argument with his father, he left. He walked to Princeton where he got a job in a newspaper office. Discouraged because he did not have enough money to continue his education, he moved to Philadelphia, where he worked for a time on *Burton's Magazine*. Daniel's father now realized that his son's will was fully as strong as his own. He wrote to his son telling him all would be forgiven and that he would be allowed to continue his education if he returned home. Daniel cheerfully agreed. In 1838, he returned to New York and took up residence with family friends, the Da Pontes, to begin his preparation for college.[6]

The Da Pontes were bohemian; their lifestyle was very different from that of the typical Victorian household. The patriarch of the Da Ponte clan was eighty-nine-year-old Lorenzo, a Venetian Jew with a brilliant intellect. Lorenzo Sr. had been the librettist of some of Mozart's most famous operas, among them *Don Giovanni*. In Europe, Lorenzo's affairs with women had been notorious. Da Ponte had three sons, the youngest being Lorenzo Jr., who followed in his father's footsteps.[7]

Daniel was not the only one taken under the wings of the Da Pontes: Another couple, the Bagiolis, joined the household as well. The young couple had just given birth to a baby girl, Teresa, when Sickles was nineteen years old.

The younger Da Ponte found Sickles a student of remarkably quick perception; with his help and tutoring, Daniel was able to enter New York

Although a politically appointed general, Major
General Daniel E. Sickles was an energetic recruiter
and courageous fighter; however, he lacked prudence and humility and was always ready to fight
to settle an argument.

COURTESY OF THE LIBRARY OF CONGRESS

University. A frequent visitor to the multilingual Da Ponte residence,
Sickles became acquainted with French, Spanish, and Italian, which would
prove helpful later on. When his mentor, Lorenzo Sr., was stricken with
pneumonia and died, Sickles was filled with sorrow. He lost interest in college and left with the same impulsiveness that would characterize his later
life.[8]

In 1840, Sickles entered the law office of the noted Benjamin F. Butler,
attorney general under Van Buren. He mastered the law with the ease with
which he did everything he tried. Three years later, he was admitted to the
bar.

As an up-and-coming young lawyer who had not completed college,
Sickles saw politics as his entrée into the world of power. In the 1830s, he
began to make connections with Tammany Hall, the Democratic Party
machine of New York. During the mid-nineteenth century, Tammany Hall
was located on East Fourteenth Street. Sickles quickly learned that he could

benefit from his association with Tammany Hall; therefore he adjusted to their politics. He soon became linked to stories of tampering and stealing ballot boxes. Sickles took part in some of the brawls and deceptions that his party was known for. Sickles was very congenial and had little difficulty getting along with people. At the same time, he was a fighter and strongly supported his friends. His loyalty to the politicians at Tammany Hall was beyond question. Here he made and exploited connections. With their help, he would be able to move from New York to Washington, from the back rooms of Tammany to the floor of Congress.[9]

Sickles was constantly in need of money; it seemed to flow through his fingers like water. Because his father refused to finance his extravagant tastes for clothing, gourmet food, gambling, and "agreeable women," he was always hard pressed for cash. One of his expensive pastimes was an association with a vivacious brunette prostitute named Fanny White. Fanny's charms were for sale to all, but Sickles wanted her for himself. This did not come cheap, particularly since she enjoyed many of the finer things in life. There were also rumors that their relationship was a two-way affair and that he accepted money from her earnings to help him in his election campaign—a report that allowed him to be labeled a "pimp" by his opponents.[10]

In 1847, Sickles began his political career as a member of the New York State Assembly. He rose rapidly through its ranks to become the youngest member of its General Committee. In 1848, he was elected to the Democratic National Convention.

Much of Sickles's reputation came from scandals. His private life was even more corrupt than his political and business affairs. He patronized houses of prostitution, kept a mistress for a while, and generally ignored the norms of decency.[11] His most infamous escapade occurred two years before the Civil War, while he was a still a U.S. congressman. It involved Sickles's beautiful young wife, Teresa Bagiolis.

Sickles first met Teresa about the time she was learning to talk, when the Bagiolis moved in with the Da Pontes. Although Teresa probably was aware of the scandals in Sickles's life, she fell in love with him as a young woman. When she grew into a dark beauty, Sickles fell in love with her. They were married in 1852, when she was sixteen and pregnant. He was twice her age.

Teresa was a carefree teenager, full of the vivacity that had been encouraged and nurtured by her upbringing. Teresa had grown up surrounded by the intellectual and artistic society of New York. As a child, she had learned Italian, French, and Spanish as well as English. She was raised in a place where the enjoyment of life's pleasures was considered normal. Sins of the flesh were understandable weaknesses rather than crimes that could not be forgiven.[12] Teresa was once described as a "beautiful, voluptuous siren, without brains or shame," whose "damning effect was a lust for men."[13]

Sickles's devotion to party and precinct brought him a coveted position in 1853: corporation counsel for New York, a position that paid well and allowed for legal work on the side. Eight months later, he resigned his post to accompany Ambassador James Buchanan to England as secretary of the American legation in London. He left his wife behind because she was pregnant, but, according to local gossip, he did take a former mistress along with him for companionship. According to rumor, he had returned to his old habits after only a year of marriage.

Sickles spent six months in London before sending for his wife. When Teresa arrived with her newborn daughter, she had to entertain guests frequently. Although only eighteen, she was greatly admired by the English. Yet, she remained "in her manner more like a school girl than a polished woman of the world."[14]

In 1855, Sickles returned to the United States with Teresa to begin working for the presidential nomination of his friend James Buchanan. When Buchanan was elected president in 1856, Sickles was elected to a seat in Congress. He went to Washington with the closest possible connections to the White House. Teresa accompanied her husband, but she never became part of the Washington social circle. She was left virtually alone as Sickles pursued his career.

The social scene in the capital consisted of a series of parties, but most congressmen were too busy to attend. It was customary and considered acceptable behavior for the wives of congressmen to attend these social functions, escorted by any of the bachelors in the city.[15]

Being a beautiful young woman, Teresa had no difficulty finding escorts; Sickles even gave his blessings to these escorts. Sometimes he would ask Philip Barton Key, a prominent Washington attorney, to accompany her to the functions he was unable to attend. Key was tall and handsome and the son of Francis Scott Key, author of "The Star-Spangled Banner."[16]

Teresa had become a very unhappy young woman with a husband who had lost interest in her. As a result, Teresa transferred her affections to Philip Key, and a love affair developed. The two designed a signal to schedule their meetings. When Key wanted to meet with Teresa, he would walk past her house with a white handkerchief in his hand and wave it at her window. Key would then go to a house he had rented nearby and, in a few minutes, Teresa would arrive. The arrangement went on for more than a year with many people in Washington aware of it. Sickles, however, was not one of them.[17]

Sickles might never have found out about his wife's unfaithfulness had it not been for an anonymous note. It read: "Dear Sir, with deep regret, there is a fellow who rents a house for no other purpose than to meet your wife. And sir, I do assure you he has as much the use of your wife as you have. With these few hints, I leave the rest for you to imagine."[18] Key also received an anonymous note, probably from the same source as Sickles. It warned him to beware; his secret affair was known.[19]

When Sickles learned of his wife's illicit affair with Key, he immediately confronted her and demanded that she write a confessional note. It was an amazing document for the time and eventually appeared in newspapers across the country. Teresa gave the details of the affair in complete candor. She wrote: "I have been in a house on Fifteenth Street with Mr. Key. . . . There was a bed on the second story. I did what is usual for a wicked woman to do. . . . An intimacy of an improper kind. I undressed myself. Mr. Key undressed also. . . . Mr. Key has kissed me in this house a number of times. . . . [We] went to bed together." Sickles was a lawyer; he wanted written proof, and now he had it in his wife's own hand.[20] He demanded Teresa's wedding ring back and told her to send for her mother to come and get her. That night, Teresa slept on the floor of the guest room.[21]

The next day, Key, who had no knowledge of Teresa's confession, appeared outside her house waving his handkerchief. When Sickles saw him, he went into a rage, running down the steps and across to the park where he intercepted Key.[22] "Key, you scoundrel," Sickles shouted, "you have dishonored my bed—you must die." As he spoke, Key turned away. Sickles drew a pistol and fired, the shot grazing Key. The two men struggled briefly with each other, and Sickles dropped his gun. As Key tried to get away, Sickles pulled another gun from his coat. Key threw a pair of opera glasses at Sickles, and Sickles fired a second shot that struck Key in the upper leg, knocking him to the ground. As Key begged for his life, Sickles placed his gun against his chest and fired again. As Key's body fell back, Sickles tried to fire again, but the pistol misfired.[23]

Key was taken to a men's club by friends where he died on the floor of the parlor. Meanwhile, Sickles walked calmly to the home of his good friend, the attorney general of the United States, to surrender himself. Later that afternoon, Sickles entered a jail that was described as "the worst in the land." "Don't you have a better room?" Sickles asked the jailer who led him to his cell.[24]

That same afternoon, the minister who served in the city jail visited Teresa. She asked him to take a message back to Sickles begging for forgiveness and the return of her wedding ring. Sickles returned the ring—broken in half. Before Teresa left for New York to be with her mother, she begged her husband for permission to visit him in jail. He refused.[25]

The Sickles murder trial was front-page news in the papers across the country for several weeks. It attracted a great deal of attention because of the prominence of the people involved and the lurid details.[26]

At first the newspapers were harsh toward Sickles; but after he revealed Teresa's confession, he became the injured party, and Key became the villain. The outcome was a foregone conclusion. In the 1800s a man could be indiscreet, but a woman was held to a different standard. The newspaper coverage expressed the belief that Sickles had acted properly to save his family's honor.[27]

Sickles's attorney was Edwin M. Stanton. For the first time in the history of American jurisprudence, the defense of temporary insanity was used. Stanton argued that, when Sickles saw Key outside his house, he temporarily went crazy and killed him. He claimed that anyone under the influence of such emotional distress was not fully responsible for his behavior. The jury agreed, and Sickles was acquitted.[28]

In the months after the trial, Sickles became a hero. When he left the courthouse, he was mobbed by well-wishers. At a reception after the trial, 1,500 people stood in line to congratulate him on his victory.[29]

Then, three months after the trial, Sickles shocked his friends when he and his wife were reunited. His friends warned him that returning to his wife would be political suicide—a prediction that proved correct as soon as the newspapers got wind of the story. They had believed Sickles to be the defender of the American home. When they learned that he had changed his attitude toward his wife, they were disappointed and turned on him. After taking Teresa back, Sickles soon lost interest in her again. When he returned to Washington for the fall session of Congress, he left her at home and resumed his philandering.[30]

For Dan Sickles, the press attacks were not new; he easily ignored his critics and in time regained his social status. But for Teresa, it was a different story. She could not take the criticism and never outgrew the shame. Her health began to fail, and she suffered from insomnia. Then she contracted tuberculosis. Finally, in 1867, at the age of thirty-one, she died.[31]

For a while Sickles's lifestyle was subdued. It looked as if his political career had been ruined by the scandal, and for a short time he did settle down. His top priority, however, was promoting himself and striving for power and fame.[32]

When Sickles returned to Washington late in 1859, his arrival lacked the fanfare it had stimulated two years earlier. Many had believed he would not have the nerve to show his face in Washington again, but they underestimated his grit and determination. He took a suite at Willard's Hotel and soon learned how few friends he had.[33] A few of his friends, however, did not desert him. Buchanan was in the White House, and he was still friendly. Edwin Stanton and a few others remained loyal to him. As long as he lived he would never forget their friendship at this critical time in his life.

In Congress, things were worse. He sat by himself and spoke very little. Mrs. Chesnut, the diarist from South Carolina, wrote: "In Washington, I saw Mr. Sickles sitting alone on the bench of the House of Representatives. He was left to himself as if he had smallpox." Mrs. Chesnut made it clear that this cold treatment was not because he had killed Key but because "he condoned his wife's profligacy and took her back."[34] It is ironic that Sickles was condemned for an act of forgiveness, a quality he was seldom accused of having.

By the summer recess of 1860, some of the legislators, either because they admired his courage or felt he had suffered enough, began to talk to him. He, too, had broken his silence.

The long period of discussion about the issue of slavery was coming to a head. With the election of Lincoln, hope for a peaceful settlement of the issue ended. There were new and stronger threats of secession.

Sickles had always been a Democrat who supported Buchanan, a New Yorker defending his state's interest, and a voter with the Southern bloc. In December, he still supported the South, delivering a strong speech attacking "the illusion . . . that the Union can be preserved by force" and defending a state's right to secede from the Union. He even went so far as to make the unbelievable threat that New York City might one day secede from the state.[35]

When war appeared imminent, however, Sickles sensed that the conflict would provide a new way to make amends for his past blunders. Sickles now became a staunch anti-secessionist. He advised Buchanan not to listen to those who would allow states to secede from the Union peacefully. Along with the attorney general, Sickles convinced the president to keep a garrison at Fort Sumter in Charleston Harbor, a move that led to hostilities in April 1861.[36] For years afterward, Sickles and Stanton shared a private joke about how they kept troops at Sumter and thus were responsible for the start of the Civil War.[37]

Barely had the last shot been fired at Sumter than Sickles was back in Manhattan, recruiting volunteers for the army. His patriotic efforts overshadowed his scandalous past. His renewed popularity enabled him to attract more than the 1,000 men Governor Edwin Morgan had authorized him to raise. Within a month, he had enlisted enough men to fill a large brigade. At first the Republican governor refused to accept the five regiments Sickles had organized; but, by September, President Lincoln, grateful for his services, nominated Sickles a brigadier general of volunteers to command his "Excelsior Brigade." The Senate tabled the nomination and then rejected it altogether; however, two months later, with pressure from Lincoln and Stanton, the Senate approved Sickles's appointment.[38]

Even in uniform, Sickles found it difficult to live down the past. Politicians and editors opposed his appointment and labeled his troops disreputable, like their commander. Eventually Sickles's brigade acquired a more enviable reputation and proved they could fight. During Major General George McClellan's spring 1862 Peninsula Campaign, Sickles's brigade was at the head of "Fighting Joe" Hooker's division of the Third Corps at Fair Oaks. Here his troops repulsed an attack on the Union left flank; in the Seven Pines sector, his brigade also acquitted itself well. In a report of the battle, he said his advance had been "as if on parade," sending "the enemy flying before them" while others made a "dashing charge" and a "bold and vigorous movement" by which they "took prisoners." Although Sickles was new at leading men in battle, he already knew the rhetoric that veteran commanders used to place a spin on their accomplishments.[39]

Sickles's brigade had demonstrated that it could perform well and so had its leader. Sickles showed leadership qualities and a flair for the dramatic, all of which kept his name in the news. Other people noted it, but more important for Sickles, his men were aware of his leadership qualities. Throughout the war, he often was at odds with other officers, but it was difficult to hear a negative word about him from his men. They recognized that, despite his aggressive manner, he had a genuine concern for their welfare and was interested in the Union cause.[40]

Sickles's brigade was a part of Joseph Hooker's division. Although Hooker was a West Point graduate with little regard for political generals, the two soon formed a friendship. They were similar in personality and shared similar tastes. Both men were heavy drinkers and womanizers. Sickles was extremely loyal to Hooker, perhaps in hopes of receiving a reward. If that was the case, it paid off. When Hooker was elevated to the command of the Army of the Potomac, he placed Sickles in charge of the Third Corps.[41]

Almost a month passed before the Excelsior Brigade saw its next action at Oak Grove, first of the Seven Days battles. Here Confederate Brigadier General Robert Ransom's brigade put great pressure on Sickles's line, threatening to weaken Hooker's position. Sickles stepped forward to lead his brigade in a desperate struggle to hold off the Confederates until he was reinforced. Because of his action, the once-maligned congressman earned a reputation as a front-line commander who was not afraid to lead his men in a crisis.[42]

Sickles's brigade saw limited service during the rest of McClellan's unsuccessful campaign outside Richmond. Following the Union withdrawal south to the James River, Sickles returned to New York. Some of his supporters felt his battle exploits had cleared his reputation, making him eligible for another attempt at public office. In late July when he reached New York, he was given a hero's welcome, something he could not have imagined months earlier. Although accepted by New Yorkers as a war hero, his reception at Tammany Hall was less than cordial. His "total-war" position, his closeness to Republicans Lincoln and Stanton, and his long separation from Democratic circles had caused him to lose favor with Tammany Hall. Sickles spent the remaining part of his leave speaking on behalf of the war and recruiting for his brigade.[43]

"Every man . . . can put implicit reliance in the good faith, and integrity, the intelligence, the patriotism, and the nerve of Abraham Lincoln," Sickles told an audience. "I did not vote for him, but I will fight under his orders, and I will trust him everywhere, and pray for him night and day. . . . All that the army has to say to the people is, 'Give us men and we will give you victories.'" The reason the South was winning battles, he stated, was that it was fully committed, which not true in the North. "A man may pass through New York, and, unless he is told of it, he would not know that this country was at war. . . . In God's name, let the state of New York have it to say hereafter that she furnished her quota to the army without conscription and without resorting to a draft."[44]

Sickles's stay in New York helped strengthen his battle-torn regiments and the city's resolve to support the war. In his absence, his brigade saw heavy action at Bristoe Station and at Antietam. One brigadier who remained in the field during this time noted that his colleague "would beat Napoleon in winning glory not earned."[45]

In October, Sickles rejoined the army at Alexandria. He was given command of Hooker's division, Hooker having moved up to corps commander. Some officers in the Army of the Potomac questioned his promotion, believing it was politically motivated and not earned in battle. His standing with other officers sunk even lower after a quarrel with a popular brigadier general, Francis E. Patterson, whom he accused of cowardice for leaving an exposed position at Warrenton Junction. When Patterson committed suicide rather than face a court-martial, Patterson's men accused Sickles of murdering a second man.[46]

At the Battle of Fredericksburg, Sickles's division was assigned to support Burnside's left flank. Because of the army's conspicuous defeat at Fredericksburg, General Burnside was replaced by Joe Hooker. One of Hooker's first acts as the new commander of the Army of the Potomac was to appoint Sickles commander of the Third Corps, a position that brought promotion to major general. Hooker's headquarters soon became a "pleasure palace," where Sickles and his companions spent their free time drinking and carousing. Years later, Captain Charles Adams Jr. recalled: "During the winter when Hooker was in command . . . the Headquarters of the Army of the Potomac was a place to which no self-respecting man liked to go, and no decent woman could go. It was a combination of barroom and brothel."[47]

Sickles did not let the war interfere with his social life. About his headquarters, one general reported that "the champagne and whiskey ran in streams." At times, Sickles would entertain as many as two hundred guests with sit-down dinners catered by the famous New York restaurateur, Delmonico. Occasionally, Sickles would take leave from his wining and dining to promote his career in Washington. His friends included not only Democrats but some notable Republicans, including congressmen and cabinet members as well as the first family. He was a special favorite of Mrs. Lincoln.[48]

Sickles's first battle as corps commander came at Chancellorsville in May of 1863. When Sickles detected Stonewall Jackson's flanking attack near Hazel Grove, he occupied the plateau and sent word to Hooker that Jackson was retreating, requesting permission to attack him. Hooker, however, saw things differently. Instead of reinforcing Sickles at Hazel Grove and maintaining his wedge between Lee's divided army, Hooker ordered Sickles to evacuate the position, thus giving up the high ground on the battlefield. Sickles later contended that, had his position at Hazel Grove been supported as he had requested, the outcome of the battle would have been different. He believed he had seized the initiative and improvised his own strategy on the spot but was denied an opportunity for victory due to lack of support.[49]

After his defeat at Chancellorsville, Hooker looked for someone to blame. The man selected was Major General George Meade, commander of the Fifth Corps. Sickles supported Hooker in his condemnation of Meade. Although the attempt to shift the blame to Meade was unsuccessful, Sickles always defended Hooker's conduct at the battle. The difference of opinion between Meade and Sickles continued throughout the war. Once again Sickles had identified someone he thought was on the rise and joined with him. Sickles hoped to gain power through his connection with Hooker, but this time he had unwisely chosen his friend.[50]

It was almost certain that Hooker would be relieved from command of the Army of the Potomac; speculation about his replacement was rampant, both at home and in the army. The editors of the influential *New York Herald* supported Sickles for the post. But Major General Oliver O. Howard, speaking for the army, was not as positive: "If God gave us Sickles to lead us I shall cry with vexation and sorrow and plead to be delivered."[51]

General Hooker's replacement was Major General George Meade, who received the command on June 28, when both the Army of Northern Virginia and the Army of the Potomac were in or near Pennsylvania. From the outset, Sickles and Meade clashed. The religious Meade and the rebellious Sickles made a volatile mix, and that mixture exploded in the Pennsylvania town of Gettysburg.

Sickles arrived at Gettysburg on July 1 with his Third Corps. That night Meade assigned him to the left flank, about 400 yards short of the hill known as Little Round Top, and told him to go forward to Cemetery Ridge to join with the left flank of Winfield Scott Hancock's Second Corps. After Sickles's corps was in position, he discovered that the high ground was in front of his position. At Chancellorsville, he had given up the high ground on Hooker's orders, and the Army of the Potomac had paid dearly for it.[52] He did not want this to happen again.

In his initial orders, Meade had granted Sickles the authority to choose his own ground and position his troops in the manner most suitable to him, as long as he stayed within the limits of his general orders.[53] Feeling the change of position he desired was beyond the scope of his orders, Sickles rode to Meade's headquarters and reported his concern. Meade sent Brigadier General Henry Hunt, chief of artillery, to look into the matter. Although Hunt had no authority to change the Third Corps' position, he did mention that a move forward might strengthen their position, particularly for his artillery.[54]

Sickles agreed and asked Hunt if he should move his corps forward. "Not on my authority," he replied, "but I will report to General Meade for his instruction." Although the position proposed would improve the location of Sickles's artillery, it would produce a salient angle or projection, exposing both of his sides to raking fire. It would also increase the ground his corps would have to defend, thus improving the enemy's chance of breaking the Union line.[55]

Hunt's departure left Sickles in a quandary. When Meade did not respond, seemingly ignoring his request, Sickles made the most important decision of his military career. Without notifying either Meade or Hancock, he moved his corps through the woods and fields to the Emmetsburg Road, creating a huge gap in the Union line and leaving the high ground on Little Round Top exposed for the enemy to occupy. From this position the Confederates could fire upon the entire Union position along Cemetery Ridge.[56]

Sickles would later claim he had acted within his authority as a corps commander and under orders issued by General Meade. In his mind, the best ground was the high ground in front of him. Although Sickles may have been correct in his assessment of the situation, his mistake at Gettysburg was in not notifying Meade and Hancock of his movement so they could take appropriate action.[57]

Before Meade could do anything to countermand Sickles's deployment, James Longstreet attacked. The fighting lasted for more than four hours and was costly to Sickles's corps, resulting in over 4,000 casualties, including a heavy toll on the officer staff. Sickles himself did not go unscathed: while trying to rally his men, a Confederate cannonball crashed into his lower right leg, almost severing it from the rest of his body. Sickles refused to leave the field even though he was badly wounded. He asked for a cigar, placed it in his mouth, and began to smoke it. During the whole ordeal, Sickles never lost his composure. Finally, when he was being carried from the field, still puffing on his cigar, he lifted himself up on the stretcher to shout encouragement to his men. Everyone on that battlefield had to admit that Sickles was a courageous soldier and commander—nothing intimidated him.[58]

Sickles's leg was amputated that evening. Later, critics claimed that only the wound saved him from being court-martialed for the unauthorized movement of his corps. Meade remained highly critical of Sickles's deployment long after the war. Some military critics have argued that his impulsive move absorbed the fury of Longstreet's attack, slowing him down before he could reach the Union's main line. Long after the battle, Sickles received support for his actions from Philip Sheridan and, interestingly, from James Longstreet. Later, Sickles would be awarded the Congressional Medal of Honor for his service at Gettysburg.[59]

A few days after the amputation of his leg, the Medical Museum in Washington received a wooden box containing a note that read: "With the compliments of Maj. Gen. Daniel E. Sickles." Inside the box was his amputated leg, which he had donated to the museum. For many years following the war he would take friends to the museum to visit the display.[60]

To Sickles, the loss of his leg became a badge of honor. He gloried in it. Though he learned to move about with an artificial leg, he preferred not to use it, choosing instead to use crutches. The loss of a leg did not hamper his spirit. In fact, it would serve him and others as a constant reminder of the important part he had played in the war.

Although the Battle of Gettysburg resulted in a Union victory, a political battle and a war of words immediately followed the event. Initially, there was strong belief in the military that Sickles should be court-martialed for disobeying orders. To his dying day, however, Sickles believed he had acted properly at Gettysburg. The placement of his corps, he argued, had slowed Longstreet's heavy assault and had broken up his attacks into individual ones, enabling them to be dissipated. Furthermore, he reasoned, had he not moved, the Confederates could have placed their artillery into position to blast away at the Union line. If Longstreet had taken Cemetery Ridge, Sickles believed, he could have easily broken Meade's line.[61]

By the time Sickles reached Washington, the Gettysburg controversy had reached huge proportions. Throughout his convalescence, he continued to claim that he had acted responsibly on July 2. From his bed, he challenged Meade and others who claimed he had acted rashly, defending his position to visiting politicians and newspaper reporters. He claimed Meade had not paid proper attention to his left flank and that it had been necessary for him to correct the oversight. Sickles's story made a hero out of the Third Corps and, thus, himself. His actions, he believed, had compensated for Meade's errors. These accusations were printed in the newspapers (as was an erroneous report that Lincoln had endorsed them).[62]

By mid-October, the Meade–Sickles controversy had intensified. When Sickles, hobbling about on crutches, returned to the Third Corps' winter camp to be reinstated into command, Meade refused, using as an excuse the fact that he had not fully regained his health. Returning angrily to Washington, Sickles stepped up his anti-Meade campaign. He charged that Meade had been preparing to retreat on the second day at Gettysburg rather than to stay and fight. Sickles claimed that it was only after his Third Corps had moved to the Emmitsburg Road that Meade committed the Army of the Potomac to stay and fight. When Meade heard this accusation, he was infuriated.[63]

In February 1864, Sickles testified before the U.S. Congress's Joint Committee on the Conduct of the War. This committee, consisting of radical Republicans, was critical of Meade's generalship during the campaign and desired to see him removed from command, hoping to rehabilitate the reputation of their political ally, Joseph Hooker. In both efforts, Daniel Sickles was more than willing to help. In the end, neither of their efforts was successful. Meade continued in command of the Army of the Potomac until the end of the war, and Hooker was relegated to a lesser command in the Western theater.[64]

Because of the controversy over Gettysburg, Meade was concerned about his reputation as a soldier. His spirits were lifted by letters from Generals Gibbons and Hancock, who reaffirmed their confidence in him as an army commander. Talk of Meade's replacement was widespread, but much to Sickles's dismay, he would retain his position.[65]

Recognition of the accomplishments of various generals became an important political issue for Congress. Hooker's supporters asserted that he was the one who had planned the Gettysburg campaign and that the actual fighting had been at the direction of the corps commanders; therefore, credit for the victory should go to Hooker rather than to Meade. As a result, Congress passed a resolution honoring Hooker for the Union success at Gettysburg and giving Meade secondary mention "for skill and heroic valor."[66]

The resolution lingered for several weeks in committee while Sickles campaigned to have Meade's name eliminated in favor of his own. Sickles contended that he had led his Third Corps until he was disabled, implying that, had he not been wounded, the Battle of Gettysburg would have been won in two days instead of three. But there were still some in Congress who did not like Sickles. Although he was unable to win official recognition for himself, he was able to get his comrade and friend, General Howard's, name included in the Gettysburg resolution. The final resolution cited Hooker, Howard, and Meade, in that order, for their contributions at Gettysburg.[67]

Meade made certain that Sickles was kept out of his army, but life was far from over for him. In December 1864, he wrote to Lincoln requesting an assignment. The president responded by sending him on a diplomatic mission to South America. Later, he completed inspection duties for Major General William Sherman's armies in the West.

Ironically, as Sickles left his military career, he found that his exploits on the battlefield and the loss of his leg had reopened the doors to his political career. In 1865, President Andrew Johnson appointed him the military governor of the Second Reconstruction District, comprising North and South Carolina. In a short time Sickles found himself at the center of controversy. He challenged Johnson's authority by advocating that Congress, rather than the president, supervise Reconstruction. Sickles also overextended his authority when he tried a local lawbreaker via military commissions when federal courts failed to do so. As a consequence, Johnson had no choice but to remove him from office. Thereafter, Sickles promoted the candidacy of northern radicals and worked unsuccessfully for Johnson's impeachment and removal from office.[68]

After leaving the army, Sickles campaigned for Ulysses S. Grant when he ran for president in 1868. To show his appreciation, Grant appointed him minister to Spain. Despite the responsibility entrusted him, Sickles never let his work interfere with his social life and philandering. Not long after he arrived in Spain rumors started to circulate about Queen Isabella II and Sickles. In 1871, Sickles married Caroline de Creagh, an attendant at the Court of Isabella II. Some rumors hinted that the arrangement had been made to conceal the relationship between the queen and Sickles.[69]

As minister to Spain, Sickles soon became entangled in Spanish politics involving Cuba. His intervention into Spanish politics and his purported affair with Queen Isabella led the Spanish government to request that he be recalled to Washington.

After returning to America, Sickles again became involved in politics and was named chairman of the New York State Civil Service Commission in 1887 and sheriff of New York County in 1890. His ultimate redemption as a politician came in 1892 when he was once again elected to the U.S. House of Representatives. Sickles was defeated when he ran for reelection in 1894, but, as a solace, he was awarded the Congressional Medal of Honor for his actions at Gettysburg.[70]

In 1887 Sickles's father died, leaving him an estate of $5 million. By 1912, Sickles had managed to squander all of it on long-shot business deals, card games, and women. Daniel Sickles was used to living to the fullest, his critics be damned. After all, he thought, dying rich would be a tremendous waste.[71]

In later life, Gettysburg absorbed a large part of Sickles's time. He visited the battlefield many times and was the driving force behind the creation of a national park there. He was also appointed chairman of the New York Monuments Commission. In 1912 Sickles was removed from the commission amid charges that he had embezzled its funds. Amazed New Yorkers were shocked when the news reached them that Sickles was to be arrested. One admirer, William Dodge of Indiana, stepped forward to assist him. He announced that he would take Sickles's note for the entire deficit.[72]

In 1892, Sickles and James Longstreet were guests at a Saint Patrick's Day dinner hosted by the Irish Societies of Atlanta. Both men drank a lot of Irish whiskey during the evening, and, before long, they became fast friends. This friendship was not surprising since Sickles was blamed by many Northerners for preventing a greater Union victory at Gettysburg, and Longstreet was blamed by Southerners for Lee's defeat in that battle.[73]

Sickles never gave up his opinion that he had acted properly at Gettysburg. In 1902, he received a communication from James Longstreet that confirmed everything he had been saying for almost half a century: "I believe that it is now conceded that the advanced position at the Peach Orchard taken by your corps and under your orders saved the battlefield for the Union cause." Sickles had the letter published and continued to do so as often as he could.[74]

Sickles continued to revisit the Gettysburg battlefield, showing up at all reunions. At the fiftieth reunion in 1913, Sickles was confined to a wheelchair but insisted on being pushed all over the battlefield. Among the many memorials on the field, there was none for him. When asked about the omission, Sickles responded, "Hell, the whole damn battlefield is my monument."[75]

Sickles died the following year at the age of ninety-four. He could have been a pitiful figure in his last years. He had squandered his fortune, was crippled by wounds, and did not have a close relationship with his family. Yet, there was a kind of nobility about him. Although there was much about him that could be despised, most people found it difficult not to like him. He was charming and always had a sparkle in his eyes that won him friends of both sexes. To most, Sickles was a fascinating person.[76]

To the very end, Sickles took pride in his pinned-up trouser leg, and it was said that he occasionally returned to the medical museum to see his other leg. It was one of Sickles's friends, Mark Twain, who understood how important this "badge of honor" had been to him. "I noticed," wrote Twain, "that the general valued his lost leg way above the one that is left. I am perfectly sure that if he had to part with either of them, he would part with the one he has got."[77]

15 *William Tecumseh Sherman*

Advocate of Total War

On April 9, 1865, Robert E. Lee surrendered to Ulysses S. Grant at Appomattox Court House. Several days after Lee's surrender, Confederate General Joseph E. Johnston, commander of the Army of Tennessee, asked for a truce so that "further effusion of blood and devastation of property might be avoided." Major General Sherman quickly agreed to a meeting with Johnston to negotiate an end to the hostilities. On April 17, the two generals' parties met under white flags. Both generals rode ahead of their escorts and greeted each other with warmth and respect. As the pair rode toward a small house owned by a farmer named Bennett, Sherman must have momentarily reflected on the events leading up to Johnston's surrender. He was now at the pinnacle of his career. Sherman had spent his entire life preparing for just this moment.[1]

Sherman's father, Charles R. Sherman, was well educated in the liberal arts, having attended Dartmouth College, and Charles practiced law in his father's office. In 1810, he married Mary Holt, a graduate of a female seminary in Poughkeepsie, New York, and the daughter of a successful Norwalk merchant. Charles rode the circuit from 1817 to 1829, first as a lawyer and then as a justice of Ohio's Supreme Court.[2]

Although Charles was regularly away from his home in Lancaster, Ohio, he was home enough to father a family of eleven children. On February 8, 1820, the sixth Sherman child was born. His father named him Tecumseh after the Shawnee Indian leader, who Charles admired for his courage and military prowess.[3]

Young Sherman spent the first years of his life in a comfortable home with his brothers and sisters, an affectionate mother, and a domineering grandmother. In June 1829, while on the circuit, Charles developed a high fever and, a few days later, died. Charles Sherman left his family only the house, its furnishings, and some bank stock worth about $200 a year; most of his earnings had regularly gone to pay off debts he had accrued from an earlier disastrous business venture. As Sherman's brother John later expressed it, his father had "left his family poor in everything but friends." Fortunately, these friends stepped forward to take responsibility for the family. The children were taken in and provided for by these friends. Sherman went to live with his neighbor, Thomas Ewing.[4]

The financial difficulties resulting from his father's death and the breakup of his family were pivotal events for Sherman. Throughout his life, he worried about his financial situation, fearing that the same might happen to him. But young Sherman had been fortunate; his foster parent, Thomas Ewing, was one of the leading citizens of early Lancaster. He was known for his intelligence, professional success, and happy family life. Sherman grew to admire and respect his foster father. His foster mother, Maria Ewing, was a devout Catholic, and she insisted on having Sherman baptized.[5]

Father Dominic Young baptized Sherman in the front parlor of the Ewing home. Father Young insisted, however, that young Sherman add a good, Christian name to his Indian one. Since the event occurred on June 28, St. William's Day, the priest baptized him "William Tecumseh."[6]

Thomas Ewing saw to it that Sherman was raised in the same fashion as his own children and made sure that he received a good education. Although Thomas Ewing made Sherman an equal member of his family, Sherman never called the Ewings "mother" and "father"; they always remained Mr. and Mrs. Ewing. William longed for a family of his own, one like the Ewings. As he grew older, he wanted to make certain his family did not experience the same hardships he had.[7]

Young Sherman was a good student and a fine athlete. In 1836, at the age of sixteen, he was appointed to West Point by Senator Ewing, his foster father. Sherman did not really desire a career in the military but embarked on one out of a sense of obligation to his foster father.[8]

At the Academy, Sherman was a good student, but he accumulated so many demerits for discipline and infractions of the dress code that he finished sixth in a class of forty-three rather than fourth as he was entitled by his academic record.[9]

One of the most valuable of Sherman's courses was on moral philosophy, which included the reading of James Kent's *Commentaries on American Law*. Kent wrote that war eliminated all morality, and, during a civil war, he argued that "the central government had to defend the laws of the union by force of arms." Sherman's actions during the Civil War reflected this idea.[10]

After graduating in 1840, Sherman's army service took him from New York to San Francisco, then to Pittsburgh and New Orleans, but provided

Upon Grant's inauguration as president in 1869,
Sherman became general-in-chief of the army, a
post he held for thirteen years.

COURTESY OF THE LIBRARY OF CONGRESS

him no opportunity for combat experience other than a few skirmishes in
Florida with the Seminole Indians. During the Mexican War, when so many
West Pointers were gaining fame and rank on the battlefield, Sherman was
assigned routine duty in Pennsylvania and California. Thirteen years after
graduating from West Point, he held only the rank of captain in the Commissary Department with no foreseeable opportunity for advancement.[11]

In a letter to Hugh Ewing, his foster brother, Sherman expressed his
feelings about the army: "I have often regretted that your father did not
actually, instead of sending me to West Point, set me at some useful trade
or business." There was no prestige in serving in the army while commer-
cial life was looked upon with esteem.[12]

In 1850, Sherman married his foster father's daughter, Ellen Ewing.

Together they had eight children. Although his marriage strengthened his ties to the Ewing family, it also increased the pressure on him to prove himself worthy of such an alliance. With the addition of children to the family, Sherman's financial problem increased. His meager army salary was not sufficient to support Ellen and their children in good style, so he was forced to accept financial assistance from his foster father.[13]

Sherman took a leave from the army to accept a job offer from a former army friend to manage a bank in San Francisco, later resigning his commission. For a while, he was able to support his family and provide many of the fine things in life for them, including a large house. In 1857, a business panic struck California, and his bank was closed, leaving Sherman unemployed and in debt. He blamed himself for this dismal outcome but managed to pay off most of his debts by selling all of his property.

Sherman considered reentering the army, but only if he could receive a higher rank. Again his family came to his aid. This time Ewing's oldest son, Thomas Jr., asked him to join his law firm in Leavenworth, Kansas Territory. Sherman was admitted to the bar "on the grounds of general intelligence and reputation." Clients were few, and he lost his only case. Having failed again, he returned to his family in 1859. "I look upon myself," he wrote to Ellen before leaving Kansas, "as a dead cock in the pit."[14]

Although unfortunate in business, Sherman was lucky in having good friends. One of them, Major Don Carlos Buell, told him of an opening for a superintendent in the newly established Louisiana Seminary Academy (the present-day Louisiana State University). With the recommendation of two army buddies, P. G. T. Beauregard and Braxton Bragg, he received the appointment. During the months that followed he proved to be a capable administrator and a popular teacher. Sherman believed he had finally found his proper niche in life, but not for long.[15]

When Sherman learned that South Carolina had seceded from the Union, he was brought to tears. He loved the South. Since entering West Point, his closest male friends had been Southerners. During the twenty-five years since leaving home, he had been under the social influence of the South. At West Point, Southern ideals were prevalent. His stay in Florida and South Carolina, his four years of working closely with Southern-born army officers in California, six years representing Missouri bankers, and now his last year as superintendent of an academy in Louisiana had all left him with a favorable impression of the South.[16]

In reality, Sherman considered himself a Southerner. He was hoping to spend his life there and was in the process of building a house in Louisiana. His old army comrades, he knew, were preparing to follow South Carolina's lead. But Sherman could not join them. It was not the slavery issue that stopped him; he considered slavery the appropriate status for blacks. But he was passionately devoted to the Union and regarded secession a form of revolution and anarchy. Within three weeks, Sherman sadly resigned his position.

To the governor of Louisiana he wrote: "I prefer to maintain all allegiance to the Constitution as long as a fragment of it survives."[17]

Sherman returned to the North with his brother, who was now a Republican senator, and offered his services to the Union. President Lincoln informed him that he would not be needed because the Union could be restored peacefully with compromise. Sherman disagreed, predicting that a long bloody war would be needed to restore the Union.[18]

After the Confederates fired on Fort Sumter, Lincoln's dream of a peaceful resolution to the problem disappeared. The War Department offered Sherman a commission as colonel in the regular army. Sherman believed, as other West Pointers did, that only trained and disciplined regulars could squash the rebellion. He distrusted politicians who would make scapegoats of those generals who might fail through no fault of their own. Surprisingly, he had no love for democracy itself, equating it to mob rule; he preferred a monarchy or dictatorship.[19]

Sherman was assigned to a brigade of volunteers under Brigadier General Irvin McDowell's command. He did not have a high opinion of the raw recruits, many of whom were ninety-day enlistees who could not wait to go home. "With regulars," he wrote to his wife, "I would have no doubt, but these volunteers are subject to stampedes." On July 21, at Bull Run, Sherman's prediction came true. His recruits, however, proved to be the exception. They performed well considering this battle was their first. Although the army was in a complete rout, Sherman was able to keep his brigade in good order while it retreated from the field. Finally, upon reaching Washington, Sherman rallied and reorganized his troops to defend the capital in the event the Confederates should attempt to follow up their victory.[20]

Late in August, Sherman was promoted to brigadier general and transferred to Kentucky. He was delighted with both his promotion and his transfer. He believed that the war would be won in the West and that reputations could be made there. Lacking confidence in his ability to lead, Sherman requested to serve in a subordinate role. "Not till I see daylight ahead," he confided to Ellen, "do I want to lead."[21]

The War Department responded to his request by assigning him second in command to Brigadier General Robert Anderson, commander of the Department of the Cumberland. Shortly afterward, Anderson fell ill and asked to be relieved. As a result, Sherman was thrust into exactly the position he had tried to avoid; he became the head commander in a vital theater of the war.

Fearing attack by Confederate General Albert Sidney Johnston, Sherman requested to be reinforced. Instead of complying with his request for reinforcements, Washington urged him to "liberate" east Tennessee. This response convinced him that he was being deliberately "sacrificed." In a letter to Ellen, he wrote that to take this action would be madness. "The idea of going down in History with a fame such as this threatens me," he said, "nearly makes me crazy, indeed I may be so now."[22]

People who observed Sherman's appearance while he was staying at a Louisville hotel concluded that he was demented. Tall, thin, and in need of a shave, he spent hours pacing back and forth, smoking cigars, head bent forward, staring straight ahead.

When Secretary of War Cameron met with him to discuss the assignment of troops, Sherman's demeanor and request for troops was outlandish. Cameron told a reporter that the general was "unbalanced and that it would not be wise to leave him in command." Cameron soon replaced him with Sherman's old friend Brigadier General Don Carlos Buell. Sherman himself was labeled by the newspapers as being "unbalanced and not fit for command." As a result, Sherman would maintain a strong dislike for the press. A despondent Sherman wrote to Ellen, "I am almost crazy."[23]

After General Buell's arrival, Sherman reported to Major General Henry Halleck in St. Louis. Halleck, who was a friend of Sherman's, ignored the reports about his instability and assigned him to central Missouri to take command of Union forces there. After evaluating the situation, Sherman reported to Halleck that the Confederate forces were too strong to be beaten, despite other reports that they were too weak to pose a problem. Halleck immediately ordered Sherman back to St. Louis and declared him unfit for duty, giving him a twenty-six-day leave.[24]

Again the newspapers attacked Sherman; one headline read, "General William T. Sherman Insane," the article asserting that he was "stark mad." Sherman was crushed and again felt he had failed and disgraced himself. Sherman wrote to John Ewing, "I am so sensible now of my disgrace . . . that I do think I would have committed suicide were it not for my children. I do not think I can be entrusted with a command."[25]

Despite the newspapers, Halleck did not give up on Sherman. On December 23, Halleck assigned him to the Union base at Benton Barracks in St. Louis, placing him in charge of recruiting, training, and logistics. In February 1862, Sherman was given an independent command at Cairo, Illinois, serving under Grant. Halleck's patience and help in building Sherman's confidence eventually paid off. Sherman soon enjoyed his first military success at Shiloh. It proved to be a valuable one, giving Sherman the confidence he needed to lead.[26] Starting in 1862, a very special relationship would develop between Grant and Sherman, one that was useful to Grant but essential to Sherman.[27]

Halleck recognized Sherman's talent for strategic planning when he assigned him to Grant's command. Sherman proved to be an asset for Grant, planning the attacks on Forts Henry and Donelson. The two men quickly developed a strong friendship and mutual admiration. War seemed to give Sherman purpose. He had found the one thing that he did well: leading men in battle. Before the war, Sherman had been a good student and had worked hard, but he had not been successful in his career. With the war, however, he came into his own. As a military innovator, Sherman became a major advocate of modern warfare, introducing the concept of total war in America.

Under Grant, Sherman commanded brilliantly at the battle of Shiloh. Although his division was made up of raw recruits, it was among the most effective and disciplined of the entire line of battle. Placed on the extreme Union right, Sherman's division held its position when it was attacked. Sherman's coolness under fire inspired his men to fight on. For several hours, they fought off fierce Confederate charges, inflicting heavy losses on the enemy. During the evening, Grant received reinforcements, and, in the morning, his counterattack drove the Confederates back to Corinth.[28]

In Grant's battle report, he singled out Sherman for having "displayed great judgment and skill in the management of his men." General Halleck also praised Sherman's efforts: "It was the unanimous opinion here that Brig. Gen. W. T. Sherman saved the fortunes of the day on the Sixth and contributed largely to the glorious victory on the Seventh."[29]

As a result of his success at Shiloh, Sherman was promoted to major general. A modest Sherman made no claim to exceptional accomplishments at Shiloh, writing to his wife: "I received today the commission of Major General, but I know not why it gives me far less emotion than my old commission as First Lieutenant of Artillery. The latter, I know I merited; this I doubt." The promotion and the commendations from Grant and Halleck restored Sherman's reputation and bolstered his self-confidence. Shiloh, for Sherman, was the turning point in his life.[30]

Sherman continued to make a name for himself. Late in April 1863, Grant began a campaign that resulted in the capture of Vicksburg on July 4 and the surrender of General John Pemberton's army. Sherman played a major role in Grant's success. Now commanding the Fifteenth Corps, he kept Pemberton off balance by bluffing another attack on Vicksburg while Grant moved south of the city. Sherman then moved quickly to reinforce Grant, bringing badly needed supplies. Vicksburg fell after several assaults and a siege. Grant gave Sherman credit for the major part he played in the victory. To his brother, Sherman wrote, "The share I have personally borne in all these events is one in which you may take pride for me."[31]

During the Vicksburg campaign, Sherman learned from Grant the importance of training his army to live off the land, which allowed them more freedom of movement. Sherman would later use this tactic to great advantage in Georgia and the Carolinas.[32]

During the lull after the victory at Vicksburg, Sherman sent for Ellen and two of their children, Minnie and Willy, to join him at his camp. While visiting with his father, Willy took sick with typhoid fever and died shortly afterward. Sherman took the loss of his son hard, mourning his death deeply.[33]

In October 1863, when Grant was promoted to commander of all armies in the West, Sherman succeeded him as the Commander of the Army of the Tennessee. In March 1864, Grant became commander of the entire Union army and was promoted to the rank of lieutenant general. In announcing his promotion, Grant expressed thanks to Sherman and McPherson "as the men to whom, above all others, I feel indebted for whatever I have had of success." When Grant moved his headquarters to the East, he named Sherman to succeed him as commander in the West.[34]

Lincoln and Grant's plan for ending the war involved attacking the Confederates on two fronts. Sherman was to move into Georgia against General Joseph Johnston's army, while Grant attacked General Lee's Army of Northern Virginia. Sherman was to destroy the enemy's interior and inflict damage on the South's resources. Both Grant and Sherman were to attack simultaneously, keeping the pressure on both armies so that the Confederates could not move troops from one front to the other.[35]

In May 1864, with an army of 100,000, Sherman left Chattanooga, Tennessee, and began his invasion of Georgia. He was opposed by Confederate General Joseph Johnston. To move rapidly, he divided his army into three groups. His troops and officers were tough, seasoned veterans; however, their discipline off the battlefield was poor and would grow increasingly worse as the army continued its march. Despite this flaw, Sherman was confident that he could carry out Grant's plan. He believed he had one of the best armies in the world.[36]

By mid-June, Sherman believed Johnston's line was close to breaking, so he decided to strike it head-on at Kennesaw Mountain. Although his officers were opposed to the attack, he ordered the Army of the Tennessee to advance anyway. When the attack failed, leaving 2,500 of some of the North's best soldiers dead or wounded, Sherman was apparently unphased. He was becoming hardened to war, writing to Ellen two days later: "I begin to regard the death and mangling of a couple of thousand men as a small affair, a kind of morning dash."[37]

As Johnston continued to retreat toward Atlanta, President Jefferson Davis became convinced Johnston had no intention of holding Atlanta. On July 17, he replaced Johnston with General John Bell Hood. Hood was able to hold off Sherman for a while, but, on September 1, Atlanta fell.

Hood marched his army toward Tennessee, hoping that Sherman would pursue him and interrupt his rampage through Georgia. This, however, was exactly what Sherman had hoped Hood would do. "If he will go to the Ohio River, I will give him rations. My business is down south," he said. When Hood moved into Tennessee, the people of Georgia felt they had been abandoned and left to the mercy of Sherman, whose cavalry had a free range of operation one hundred miles south of Atlanta. Sherman split his army, sending a contingent to deal with Hood, while he embarked with 62,000 troops on his famous March to the Sea.[38]

On November 15, Atlanta was torched. This act set the pattern for Sherman's March to the Sea and shocked the South by its ruthlessness. It marked the end of an era in which contending armies were involved only in battles. Major Henry Hitchcock observed, "Immense and raging fires light up the whole heaven. First, bursts of smoke, dense black volumes, then tongues of flame, then huge waves of fire roll up into the sky. Presently the skeletons of great warehouses stand out in relief against sheets of roaring, blazing, furious flames."[39]

Sherman believed that the war was not just a conflict between armies but a campaign between societies. "They [the Southerners] cannot be made to love us," Sherman said, "but they can be made to fear us." By marching his army through the center of the Confederacy, destroying the countryside as he went, he would show the people that their army could not protect them. This demonstration, Sherman felt, would break the South's will to fight and bring the war to a speedy end.[40]

Before Sherman started his march, Lincoln expressed concern about whether the plan would shorten the war. Grant trusted Sherman and convinced Lincoln and Secretary of War Stanton to give their approval. Sherman carefully planned for the march. He obtained the census records for each county in Georgia and information about where food was produced. Using this information, he planned his route. Attacking both civilian and military targets, Sherman wanted to destroy the South's will to win and its means to fight.[41]

Sherman began the march without informing the army where they were going. No one but Sherman, himself, knew that their final destination was Savannah, 275 miles away. Facing little military resistance, Sherman's army moved quickly, foraging and destroying everything in their path. Behind them they left a trail of devastation sixty miles wide. With an abundance of food available, Sherman's vague order to "forage liberally" allowed his troops a great deal of latitude. The men ransacked houses along the way despite orders to the contrary, removing valuables, breaking dishes, smashing furniture, and stealing what money they could find. Their excuse was that they were "foraging liberally." Southerners charged that Sherman only winked at the abusers, allowing them to do exactly what he wanted them to do—terrorize the countryside. In most cases, the soldiers were operating miles from their commanders' influence and supervision and felt that this was their opportunity to punish the South. The worst of Sherman's raiders were called "bummers." They wreaked havoc wherever they went and created the popular image today of the March to the Sea.[42]

Traveling with Sherman's army came a large number of freed blacks who had been recently liberated. Their presence annoyed Sherman, who considered the Emancipation Proclamation a mistake. On December 21, the Union troops entered the city of Savannah, and Sherman telegraphed

Lincoln: "I beg to present to you a Christmas gift, the city of Savannah, with 150 heavy guns, plenty of ammunition and 25,000 bales of cotton."[43]

Lincoln was elated and responded with a letter to Sherman: "When you were leaving Atlanta for the Atlantic coast," he wrote, "I was anxious, if not fearful; but feeling that you were the better judge. . . . Now, the undertaking being a success, the honor is all yours. . . . It is indeed a great success."[44]

The destruction during Sherman's March to the Sea has been greatly exaggerated. Among whites, there are no known murders, and there are only a few reports of rape. Some atrocities did occur to African Americans. The worst incident occurred on December 9, when General Davis marched his troops across the rain-swollen Ebenezer Creek. After his troops crossed the waterway, he ordered the pontoon bridges removed, leaving hundreds of fugitive slaves on the opposite shore. With the Confederate cavalry close behind, the slaves panicked and tried to swim across the creek. Unfortunately, many drowned. Even Sherman's hardened troops disapproved of Davis's act of cruelty.[45]

Sherman did not attempt to protect the freed slaves on his march. His proslavery and racist views were well known. When Halleck cautioned him about what he said to others, particularly the press, on this issue, Sherman responded, "Military success, not protection of 'Sambo,' is my main priority." When others called for better treatment of African Americans, his answer was, "The Negro should be a free man, but not part of any equality with whites. . . . Indeed it appears to me that the right of suffrage in our country should be abridged rather than enlarged."[46]

As a result of his march, Sherman estimated the damage done to the state of Georgia and its military resources at $100 million. Of this amount, at least $20 million was military related. The rest, he confessed, "is simple waste and destruction."[47]

By the end of January 1865, Sherman's army had moved into South Carolina. The mood of the men as they entered the state was described by one soldier: "The whole army is burning with an insatiable desire to wreak vengeance upon South Carolina. I almost tremble at her fate, but feel that she deserves all that seems in store for her." The soldier's estimate was correct; the result was what Sherman would call "minor depredations." A Pennsylvania soldier wrote that, after his unit crossed into South Carolina, the division commander rode along the line of troops saying, "Boys, are you well supplied with matches as we are now in South Carolina?" At the end of the march, a soldier wrote, "We burnt every house, barn and mill that we passed."[48]

Sherman's men devastated the countryside, even though he had ordered his troops to spare dwellings that were occupied, be courteous to women, and take only the provisions and forage necessary. In Georgia, few houses were burned; in South Carolina, few escaped. Sherman was too intent upon the army's safety to worry about the conduct of his men and to enforce his orders.[49]

In South Carolina, Sherman encountered little opposition, but when he entered North Carolina, he was confronted by Joseph Johnston. Grant ordered Sherman to move against Johnston, now back in command of the Confederate army, to prevent him from joining Lee in Virginia.

Later, reflecting on his march to the sea and beyond, Sherman believed he was justified in his wartime action. He did, however, have some concern about the way children felt about him. "They were taught to curse my name, and each night thousands kneel in prayer and beseech the Almighty to consign me to perdition," he said.[50]

The Southerners may have hated Sherman, but his men idolized him. To them he was known as "Uncle Billy." He would join them around the fire in their camps, smoke a cigar, and exchange stories. Because Sherman was not a spit-and-polish soldier, he was able to establish a bond with his troops. Sherman was a hero to his men and to the nation.[51]

Early in April, Grant forced Lee out of Petersburg and Richmond and, on April 9, accepted his surrender at Appomattox. On April 14, Joseph Johnston, who saw no point in continuing a war that was lost, asked to meet with Sherman to discuss the surrender of his army. The joy in the North that followed the news of Lee's surrender was suddenly stifled by the news of Lincoln's assassination. Sherman instructed the telegrapher not to tell anyone of the president's death until he had met with Johnston. The two generals met in a little farmhouse. When Sherman showed Johnston the dispatch about Lincoln's assassination, Johnston was visibly shaken. The two agreed to meet the next day with John C. Breckinridge, the Confederate secretary of war.[52]

Sherman ordered all soldiers to their camps and issued a carefully worded announcement about the president's assassination. He stated clearly that the Confederate army was not involved in Lincoln's death. The Union troops were shocked. Some wanted vengeance, but Sherman was able to maintain order and prevented his troops from acts of reprisal.[53]

Thinking he was acting in the spirit of Lincoln's policy for Reconstruction, Sherman was more generous with his terms to Johnston than Grant had been with Lee. He negotiated a political plan for Reconstruction, something he had no authority to do. Under his terms, Confederate armies were to turn in their weapons and promise to obey federal authority. Existing state governments were to be recognized, and federal courts reestablished. Political rights of individuals were to be guaranteed, and no one was to be punished for his role in the war as long as they obeyed the law. With the end of the war, there was to be a general amnesty.[54]

Sherman, who had terrorized the South, now made the terms for peace as painless as he could. In doing so, he negotiated political matters beyond his realm of authority that were unacceptable to the radicals in Washington.

Andrew Johnson, now president, had no choice but to repudiate Sherman's agreement with Johnston. Sherman rather expected this and was not offended, but he was incensed by the way Secretary of War Stanton and General Halleck handled the affair. They implied that Sherman had betrayed the Union and was seeking to make himself a military dictator.[55]

Stanton accused Sherman of insubordination, stupidity, and treason. When papers across the nation reported Stanton's accusations, Sherman was outraged, as were his soldiers. To speak unkindly of "Uncle Billy" was to show disrespect to them as well. In Raleigh, soldiers burned a collection of Northern newspapers that had been brought into town and threatened to burn the newspaper office. Sherman's Western army had devastated the South; now there was fear they might march to Washington to do the same there. To defuse the anger of Sherman and his men, the government decided to hold a "grand review" in Washington. The Eastern and Western armies would march separately on successive days. The event turned out to be the greatest parade in American history.[56]

On May 23, the Eastern Army of the Potomac marched. This army was Washington's own, the men who had defended the city in many desperate battles. General Meade, the hero of Gettysburg, led the parade. Everyone agreed that the troops gave a splendid military performance. The *New York Times* assumed Meade's men would be much better received than Sherman's Western army and predicted thin crowds for the next day's march.[57]

The next morning, the Army of the Tennessee marched down Pennsylvania Avenue before a crowd estimated at 200,000. At the head of the column was their leader, William Tecumseh Sherman. The Westerners quickly won the hearts of the crowd, and the army received an overwhelming reception. As Sherman passed the presidential stand, he raised his sword in salute. One New York paper reported that the acclamation was "without precedent. . . . Sherman was the idol of the day." Ironically, this newspaper was the same one that had called Sherman a traitor only ten days earlier.[58]

After passing the reviewing stand, Sherman dismounted and joined the dignitaries. He embraced his wife and son, and shook hands with his father-in-law, Thomas Ewing, and with President Johnson and General Grant. When Secretary of War Stanton put out his hand, Sherman refused to shake it. "I declined it publicly," he wrote, "and the fact was universally noticed." Then he sat down to enjoy the parade.[59]

When the war ended, Sherman's attitude toward the South changed completely. Sherman had once loved the South and was now ready to renew his friendship. In doing so, he followed Lincoln's conciliatory views. Later, Sherman stated that to persecute the beaten South would be like slashing the crew of a sinking ship. He told President Andrew Johnson he would "risk person and reputation to heal the wounds he had helped make."[60] Sherman proved his benevolent attitude toward the South by collecting money and supplies for the civilians of Atlanta; at Savannah, he instituted a system of barter that kept its people from starvation.

On May 30, Sherman issued his farewell to his troops, saying, "Our work is done, and armed enemies no longer defy us. . . . You have done all that men could do." He urged them to be good citizens. Sherman now looked forward to peaceful days.[61]

Sherman's tumultuous reception at the Grand Review and during a tour that he and Ellen took in June demonstrated the nation's affection for him. When they reached New York, the crowds were so large that the police had difficulty controlling them. It was an impressive sight: a grateful nation expressing its thanks.[62]

Sherman's friends did more than shout and cheer. The citizens of Lancaster undertook a $100,000 testimonial fund drive throughout Ohio. Later, people in St. Louis raised money to buy him a $24,000 house and provided an additional $5,600 for his bank account. In 1889, when he became the commanding general, prominent businessmen bought him Grant's former home for $65,000 and banked an additional $37,000.[63]

Many Southerners remembered Sherman's destructive march during the war but also appreciated the lenient peace terms he had offered Johnston. When he visited the South in the postwar years, his receptions were always cordial.[64]

When the Civil War was over, American energies returned to their plan of economic development and westward expansion. The chief impediment to this objective was the Indians of the Great Plains. A postwar army of 25,000 men was given the responsibility of making certain that the Native Americans did not impede progress. When Grant went to Washington as commanding general of the army, Sherman was sent to St. Louis to serve as the leader in the field. Sherman understood that his central focus was to gain "absolute and unqualified control of the Indians."[65]

The removal of the Indians would be a war of extermination if no other way could be found. Sherman had no difficulty carrying out his assignment, believing that he was an "Agent of Progress" and that his enemies were an impediment to America's future.[66] Sherman admitted he had "no doubt our people have committed grievous wrong to the Indians," but he felt that both races could not share the country; one or the other must withdraw. "We cannot withdraw without checking the natural progress of civilization," he said.[67]

Grant agreed with Sherman about the means and ends of his Indian policy and gave him his complete support. In 1868, when Grant went to the White House, he appointed Sherman commanding general of the army and promoted him to the rank of full general. Sherman gave his replacement in the West, Phil Sheridan, full authorization to carry on his policy of Indian extermination.

Acting as the commanding general of the army was not easy for Sherman.

When he gained the position in 1869, he found himself battling politicians in Washington and Indian agents in the West. Even Grant, the new president, sided with his new political friends rather than his old army comrades. Sherman had hoped that Grant would maintain the same relationship with him in peacetime as he had during the war. He was disappointed with Grant as he became more political and less supportive of the army.[68]

Sherman was not a politician and wanted no part in politics. He viewed politicians as adversaries he was forced to tolerate but not with whom he was required to work. He was absent from Washington regularly and did not involve himself in the political battles necessary for the army to thrive.[69]

Sherman felt things would improve with the army when Rutherford Hayes took office in 1877; however, Congress pressured him to reduce the size of the army to less than 25,000. He tried to hang on to the old army rather than change with the times. No matter what he tried, he could not free the army from political influence.

Sherman often talked of retiring when he became frustrated. He was finally convinced to leave the army when Congress expressed its willingness to let him retire at full pay and benefits for the rest of his life. In November 1883, Sherman turned the army over to Phil Sheridan, retiring officially in February 1884.

Because of Sherman's reputation for being politically independent, both parties spoke of nominating him to run for president. No American so likely to be elected president ever rejected the idea so many times. During the 1884 Republican convention, Sherman sent two telegrams to a friend among the delegates. The first read: "Please decline any nomination for me in language strong but courteous." The second, two days later, said: "I will not accept if nominated, and will not serve if elected." Sherman believed that the presidency destroyed those who held it. He also feared that, if he were a candidate, his family would come under fire because of their Roman Catholic faith.[70]

As a veteran, old soldiers and their welfare became one of Sherman's chief concerns. Veterans often appeared at his door, usually in search of a handout. It was reported that he gave about a third of his income to needy veterans. When he marched in veteran parades, he always dressed in the plain blouse of a private with his four silver stars. It was to a veterans' group in 1880 that he made his famous remark, "War is hell." "War is usually made by civilians, bold and defiant in the beginning, but when the storm comes, they generally go below." The only office Sherman ever sought was that of president of the Army of the Tennessee, which he held from 1869 until his death.[71]

In 1875, Sherman wrote his memoirs. His two-volume work was a model of its kind, candid and outspoken, assessing the roles of individuals and governments alike. The book angered Jefferson Davis and a number of Federal generals. Southerners were outraged by his account of his march and description of the Confederacy as a criminal and senseless conspiracy. In the North, however, the book was well received, and there was an immediate move to have Sherman run for president.[72]

By 1887, Ellen's health was deteriorating rapidly. Sherman hired a nurse to care for her, but it was difficult for him to accept the fact that his wife was going to die. On November 28, as he was reading in his office, the nurse called to him that Ellen was dying. He ran upstairs calling out: "Wait for me Ellen; no one ever loved you as I loved you." It was too late; she was dead.[73]

General William Tecumseh Sherman and Joseph E. Johnston both lived for a quarter of a century after the Civil War. Their mutual respect led to a genuine friendship. They corresponded and occasionally met with each other. At General Grant's funeral in New York, Sherman and Johnston stood side by side.[74]

Sherman lived to be seventy-one years old. He had many ailments, but it was asthma that finally caused his death on February 14, 1891. On February 18, thousands viewed his remains. Members of the Grand Army of the Republic, many of them Sherman's veterans, participated in the funeral. President Harrison and former Presidents Hayes and Cleveland were present, along with members of the cabinet, congressmen, senators, governors, and friends. Also present at the funeral was Joseph Johnston, who had observed his eighty-fourth birthday on February 3.[75]

General Johnston was an honorary pallbearer. It was a very cold day following a winter rain. Johnston stood bareheaded with the other pallbearers while the flag-draped coffin was carried. A friend, concerned about Johnston's health, urged him to put on his hat. Johnston replied: "If I were in his place and he were standing here in mine, he would not put on his hat." Johnston developed a bad cold that aggravated his heart condition. A month later, he was dead.[76]

William Tecumseh Sherman was buried in Calvary Cemetery, St. Louis. He chose his own epitaph, "Faithful and Honorable," and it was an accurate assessment of his life. He had been true to his word, in both war and peace. Sherman was considered by many to be a military genius. He possessed an extraordinary mind and was quick to grasp major military problems. The Civil War was the defining moment of his life. He helped preserve the Union and was proud of it. He remained a soldier and patriot always.

16 John Sedgwick

"Uncle John"

They called him "Uncle John," a term of endearment indicating he had been accepted by his men with esteem and affection. Soldiers expect a general to be brave but not foolhardy; a firm disciplinarian but not unfair; someone who makes certain his men are treated well and with care. Major General John Sedgwick met all these qualifications and became one of the best-loved generals in the Army of the Potomac.[1]

One episode illustrates why Sedgwick's men had such a high regard for him. Wheaton's Brigade, a part of Sedgwick's Sixth Corps, had been detached on duty for several months in western Virginia. They returned to the corps during the winter of 1863 to 1864 only to find all the desirable bivouac areas taken by other troops. The only available spot was a muddy field. Nearby was a dry area under a grove of trees that was occupied by a brigadier general and his staff. When Sedgwick learned of their plight, he rode over to the grove and told the brigadier to pack up and move to another place. Then he invited Wheaton to move his brigade to the campsite.[2]

Born on September 13, 1813, in Cornwall Hollow, Connecticut, John Sedgwick was robust, strong-willed, and a natural leader. He was the son of Benjamin and Olive Sedgwick. His father was a hard-working farmer and an active Congregationalist; his grandfather, a major who served under George Washington at Brandywine and Valley Forge during the Revolutionary War.[3]

Young John attended public schools and spent a semester at Sharon Academy, later teaching in the one-room school in his home town. Just before his twentieth birthday, John entered West Point. In 1837 he graduated, finishing twenty-fourth in a class of fifty, which included future Civil War generals such as Braxton Bragg, Jubal Early, John Pemberton, and Joseph Hooker.[4]

After graduating, Sedgwick was assigned to the artillery, serving in Florida where he saw action in the war against the Seminoles. Later, he saw duty in Georgia as part of the removal of the Cherokees from their homeland, later known as the "Trail of Tears" because of the brutal way the Indians were treated.[5]

In 1846, Sedgwick was assigned to General Zachary Taylor's army on the Texas border. Later, he served in Mexico under General Winfield Scott at Vera Cruz, seeing action in all the battles of the Mexican War, including the final assault on Mexico City. Sedgwick was brevetted captain for "gallant and meritorious conduct in the Battles of Contreras and Churubusco." On September 13, 1847, he was brevetted major for distinguished service in the Battle of Chapultepec. One officer said of him, "Sedgwick, under fire, was the coolest man I ever saw."[6]

In 1855, when the First Cavalry Regiment was organized, Sedgwick was promoted to major. He later participated in the Utah expedition in 1857 to 1858 and in the Indian Wars with the Kiowa and Comanche in 1858 to 1860. During his service in the army before the Civil War, Uncle John gained a reputation as an officer who was fair to his troops. Though slow to make a decision, he was resolute in carrying it out once he did.[7]

When Lincoln was elected in 1860, Sedgwick was engaged in the construction of Fort Wise, Colorado. A lifelong bachelor, now forty-seven years old, he was planning to retire to his childhood home in Cornwall Hollow. The Indian campaigns and the drudgery of constructing forts were so exasperating that he was determined to resign his commission the following spring. The national crisis, however, would upset his plans.[8]

Sedgwick was still hopeful that the sectional difference could be resolved peacefully, writing that "a remedy will be found to forge the links of the Union stronger than ever. All other evils compared with disunion are light." But as the months passed, the hopes for peace were dashed as South Carolina seceded from the Union in December 1860. Other Southern states quickly followed, forming the Confederate States of America.[9]

When the war began, the need for experienced officers was great. As a result Sedgwick was commissioned lieutenant colonel of the Second Cavalry and assigned to Fort Leavenworth, Kansas. Sedgwick said to his cousin, "I had hoped to leave military life, but this cannot be now, for my country needs my service."[10]

Such feelings of responsibility and patriotism were characteristics of John Sedgwick. He was a solid man; his modest and straightforward manner quickly won him support and respect in the Union army. His personal appearance was unpretentious. Sporting a full beard and curly hair, he was short but muscular, weighing over 200 pounds. He frequently wore plain clothes without an insignia of rank and was often mistaken for a common soldier. Confederate J. E. B. Stuart's trademark was a plumed hat; for Uncle John it was a round straw hat. Simple in his habits, he preferred to

Major General John Sedgwick was one of the Army
of the Potomac's most experienced officers. He
was killed by a sniper after stepping into the open
to reassure his men. Just seconds earlier, he had
said to a cowering soldier, "They could not hit an
elephant at that distance."

COURTESY OF THE LIBRARY OF CONGRESS

keep his headquarters in a tent, roughing it with his men, rather than in
the comforts of a house. He rode the same horse, called "Tom," that he had
had for the last ten years. It was easy to see why he was popular with his
men—he was one of them.[11]

During the spring of 1861, Sedgwick was struck with a severe case of
cholera that prevented him from active field duty. During the disastrous
Union defeat at the Battle of Manassas, he was still confined to a sickbed.
After his recovery, Sedgwick was promoted to colonel and ordered to Washington. During the winter of 1861 to 1862, he remained at brigade headquarters while the Army of the Potomac prepared for their spring offensive.

In February 1862, Major General George McClellan relieved Brigadier
General Charles Stone of his command and replaced him with Sedgwick.
To lead Stone's division of 13,000 men, Sedgwick was promoted to brigadier
general. Although a little apprehensive at first, he accepted the responsibility, writing to his sister that "I enter upon the duties with a great deal of

diffidence. It is a large command, occupying an important position, and, I fear, above my capacity; however, I shall do my best."[12]

Sedgwick's first assignment as division commander was to guard the B&O Railroad near Harper's Ferry. When McClellan's spring campaign began, Sedgwick's command was ordered to the peninsula, his division becoming a part of Major General Edwin Sumner's Second Corps. The Second Corps was divided into three divisions, with Sedgwick commanding the First Division. One of his brigades saw action at Eltham's Landing, but it was not until May 31 that his entire division was engaged at the Battle of Fair Oaks. While the Chickahominy River was at flood height, Confederate corps attacked a part of the Union army under Major General Samuel Heintzelman and Brigadier General Erasmus Keys while they were separated from the rest of the main force. Sedgwick and Brigadier General Israel Richardson were able to improvise bridges and cross the river to join them in the battle; it was their assault that sent the enemy reeling and saved the day.[13]

At the beginning of the Battle of Seven Days, Sedgwick was stricken with a prevailing camp fever and should have been in the hospital, but he insisted on remaining with his division. On June 29, still sick, he mounted and rode with his men. At the Battle of Glendale he was wounded twice, though not seriously.[14]

Early in July, McClellan became alarmed over the shortage of supplies and ordered an immediate retreat. When Sedgwick's troops were notified of the withdrawal, they were critical of McClellan's actions. One of his officers, Francis W. Palfrey, noted, "I regard McClellan as a failure. He is not only a disappointment, but his 'tall talk' makes him an aggravating disappointment."[15]

After McClellan's failure on the peninsula, the morale of Sumner's Second Corps and Sedgwick's division sank. In a letter home, Sedgwick wrote, "Our men were without rations and without blankets, and in one of the severest storms. Rumors speak of changes in the cabinet and in the army." Sedgwick, however, was proud of his division's accomplishments, sympathetic for McClellan's situation, and thankful for having survived the ordeal. A new commanding officer was selected to take the fight to Lee— Major General John Pope and the Army of Virginia.[16]

On July 4, Sedgwick was promoted to major general of U.S. Volunteers. This rank was only temporary; when the war was over, the Union volunteers would be mustered out and his commission would expire, while his permanent rank would revert to that of colonel in the regular army.

Sedgwick's division saw very limited action during the Second Battle of Manassas, but on August 30, he received urgent orders to join the main body of General Pope's army, which had been badly defeated and was in danger of annihilation. Their retreat had quickly become a rout. Sedgwick drove his men forward to Centreville, hoping to arrive in time to slow down the Confederate advances. That night it rained, and despite periods of rest, the men were exhausted. One of Sedgwick's men, Alfred Gray Gardner of the First Rhode Island Light Artillery, recorded the moment: "An awful battle yesterday. Prisoners on both sides coming in, first about six hundred of our paroled men, then seven hundred Rebel prisoners, dirty, ragged, and bare-footed . . . thousands of soldiers lying on the ground, so common it's not thought of. . . . Saw about thirty wagons loaded with wounded soldiers; they looked sad enough."[17]

As Pope's stragglers came streaming back toward Washington, Sedgwick deployed his division as a skirmish line and advanced. Believing Sedgwick had a large force in reserve, the Confederates halted their advance to regroup. Sedgwick's strategy had worked, slowing Lee's thrust for several hours and allowing the Union army to make good their escape. Sedgwick's division had performed admirably in his relief of the battered Army of Virginia, but they were unable to reverse the effects of this overwhelming defeat. Pope's campaign was over, and so was his command of the armies in Virginia.[18]

Pope's army and the rest of McClellan's army now crowded together outside Washington. Despite Lincoln's frustration with McClellan's caution, he had no one else to whom he could turn. In September, the president restored McClellan to his position as commander of the Army of the Potomac. Although the move was counter to the wishes of his cabinet, Lincoln insisted that McClellan "had beyond any officer, the confidence of the army." "There is no man in the army who can lick these troops of ours into shape half as well as he. . . . McClellan has the army with him," Lincoln said.[19]

When the news of McClellan's reinstatement reached the Union troops, they were elated; the affect on their morale was electrifying. McClellan struggled to reequip and to reorganize the consolidation of the Army of Virginia and the Army of the Potomac. Although happy that McClellan was back in command, many officers had doubts about his ability to lead them to victory in the future. Sedgwick was disgusted with all the political appointments and the caliber of Union troops, writing: "The enemy has out generalled [sic] us. Their hearts are in their cause; our men are perfectly indifferent. . . . I am in despair of our seeing a termination of the war till some great change is made." It was up to McClellan, Sumner, and Sedgwick to make the change and to restore confidence to the beaten army.[20]

While the Army of the Potomac was regrouping and licking their wounds, Robert E. Lee was planning to carry the war into the North, to draw the war away from Virginia, and to entice Maryland to join the Confederacy. To execute this bold plan, Lee wanted to strike the Union army while morale was still low from their recent defeat at Second Manassas. The stakes were high. The military, political, and diplomatic consequences of the outcome were critical for the survival of the Lincoln administration. The country's future lay in the hands of McClellan and his command.

The next great battle of the Civil War was in Maryland, along the Antietam

Creek near Sharpsburg. Planning to fight a defensive battle, General Lee formed lines east of Sharpsburg, with his back to the Potomac River. McClellan took up a position north and south along Antietam Creek, a tributary of the Potomac River. Thus, the site for the bloodiest one-day battle in American history was established.

The Battle of Antietam was the next major engagement for Sedgwick's troops. Although outnumbering Confederate forces two to one, McClellan responded to events rather than initiating them. When Sedgwick arrived at Sharpsburg, McClellan's battle plan was already in shambles. Major General Ambrose Burnside had not yet launched his diversionary assault on the Confederate right, and McClellan's main attack on the left had degenerated into a series of uncoordinated assaults. His deployment of General Sumner's Second Corps, assigned to support the Federal right, had also resulted in a series of disjointed assaults.[21]

Sumner was ready to cross the Antietam Creek well before daybreak, but he delayed doing so when he was unable to see McClellan's main force. Finally he was ordered to move his two divisions—under John Sedgwick and Brigadier General William French—across the Antietam just east of the Dunker Church. Near the East Woods, Sumner deployed his men. Sedgwick's three brigades were formed into three battle lines in a front about 500 yards wide. Sumner's plan was to smash through the West Woods and turn the Confederate left flank; however, he had no knowledge of the tactical situation. When Brigadier General Alpheus Williams of the Twelfth Corps tried to brief Sumner on the situation, he was in too much of a hurry to stop and listen. Had he taken time, he would have learned that units from the First and Twelfth Corps were available to take part in the assault. Rather, Sumner rushed on, personally leading Sedgwick's division across the cornfield and not waiting for French's division to join them. When French's division arrived twenty minutes later, Sumner and Sedgwick's division were not in sight. Seeing other troops nearby, French veered off southward to the left to join them. Without French's division available to assist in the attack, Sumner's force was reduced to just Sedgwick's division of 5,400 men.[22]

Sumner's impulsiveness led to tragedy. For twenty minutes, Confederate divisions poured fire on Sedgwick's troops from three directions. Union soldiers in Sedgwick's second and third ranks were afraid to shoot for fear of hitting their own men. The Confederate artillery batteries found their range. Shells, grape, and canister tore into the Yankee ranks. As one regimental historian later wrote, "A shot fired at Sedgwick's division would hit it somewhere and hurt somebody. The Division was as easy to hit as the town of Sharpsburg." When Sumner realized his mistake, he shouted, "My God! We must get out of this." Taking off his cap, he waved it as a signal to retreat.[23]

Sedgwick was everywhere during the slaughter, rallying his men. A bullet pierced his leg, but he ignored it. Then another shot hit his wrist; somehow, he was able to hang onto his horse. Almost faint from loss of blood, Sedgwick continued his efforts. When his horse was shot out from under him, he still refused to take the advice of his doctor to go to the rear. When he received a third wound in his shoulder, he was forced to turn the command of his division over to Brigadier General Oliver Howard. Sedgwick was finally carried off the field; it was over an hour after receiving his first wound.[24]

Sedgwick's division was finally able to escape the death trap by retreating to the north, but at a terrible cost. Of the 5,400 men engaged, his division had suffered 2,210 casualties, the highest of any Union division at Antietam. Under the impossible situation that Sedgwick found himself, he had fought as well as he could. Sedgwick's aide, Captain Charles Whittier stated, "Rarely during the war, in my judgment, has an experienced officer so bungled as Sumner did here."[25]

During the evening, Lee took the opportunity to slip away, leaving the battlefield in control of Union forces and providing McClellan with a strategic victory. Controversy, however, surrounds the Battle of Antietam in that there was no Federal attack the following day. Although Lee's invasion had failed and he was forced back to Southern soil, Lincoln expected McClellan to follow up on his victory. Ten days after the battle, McClellan had still not moved his army. On November 7, after visiting him in the field, Lincoln relieved McClellan of his command, replacing him with Major General Burnside.

Although Sedgwick's wounds were painful and disabling, they were not life threatening. "If I am ever hit again, I hope it will settle me at once," Sedgwick said. "I want no more wounds."[26] He returned to his home town of Cornwall Hollow to recuperate. Here the food was good, and the peaceful surroundings worked wonders on his shattered body. His home had burned down while he was away, so he supervised the construction of a new home across the road from where he was born. It had a beautiful view, and he loved to walk across its fields and through the pine woods. If Sedgwick ever thought of leaving the army, the fall of 1862 was the proper time. The public would not have questioned his decision. After almost thirty years of service, severe wounds, and the removal of his friend McClellan from command, he seriously considered retirement. Despite the temptation, however, his overwhelming sense of duty prevailed. On December 22, 1862, he reported to the Army of the Potomac headquarters at Falmouth, Virginia.[27]

It was a depressing time for the Army of the Potomac after another overwhelming defeat in December at Fredericksburg. The Second Corps had suffered tremendous losses and was completely demoralized. Many soldiers were feigning sickness and had lost all confidence in General Burnside. In January, Burnside offered his resignation, but Lincoln refused to accept it. Finally, at Burnside's request, the president relieved him of duty, replacing him with Major General Joseph Hooker.[28]

Hooker immediately began to reorganize the Army of the Potomac. He appointed Sedgwick to replace Major General William Smith as commander of the Sixth Corps, the largest corps in the Union army, containing 23,000 men. During the spring of 1863, Uncle John devoted his time to restoring the confidence of his badly demoralized corps.[29]

As a new corps commander, Sedgwick was received rather coolly when he replaced the popular General Smith. The soldiers soon found him to be warm and down-to-earth, although a strict disciplinarian. One day, while the general was out of uniform, he was approached by a soldier who asked him if he lived near headquarters. When Sedgwick asked why he wanted to know, the soldier replied that he "wanted an order on the commissary for a canteen for some friends who had come to see him." "Well," said Sedgwick, "the commissary is a friend of mine," and he wrote a note on the back of an old letter and handed it to the soldier. When the soldier saw the signature "John Sedgwick" on the bottom, he was speechless. The embarrassed soldier gazed respectfully at his corps commander, then carefully folded the note and put it in his pocket. The commissary never received the note; to the soldier this memento was a priceless piece for his scrapbook. This and other stories soon spread throughout the corps, and skepticism about Sedgwick was replaced by respect and admiration.[30]

Hooker realized his first priority was to improve the morale and health of his army. He saw to it that the medical department and food services were improved. He hoped that fresh vegetables and an occasional change of diet would help enhance the health and efficiency of the army. Sedgwick instituted Hooker's reforms with enthusiasm; his mess soon became well known throughout the Army of the Potomac. Hooker worked out a system of granting leaves to help reduce desertions. Realizing that idle hands often lead to poor morale, Hooker and Sedgwick kept their troops busy with drill and inspections. To develop corps pride, Hooker designed distinctive badges for each corps. Sedgwick's men wore the Greek cross with pride for the rest of the war. Although still experiencing some pain from his wound, Sedgwick worked hard to set an example for his men. Hooker and Sedgwick slowly built army pride and helped bring fresh vigor to their men. One reporter wrote, "The name of McClellan has vanished from the minds of the soldiers." The Army of the Potomac was now as much Hooker's as it once had been McClellan's.[31]

Sedgwick's popularity with his men continued to grow. Few would dispute that he was the most deeply loved of all the commanding officers in the Army of the Potomac. One staff officer said that he was a "pure and great-hearted man, . . . a brave and skillful soldier. From the commander to the lowest private, he had no enemy in the army." Another officer claimed, "His whole manner breathed of gentleness and sweetness, and in his broad breast was a boy's heart."[32]

There were some doubts, however, about Sedgwick's ability to command a corps. Although he assigned him to command the largest corps in the army, Hooker did not believe he was able to carry out important commands in battle. Despite Hooker's less than glowing opinion of Sedgwick's leadership ability, he nevertheless placed him in a semi-independent command at Chancellorsville in May 1863.

Sedgwick with his Sixth Corps, Major General John Reynolds's First Corps, Major General Daniel Sickles's Third Corps, and Brigadier General John Gibbon's division of the Second Corps were directed to cross the Rappahannock below Fredericksburg and make a strong demonstration, hoping to convince Lee that this incursion was Hooker's main thrust. In the meantime, the main body of Hooker's army would cross the Rapidan and assemble at Chancellorsville. In this way, Hooker hoped to pin Lee down between both parts of his army. If Lee remained at Fredericksburg, Sedgwick was to attack; if Lee moved, Sedgwick would pursue him.[33]

Hooker's plan seemed to have great merit; he already had a numerical superiority with about 130,000 troops to Lee's 60,000. The only flaw in the plan was the impractical assignment given to Sedgwick's corps. Major General Darius Couch believed that the assignment was excessively difficult and that Sedgwick would never be able to carry it out. "I pitied him from the bottom of my heart," he said.[34]

On April 30, Hooker moved the main part of the army eastward toward Fredericksburg. When he learned that Lee planned to attack him, he pulled back to his original position in the Wilderness and ordered Reynolds's and Sickles's corps to join him at Chancellorsville, leaving Sedgwick with only his Sixth Corps and Gibbon's division. When Hooker faltered, Lee took the opportunity to attack. On May 2, "Stonewall" Jackson, with 32,000 Confederate troops, completely surprised Howard's Eleventh Corps and routed them. Hooker ordered Sedgwick to relieve the pressure on the main body of the army by attacking the Confederate lines at Marye's Heights—the same spot where the Union army had failed during the Battle of Fredericksburg. After Sedgwick captured the heights against thin opposition, he turned his troops toward Chancellorsville to join Hooker.[35]

General Lee dispatched Major General Lafayette McLaws's division to intercept Sedgwick. McLaws marched to the Salem Church, about four miles west of Fredericksburg and formed a line on the edge of a wooded area. There they were joined by five regiments of Alabama infantry, increasing McLaws's forces to 10,000. Sedgwick was slow in getting his force in place before launching his attack, which limited his assault to only one division—4,000 of the 19,000 men under his command. It was only after two of his fresh divisions arrived that he was able to stabilize his shattered line. Lee, now confident that Hooker was not going to attack, ordered Major General Richard Anderson's division to reinforce McLaws.[36]

Lee hoped to destroy Sedgwick's forces, but Anderson's division became entangled in the thick underbrush, and Sedgwick was able to safely withdraw across the Rappahannock. In the days that followed, Hooker tried to shift responsibility for the disaster at Chancellorsville on others and to present his debacle in the best possible light. The cavalry and General Sedgwick received the largest share of the blame. Major General Daniel Butterfield, Hooker's chief-of-staff, informed the president that "the cavalry have failed in executing their orders. General Sedgwick failed in executing his orders." Lincoln was distressed to learn that the Army of the Potomac had been defeated again: "My God! My God! What will the country say?"[37]

On May 7, President Lincoln and Major General Henry Halleck arrived at Falmouth to discuss matters with Hooker and his officers. Speculation in the Northern press was that Hooker would be replaced and that McClellan might be coming back. Shortly after Lincoln's visit, Sedgwick and other officers indicated that they had lost confidence in Hooker's ability to lead the army and sent word to Major General George Meade that they would be willing to serve under him. Meade, however, was not seeking the position and was reluctant to undermine Hooker.[38]

Unlike many generals in the Army of the Potomac, Sedgwick never campaigned for promotion. Many thought he could have succeeded Burnside as the commander of the Army of the Potomac had he attempted to cultivate friends in Washington, but this was not his nature. John Sedgwick disliked needless conflict and political squabbling, a consequence of commanding the Army of the Potomac. In all his letters home, he wrote of his desire to retire in the quiet Connecticut River Valley. He was not daring; rather, he was careful, cautious, and conservative, but he was a hard fighter whose men would do anything for him.[39] After Hooker's defeat at Chancellorsville, Sedgwick was approached about leading the army, but he deferred, saying, "Meade is the proper one to command this army."[40]

In June 1863, Lee's Army of Northern Virginia was at full strength, numbering 75,000 men. Needing supplies, he decided to seek them where they were more abundant, and on June 3, his army began moving up the Rappahannock. By mid-June, it was clear that Lee was planning a full-scale invasion of the North. On June 15, the Sixth Corps started their march to intercept the Army of Northern Virginia.[41]

On June 28, General Meade replaced Hooker as commander of the Army of the Potomac. Many in the Union army were surprised by Hooker's sudden dismissal. Sedgwick's personal relations with Meade were smoother than with Hooker, but with the impending battle, he worried about the new commander's ability to coordinate troop movements and strategy before engaging Lee.[42]

In the three days before the Battle of Gettysburg, Meade advanced the army on a broad front to prevent Lee from slipping around him and threatening Washington. At the same time, he decided to concentrate his army around Gettysburg. Meade sent a dispatch to Sedgwick to hurry his men to

Gettysburg, and hurry he did. They were at least a day's march away, to the southeast of Manchester, Maryland, when he received the order to move to Gettysburg. The march began at 9:30 p.m. and continued all through the night. The corps plodded on without stopping for breakfast or lunch, reaching the battlefield at 4:00 p.m. the next day. They had covered the distance in eighteen-and-a-half hours. As a result, the corps adopted the name "Sedgwick's Foot Cavalry."[43]

At Gettysburg, the Sixth Corps was held in reserve, although several brigades were used chiefly in support roles. After the battle, Sedgwick's corps was ordered to follow the Confederates, fighting several rear-guard actions with Confederate Major General Jubal Early's division.[44]

To ensure an orderly withdrawal, Lee put up a stiff resistance, ordering his rear guard to attack when possible. Time was running out for General Meade if he hoped to destroy Lee's army before they could return to Virginia. At Williamsport, Lee had his engineers construct a strong defensive position and was able to obtain supplies from Virginia. Lee was prepared if Meade should attack.[45]

During Meade's pursuit of Lee, he met regularly with his corps commanders to discuss strategy. On July 12, he asked his seven generals to vote on attacking Lee's entrenched position, saying he would abide by their decision. The vote was five to two not to make a direct assault against Lee's position. Sedgwick voted against the attack, remembering his experience at Fredericksburg and the inadvisability of sending troops across exposed ground to attack a fortified position. When Meade failed to attack, Lee crossed the Potomac during the night to the safety of Virginia.[46]

When the news of Lee's escape into Virginia reached the North, there was a feeling of frustration—Meade's victory at Gettysburg was not sufficient. Lincoln expressed his disappointment at the actions of the Army of the Potomac: "Our Army held the war in the hollow of their hand and they would not close it." Brigadier General James Wadsworth, commanding general of the First Corps who had voted for attacking Lee at Williamsport, expressed his views at the White House on July 16, 1863. When asked how Lee escaped, Wadsworth replied, "Because nobody stopped him."[47]

Sedgwick came to Meade's defense. In a letter on July 26, Sedgwick stated that the Army of the Potomac, with reinforcements, could have routed Lee's army but that the people of Pennsylvania did not offer their full support. "Not ten thousand men turned out and then [those that did] refused to follow [Lee] into Maryland," Sedgwick said. The Gettysburg campaign was over, and General Meade summed up his feelings: "I start tomorrow to run another race with Lee."[48]

In November, Sedgwick was placed in command of the right wing of the Army of the Potomac, comprising the Fifth and Sixth Corps. When Meade left for Washington to consult with the president, Sedgwick became the temporary commander of the army, a position that proved to be more than he could handle. In Meade's absence, Sedgwick did not demand the tough discipline that his predecessor had, and some of the officers and troops took liberties, including desertion and malingering. This short period of army command helped Sedgwick decide that the most responsibility he wanted was that of a corps commander.[49]

With the suspension of most military operations during the winter, many of the high-ranking officers became unwillingly involved in politics. Since George McClellan had left his command of the Army of the Potomac, he had become actively involved with the Democratic Party and quickly became an anathema to the Republican Party. During the winter, some of McClellan's army friends made plans for a "McClellan testimonial." To Sedgwick, who was a Democrat and an admirer of McClellan, it was purely a private affair and nothing more. When a circular was developed with subscription rates for each rank, Sedgwick pledged $20,000 for himself and his corps.[50]

When the radical Republicans got word of the plan to honor McClellan, they immediately took steps to put a stop to it. A circular was sent to the Army of the Potomac stating that the proposed testimonial violated army regulations and ordering its supporters to proceed no further. General Meade was persuaded to put an end to the testimonial, which he did. Secretary of War Edwin Stanton drew up an order summarily dismissing Generals Sedgwick, Sykes, and Hunt from the army for their part in the testimonial. Although calmer heads prevailed and Sedgwick was not dismissed, he knew that there would be no opportunity for further promotion and that he might be dismissed at any time.[51]

On January 9, 1864, Meade went on furlough, and he again placed Sedgwick in charge of the army. Sedgwick realized there was more to running an army than fighting battles. The constant bickering between military and civilian authorities, maintaining troop morale, and problems related to feeding and quartering the army were frustrating to him. In a letter to his sister, he wrote, "We hear there is to be a reorganization in the army. . . . I shall not be sorry to hear that I am one of them. . . . I could even leave altogether without many regrets."[52]

Before the reorganization, Sedgwick's Sixth Corps was called on to support Brigadier General Judson Kilpatrick's raid on Richmond. The plan called for Sedgwick's corps to create a diversion, while Kilpatrick made his raid. Although Sedgwick's feint was successful, Kilpatrick's raid failed and resulted in the loss of lives with no material gain.[53]

In the spring of 1864, Ulysses S. Grant was promoted to the rank of lieutenant general and named general-in-chief. Sedgwick, who had known Grant during the Mexican War, went to see his old friend. After talking with Grant, Sedgwick came away from the meeting a bit disappointed, both with Grant's appearance and his method of expressing himself. The same feelings seemed to exist among the men of the Sixth Corps. Colonel Selden

Connor wrote: "There is no enthusiasm for General Grant; and on the other hand, there is no prejudice against him."[54]

Shortly after Grant's assumption as overall commander, Secretary of War Stanton removed Sedgwick from command of the Sixth Corps; his rationale was political. Sedgwick's allegiance to the Democratic Party, his friendship with General McClellan, and the presence of McClellan's brother, Major Arthur McClellan, on Sedgwick's staff, contributed to Stanton's decision. His solution to the situation was to remove Sedgwick from his command.[55]

When Meade heard of this removal, he protested vigorously, insisting that he did not know what Sedgwick's political position was and did not care. He said he was sure of Sedgwick's loyalty and efficiency and insisted that he was more important to his army than any other of his officers. Stanton's position remained unchanged, but he did promise to assign Sedgwick to an independent command in the Shenandoah Valley. Meade and Stanton parted with the understanding that orders would be issued the next day. Lincoln, however, intervened, ordering Major General Franz Sigel to the valley and seeing to it that Sedgwick remained as commander of the Sixth Corps.[56] When the Army of the Potomac was reorganized again, Sedgwick's Sixth Corps was increased to 25,000 men.

The months of March and April 1864 were unusually wet and stormy, and the rate of illness among the troops increased. Concerned about the welfare of his men, Uncle John Sedgwick insisted that the corps surgeons establish field hospitals for the divisions near the encampment of the troops.[57]

In the spring of 1864, Grant planned a major, coordinated assault on General Lee's army. Unlike prior Union strategy, Grant hoped to destroy Lee's army in the field. To accomplish this task, he would do something all previous Union commanders had been unable to do: Despite logistical and topographical problems, Grant advanced across the Rapidan River with a force almost double that of Lee's.

The campaign of 1864 began in the Wilderness of Virginia, with the Sixth Corps holding the right flank of the Union army. In the early stages of fighting, the corps suffered heavy casualties when Confederate General Jubal Early attacked the right flank. When the action finally ended on May 5, both sides had suffered heavy losses.[58]

Brigadier General Alexander Webb described the action in a letter home to his family: "I have lost most of my brigade, have had a fearful battle. . . . Lee is very strong. God alone saved me. . . . I had a terrible defeat."[59]

The Battle of the Wilderness proved costly to both armies. The Union army suffered nearly 18,000 casualties. The losses to the Sixth Corps alone were 5,035, of which 719 were killed. Although Lee's casualties were half those of Grant's, he could ill afford to lose men at that rate; a war of attrition definitely favored Grant. In the past, after such heavy losses, Union commanders would retire to regroup, allowing Lee to slip away, but not

Grant. Despite his ordeal in the Wilderness, Grant moved forward, pressing the enemy.[60]

Disregarding his personal safety, Sedgwick had thrown his full energy into the campaign, his men responding to his leadership with renewed enthusiasm. In times of danger, his men often said, "It must be all right. Uncle John is there."[61]

On May 7, the army moved to Spotsylvania Court House. On the 8th, Sedgwick's corps, along with the Fifth Corps, attacked the Confederates but were repulsed. On May 9, when there was light fighting, Grant took the opportunity to visit Sedgwick. Sedgwick's efforts had not gone unnoticed. Grant complimented him on his recent service and mentioned all the hardships Sedgwick had encountered. It would be the last time Grant would ever see Sedgwick alive.[62]

Later in the day, a Confederate sniper dealt the Army of the Potomac a costly blow. While overseeing the placement of artillery in his corps' forward line, Sedgwick and his men were under constant rifle fire. Attempting to reassure his men who were unnerved by the Confederate sharpshooters, he jokingly said, "They couldn't hit an elephant at this distance." Just then a bullet struck Sedgwick's face below the left eye, and he fell to the ground. Members of his staff rushed to his aid, but there was nothing they could do for him. Captain Richard Halstead felt vainly for a pulse, but to no avail. Uncle John was dead.[63]

When General Grant learned of the tragedy, he declared the loss as costly as that of a whole division. "Never had such a gloom rested upon the army on the account of the death of one man as came over it when the heavy tidings passed along the lines that General Sedgwick was killed," wrote George Stevens of the Sixth Corps.[64]

Secretary of War Stanton issued an official dispatch announcing the sad news to the nation. In Sedgwick's home state of Connecticut, the *Hartford Courant* commented, "His loss at this juncture is a sad national calamity." Sedgwick's loss was felt even by his friends in the Confederate army. Colonel Charles Venable of Lee's staff wrote, "He was much liked and respected by his old West Point comrades in the Confederate army, and his death was a real sorrow to them."[65]

John Sedgwick was buried in his beloved Cornwall Hollow. In 1868, a bronze statue of him was cast from a cannon captured by the Sixth Corps and unveiled at West Point. Tradition has it that a cadet in danger of failing his academic coursework will pass his examinations if he sneaks out of the barracks after taps and spins the rowels of Sedgwick's spurs. Sedgwick would have found this story amusing; as a cadet, it is something he would have done himself.[66]

17 *Joseph Hooker*

"Fighting Joe"

Early in 1863, a weary and disheartened President Lincoln sat in his White House study. His attempt to unite the country by military force, which had at one time seemed so certain to succeed, now seemed close to failure. The Confederates had been victorious, almost invincible, during the last two months of fighting. In the East, the Army of the Potomac was still demoralized from their disaster at Fredericksburg, which had followed a series of other Union defeats. In the West, the war was not progressing much better. Desertions were decreasing the effectiveness of the armies, and the ranks could not be filled because the flow of volunteers had all but ceased. Support on the home front was crumbling as a result of the reverses in the field and the unanticipated length of the war.[1]

Abraham Lincoln realized he had to appoint a new commander for the Army of the Potomac. No other Federal army was more important to the preservation of the Union, yet none was as badly in need of reorganization and a strong leader. The man the president selected was a friend of his, Major General Joseph Hooker. Hooker was unquestionably a fighter, having earned the title "Fighting Joe," and was as popular with the troops as any general available. But Lincoln also realized that Hooker possessed some troubling weaknesses he could not overlook.[2]

Still fresh in Lincoln's mind was the way Hooker had denigrated his commanding officer, Major General Ambrose Burnside, after the Union defeat at Fredericksburg. Hooker went so far as to appear before the Joint Congressional Committee on the Conduct of the War to denounce Burnside's competence in leading the army. An already demoralized Union now faced infighting and distrust among its officers. Lincoln had to act quickly, lest he lose the entire army.

Before turning over the command of the Army of the Potomac to Hooker, Lincoln wanted to make certain Hooker knew how he felt about this issue. In a letter, Lincoln first praised Hooker for being "a brave and skillful soldier," but added, "I must fear that the spirit which you have aided to infuse into the Army, of criticizing their Commander, and withholding confidence from him, will now turn upon you. . . . Neither you, nor Napoleon, if he were alive again, could get any good out of an army while such a spirit prevails in it." Lincoln ended his letter with both advice and encouragement: "And now, beware of rashness, but with energy, and sleepless vigilance, go forward, and give us victories."[3]

The man who was to take over the command of the Army of the Potomac was born on November 13, 1814, the fourth child of Mary and Joseph Hooker. The Hookers lived in a comfortable home on the main street of Hadley, Massachusetts. For 125 years, the Hookers had played a major role in the expansion and development of the state. The infant was christened Joseph, the fifth in a line of farmers, prominent landowners, town officials, and soldiers to bear that name.[4]

During the war of 1812, the Hooker family suffered financial loss, forcing Hooker's father to take a job as a cattle purchaser. Joseph was depressed by the change in his fortune, and it was only Mary's perseverance that held the family together. Her three daughters and Joseph Jr. worked at odd jobs to earn additional money for the family. Mary was determined that her children receive a good education. Despite their financial difficulties, the Hooker children attended the Hopkins Academy in Hadley.[5]

Joseph's mother hoped her son would prepare for the ministry, but young Joseph was more interested in studying law. When it came time for college, it looked as though he would not be able to attend because of financial circumstances. Although Joseph was not able to go to the school of his choice, one of his teachers was able to acquire an appointment to West Point for him. In June 1833, at the age of eighteen, Joseph left home for West Point. It was a sad parting for both mother and son, for their relationship was very close.[6]

The rigid life of the Academy agreed with young Hooker. He applied himself with zeal and industry. Although he was quick to learn, he was often critical of the ideas and facts presented to him. This assertiveness was not limited to the classroom but manifested itself in his daily associations with other cadets. In discussions with those from the South, Joseph had no hesitation in expressing his antislavery position, causing friction among the cadets.[7]

Hooker ranked well above the average for his class in final grades but accumulated a large number of demerits. He was independent, outspoken, and quick to take offense, traits undoubtedly responsible for many of his demerits. As a result, he ranked twenty-ninth out of a class of fifty upon graduation.[8]

During the Peninsula Campaign, someone at a
New York newspaper titled a story "Fighting—Joe
Hooker." The title, when it was published, was
erroneously printed without the dash, so the heading appeared as "Fighting Joe Hooker." The
name stuck from then on.

COURTESY OF THE LIBRARY OF CONGRESS

The class of 1837 would distinguish itself during the Civil War. Among
the graduates were John Sedgwick, Braxton Bragg, Jubal Early, John Pemberton, and William Walker. Among the underclassmen with whom Hooker
would have contact during the war were Henry Halleck, William T. Sherman,
and George Thomas.[9]

Upon graduation, Hooker was commissioned a second lieutenant in the
First Artillery and sent to Florida to fight the Seminole Indians. Skirmishes

were frequent, but it was difficult to engage the Seminoles in an all-out battle. The Indians were elusive and adept at disappearing into the swamps. Finally, in April of 1838, active operations ended when Chief Osceola was captured and the Indians temporarily subdued.[10]

In 1841, now a first lieutenant, Hooker was appointed adjutant at West Point. By outward appearances, Hooker seemed well suited to command. He was described by a fellow officer as a "handsome fellow, polished in manner, the perfection of grace in every movement, . . . the courtesy of manner we attribute to old-time gentlemen. . . . He was simply elegant, and certainly one of the handsomest men the army ever produced." But there was more to Hooker than his good looks. As Lincoln noted, he was ambitious and at times reckless and brash; he was also immodest and had a reputation for hard drinking and high living.[11]

On May 13, 1846, the United States declared war on Mexico. War was welcomed in some parts of the country, but many Northerners feared the war would result in an expansion of slavery. Although Hooker's home state of Massachusetts was opposed to the conflict, Hooker looked upon the war as a great opportunity. For him and others in the fraternity of West Point, it would be a proving ground for them and a chance for promotion.[12]

During the Mexican War, Hooker distinguished himself. His bravery while serving under Zachary Taylor at Monterrey was recognized. In Taylor's report to the secretary of war he stated, "I am under particular obligation to the chief of my staff, Lieutenant J. Hooker. . . . By his soldierly conduct and fine military acquirements, [he] had been invaluable to me through the whole campaign; and his coolness and self-possession in battle set an example to both officers and men that exerted a most happy influence." Recognition of Hooker's courage also came in the form of a promotion to the rank of brevet captain.[13]

After action at Monterrey, Hooker was transferred to Brigadier General Gideon Pillow's division as adjutant and professional adviser to the politically appointed general. Pillow's division was at the storm center of the battle at the Mexican fortified heights of Chapultepec, where the general was wounded. Assuming command, Hooker led a regiment in an attack against the enemy's flank. Finding the approach too steep, he returned in time to see the other regiments break the Mexican line and reach their objective at the top of the heights. In the meantime, Thomas Jackson was able to silence the Mexican artillery and drive off an enemy charge with his cannon. That evening, General Scott's troops stormed the city, and in a short time the American flag flew over the capital.[14]

By the war's end, Hooker had won all the glory he could have hoped for, earning his third brevet of the war, that of lieutenant colonel. General Scott mentioned his role in the capture of Mexico City, and Pillow testified that he had "distinguished himself by his extraordinary activity, energy, and gallantry."[15]

During a court of inquiry in March 1848 involving Winfield Scott and Gideon Pillow, Hooker testified for Pillow. From a professional standpoint, as he would learn later, it was a serious mistake. Hooker earned the enmity of a commanding general who would have a long career and commensurate memory.[16]

Hooker returned from the Mexican War with a proud record. With three battlefield promotions, Hooker requested and received duty on the West coast, assigned as adjutant general for the Pacific Division. After the excitement of the war in Mexico, Hooker found service in the West disappointing. Boring peacetime army life and its modest pay scale were major causes of dissatisfaction. The discrepancy between the pay of officers and soldiers of the army and civilians was disconcerting. A common soldier might make $14 per month, whereas a common laborer could earn $16 per day. Hooker's salary fell far short of the wages received by a domestic servant.[17]

In 1851, faced with gambling debts, Hooker took leave from the army. He is reputed to have borrowed money from fellow officers Henry Halleck and William T. Sherman and to have never repaid them; like his mistake in testifying during the Scott–Pillow dispute, this miscalculation would come back to haunt him.[18]

Hooker established a reputation for fast living. He was a regular at a local tavern where the clientele included famous outlaws and politicians. Still unmarried, Hooker "became famous for his 'glad eye' for ladies of easy virtue," which led to the story that prostitutes took their nickname from him.[19]

When his leave was up, Hooker resigned his commission, leaving the army and accepting an appointment as colonel of California state volunteers. As war approached in 1861, he organized a regiment of volunteers, hoping they could join the ranks of the Union army. When he learned that his regiment would not be sent East, he was determined to go on his own. Hooker wrote to General-in-Chief Winfield Scott and offered his services. When Hooker received no answer, he decided to go to Washington and plead his case in person.[20]

Using his political connections, Hooker was able to bring his credentials to the attention of President Lincoln, who passed them along to General Scott. Scott had neither forgotten nor forgiven Hooker's testimony ten years earlier, and he pigeonholed his request for a command assignment. After the Union's defeat at the First Battle of Manassas, Hooker went personally to see the president. With his characteristic self-assurance, Hooker informed Lincoln: "I was at the Battle of Bull Run the other day, and it was neither vanity nor boasting in me to declare that I am a damned sight better general than you, sir, had on that field." Hooker selected an excellent time to present his case to the president. Lincoln was still despondent over the defeat of McDowell's army and was willing to listen to Hooker.[21]

Lincoln was impressed by Hooker's forthrightness and self-confidence. After their conversation, Lincoln rose, placed his hand on Hooker's shoulder and said, "Colonel—not Lieutenant Colonel—Hooker, stay. I have use for you and a regiment for you to command." Later Lincoln would comment on the meeting: "His eyes were steady and clear—his manner not half so confident as his words, and altogether he had the air of a man of sense and intelligence, who thoroughly believed in himself and who would at least try to make his words good."[22]

At last Hooker was able to rejoin the army, but he thought he deserved more than the command of a regiment. With the help of political friends, he was promoted to the rank of brigadier general and given command of a brigade. On August 3, 1861, Hooker became the thirty-second ranking general in the Union army.

While Hooker's brigade was camped outside of Washington, he imposed strict discipline on his troops and drilled them rigorously. At the same time, he cared for the needs of his troops, making certain they were well supplied with rations and clothes.[23]

Within two months, Hooker was given a division to command and ordered to southern Maryland to clear the lower Potomac of Confederate spies and supplies. During the winter of 1861 to 1862, Hooker proposed numerous raids against the Confederates across the river, but Major General George McClellan restricted his activities to routine picket duty. With the monotony of the winter months, Hooker took to drinking hard liquor. His men noticed his drinking and soon were singing a ditty: "Joe Hooker's our leader, he takes his whiskey strong."[24]

As 1862 began, McClellan prepared to attack the Confederate army in Virginia, moving the Army of the Potomac down the Chesapeake and landing on the peninsula near Yorktown. Hooker's division arrived on the peninsula in April and began to entrench in preparation for the siege of Yorktown. Because the task of digging trenches at night was so grueling, Hooker ordered a special ration of whiskey for the men. In the course of delivering the liquor to the troops, it had to pass through the officers first. They filled their own canteens and diluted the remainder with water. When one of the disgusted privates brought a sample of the diluted whiskey to Hooker, the general took a swig and immediately spit it out. He promised the men this would not happen again, making certain that his promise was carried out by issuing liquor from his own headquarters.[25]

Early in May, Confederate General Joseph E. Johnston withdrew his troops from Yorktown, retreating toward Richmond. Quickly, without support and without considering the consequences, Hooker attacked the Confederate rear guard commanded by Major General James Longstreet. As a result, his Second Division was badly mauled. During the engagement, Hooker rode his horse among the men, personally directing the placement of his artillery. His horse reared when the first cannon fired, throwing him to the ground and falling on top of him. Hooker crawled out from under his horse, ordered more troops forward, and continued to inspire his men until reinforcements arrived. Hooker complained of a lack of support, claiming he had been forced to carry on the fight for most of the day while 30,000 nearby troops were not used.[26]

As a result of his aggressive action, Hooker became a favorite of the press. Someone at a New York newspaper, writing about the Peninsula Campaign, titled the story "Fighting—Joe Hooker." The title, when it was published, was erroneously printed without the dash, so the headline appeared as "Fighting Joe Hooker." The nickname stuck, and he became known as "Fighting Joe." Hooker himself did not like the nickname. It caused him "incalculable injury," he said, by having people think he was "a hot-headed, furious young fellow, accustomed to making furious and needless dashes at the enemy."[27]

At Seven Pines, Hooker ordered a reluctant colleague whose troops had stalled to "get out of his way. I have two regiments here that can go anywhere." Later, near Richmond, Hooker confidently told McClellan, "I can hold my position against 100,000 men." Soon the *New York Times* assigned a reporter to follow Hooker because of his reputation for being at the location of the heaviest fighting.[28]

When McClellan reported the action at Seven Pines, he failed to mention Hooker's contribution, thereby incurring his hostility. Later, when the Committee on the Conduct of the War investigated McClellan's action during the Peninsula Campaign, Hooker did not hesitate to elaborate on his own performance and denigrate that of his superior. He went so far as to say that "if I had commanded, Richmond would have been ours."[29]

Hooker was ambitious, hoping soon to be promoted to major general. As a division commander, he had performed well during the Peninsula Campaign. When McClellan told him he was being recommended for promotion and command of a corps, Hooker temporarily softened his criticism of his commander. Now he turned his criticism to McClellan's corps commanders. In a letter to Senator James Nesmith, Hooker declared that the army was suffering because of the incompetence of McClellan's corps commanders: "If these officers are still to be imposed upon him [McClellan], God help him and his army. . . . I will sooner dig potatoes or cut down trees than belong to any army in which these officers exercise commands." He continued pressing the point of his qualification for corps command: "If I cannot be placed upon the same footing of other officers of the Army, the sooner I quit it the better. I will not fight their battles for them with the doors of promotion closed to me." Similar letters were sent to other senators. In July, Hooker was promoted to the rank of major general of volunteers.[30]

Convinced he was outnumbered, when in fact he outnumbered the Confederates, McClellan continued to request more troops as Lee initiated a series of attacks in what became known as the Battle of Seven Days. Although the Army of the Potomac acquitted itself well, McClellan seemed beaten and withdrew to Harrison's Landing, Virginia. Later in the summer, over McClellan's protestation, Lincoln ordered him to return his army to Washington.[31]

Lee was elated when he learned that McClellan was preparing to withdraw from the peninsula. He had been struggling with the problem of how to protect Richmond and still release enough men to engage a new Federal army under Major General John Pope. Now, McClellan's departure simplified the problem for him.[32]

Hooker left the peninsula with the recognition he coveted. He had established himself as a fighting officer, capable of handling at least one division in battle. Although Hooker's immediate superior, Major General Samuel Heintzelman, spoke highly of his ability, McClellan still believed he was too rash for his own good. One of McClellan's staff officers later stated: "Let Hooker go where he will, he invariably meets the enemy, and always in superior force."[33]

Returning to northern Virginia, Hooker joined John Pope's Army of Virginia in the Second Battle of Manassas. Although his division did not distinguish itself, Hooker conducted himself with the usual self-confidence. Following the battle, Lincoln and several cabinet members discussed replacing Pope with Hooker. Lincoln, however, had concerns about Hooker in that position, stating: "I think as much as you or any other man of Hooker, but—I fear he gets excited." The recommendation was quashed when Postmaster General Montgomery Blair suggested that Hooker had a drinking problem: "He is too great a friend of John Barleycorn." In the end it was McClellan who was selected to command the combined Army of the Potomac and the Army of Virginia. He was directed immediately to organize a movable army to meet the enemy in the field. On September 5, 1862, Hooker was assigned to command the Fifth Corps, replacing Fitz-John Porter.[34]

In early September, Robert E. Lee crossed the Potomac to invade the North. Hooker's troops marched westward to meet the invaders. After aggressively engaging Major General D. H. Hill at Turner's Gap, Hooker's corps advanced to the vicinity of Sharpsburg, a Maryland village near Antietam Creek. Here Hooker prepared his men to attack Lee's left flank. In the early morning of September 17, Hooker's divisions encountered stiff resistance from Brigadier General John Bell Hood's division but were able to drive the Confederates back. When Hood was reinforced, the Rebels counterattacked. During the attack, Hooker was struck in the foot by a rifle ball, incapacitating him for further action in the battle.[35]

Hooker's service was once again outstanding. General McClellan sent him a friendly letter expressing his regrets about the wound and adding, "Had you not been wounded when you were, I believe the result of the battle would have been the entire destruction of the Rebel's army." McClellan also recommended Hooker's promotion to brigadier general in the regular army. In the press, Hooker continued to receive praise as "fearless and indomitable and sagacious and prompt in his movements."[36]

During his convalescence, Hooker was visited by President Lincoln and other important officials. Hooker took the opportunity to talk freely, mostly to denigrate McClellan as being too timid and hesitant to lead the Army of the Potomac and to praise his own efforts. In a discussion about the Battle of Antietam, Hooker said that, had he been able to remain on the field three more hours, the Union victory would have been complete, "for I had already gained enough and seen enough to make the rout of the enemy sure."[37]

In early November, Lincoln selected Major General Ambrose Burnside to succeed McClellan. Burnside reorganized the army into three grand divisions, appointing Hooker to command the largest of these divisions containing 40,000 men.[38]

Hooker returned to active duty in time for the Battle of Fredericksburg. He vehemently opposed Burnside's strategy of frontal attack on a well dug-in Confederate army. At the outset of the battle, Hooker's division was held in reserve. When Burnside ordered his troops forward, he did so haphazardly. The outcome, as Hooker anticipated, was disastrous. The result of the assaults was the butchery of Burnside's army, with dozens of Union regiments torn to pieces as they struggled to cross open fields toward the heights where the Confederate army was waiting. "We might as well have tried to take hell," one Union soldier said. Confederate Major General James Longstreet described the assaults as "desperate and bloody, but utterly hopeless."[39]

Having sacrificed more than 12,000 men and gaining nothing, Burnside withdrew his battered army back across the Rappahannock. Appalled by the senseless killing, Hooker appeared before the Congressional Committee on the Conduct of the War denouncing Burnside's generalship in the debacle. Burnside was angered and exasperated by Hooker's insubordinate criticism and his obvious efforts to replace him. He asked the president to choose between Hooker and himself, offering his resignation if he chose Hooker. Although Lincoln did not accept Burnside's resignation, he did relieve him of command of the Army of the Potomac.[40]

The choice for Burnside's replacement fell between Hooker and Major General George Meade. Lincoln decided on "Fighting Joe," who to many in the army was a dubious choice. Although an aggressive and reliable leader, he was also known to be ambitious and abrasive—and known for praising himself to the press. He also had a reputation for being a heavy drinker and for making unguarded remarks. Lincoln was aware of all these deficiencies in his personality, but he wanted a general who would fight; he believed Hooker was such a general.[41]

On January 26, 1863, Hooker assumed command of the Army of the

Potomac. Surprisingly, Hooker quickly proved himself a capable administrator. He insisted on new sanitary rules, including the proper use of latrines. He reduced desertions by providing a liberal furlough policy. He greatly improved hospital services and the quality of food provided for the troops, including fresh vegetables at least twice a week. Hooker raised the morale of the army by ordering extensive drilling with frequent parades, which he personally reviewed. Within weeks after Hooker assumed command, a Wisconsin officer wrote home that "the army is in excellent condition as far as health and spirit of the men are concerned."[42]

Hooker also reorganized and galvanized the command. He dismantled Burnside's huge Grand Divisions by dividing them into seven easier-to-command corps. To distinguish one corps from another, he devised a system of badges for the men to wear on their hats. Shapes and colors were used to distinguish the corps and divisions from each other. The badges did wonders for morale, the men wearing them "like badges of honor."[43]

In April, Lincoln visited the army in the field. He was impressed by the improvement in morale but was apprehensive about Hooker's overconfidence. Hooker told Lincoln he had the "finest army on the planet," boasting that it was not a question of whether he would take Richmond but only when.[44]

Hooker began his offensive on April 27. He detached a third of his army, three infantry corps, and sent them on a wide flanking movement to meet up with Major General Darius Couch's Second Corps. Together, there would be more than 70,000 men poised to attack Lee's exposed left flank. To conceal this movement and confuse the enemy, Hooker ordered Major General John Sedgwick and his Sixth Corps to attack Stonewall Jackson's troops on the Confederate right. At the same time, Major General Daniel Sickles's Third Corps and a Second Corps division would remain in their position across the Rappahannock River, ready to move if necessary.[45]

At first, Lee was slow to see the danger, but soon it was clear to him what Hooker was planning to do. When he saw Generals Sedgwick and Reynolds crossing the Rappahannock, he sent Major General Jubal Early to engage them. Hooker's behavior during the early phase of the Chancellorsville campaign allowed Lee to gain the upper hand. For some reason, Hooker lost his self-confidence and aggressiveness. He faltered, whether due to his inability to assume the awesome responsibility of commanding an entire army or to the sudden realization that he was facing the formidable team of Lee and Jackson, allowing Lee to take the offensive.[46] Major General James McPherson described the scene: "Like a rabbit mesmerized by the gray fox, Hooker was frozen into immobility."[47]

With astonishing boldness, Lee decided to split his already outnumbered army. On May 2, leaving a small force of 14,000 to contain the 70,000 Federals at Chancellorsville, Lee sent Jackson on a fourteen-mile march around Hooker's right flank. Jackson's movement was spotted by Union scouts, but Hooker concluded that Jackson was retreating.[48]

In late afternoon, with less than three hours of daylight remaining, Jackson fell upon General Oliver O. Howard's totally unprepared Eleventh Corps. By dusk, the Federal retreat had turned into a rout, with the terrified troops streaming through the forest in chaos. Hooker tried in vain to stay the rout, but to no avail. Only darkness halted the relentless Confederate attack. Not satisfied with his victory, Jackson rode ahead to see if he could launch a night attack. As he rode back to join his forces, nervous Confederate troops mistook his party for Federal cavalry and fired into the dark. Jackson was hit three times; bullets shattered his left arm, which had to be amputated. Jackson died several days later.[49]

Time and numbers were still in Hooker's favor. There was still time to reorganize his army for a counterattack in the morning; he enjoyed numerical superiority over a divided Confederate army. But Hooker relapsed into a passive state, leaving his army virtually leaderless. When he was struck in the head by a piece of solid shot, his condition further deteriorated. Finally, when Sedgwick did not arrive from Fredericksburg in time to turn the tide, Hooker ordered his army to withdraw north of the Rappahannock. By the morning of May 6, all the Federal troops had crossed the river, and the campaign was over.[50]

Hooker tried to shift the blame to others for his defeat at Chancellorsville. The cavalry had failed in carrying out his orders, he said, "and General Sedgwick failed in executing his orders." But his troops were not fooled. One Massachusetts volunteer questioned Hooker's judgment: "How had one half of the army been defeated, while the other half had not fought?"[51]

Lincoln was not fooled either. When he learned of the defeat, he was visibly shaken. A California reporter who was a close friend of Lincoln's stated, "Never, as long as I knew him, did he seem to be so broken, so dispirited, and so ghostlike. Clasping his hands behind his back, he walked up and down the room saying: 'My God! My God! What will the country say?'"[52]

Lincoln refrained from blaming Hooker and left him in command, but many of his officers were not as charitable. Since he had previously been so critical of his own superiors, it was not surprising that his officers would do the same to him. One found Hooker's behavior "inexcusable" and recommended he be replaced. When Hooker learned that some of his officers had complained to the president, he asked to know who they were, but Lincoln declined to furnish the information. Hooker suggested that Lincoln grant leaves to all the generals in the Army of the Potomac so they could express their feelings openly to the president.[53]

Many of the corps commanders availed themselves of the opportunity to meet with Lincoln. Their reactions varied from those of Generals Couch and Reynolds, who advocated his removal, to Generals Sickles, Pleasonton, and Butterfield, who strongly supported him. Lincoln decided to give Hooker one more chance. He informed him that he was now to communicate directly with the general-in-chief before acting; Halleck was to give the orders, and Hooker was to obey them. Thus ended the five-month period in which Hooker enjoyed Lincoln's consent to bypass Halleck for his orders. Hooker must have realized that his days as commander of the Army of the Potomac were numbered.[54]

When it became clear that Lee was planning to mount another invasion, Hooker was instructed to stay north of the Rappahannock. He became increasingly frustrated as Stanton and Halleck consistently vetoed his plans and refused to send him the reinforcements he requested. Halleck seemed determined to get Hooker to resign, and when Halleck told Major General William French to "pay no attention to General Hooker's orders," his mission was accomplished. "Fighting Joe" would not suffer such humiliation and requested to be relieved.[55] Three days before the opening of the Gettysburg campaign, Lincoln replaced Hooker with Major General George Meade. Although Meade and Hooker had been on cool terms, Hooker praised Meade and asked the troops to give the new commander the same support they had given him.[56]

In September 1863, Major General William Rosecrans was defeated at the Battle of Chickamauga and forced to retreat to Chattanooga, Tennessee. Hooker was sent West with the Eleventh and Twelfth Corps to reinforce the besieged Rosecrans. Within a short time, Hooker was involved in a frivolous misunderstanding with Major General Grant. When Grant came down from Louisville to take charge of a new military division, Hooker sent one of his staff officers to meet him and escort him to Hooker's headquarters. Grant was offended by what he regarded as a breach of military etiquette and refused to go with the staff officer, sending word that "if General Hooker wishes to see me, he will find me at the train." Hooker complied, but Grant was not placated. His antipathy to Hooker increased when Sherman arrived in November. They shared a dislike of Hooker.[57]

Hooker performed admirably in the battles around Chattanooga. On November 24, he sent three of his divisions against the Confederate forces holding the northern slope of Lookout Mountain. The prospect was daunting: the Confederate lines were bolstered by log breastworks facing downward. However formidable the Confederate position seemed, Hooker's troops were able to scramble up the hill using boulders and fallen trees as shields from enemy fire and attack their flank virtually undetected. They drove the Confederates from their position and down the reverse slope, forcing General Bragg to evacuate the defenses on the mountain.[58]

Despite Hooker's efforts, Grant did not mention any of his accomplishments in his report of the battles around Chattanooga and, rather, suggested that Hooker be transferred to an inactive command. In the meantime, Hooker maneuvered to regain his old position as commander of the Army of the Potomac. His plan seemed to be gaining momentum in Washington until March 9, 1864, when Grant was appointed general-in-chief and commander of all Union armies. Rather than working out of Washington as Halleck had, Grant decided that his place was with the Army of the Potomac. That ended any chance of Hooker returning to the East to serve. Sherman was left in command of the three armies in the West.[59]

Sherman combined Hooker's two corps into a newly designated Twentieth Corps under General George Thomas's Army of the Cumberland. Although Hooker was pleased with his new command, he believed that Grant and Sherman were "out to get him." In a letter to Senator Zack Chandler, he wrote: "I am utterly disgusted and would resign today were it admissible to think of self at such times."[60]

As the war in the West continued, Confederate Bragg was replaced by General Joseph Johnston. Johnston continued to retreat toward Atlanta, and Sherman followed the retreat with his three armies. On July 20, 1864, General John Bell Hood, Johnston's replacement, attacked General Thomas's Army of the Cumberland. Hooker and his Twentieth Corps held firm against a three-hour assault.

The next day when Sherman and Thomas visited the Twentieth Corps headquarters, Hooker mentioned with pride what his men had accomplished and his heavy losses. To this comment, Sherman replied: "Oh, most of 'em will be back in a day or two." Hooker's response to Sherman's unpardonable remark is not known, but Lieutenant Colonel C. H. Asmussen was so infuriated that he begged a fellow officer for a pistol that he might shoot the "God-damned son-of-a-bitch" who defamed such brave men. Asmussen cooled down, and Sherman was spared.[61]

When Union Major General James McPherson was killed, Sherman again showed his lack of confidence in Hooker by passing over him and appointing Hooker's former subordinate, Major General Oliver O. Howard, to command the Army of the Tennessee. Hooker was incensed, not only because of the insult, but because he believed Howard had been responsible for the rout of his corps at Chancellorsville.[62]

Hooker submitted his resignation to General Thomas: "I have learned that Major General Howard, my junior, has been assigned to the command of the Army of the Tennessee. If this is the case, I request that I may be relieved from duty with this army. Justice and self-respect alike require my removal from an army in which rank and service are ignored."[63]

Lincoln agreed with Hooker and telegraphed Sherman to give the command of the Army of the Tennessee to him, but Sherman replied that he wanted Howard. Lincoln again urged Sherman to appoint Hooker. Sherman offered his resignation if Lincoln insisted on Hooker's appointment. The president was not prepared to go that far; Howard would command the Army of the Tennessee.[64]

Two days later, Sherman wrote home that he did not regret Hooker's resignation: "He is envious, imperious, and a braggart. Self prevailed with him and, knowing him intimately, I honestly preferred Howard." In their memoirs, both Grant and Sherman mentioned Hooker's practice of resisting authority. Grant said, "He was not subordinate to his superiors. He was ambitious to the extent of caring nothing for the rights of others."[65]

Fighting Joe's men, however, were saddened by his departure. They had great confidence in him and deeply regretted his leaving. It was well known that "Joe Hooker fed his men the best and fought them the best of any of the corps commanders."[66]

In September, Hooker was assigned to command the Northern Department, which included Michigan, Ohio, Indiana, and Illinois. His duties consisted of supervising the draft, providing for the security of prisoners of war, and guarding the northern frontier. During that time he courted Miss Oliver Groesbeck of Cincinnati, who he married shortly after the war.[67]

On June 27, 1865, Hooker was placed in charge of the Department of the East, comprising New England, New York, and New Jersey. Hooker was heartened by the 1865 report of the Congressional Committee on the Conduct of the War, which exonerated him from blame for the Union defeat at Chancellorsville.[68]

In November 1865, Hooker had a stroke and for some time lost the use of his right side. Nevertheless, he clung to his command, and by the summer of 1866, he had recovered enough to go back to work. In 1867, he suffered from another stroke and had to apply for a leave of absence. He and his wife sailed for Europe, hoping a change of environment might help his recovery. Shortly after they returned from Europe in July 1868, Hooker's wife died. Three months later, he retired from the army.[69]

Hooker spent his remaining years attending army reunions and working on his memoirs. On October 31, 1879, he died suddenly. Brief services were held in Garden City, Long Island, and then his body was taken to New York where it lay in state at City Hall. The turnout to view "Fighting Joe" was surpassed only by the number who paid tribute to President Lincoln and Horace Greeley. Hooker was buried with his wife in Spring Grove Cemetery in Cincinnati, Ohio.[70]

Joseph Hooker was a soldier's general who possessed good leadership and administrative qualities. Loved by his men, he was disliked by many of his fellow officers and commanders. It is unfortunate that "Fighting Joe" had but one independent command; he might have had others had it not been for his propensity to criticize his superiors.

18 George H. Thomas

"The Rock of Chickamauga"

George Henry Thomas was born near Newsom's Depot, Virginia. His family felt a primary allegiance to Virginia rather than to their country when the Civil War began. For all but Major Thomas, the decision was already clear. Earlier, Thomas had said, "I shall never bear arms against the United States, but it may be necessary for me to carry a musket in defense of my native state," a curious contradiction. On March 12, 1861, Governor John Letcher of Virginia offered Thomas the position of chief of ordnance in the Virginia militia. Thomas declined the offer, stating that, as long as Virginia remained in the Union, he would remain in the army.[1]

When Thomas learned of the attack on Fort Sumter, he sent telegrams announcing his decision to continue in the U.S. Army to his sisters and wife in Virginia. His sisters, loyal Virginians, immediately disowned their brother. They turned his picture to the wall, destroyed all his letters, and never wrote to him again except to suggest that he change his name. His wife defended his decision: "Whichever way he turned the matter over in his mind, his oath of allegiance to his government always came uppermost." Thomas had put on his uniform and taken his oath. He would not desert, despite the cost. After the war, the general attempted to reconcile with his family but to no avail. He never went home again.[2]

George Thomas was born on July 31, 1816, to John and Mary Rochelle Thomas. As a youth, George worked on the family farm, often associating with the slaves. Against his family's wishes, he taught the slaves lessons he had learned at church and school. When his father died in 1830, George took over the responsibility of managing the family farm. Many of his friends thought he might do something more engaging than farming. After graduating from the local academy, he entered the law office of his uncle, James Rochelle. He helped prepare the usual documents but showed no great desire to be a lawyer.[3]

In 1836, Congressman John Young Mason recommended George for admission to West Point. When the recommendation was accepted and the appointment made, Thomas went to Washington to thank Mason. Mason took the opportunity to remind him of the poor record of other students from his district at West Point. "If you should fail to graduate," he told George, "I never want to see your face again."[4]

George did well in his studies at West Point, finishing twelfth out of forty-two graduates in the class of 1840, while accumulating only eighty-seven demerits over the four-year period. While at West Point, he made friends with many who would serve with or against him during the Civil War. Among them were Philip Sheridan, Ulysses Grant, William Rosecrans, Don Carlos Buell, Joseph Hooker, Braxton Bragg, William Hardee, and Daniel H. Hill. After receiving his second lieutenant's commission, Thomas returned home on leave. He had exceeded Congressman Mason's highest expectations.[5]

Thomas's first assignment was with the Third Artillery at Fort Columbus in New York Harbor. In November, he and the Third Artillery disembarked to Florida to assist with the roundup of the Seminole Indians. The campaign accomplished very little as the Seminoles fled to safety in the Everglades. In February 1842, Thomas and his company left Florida for New Orleans. Later he was assigned to Fort McHenry outside Baltimore. His military service after Florida was uneventful until the outbreak of the Mexican War.

Early in the war with Mexico, Thomas had a chance to prove himself. During bitter street fighting for Monterrey, he brought a cannon into action in a narrow alley, blasting away at an enemy barricade. When fire from the front and rooftops began to cut down his crew, he was ordered to withdraw. Thomas did not retreat until he had fired a final round and repulsed an enemy charge. Then, he and the surviving cannoneers moved the artillery piece from the alley to safety.[6]

Braxton Bragg, who would later see Thomas perform a similar feat with a corps instead a cannon during the Civil War, praised Thomas. "No officer of the army has been so long in the field without relief, and to my personal knowledge no one has rendered more arduous, faithful, and brilliant service," he said.[7]

Thomas's method of operation and style of leadership were developed in Mexico, and his actions there illustrate how he served during the Civil War. As a leader, he operated on fixed principles, with absolute readiness being his first rule. Whenever in command of an independent force during the Civil War, he would first secure fixed supply bases and then establish lines of communication before advancing against the enemy, a rather conservative approach. When Thomas was compared with William T.

When George H. Thomas, a Virginian, learned of the attack on Fort Sumter, he decided to continue in the U.S. Army. His sisters, loyal to the Confederacy, immediately disowned their brother, turning his pictures to the wall, destroying all of his letters, and never writing to him again except to suggest that he change his name.

COURTESY OF THE LIBRARY OF CONGRESS

Sherman, it was said, "Thomas never lost a battle," whereas "Sherman never won a battle or lost a campaign."[8] "Old Slow Trot" was one of the nicknames Thomas would pick up—along with "Old Reliable." Once committed to a battle, he fought to the very end.

Thomas's contribution to the victory in Mexico did not go unnoticed. During the Monterrey campaign, he was brevetted to captain for his good performance and gallantry under fire. At Buena Vista, Thomas's artillery played a major role in the victory. Again he was brevetted, this time to the rank of major.[9]

After the war, there was a teaching vacancy in Thomas's field, artillery, at West Point. The position was first offered to Braxton Bragg, who, declining it, recommended Thomas. In a letter to President Polk, Bragg wrote: "The vacancy, I think would suit your young friend Brevet Major George H. Thomas, Third Artillery, and it is one for which he is eminently qualified." The appointment, however, went to Lieutenant William Shover, who outranked Thomas by two years.[10]

The position at West Point became available again in 1853, when Captain Shover died. This time, with the recommendation of William Rosecrans, Thomas received the appointment. In addition to teaching the fundamentals of artillery, he was given the duty of cavalry instruction. A little too heavy for an ideal cavalry commander, Thomas was called "Old Slow Trot" by his students.[11]

While at West Point, Thomas courted and married Frances Kellogg. She was considered a natural match for him and described as "a noble woman, good-natured, and congenial." During his honeymoon, Thomas received a much overdue promotion to captain. After three years at West Point, he was transferred, this time to the opposite side of the country—Fort Yuma, on the California–Arizona border.[12]

In 1855, the famous Second Cavalry Regiment was formed through the efforts of Secretary of War Jefferson Davis. Davis was attempting to build a mounted force of the highest caliber, staffed with the most promising of the army's officers. Of the twenty-five who held commissions in the regiment, seventeen were Southerners; twelve of them later became Confederate generals. The leader of the Second Cavalry was Colonel Sidney Johnston, with Robert E. Lee as second-in-command. Thomas was appointed to this famous outfit on May 25, 1855. The years Thomas served with the Second Cavalry in Texas were his most pleasant in active service.[13]

When Virginia seceded from the Union, Thomas was faced with a difficult decision. Turning down an offer from the Governor of Virginia to serve his state, Thomas elected to remain in the U.S. Army. The decision would cost him his family and friends in Virginia, but he would not break the oath he had taken to defend his country against all enemies.

With the departure of its Southern members, gaps in the Second Regiment had to be filled. Thomas, now a colonel, began to recruit and train new members for these positions. Within five months, Thomas was promoted to brigadier general.[14] In August, Thomas and his brigade were assigned to the Department of the Cumberland under the command of Brigadier General Robert Anderson. When Anderson resigned because of ill health, he was replaced by William Sherman. In October, Sherman's army encountered Confederate forces led by Brigadier General Felix Zollicoffer. After a decisive victory, Thomas wanted to pursue the Confederates into east Tennessee, the region Lincoln hoped to liberate, but Sherman decided to call off the pursuit.[15]

When the responsibility of army command proved too much for Sherman, he asked to be relieved and was replaced by Brigadier General Don Carlos Buell. Had Lincoln known all the facts, he might have chosen Thomas, who was better at offense, to lead the Army of the Cumberland. Buell would soon gain a reputation for being reluctant to go on the offensive.[16]

Under Buell's reorganization, Thomas's group of five brigades became known as the First Division, Army of the Ohio. On January 19, 1862, Thomas's division defeated a Confederate force led by General Zollicoffer at the Battle of Mill Springs. The engagement demonstrated Thomas's skillful use of strategy and tactics to gain a victory without heavy losses. News of the victory was greeted with celebration throughout the North. Although Thomas had thwarted the Confederate threat from east Tennessee, he received no reward as the commanding general, nor was he even mentioned in the official record. Four colonels, however, were named brigadier generals for their part in the victory.[17]

Although Lincoln had instructed Buell to invade east Tennessee, Buell elected to advance toward Nashville. By the time his army reached Nashville, the Confederates had withdrawn.

Early in April, Buell's Army of the Ohio moved to join Grant at Pittsburg Landing. On April 6, Grant's army was attacked by Confederate troops led by Generals Albert S. Johnston and P. G. T. Beauregard. The first day belonged to the Confederates, but that evening three of Buell's divisions arrived to reinforce Grant. On the morning of April 7, with the aid of Buell's fresh troops, Grant counterattacked and drove the Confederates from the field, forcing them back to Corinth. Two days later, Thomas's First Division arrived, too late to participate in the battle. The engagement, later referred to as the Battle of Shiloh, was costly for both sides. Among the Confederate army's 11,000 casualties was General Johnston, who bled to death from a bullet wound in the leg. Casualties were heavy on the Union side as well.

After the battle, Major General Henry Halleck arrived at Shiloh to take command of the combined armies, replacing Grant and recommending both Sherman and Thomas for promotion to major general. Although Thomas had not taken part in the recent fighting, Halleck appointed him commander of the right wing of a newly organized army and placed Sherman under his command. The incident would not be forgotten by Grant when he became general-in-chief. Without knowing it, Sherman had ingratiated himself with Grant at the expense of Thomas.[18]

Halleck's army now numbered 120,000 men, but its leadership was far from brilliant. Buell, with two divisions of the Army of the Ohio, commanded the center, while the left wing was headed by Major General John Pope of the Army of the Mississippi. Commanding the reserve was Major General John McClernand. Thomas found himself in the company of mediocrity.[19]

Halleck moved his army in the direction of Corinth, but his slow movement allowed the Confederates to withdraw before his troops could arrive in force. Although he possessed the larger force, Halleck failed to take advantage of it. In the meantime, Lincoln ordered Buell to advance against

Chattanooga and Knoxville in eastern Tennessee. When Halleck was named general-in-chief, succeeding McClellan, Thomas was left temporarily in charge at Corinth. On June 10, Thomas relinquished the command of the Army of the Tennessee to Grant. Within a short time, Thomas, with his First Division, was on his way to join Buell.[20]

Lincoln expected Buell to fight in Tennessee, but the only fight he had was a verbal one with Governor Andrew Johnson. After Buell refused to fight the enemy at Munfordville, he was ordered to turn his command over to Thomas. When Thomas received the dispatch, he went to see Buell, telling him he was going to decline the command. Buell later said that he did not want Thomas to decline the position "on any ground that was personal to me." Thomas did not accept the position, explaining to Lincoln that Buell's preparations had been completed and that he was ready to move against the enemy. He asked that Buell be allowed to remain in command. Later, Thomas said that he would not allow himself to be used "to do Buell an injury." Buell remained temporarily in command.[21]

On October 8, Buell's army engaged Confederate General Braxton Bragg at Perryville. Although Buell had maneuvered his army into a position to destroy Bragg's army, once the fighting started he had difficulty bringing his whole army into action. By the time instructions reached Thomas, it was mid-afternoon and too late to be of any help in the battle. That evening, realizing he was outnumbered, Bragg slipped away. Some Northern papers credited Buell with a victory since Bragg had withdrawn from the field. In his report, Buell praised Thomas "for the most valuable assistance during the campaign."[22]

Discussion continued in Washington about who would replace Buell; it centered around Thomas and William Rosecrans. Although the original plan had been to replace Buell with Thomas, Lincoln believed the appointment of Rosecrans, a devout Catholic, would help him politically and that it would be unwise to replace one Southern-born general with another. To remove any objection regarding who had seniority, the president changed the date of Rosecrans's commission from August 21 to March 31. "Let the Virginian wait," Lincoln said. "We will try Rosecrans." In the middle of October, Major General Rosecrans was ordered to take command of the reorganized Army of the Cumberland.[23]

When Thomas received the news that Rosecrans had been selected to replace Buell, he was surprised and angered. When he had been directed to take command of Buell's army just before the battle at Perryville, Thomas believed he was to be the army's next commander. Now he was notified that Rosecrans, his junior, was to be Buell's replacement.[24]

Thomas had no personal objection to Rosecrans and believed he was a competent leader; however, he resented the way he had been passed over. When Rosecrans arrived, Thomas spoke with him about the situation and informed him of the reason for his discontent. Thomas asked to be transferred, but Rosecrans, who was counting on him for help, prevailed upon him to remain. When asked about his choice of commands, Thomas said he preferred to lead a corps. At his request, he was assigned to the center.[25]

Although Thomas was by nature reserved and found it difficult to relax with his men, his detachment never seemed to trouble the men. They always found him accessible and referred to him as "Old Pap" and "Uncle George" because of his fatherly regard for their comfort and morale.[26]

Rosecrans soon began to receive pressure from Washington to move against General Braxton Bragg at Murfreesboro, but Thomas advised him not to move until Rosecrans was ready. On December 31, Bragg struck first at Stone's River. Lieutenant General William Hardee's corps attacked Rosecrans's right flank, surprising them while they cooked breakfast. Union brigade after brigade was forced to retreat before rallying at the Nashville Turnpike. Although Union troops fought valiantly, they soon began to run out of ammunition. A division under Brigadier General Philip Sheridan fought stubbornly before making an orderly retreat. Thomas directed his corps in a rally that stabilized a new Union line, and further Confederate attacks were repulsed as the day ended.[27]

That evening, Rosecrans met with his generals to decide whether to continue to fight the next day or to retire from the field. After soliciting the opinions of all his generals, Rosecrans turned to General Thomas: "General, what have you to say?" Thomas rose to his feet and said, "Gentlemen, I know no better place to die than right here" and walked out of the room. Rosecrans had decided. "Go to your commands," he said. "We must fight or die."[28]

Bragg believed he had achieved a major victory and that Rosecrans would fall back to Nashville. Overconfident and exultant, he telegraphed Richmond, "God has granted us a Happy New Year." But the battle was not over. The next day both armies held their positions, and on January 2, Bragg resumed the attack, this time meeting strong resistance and artillery support from the enemy. That night, when Bragg learned that reinforcements were being sent to Rosecrans, he retired from the field. Rosecrans declared a victory, but in truth it was a stalemate. Nothing had been settled at Stone's River. The losses on both sides had been high, almost as high as at Shiloh, which was the bloodiest battle of the war up to that time.[29]

During the spring of 1863, Rosecrans's objective was to move through eastern Tennessee and capture Chattanooga. With Chattanooga in Union hands, Lincoln wrote, "I think the rebellion must dwindle and die." Rosecrans's campaign was slow in getting underway because he wanted his larger, better-equipped army to be perfectly ready before he moved. By June, Rosecrans still had not moved. Halleck continued to bombard him with messages directing him to advance against Bragg. Finally, on June 16, Halleck wired the general: "Is it your intention to make an immediate move forward? A definite answer, yes or no, is required." Eight days later, Rosecrans began his march.[30]

On June 30, Bragg evacuated Tullahoma and began his retreat to Chattanooga. Rosecrans settled into his new headquarters at Tullahoma to plan his next move. Despite constant prodding by Halleck, not until August 16 did Rosecrans begin to move again. With Crittenden's corps on the left, Thomas's in the center, and McCook's on the right, Rosecrans's army advanced on a fifty-mile front, screened by cavalry and artillery. Bragg's army, now plagued by illness and desertions, had been greatly reduced.[31] Rosecrans skillfully maneuvered his army into position to attack the Confederate's rear. Late on September 7, the Confederates gave up Chattanooga without firing a shot.[32]

Rosecrans was elated. On the morning of September 9, he telegraphed Halleck: "Chattanooga is ours without a struggle and East Tennessee is free." Then he sent his army in pursuit of Bragg. Thomas was ordered to strike the enemy's flank and, if possible, to cut off his escape. Before moving out, Thomas suggested to Rosecrans that it would be wise to consolidate his forces around Chattanooga before going after Bragg. Rosecrans ignored his suggestion, wanting to pursue Bragg as quickly as he could; he believed this was a golden opportunity to destroy the Confederate army while they were disorganized and fleeing.[33]

In the meantime, General Bragg had reorganized his army and taken up a position a few miles south of Chattanooga near Chickamauga Creek. The creek was about to live up to its Cherokee name, "River of Death." When Bragg learned he was being reinforced by 12,000 fresh troops under Lieutenant General James Longstreet, he decided to fight at Chickamauga.[34]

Bragg realized he had a chance to destroy Rosecrans's divided army by attacking one part at a time. First, he attacked Thomas's advance guard under Major General James Negley. When the Confederates were slow getting into position, Negley suspected a trap and pulled back safely to join Thomas.[35]

Frustrated by the failure to engage Thomas's corps, Bragg ordered Lieutenant General Leonidas Polk to attack Crittenden's corps, elements of which had moved south. Polk, fearing he faced a superior force, refused to move. After having failed on two attempts to attack Rosecrans's divided army, Bragg prepared to attack the Union army with full force near Chickamauga Creek.[36]

The battle began on the morning of September 19 in the dense woods at Chickamauga. The fighting was fierce and bloody; 66,000 Confederates faced 58,000 Federals. At the end of the first day of the struggle, units on both sides moved to get into position to resume the fighting the next day. Rosecrans chose a defensive position with Thomas on the left, McCook on the right, and Crittenden in reserve.

On the second day, Longstreet launched a massive attack at the Union line, breaking through and cutting the Union army in half. The terrified Federals fled in panic, and by noon, most of McCook's and Crittenden's corps were in full retreat. Even Rosecrans was chased from his headquarters. Thomas's corps, however, stood firm, forming a defensive line on Snodgrass Hill and along the adjacent high ground called Horseshoe Ridge. His corps repulsed attack after attack, allowing the rest of the army to retreat from the field in relative safety. Through all the desperate fighting, Thomas calmly moved from one unit to another, encouraging his men. He was, Brigadier General James Garfield said, "standing like a rock," thus bestowing on Thomas the nickname he would carry with him the rest of his life, the "Rock of Chickamauga."[37]

As evening approached, Thomas began an orderly withdrawal. "Like magic," Longstreet later wrote, "the Union army melted away in our presence." Thomas gathered his battered corps at the town of Rossville and formed a line to meet any Confederate pursuit.[38]

General Garfield later recalled an occurrence near the close of the action. Thomas, he said, took the hand of a soldier in a rare moment of comradeship and thanked him for his valor and courage. The surprised soldier stood for a moment, then suddenly shouted out, "George H. Thomas has taken this hand. I'll knock down any man that offers to take it hereafter."[39]

To the dismay of his officers, Bragg failed to follow up his victory. Confederate casualties had been heavy: more than 18,000 were killed, wounded, or captured. Bragg said, "Any immediate pursuit would have been fruitless." In the meantime, Rosecrans's army slipped away toward Chattanooga, and Bragg lost the opportunity to crush the Union army.[40]

During the evening of September 20 and the next day, exhausted troops staggered into Chattanooga, the result of the bloodiest two-day battle of the war. Of the 120,000 soldiers who had taken the field, 35,000 died. Shaken by his defeat, Rosecrans wired the president that his army's "fate was in the hands of God; in whom I hope."[41]

After the carnage at Chickamauga, Union forces occupied Chattanooga, while Confederate forces moved into the surrounding mountains and ridges. Controlling the enemy's lines of supply, Bragg hoped to starve the Union troops into submission. To ease the situation, Lincoln ordered Major General Joseph Hooker to reinforce Rosecrans. Secretary of War Stanton questioned the suitability of Rosecrans continuing in command. "What the Army of the Cumberland needs," he said, "is a competent commander." At the same time, he took the opportunity to praise Thomas: "The merit of General Thomas and the debt of gratitude the nation owes to his valor and skill is fully appreciated. . . . It is not my fault that he was not in chief command months ago."[42]

Several days after the battle, the subject of promotions and changes in command was discussed at a cabinet meeting in Washington. Secretary of the Navy Welles expressed the opinion that, if a change was to be made, no one seemed more suitable than Thomas. The feeling, however, was not unanimous because Thomas was a Virginian. Many Northern politicians did not want to see a Southerner promoted. Lincoln delayed his decision for three weeks.[43]

In October, Major General Ulysses Grant assumed command of the armies in the West. His immediate concern was the Army of the Cumberland, now under siege in Chattanooga. On October 19, the problem of command was solved—Rosecrans was relieved of command and replaced with Thomas. Grant's dispatch to Thomas ordered him to "hold Chattanooga at all hazards." He wired back, "We will hold the town till we starve."[44]

Grant went to Chattanooga to get a firsthand look at the situation. Once in Chattanooga, he adopted Thomas's plan to shorten the supply line to make certain his troops could get much needed supplies. By November 13, Hooker's 20,000 troops from the Army of the Potomac and elements from Vicksburg under William Sherman arrived. Grant now had the manpower he needed.[45]

By the end of November, the Union army was ready to break the siege and take the offensive. General Hooker attacked Lookout Mountain from the west, while Thomas's 20,000 troops moved against the face of Missionary Ridge in an attempt to drive the Confederates from the heights. By November 28, the attacks had been successful, and Bragg's army was fleeing south into Georgia. Bragg offered his resignation to Jefferson Davis, blaming his generals for undermining his authority and his troops for not putting up much of a fight. It was accepted, and General Joseph E. Johnston was named as his successor.

In February, Sherman was placed in charge of three armies: the Ohio, Tennessee, and Cumberland. The first two formed the wings of his army, with Thomas's in the center. Although Thomas was disappointed at being placed under Sherman, who was his junior in rank, he never complained. The two, however, often disagreed over strategy. The first disagreement occurred in April at Chattanooga. Thomas believed it was possible to defeat Johnston in one stroke; he proposed a flanking and frontal attack at the same time. Sherman, however, had his own plans—simply to pursue Johnston and harass him—and rejected Thomas's suggestion.[46]

Because he was outnumbered, Johnston's basic strategy was to use part of his army as a shield and counterattack when the opportunity presented itself. Jefferson Davis wanted Johnston to take the offensive and recapture Tennessee, but Johnston believed his army was too weak for such a move.[47] Sherman continued to pursue Johnston through Georgia, taking 113 days to reach Atlanta. In the process, Thomas's Army of the Cumberland engaged in numerous battles, some lasting as long as four days.

As Johnston continued to retreat to Atlanta, President Davis was convinced that he had no intention of holding Atlanta. On July 17, 1864, Johnston was replaced by General John Bell Hood. Hood attempted several attacks against Sherman's army, suffering heavy losses but gaining little.

Hood was able to hold Sherman off for a while, but on September 1, Atlanta fell.

Hood marched his army toward Tennessee, hoping that Sherman would follow him, interrupting his march through Georgia. Sherman split his army, sending Thomas to deal with Hood, while he began the March to the Sea. Hood hoped he could recapture Tennessee and move over the mountains to join Lee. By moving swiftly, he was able to trap a part of Thomas's army under Major General John Schofield at Spring Hill, cutting off his escape route to Nashville. But before Hood could attack, Schofield slipped by the Confederates at night, taking up a position at Franklin, a town between Spring Hill and Nashville.[48]

When Hood discovered that Schofield's army had escaped, he was angry, blaming two of his generals, Patrick Cleburne and Benjamin Cheatham. He decided that they and their men should be punished. He did so by ordering them to make a frontal attack on the fortified Union lines at Franklin. Although there was a way to bypass the Franklin road and still block Schofield's line of retreat, Hood insisted on this suicidal attack.[49]

A Confederate force of 20,000 men marched across an open field against entrenched Union troops supported by artillery. On this day, the spirit of the Confederate Army of Tennessee was lost. The fight continued into the night until the Union troops retreated. Hood claimed victory since Schofield had left the field, but the Confederate army had suffered 6,000 casualties, including many regimental commanders and six generals. It was a price the Confederate army could not afford to pay and a battle Hood would regret.[50]

Grant wanted Thomas to attack Hood immediately after the Battle of Franklin, but Thomas waited. He held a strong position at Nashville and wanted Hood to attack him. Lincoln expressed concern that Thomas would fail to attack Hood before he dug in or moved into Kentucky. "Attack Hood and wait no longer," Grant wired Thomas. To Halleck, he wired, "If Thomas has not struck yet, he ought to be ordered to hand over his command to Schofield. There is no better man to repel an attack than Thomas, but I fear he is too cautious to take the initiative."[51]

When fog and freezing rain swept in, Thomas had to delay his move even longer. The next day, sleet and snow fell, making movement on the slopes hazardous. On December 9, an impatient Grant demanded that the War Department replace Thomas with Schofield, but Halleck protested and asked Grant to reconsider. When Grant learned of the weather conditions, he temporary suspended the order.[52]

Although the freezing weather persisted, Grant insisted that Thomas attack Hood. "I will obey the order as promptly as possible, however much I may regret it, as the attack will have to be made under every disadvantage," Thomas replied.[53]

On December 15, as Grant prepared to come to Nashville himself,

Thomas attacked Hood at Shy's Hill. The result was a crushing defeat for the Confederates, followed by a vigorous Union pursuit. As a result of his victory, the Rock of Chickamauga became the "Hammer of Nashville."[54]

Thomas's success was quickly recognized in Washington. From Stanton, he received a letter saying, "I rejoice in tendering to you and the gallant officers and soldiers of your command the thanks of this department for the brilliant achievement of this day." On December 23, Sherman, who had entered Savannah a day earlier, wrote to Thomas congratulating him for his victory and commiserating with him about the cold weather he was experiencing in Tennessee. Thomas published these telegrams to the army in general orders: "The major general commanding with pride and pleasure . . . adds thereto his own thanks to the troops for the unsurpassed gallantry and good conduct displayed by them in the battle of yesterday and today."[55]

Thomas's pursuit of the defeated Confederate army was a fight against exhaustion, but still Grant was not satisfied. To Sherman, Grant remarked: "His pursuit of Hood indicated a sluggishness that satisfied me he would never do to conduct one of your campaigns."[56] In the meantime, Stanton notified Thomas of his promotion to major general in the U.S. Army. Thomas's mood, however, could not be changed by the promotion. He found disturbing the rumor that he was to have been relieved before the battle of Nashville. Thomas showed the dispatch, which announced his promotion, to a staff member and asked him what he thought. "It is better late than never," he responded. "I suppose it is better late than never, but it is too late to be appreciated," Thomas replied. "I earned this at Chattanooga."[57]

The campaign against Hood ended on December 29 when Hood was effectively defeated and replaced by General Joseph Johnston. That spring, Thomas's army was dispersed. On May 9, he bid farewell to the men who had fought at Shiloh, Stone's River, Chickamauga, Chattanooga, Franklin, and Nashville. Thomas, however, continued in command of the army's Department of Tennessee until 1867.

After the war, many of Thomas's fellow officers entered politics and ran for office. When his name was suggested as a candidate for political office, he responded: "I have not the necessary control over my temper nor have I the faculty of yielding to policy and working to advance it unless convinced within myself that it is right and honest. . . . I have no taste whatever for politics."[58]

In 1868, when presidential impeachment was being discussed in Congress, President Andrew Johnson sent Thomas's name to the Senate for confirmation as brevet lieutenant general. Johnson hoped to remove Grant as general-in-chief and replace him with Thomas. Thomas refused to be drawn into the conflict, stating, "My services since the war do not merit so high a compliment, and it is now too late for it to be regarded as a compliment if conferred for service during the war." In 1869, at his own request, he was assigned commander of the Division of the Pacific.[59]

On March 28, 1870, Thomas died in his office of a stroke. His body was returned from San Francisco to Troy, New York, for burial in Oakwood Cemetery. President Grant, Generals Sherman, Sheridan, and Meade, cabinet members, congressmen, and thousands of soldiers and veterans attended the funeral. Yet among the thousands who came, no member of Thomas's family, except his wife, was present. "Our brother George died to us in 1861," his sisters told their neighbors.[60]

19 *Philip Sheridan*

Worth His Weight in Gold

In the middle of October 1864, Major General Philip Sheridan's army was camped near Cedar Creek, Virginia, twenty miles south of Winchester. Confederate Lieutenant General Jubal Early was not far away, but he had been beaten in two recent battles, and it was unlikely he had any intention of attacking Sheridan now. Sheridan took this opportunity to leave the army and visit Washington. On October 18, he spent the evening at the home of a local tobacco merchant, Lloyd Logan, in Winchester. His mind at ease over the situation at the front, Sheridan turned in for the evening. General Early, however, had learned that Sheridan had ordered some of his troops back to Petersburg and that he himself was absent from his army. Under cover of night, Early moved his divisions into position to attack the unsuspecting Union army before daylight.[1]

Shortly after six o'clock the following morning, almost an hour after the Confederates had begun their attack, Sheridan was awakened by his duty officer, who informed him of sporadic artillery fire at Cedar Creek. Suspicious that trouble might be brewing, Sheridan headed back to rejoin his army.[2]

Meanwhile, the opening stages of the battle had begun, and the Confederates were winning. After a few hours of fighting, Early's men had the Federals reeling. Sheridan's trip back toward his army was casual and unhurried until he met the first wave of retreating soldiers. Sheridan later described the event: "Just as we made the crest of the rise of the stream (Mill Creek) there burst upon our view the appalling spectacle of a panic-stricken army—hundreds of slightly wounded men, throngs others unhurt but utterly demoralized, and baggage-wagons by the score, all pressing to the rear in hopeless confusion, telling only too plainly that a disaster had occurred at the front."[3]

At that moment, he was met by Major General William Emory, who reported that a division of his corps was ready to cover the retreat to Winchester. "Retreat, Hell!" Sheridan declared. "We'll be back in camp tonight." Then he went to work to re-form his army.[4]

After he had completed his preparations, Sheridan rode along the two-mile front, cap in hand, showing himself to all the troops along the line. "I'll get a twist on those people yet," he shouted. "We'll raise them out of their boots before the day is over!" As he passed by, his men cheered and threw their hats in the air. Sheridan then led a counterattack that drove the Confederates back. By the end of the day, Early's army was so badly damaged that they would never again threaten the North by way of the Shenandoah Valley.[5]

Moments such as these require split-second decisions and most severely test a commander's competence and fortitude. Sheridan passed the test at Cedar Creek. He was a man who had risen by sheer merit to command an army, an officer of sound judgment who his men trusted completely.

Sheridan's appearance belied his ability as commander of an army. He was an unimpressive little man, only five-feet-five-inches tall with a large, bullet-shaped head. Abraham Lincoln described Phil Sheridan as a "brown, chunky little chap, with a long body, short legs, not enough neck to hang him, and such long arms that if his ankles itch he can scratch them without stooping." All his life, until his victories on the battlefield, people had underestimated his ability. It was not until Ulysses S. Grant put the matter in proper perspective that Sheridan received the respect and recognition he deserved. When told that his subordinate was "rather a little fellow," Grant stated, "You will find him big enough for the purpose before we get through with him."[6]

"Put your faith in the common soldier," Sheridan said, "and he will never let you down." He knew because he himself was a common soldier. Relatively speaking, of all the Union generals, Sheridan accomplished as much as any, when one considers the poor background from which he came.

Sheridan was born on March 6, 1831, the third of six children born to John and Mary Meenagh Sheridan. The Sheridans were second cousins who had lived as tenant farmers on the Cherrymount estate in northern Ireland before immigrating to America. Hoping to improve their lot, they made their way to Albany, New York, but were disappointed not to find work as they had been led to believe they would. There was no work in Albany, but construction gangs were hiring on the National Road, the thoroughfare from the Chesapeake Bay to the Mississippi River. Somerset, Ohio, with its large Catholic population and crossroads, seemed a good place to settle.[7]

Young Phil was raised mostly by his mother. She was quiet, devout, and patriotic. Phil saw very little of his father, who was always off somewhere

Philip Sheridan galloped to Cedar Creek, where his army had been attacked in his absence. There, he rallied his men and repulsed the Confederate advance.

COURTESY OF THE LIBRARY OF CONGRESS

working on a road, canal, or railroad project. At the age of ten, Phil began attending the one-room schoolhouse in Somerset, where he received a typical nineteenth-century frontier education—four years in length. Sheridan learned to read and do a little arithmetic; the rest, in the tradition of American education of the time, was left to him.[8]

Phil's childhood was very similar to that of other people living in small towns. Sheridan's small size and unconventional appearance made him a target for the town bullies. Some children respond to such abuse with clowning or seclusion, but little Phil fought back. He learned that a quick assault, catching the adversary off guard, usually overcame heavy odds, and before long only newcomers risked igniting his explosive temper.[9]

School was not the only ground for young Phil Sheridan's education; Finch's Tavern on the town square proved just as valuable. Sheridan enjoyed the stories told by the tough-talking Conestoga wagon drivers who told tales in a style all their own. Their creative use of language was legendary, and Sheridan enjoyed their colorful way of expressing themselves.[10]

Sheridan was too young to fight in Mexico, but his intention to become a soldier was set by the time the war was over. To be considered for West Point, he would have to be nominated by a member of Congress, but neither he nor his family were in a position to exert much political influence. A chance came in 1848, when a young man who had been nominated failed the entrance examination. Sheridan wrote to his congressman asking for the appointment. The response was prompt, and he received an appointment to the class of 1848.[11]

Sheridan recognized his educational deficiencies, particularly in mathematics, and applied himself to his studies. He was fortunate to have a scholarly New Yorker named Henry Slocum for a roommate. At night, long after lights out, the two cadets would hang a blanket over their window and continue to study. Like most Midwesterners and Southerners, Sheridan found himself at an educational disadvantage when compared to Eastern cadets. Contrary to the popular belief that West Point was dominated by aristocratic Southerners, most of the faculty and highest ranking cadets came from the East, where better schooling gave them an academic head start.[12]

Sheridan was something of an outcast among the cadets. Not only was he short, unattractive, and argumentative, he was also Irish Catholic—traits that left him open to teasing by his classmates. On September 9, 1851, he was involved in a fight with a Virginian, Cadet Sergeant William Terrill. A nearby officer stepped in and saved Sheridan from a beating at the hands of the larger cadet. As a result of his actions, he was suspended from West Point for the rest of that year.[13]

A year later, Sheridan was back at West Point, but, in the interim, his original class had graduated. Sheridan's time away from the Academy did not help his disposition; he received more demerits in his last year than he had during the previous three years. When he graduated, he ranked thirty-fourth in a class of fifty-two, which was actually higher than most people had expected.

Sheridan was assigned as a brevet second lieutenant to Company D, First Infantry Regiment, garrisoned at Fort Duncan, Texas. There he developed two habits that would prove helpful to him during his military career: he studied the local ground, making maps where none were available, and he attempted to learn the local language.[14]

In November 1854, Sheridan was promoted to second lieutenant and transferred to the Fourth Infantry Regiment at Fort Reading, California. The frenzy of the gold rush of 1849 was over, and the mining corporations had taken over. The West was becoming civilized. The major barrier to this process was the original inhabitants of the land, the Native Americans.[15]

Young Sheridan had no difficulty carrying out his duties in fighting Indians. His ability to accomplish the task was not hampered by his feelings of sympathy for his opponent. "They were a pitiable lot," he said, "almost naked, hungry, and cadaverous." Sheridan, however, had little opportunity to test his military prowess against them. The army's various expeditions turned out to be uneventful; however, Sheridan was involved in a few minor skirmishes, allowing him to gain fighting experience. For the next five years, Sheridan's job was primarily the policing of an Indian reservation in western Oregon. He showed no signs of discontent, however. He spent his time learning to speak Chinook, making maps, and preparing himself for future assignments.[16]

By the spring of 1861, Sheridan had been a second lieutenant for almost eight years. His experiences during that time had been extensive. He had commanded men in battle, been wounded, and seen both good and bad examples of how an army officer should conduct himself. In the process, he had impressed his superiors with his work ethic, ingenuity, and diplomacy. Now, at the age of thirty, he was ready to play a major role in the Civil War.[17]

News of the firing on Fort Sumter and the Battle of Bull Run reached the West Coast. As the Union military efforts expanded in the months that followed, Sheridan was promoted to captain and awaited orders for active duty in the East. Later, he said that "my patriotism was untainted by politics." To him, the "preservation of the Union" was his prime consideration, not the question of slavery.[18]

After the Union defeat at Manassas in September, Sheridan was assigned to the Thirteenth U.S. Infantry, located in Missouri. His assignment was to audit the books of Major General Halleck's predecessor, Major General John Frémont. Sheridan did his best to straighten out the enormous confusion left behind by Frémont and untangle the snarled supply and transportation system. During 1862, Sheridan was still deeply involved in inventories and supplies. When Sheridan discovered an illegal transaction involving the sale of horses, he refused to pay the thieves. Major General Samuel Curtis, his superior, ordered him to make the payment. When he refused, Curtis threatened to have him court-martialed. Appealing to General Halleck, Sheridan was transferred out of Curtis's command.[19]

In the spring of 1862, Sheridan's chance for action finally came. The governor of Michigan offered him a colonelcy in the volunteer Second Michigan Cavalry. If Sheridan wanted action, he would have it. In the next thirty-five days, he led his regiment in six skirmishes and one full-scale battle.[20]

On June 11, Sheridan's brigade commander was promoted, and Sheridan was given command of the brigade. He immediately established a rapport with his men. "I had striven unceasingly to have them well fed and clothed, had personally looked after the selection of their camps, and had maintained such discipline as to allay former irritation," he said. His care extended beyond physical needs: "Whenever my authority would permit, I saved my command from needless sacrifices and unnecessary toil; therefore, when hard or daring work was to be done, I expected the heartiest response and always got it." Within a few weeks, he said, "I had gained not only their confidence as soldiers, but their esteem and love as men."[21]

Sheridan's first important command situation was at Boonesville, Mississippi, during the Corinth campaign. After Shiloh, Confederate General Beauregard withdrew his army back toward Corinth to await reinforcements and additional supplies. Grant did not pursue the enemy, believing his troops were too exhausted. Sheridan, however, was sent on a probing action with a small cavalry brigade. When Sheridan found himself under attack and outnumbered four-to-one, he responded by detaching several companies for a ride that sent them loudly into the Confederate rear. Then he led a frontal attack. The two Federal attacks were well coordinated, and the Confederate force broke rank and ran.[22]

It was not an important engagement, but it did identify Sheridan as a potential leader. In a telegram sent shortly afterward to General Halleck, signed by no fewer than five brigadier generals, his efforts were recognized. "Brigadiers scarce; good ones scarcer," it read. "The undersigned respectfully beg that you will obtain the promotion of Sheridan. He is worth his weight in gold."[23]

The only change made, however, was to add other regiments to his brigade and to transfer him and his troops to Louisville to help oppose Confederate forces there. Grant had just replaced Halleck as department commander when he learned of Sheridan's transfer. Not wanting to lose a good fighter, he met with Sheridan, hoping to convince him not to accept the transfer. But Sheridan refused to stay, as he wanted to go where the action was.

When Sheridan reported to the commanding general at Louisville, he was surprised to learn that he had been promoted to brigadier general. Sheridan, who had hoped the war would last long enough for him to become a major, was now a brigadier general and a division commander in the Army of the Ohio.[24]

In October 1862, at the battle at Perryville, Sheridan's division held the center. On the left flank was another newly appointed brigadier general, William Terrill, the Virginian with whom Sheridan had fought at West Point. When Terrill decided to remain in the Federal army, his father had been so incensed at his son's action that he wrote to him: "Your name shall be stricken from the family records." Meanwhile, his brother James was serving as colonel of a Confederate regiment fighting in Virginia under Jubal Early. Earlier Sheridan and Terrill had met, shaken hands, and put their past feud behind them. Hours later, Terrill was killed. Two years later his brother was killed in the Battle of Cold Harbor. After the war, the Terrill family viewed the situation differently. They erected a memorial in remembrance of their fallen sons, bearing the inscription: "God Alone Knows Which Was Right."[25]

Sheridan believed the Battle of Perryville was an example of lost opportunities. "Had a skillful and energetic advance of Union troops been made, instead of wasting precious time in slow and unnecessary tactical maneuvers," Sheridan said, "the enemy could have been destroyed before he quit the state." Although dissatisfied by the results, Sheridan enjoyed his first taste of military glory. Some newspapers wrote of his achievement, calling him "The Paladin of Perryville."[26]

After Perryville, General Buell was replaced by Rosecrans. On Christmas Day, Rosecrans advanced the army to confront Bragg along Stone's River, near the town of Murfreesboro. Rosecrans intended to attack the Confederate right, but, before he could, Bragg attacked him. Outnumbered and outgunned, Sheridan was forced to retreat. Angered by the situation, Sheridan was swearing as he led his men to the rear. Even in the midst of disaster, the religious Rosecrans could not resist an admonition: "Watch your language. Remember the first bullet may send you to eternity."[27]

During the battle at Stone's River, Sheridan's division was involved in savage fighting and acquitted itself with honor. Sheridan had confirmed the truth that soldiers are not disheartened by death, only by pointless death.

Eight months later, at the Battle of Chickamauga, Bragg was reinforced by two divisions from Lee's Army of Northern Virginia under the leadership of James Longstreet. Sheridan's division was overwhelmed and driven from the field. It was Major General George Thomas, holding against impossible odds, that saved the Union army. As a result, Thomas earned his title the "Rock of Chickamauga." The Army of the Cumberland had been beaten in the bloodiest battle of the war in the Western theater.[28]

Rosecrans's army withdrew to the safety of Chattanooga, where it was then bottled up by Bragg. Grant joined the besieged army, replaced Rosecrans with General Thomas, and summoned reinforcements from Sherman and his own Army of the Tennessee. With the aid of Sheridan's division, the Federals were able to break through the Confederate center and send Bragg's army to a quick retreat.

Grant's victory at Chattanooga convinced Lincoln that he was the best general in the Union army. On March 12, 1864, Grant was named general-in-chief of the Union armies, and Sheridan was ordered to Washington. Sheridan arranged to leave the next day without making the usual formal farewell to his troops. "I could not do it," he wrote. "The bond existing between them and me had grown to such depth of attachment . . . from our mutual devotion . . . and by general consent within and without the command were called 'Sheridan's division.'" His men found out that he was leaving anyway. As Sheridan boarded the train, he was surprised to see the hillsides around the station lined with his troops, there to say farewell and to show their affection.[29]

When Sheridan learned he had been named the chief of cavalry for the

Army of the Potomac, he was "staggered" by the thought of the "great responsibilities." Moreover, he was bothered by the political infighting for which the Army of the Potomac was famous. General George Meade was the center of the controversy. He had little use for cavalry, and Sheridan's predecessor, Major General Alfred Pleasonton, had been replaced because of his difference of opinion with Meade over its use. Like Pleasonton, Sheridan wanted his cavalry to be permitted to act independently of the main army. He, too, had problems with Meade, who believed cavalry was fit for little more than guard and picket duty.[30]

Their disagreement came to a head on May 6. Grant ordered Meade to prepare for a night march to Spotsylvania Court House. It was important that the Union forces get there before Lee's army and hold it. The night was foggy and rainy, and the bulk of the army did not leave until evening. The weather and road slowed their movement. For Lee to reach Spotsylvania, he had to cross the Po River. Meade should have sent Sheridan immediately to block or destroy the bridge crossing the river, but Lee was left to use it as he pleased. As a result, the Confederates reached Spotsylvania before the Union troops and were able to repulse Sheridan's cavalry.[31]

Meade blamed Sheridan for not carrying out his orders and told him so in no uncertain terms. Sheridan, who was just as outspoken as Meade, if not more so, responded with anger. It did not matter that Meade outranked him. He was not going to take the blame for something he saw as Meade's fault. Sheridan concluded angrily, "I could whip Jeb Stuart if you would only let me. But since you insist on giving cavalry directions without even consulting or notifying me, you can command the cavalry corps yourself. I will not give it another order." He said he was resigning and stormed out.[32]

Meade went to see Grant, expecting him to reprimand Sheridan for his insubordination. When Grant did not react the way he expected, he repeated Sheridan's boast about defeating Stuart if given the opportunity. "Did he really say that?" Grant asked. "Well, he usually knows what he's talking about. Let him go ahead and do it."[33]

By nightfall, Sheridan was back in the saddle and leading 10,000 of his men to the outer suburbs of Richmond, where he encountered Stuart at Yellow Tavern, six miles north of the city. Outnumbering Stuart's cavalry three to one, Sheridan ordered a charge. Stuart tried desperately to rally his men. This time his luck ran out; he was shot by a dismounted Michigan cavalryman. Sheridan not only made good his boast but was instrumental in the death of Stuart. Nothing Sheridan accomplished, however, helped Grant as he tried to capture the crucial crossroads at Spotsylvania. But by separating Meade and Sheridan, Grant had been able to maintain the peace and services of both men.[34]

As cavalry commander, Sheridan retained all Pleasonton's leaders, most notably George Custer, Wesley Merritt, and James Wilson. All three men were young and became known as the boy generals. They served Sheridan well, but it was Custer with whom he developed the closest bond. Sheridan admired Custer's dash and respected the fact that he was as aggressive as Sheridan himself.[35]

With his victory over Stuart, Sheridan made a dramatic point about the proper use of cavalry and helped destroy the belief that Southern horsemen were superior to those of the Union. In July 1864, Jubal Early frightened the bureaucrats in Washington when his raid threatened the capital. At the same time, both Grant's offensive at Petersburg and Sherman's movement through Georgia had stalled. With the presidential election coming up in the fall, Lincoln could not afford another setback. While in Washington, Sheridan was informed that his main task was to avoid being beaten; a defeat of his army could cost Lincoln the election.[36]

Grant did not share the administration's concern. He was well aware of Sheridan's capabilities and knew he could count on him. He gave Sheridan the task of clearing the Shenandoah Valley of all Confederate forces. The Shenandoah Valley had twice before been used as a corridor for the invasion of the North, and it was known as the breadbasket of the Confederacy. Its food supply was vital to the South's war effort.[37]

Grant hoped to block the Confederates from the valley once and for all, instructing Sheridan on the type of warfare to conduct there: "In pushing . . . it is desirable that nothing should be left to invite the enemy to return. Take all provisions, forage, and stock wanted for use of your command. Such as cannot be consumed, destroy. . . . The people should be informed that so long as an army can subsist among them, recurrences of these raids must be expected."[38]

With 40,000 men, Sheridan moved cautiously into the valley, probing and skirmishing with Jubal Early's 12,000 Confederates. Gradually, he made progress, mostly by attrition. Sheridan issued orders for the destruction of all wheat and hay and for the seizure of all mules, horses, and cattle that might be useful to the army. The campaign became known as the Burning. Sheridan, like Sherman, believed in total war. If the inhabitants were made to suffer, he believed, they would force the government to seek peace. To Sheridan, the torch was as important a weapon as the sword. When he left the valley in late 1864, there were no crops left.[39]

By the middle of October, Sheridan's army was camped near Cedar Creek, twenty miles south of Winchester. Jubal Early was not far away, but it was unlikely that he had any intention of attacking. When Sheridan was absent from the field, Early launched a surprise attack on the Union army. Sheridan was on his way back from Washington when the fighting began. Once he realized what was happening, he rallied his men by riding along the line, inspiring them to victory.[40]

Early's army was so badly damaged that they were no longer a menace. The battle cost the South one of its brightest stars, young Major General

Stephen D. Ramseur. The Confederacy would never again threaten the North by way of the Shenandoah Valley.[41]

After a final engagement at Waynesborough, Sheridan joined Grant for the final weeks of the war. Sheridan's army acted as Grant's shock troops, helping to force Lee's Army of Northern Virginia from Petersburg. The battle at Five Forks on April 1 ended the siege at Petersburg, forcing Lee to abandon his position and retreat back to Richmond.[42]

On April 3, Union troops marched into Richmond unopposed and occupied the town. As the Confederates retreated, they were repeatedly harassed by Federal cavalry. When Lee learned that his supply trains had been captured, he made one last effort to break away from Grant's army. Custer and his troopers moved in quickly to cut off Lee's retreat. Sheridan's cavalry held the Confederates at bay long enough for the Union infantry to advance. Lee had no choice but to surrender.[43]

Grant was magnanimous in his terms and would not allow the firing of victory salutes or cheering in the Union lines. There would be many incidents in the future, however, when the South would forget its dignity and the North, this example of magnanimity. Some of these incidents would involve Sheridan, who could not easily forget the bloodshed and destruction he had witnessed during the war.

Sheridan's contributions to the Union victory did not go unnoticed. Lincoln said of him after Cedar Creek, "Phil Sheridan is all right." General Grant was more generous in his praise of Sheridan: "I believe General Sheridan has no superior as a general, either living or dead, and perhaps not an equal." Sherman described his Ohioan neighbor as "a persevering terrier dog, honest, modest, plucky, and smart enough."[44]

After the war, the army turned its attention to the Indians on the Western frontier and to a problem developing in Mexico involving the French. There was concern about the presence of 40,000 of French Emperor Napoleon III's troops in Mexico. Without actually sending his troops across the Rio Grande, Sheridan did all that was possible to let the French know that armed intervention was possible if the troops were not removed. In April 1866, Napoleon III announced that he would begin to pull his troops out of Mexico. Sheridan believed his display of force at the border had been responsible for the French withdrawal.[45]

In March of 1867, Congress divided ten of the eleven former Confederate states into five military districts. The Southern states were to be administered by the army until they met the requirements for being readmitted into the Union. President Johnson gave Sheridan command of the Fifth Military District, composed of Texas and Louisiana. His harsh policies as military commander resulted in his removal from the position six months later and his transfer to the Department of Missouri with headquarters at Fort Leavenworth.

Sheridan left for his new assignment, exchanging commands with General

Winfield Scott Hancock. For many years, the Plains Indians had been gradually pushed across the Mississippi and were being settled "permanently" on a vast range of reservations west of the Arkansas, Missouri, and Iowa borders. They were promised they could live and roam there forever. Unfortunately, the terms of the treaties were broken by the United States.[46]

There was an uneasy quiet in the Department of the Missouri when Sheridan took over the command. When rumors of renewed bloodshed by the Indians swept through the post, Sheridan had only a small force on hand. His command was less than half of the combined might of the Indians—and even that force was scattered among eight forts. Sheridan, who at the end of the Civil War had commanded well-trained, battle-worn troops, now had a depleted army of regular recruits.[47]

The Indians were more than a match for Sheridan's troops. It was Sheridan's task to use his smaller force so to take advantage of their firepower, discipline, organization, and leadership. The Indian tribes could put 6,000 warriors in the field, whereas Sheridan's command totaled only about 2,600. Nevertheless, he laid down the principle: "Punishment must follow crime." To punish the Indians who preferred raiding to farming, however, Sheridan could not fight them on their terms.[48]

As always, Sheridan made a careful plan. He selected George Armstrong Custer, now a lieutenant colonel, and his Seventh Cavalry to lead the attack. Custer was one officer that Sheridan felt he could rely on for quick and aggressive action. Custer, however, had little regard for the Indians. He slaughtered women and children as well as braves. Custer burned and destroyed entire villages without feeling or regret.[49]

The aftermath of Sheridan's rigorous Indian campaigns brought controversy, drawing an outcry of protest in the East. Sheridan assured General Sherman that future fears of massacres were groundless. He also made it clear that the Indians who complied with the terms of the treaty and lived on the reservations should be adequately clothed and fed. Those that spent their summers in war parties, Sheridan said, should be quickly and sternly punished.

In November 1868, when Ulysses S. Grant was elected president of the United States, he appointed Sherman commander of the army and Sheridan commander of the frontier, promoting him to lieutenant general. This change in assignment meant that Sheridan would be farther from the action and tied to a desk in Chicago. He would never again come as close to an Indian fight as he had during recent campaigns.[50]

The army's action against the Indians continued to provoke a firestorm of protest back East. Sheridan lashed out quickly and instinctively at his critics, claiming that, since 1862, at least eight hundred men, women, and children had been murdered within the limits of his command, and some in the most fiendish manner; the men were usually scalped and mutilated, women raped, then killed and scalped. During the controversy, Sheridan was quoted as having said, "A dead Indian is the only good Indian." Although he immediately denied the statement, it continued to be attributed to him and used by his enemies ever since to characterize and denigrate his Western career.[51]

Sheridan was in Chicago during the Great Chicago Fire of 1871. At ten o'clock on the night of October 7, a fire broke out that continued to burn for five days. By the time the fire was brought under control, 250 people were dead, and property losses reached $200 million. Sheridan's quick assistance with the army aroused a political controversy. During the fire, he directed his soldiers to assist civilians in fighting the fire. When he learned that a hotel owner, whose establishment had not been damaged by the fire, had raised his daily rates from $2.50 to $6.00, he dismissed the proprietor, replaced him with one of his orderlies as manager, and dropped the rates to their original level.

His troops patrolled the city with bayonets, routing gangs of hoodlums and looters and restoring order as quickly as possible. Sheridan had his men supply blankets, set up tents for the homeless, and distribute food rations. Governor Palmer was upset by Sheridan's intervention and claimed that the mayor should have called out the militia. He charged Sheridan with unconstitutional acts.[52]

When Palmer took the matter to the state supreme court, the citizens, who were grateful to Sheridan for his assistance, rallied to his support. He received thousands of letters of thanks and the support of Secretary of War Belknap, but the Illinois Supreme Court upheld Palmer. Some believe that Palmer's actions were the result of some personal difference that he and Sheridan had had while serving together during the Civil War.[53]

When gold was discovered in the Black Hills of Montana, many prospectors began moving into the hills, trespassing on land that had been set aside for Native Americans in 1868. When Sheridan learned of the intrusion, he issued orders to burn wagon trains, destroy equipment, and arrest those involved in expeditions into the hills. The treaty of 1868, he pointed out, "deeds this portion of the Black Hills to the Sioux." He suggested, instead, that miners and homesteaders try their luck farther west in the unceded lands of Wyoming and Montana.[54]

While in Chicago, Sheridan turned his attentions to a young lady. She was Irene Rucker, the youngest daughter of General Daniel Rucker, quartermaster general of the Division of the Missouri. Irene was described as "young, beautiful, bright and accomplished, blond, and vivacious." She was twenty-two at the time, only half his age. On June 3, 1875, they were married at the home of her father. Their marriage was a happy one and blessed by four children.[55]

For the next eight years, Sheridan continued to be involved with the Plains Indians as civilization spread to the West. The Sioux were outraged by the invasion of gold-seekers in their old hunting grounds in the Black

Hills and the slaughter of the buffalo herds by white hunters. Sheridan was aware that settlers, prospectors, and corrupt bureaucrats were preying on the Native Americans and inviting a violent reaction. He recommended the enactment of laws that would punish marauding whites who encroached on Indian lands as well as punish Indians for their criminal acts. Congress, however, did little to solve these problems.[56]

In June of 1876, Sheridan sent Custer to crush all resistance from the Sioux. When Custer discovered a Sioux encampment on the banks of the Little Bighorn, he decided to attack. Although outnumbered, he divided his command. In the battle that followed, Custer and 225 of his men were killed in what became known as Custer's Last Stand.[57]

When news of the massacre reached Sheridan in Philadelphia, there was an outcry for vengeance. The nation was not ready for such a disaster and demanded to know what had happened. Sheridan investigated the matter and concluded it had been caused by Custer's bravado, his faulty tactics, and his failure to determine the strength of the enemy before attacking.[58]

At least three times in his later years, Sheridan's name was proposed as a candidate for president, but he turned down all offers. He told an Associated Press reporter, "I don't want that or any other civil office." In the autumn of 1883, when General Sherman retired as general-in-chief, Sheridan was appointed in his place.[59]

In the spring of 1888, Sheridan was struck by a series of heart attacks. He was fifty-seven years old, and his luck was running out. In June, a bedridden Sheridan was promoted to full general. He spent the remaining days of his life at his summer cottage at Nonquit, Massachusetts. On August 5, he died.[60]

Sherman eulogized Sheridan, saying, "He was a great soldier and a noble man." Earlier Grant had said that Sheridan was "the embodiment of heroism, dash, and impulse." But the most memorable tribute came from his wife. When asked by a friend why she did not remarry, she responded, "I would rather be the widow of Phil Sheridan than the wife of any man alive."[61]

20 John F. Reynolds

Man of Honor

By the summer of 1863, John Reynolds, commander of the First Corps, was among the most respected and admired officers in the Army of the Potomac. After the Union debacle at Chancellorsville in May, President Lincoln wanted to replace "Fighting" Joe Hooker. Aware of the high regard that the men of the Army of the Potomac had for Reynolds, he invited him to the White House for a conference. What was discussed at that meeting is not known for certain, but it is believed that Lincoln offered the command of the Army of the Potomac to Reynolds. Reynolds would not accept the position unless he could be certain he could be protected from the political interference that had hindered his predecessors. Lincoln, however, was unable to give him that assurance. As a result, three weeks later, just before the crucial battle at Gettysburg, the command of the army was turned over to Major General George Meade.[1]

When Reynolds learned of Meade's appointment, he went to see the general at his headquarters. Meade rose to greet Reynolds, searching for words to express his discomfort at the awkwardness of having been promoted over the man who, the day before, had been his superior. Reynolds put Meade at ease, assuring him that the job had gone to the right man and that he could count on his support.[2]

Perhaps no Union general was more widely respected and highly admired by his associates, superiors, and subordinates than John Reynolds. Brave and dynamic, he was held in esteem by virtually everyone who came into contact with him. To one officer he was "impetuous without rashness, rapid without haste, ready without heedlessness." A close colleague of his, Major General Oliver Howard noted, "From soldiers, cadets and officers, junior and senior, he always secured reverence for his serious character, respect for his ability, care for his uniform discipline, admiration for his fearlessness, and love for his unfailing generosity."[3]

Reynolds was a born soldier, displaying at all times a sober and judicious use of authority. He rarely made tactical mistakes. He was a dependable corps commander who was able to move his units into the right place at the right time. He always showed concern for the well-being of his men and went out of his way to instill confidence and enthusiasm in all those under his command. John Reynolds looked the part of a leader. Standing six-feet tall, he was darkly handsome, with a thin face hidden behind a neatly combed and trimmed beard. His deep sensitivity seemed to be at odds with his stern image; his stare easily indicated when he was displeased with one's actions. One of his few shortcomings was his lack of a sense of humor.[4]

John Reynolds was a complex man with a varied personality. To staff officers and close subordinates, he seemed reticent and aloof. He was, as General Meade described him, "a man of very few words." To his family and sisters, he was a warm, protective man who wrote long affectionate letters in which he expressed all his inner thoughts. To the officers and men he commanded, he was charismatic. Colonel Fred Hitchcock said, "Reynolds was a superb looking man, . . . the ideal soldier." In the words of a First Corps aide, ". . . the love we had for him is beyond expression."[5]

Reynolds deeply distrusted the politicians who tried to direct the war and the writers who reported the movement of troops. He was a stickler for details and rarely left even the minor ones to subordinates. Occasionally, when angered, he would resort to the use of profanity. Nevertheless, these shortcomings did not offset the many good qualities that won him fame, glory, and the most prestigious opportunity of his career: the chance to command the Army of the Potomac.[6]

John Reynolds was a Pennsylvanian, born on September 20, 1820, in the town of Lancaster, only fifty miles east of Gettysburg, where he would die in battle. He was the fifth of thirteen children, four of whom died at an early age. His Irish and French Huguenot ancestors migrated to America in the mid-eighteenth century. His father was a well-known Lancaster business-man and journalist who owned a local newspaper, the *Lancaster Journal*. He also served in the state legislature and had been captain of the local militia company.[7]

Lancaster was a pleasant place for a boy to live. In the summer he could swim or fish; in the winter there was skating, and the snow-covered hills made ideal runs for sledding. All in all, it was a comfortable life for young John. He enjoyed sports, riding, and gardening. John's parents were inter-ested in having him obtain a good education, sending him to a well-known public school in Lititz, Pennsylvania. His letters home indicate that he was an enthusiastic student: "I think I have improved very much since I am here." He and his brother later attended Long Green Academy in Balti-more, but John did not enjoy his stay there as much.[8]

By the summer of 1863, Major General John F. Reynolds, commander of the First Corps, was among the most respected and admired men in the Army of the Potomac. When offered the command of the Army of the Potomac, he turned it down because Lincoln could not assure him he could be protected from the political interference that had hindered his predecessors.

COURTESY OF THE LIBRARY OF CONGRESS

John finished his final year of school and graduated in 1835 at the age of fifteen. So far, nothing suggested that he would become a soldier. John's father was not wealthy, but he did prize education. In 1836, he began looking for a means of furthering his son's education without straining family resources. He turned to his friend, future president James Buchanan, seeking his help in securing a position for John at West Point. Attending West Point was his father's idea, not John's.[9]

Buchanan's first attempt to get John an appointment to West Point was unsuccessful. John was still too young to meet the regulation age, and

Buchanan's request was denied. When Buchanan tried again the following year, he was able to secure the appointment. On March 6, 1837, John wrote to the secretary of war, accepting the position.[10]

John began his cadet years in training camp that summer. In one of his first letters home, he said, "I am very pleased with my life here and think I shall continue to like it." Reynolds proved to be an average student, graduating twenty-sixth in a class of fifty-two.[11]

In his own quiet way, Reynolds made many friends. William T. Sherman knew him at the academy and liked him. As a cadet, John impressed Henry Kendrick by his clear and independent thinking, his even temperament, and his courtesy. Along with Reynolds, the class of 1841 included several cadets who would play significant roles in the Civil War: Nathaniel Lyon, Don Carlos Buell, and Richard Garnett. The class behind him included James Longstreet, William Rosecrans, John Pope, Abner Doubleday, George Sykes, D. H. Hill, and Lafayette McLaws. Preceding him by a year were Sherman, George Thomas, and Richard Ewell. Two fellow Pennsylvanians, Winfield Scott Hancock and Alfred Pleasonton, had entered as plebes during Reynolds's last year.[12]

In the fall of 1841, Brevet Second Lieutenant John F. Reynolds moved happily into his first assignment: Battery H, Third Artillery, at Fort McHenry, Baltimore. He spent the next four years in Maryland, Florida, and South Carolina. At the last post, he served with two future military greats, Lieutenants William T. Sherman and George Thomas. Afterward, he was transferred to Corpus Christi, Texas. He was there when the war with Mexico broke out.[13]

Now a first lieutenant, Reynolds served under General Taylor in Mexico, winning two brevet commissions: captain, for bravery in the Battle of Monterrey in September 1846; and major for "special gallantry" during the decisive fighting at Buena Vista on February 23, 1847.[14] Brevets were given for gallantry in action or for meritorious service, but except under the most special circumstances, they remained purely honorary. The recipient received neither more pay nor a permanent increase in rank, but a brevet did serve to single a man out, especially when it was a reward for gallant fighting.

After the Battle of Monterrey, Abner Doubleday found Reynolds leaning on a cannon near the spot of attack and asked him what his thoughts were when he was under attack by the Mexican troops. Reynolds replied that he did "not allow himself to think of the subject, for I might have thought wrong." At a later date he wrote that "this [Aqua Nueva] has been the greatest battle yet. I thought that at Monterrey I had been in pretty tight places, but it was nothing to this. . . . We are pretty well used up, both men and horses."[15]

As the Mexican War dragged on, Reynolds was anxious to return home for a special reason. At the age of twenty-seven, he was still a bachelor and wanted a wife. Writing on New Year's Day, 1848, he told his sister June that he would consider proposals from any of the female population at home. He had, however, three requirements: "the applicant must be good looking, amiable, and have a small portion of what is usually termed common sense." He also added that he would not object if the applicant had a bit of money.[16]

After America's victory in Mexico, Brevet Major Reynolds returned to the more routine business of garrison duty. He served at numerous forts in New England, Louisiana, and New York, where the monotonous routine and low pay depressed him. Although many of his friends left the service for civilian life, he remained in the army. In the summer of 1854, the two companies of the Third Artillery, of which Reynolds was temporarily in command, were ordered to accompany a 1,200-mile overland expedition along the Oregon Trail to Salt Lake City. In May 1855, he traveled on the final leg of his trip to California sporting a new rank, that of captain.[17]

Although happy with his promotion, there was one position that he coveted: command of a light artillery company that his old friend Braxton Bragg had commanded. When he learned that Bragg had been promoted to major and would be giving up his command, he wrote to his brother James, a lawyer with political clout and the ear of James Buchanan, soon to be elected president: "I wish you could use any and all of the political influence you may have to get me that company." Despite his brother's efforts, General Scott recommended Robert Anderson to replace Bragg. In another letter to his brother James, Reynolds clearly expressed his feelings: "Merit is no recommendation and political influence everything. . . . I may say that I have never been so disgusted with this army as within the last twelve months." He might have threatened to resign, but he never did. For months to come, his letters would reflect a sense of frustration.[18]

Instead of the assignment he had hoped for, Reynolds was ordered to Fort Orford, Oregon, to take command of Company H, Third Artillery. In March 1856, he was involved in his first Indian war, which required him to chase a band of Native Americans through rugged, mountainous country. His efforts were successful, and many of the enemy combatants came in and gave up their arms. Orders soon arrived for Reynolds, giving him command of the light artillery company he had desired earlier. The War Department had decided to replace the light artillery with long-range guns and, according to Braxton Bragg, destroyed their "finest battery." With the new assignment came the order to move to Fort Monroe, Virginia.[19]

By 1859, Reynolds was reassigned to the West Coast again. Although far from home, he kept up-to-date with the mounting tensions in the East, including John Brown's raid at Harper's Ferry. Reynolds was a Democrat whose family had close ties with the Buchanan administration, but for him slavery did not pose a moral dilemma. He believed that "if they hang, along with old Brown . . . a few more of the abolitionist stripe, it would effectively stop the agitation for a time." Reynolds, however, was a strong Unionist, and there would be no question about which side he would fight on when war came.[20]

As the country moved toward war, Reynolds's private life was undergoing change. When thirty-nine years old and still a bachelor, he met and fell in love with Catherine (Kate) Mary Hewitt, a twenty-year-old Catholic girl. When Reynolds was ordered East the next year, she followed him and took up residence at a Catholic school near Philadelphia. Reynolds kept their relationship a secret, and it was only at his death that his family learned of her existence.[21]

During the summer of 1860, Major Reynolds was assigned as the commandant of cadets at West Point. This was a prestigious position. Although he had regarded West Point a desirable assignment in 1845, by 1860 he was having second thoughts: "I have been on duty for a week trying to persuade myself that I shall like it." With the great number of Southern cadets and high tension between units, Reynolds knew he had stepped into a hornet's nest.[22]

The commandant of cadets had many responsibilities, including the teaching of artillery, cavalry, and infantry tactics, equitation (veterinary science), art, outpost duty, strategy, grand tactics, and army administration and organization. This was a tall order, but not as difficult as it sounded. The commandant had assistant instructors under him who did most of the teaching. In addition, he was responsible for all corps formations, parades, and ceremonies. He was also the chief disciplinary officer at the Point.[23]

Maintaining discipline was difficult enough during normal times, but under the current conditions, it became almost impossible. Reynolds's discipline fell heavily on one cadet in particular: George Armstrong Custer. In June 1861, as Custer's class left for Washington and the war, Custer was under arrest for dereliction of duty. Custer was academically last in his class and three demerits short of expulsion. He had been brought before Reynolds for a number of offenses, but he had never been court-martialed. Reynolds would have liked to expel him from the army, but the times did not permit it. Custer was not the only cadet to feel Reynolds's disciplinary action. Over the months, Reynolds had established a reputation for strictness, and his actions were viewed by some as tyrannical. This reputation did not seem to bother him. To the contrary, he was pleased that, when he left, there was "great rejoicing among the cadets at their being relieved of me."[24]

Reynolds's stay at West Point was not destined to be long. Within a year, he and some of the cadets would be fighting on opposite sides. The election of November 1860 placed Pennsylvania into the Republican column. This put a strain on Reynolds's neutrality, but throughout the winter, he still hoped for a settlement that might avoid war. When Fort Sumter was fired upon in April 1861, Reynolds wrote to his sister Ellie: "What history will say of us, our government, and Mr. B's [President Buchanan's] administration makes one wish to disown him." For him, this was hard to say; old loyalties were not easily forgotten.[25]

With the outbreak of war, Reynolds received an offer to serve as aide-de-camp to General-in-Chief Winfield Scott. During peacetime, he would have jumped at the chance, but now he turned it down and stayed at West Point. He was discouraged by the thought of being "tied to a desk" in Washington when the war heated up. He wanted to be where the fighting was.[26]

The attack on Fort Sumter had made Reynolds's job at West Point all but impossible. He assured the Southern cadets that they would be allowed to complete their studies. On May 2, orders came to graduate the first-class cadets at once. Reynolds wondered about his own future: "How long I will remain [at West Point] is uncertain."[27]

Active field command for Reynolds came less than four months later, in July 1861, when he was commissioned lieutenant colonel in the newly reactivated Fourteenth U.S. Infantry. "I would, of course, have preferred the artillery arm of the service," he wrote his sister, "but could not refuse the promotion offered me under any circumstance, much less at this time, when the Government has a right to my services in any capacity."[28]

Reynolds hardly had time to enjoy his new promotion before being commissioned as a brigadier general of volunteers. Soon afterward, he received a telegram from Major General George B. McClellan, commander of the Army of the Potomac: "Do you accept your appointment of brigadier general, and if so, when will you be here?" On September 12, Reynolds reported to the headquarters of the Army of the Potomac and was assigned the First Brigade of the Pennsylvania Reserve Division, commanded by General George McCall.[29]

General McClellan was determined to whip the volunteer army into shape before they were forced to fight, thereby avoiding the mistakes made by McDowell at Bull Run. Reynolds, however, had some doubt about whether he would be able to make soldiers out of volunteers. Not until March 1862 did the Pennsylvania Reserves, now part of the First Corps, leave for the Virginia peninsula. As McClellan's army moved up the peninsula, Reynolds's brigade remained in the rear, along the banks of the Rappahannock River. Reynolds was disappointed when his brigade was not involved in the fighting. Anxious for action, Reynolds considered resigning his volunteer commission and returning to the regular regiment that he had been ordered to the year before.[30]

In May, when Major General Irvin McDowell's First Corps occupied Fredericksburg, McDowell appointed Reynolds military governor of the area. He was well suited for this position; his temperament and method of dealing with people were both humane and fair. His regime lasted only sixteen days, but in that short time he won the respect and admiration of many of the citizens of Fredericksburg. The kindness and fairness he showed them would be returned to him later in the war.[31]

Action finally came on June 26, when Robert E. Lee's Army of Northern Virginia attacked Reynolds's right flank. His men turned back the Rebel attack and, by their action, convinced their commander that volunteer troops could be good soldiers. The next afternoon, Reynolds's battle-tested men were involved in the battle at Gaines's Mill. In desperate fighting, the reserves suffered heavy losses, and the Federal center caved in. Reynolds's troops accounted well for themselves, but Gaines's Mill was an ill-fated engagement for the general. That evening, while supervising the retreat, he became separated from his brigade and surrounded by Confederate pickets. He hid in dense woods through the night, but the next morning the Rebels discovered his whereabouts and took him prisoner.[32]

Reynolds was taken away to the field headquarters of Confederate Major General D. H. Hill, once his tent mate in the prewar army. Hill later described Reynolds as "confused and mortified at his position" and noted that, in his anguish, "he sat down and covered his face with his hands and at length said: 'Hill, we ought not to be enemies.' I told him there was no bad feelings on my part, and that he ought not to fret at the fortunes of war, which were notoriously fickle."[33]

Charles Lamborn, Reynolds's aide, assured Reynolds's sisters that their brother was greatly missed by his men. "His coolness and bravery and his admirable disposition of the forces at Mechanicsville . . . are yet the constant theme of conversation about the camp fires. It is the highest aspiration of these men to fight again under General Reynolds." After a time, Reynolds was sent to Richmond, along with other captive officers, including his division commander, Brigadier General McCall. For a week he was held under arrest at the Spotswood House, a hotel in Richmond. After the end of the Battle of Seven Days and General McClellan's withdrawal, Reynolds was moved to the notorious Libby Prison. When the captives were moved, they were forced to march through the streets to the prison. Reynolds had made and would make longer marches, but none during which his pride was hurt as much as this one.[34]

At Libby Prison, the officers and men were quartered together regardless of rank. They all washed, ate, and slept in the same room, described by Reynolds as filthy. He and his commanding officer, General McCall, however, were allowed to buy their own food, which was sent into the prison from a boardinghouse. For Reynolds, the greatest indignity was to be kept constantly under guard after having given his word of honor that he would not try to escape. He had wanted to fight this war "old army" style, and General Hill's courtesy had supported this notion, but the authorities at the prison preferred to take no chances.[35]

When the news of Reynolds's imprisonment became known, many of the residents of Fredericksburg were concerned about his welfare. The mayor of Fredericksburg brought a petition signed by twenty-seven of the city's most influential citizens asking for Reynolds to be exchanged or paroled as quickly as possible. Recalling his humane regime as military governor, the citizens requested that his "treatment be as kind and considerate as was extended by him to us." Whether their petition had an effect on Reynolds's release or not is uncertain, but he was involved in a general exchange of prisoners on August 13. On his return to the Pennsylvania Reserves, he was welcomed back by his men who had taken up a collection to purchase a sword for him.[36]

General McCall was also released by the Confederates, but, because of poor health, he resigned his position and returned home. Reynolds assumed command of the Pennsylvania Reserves, now mustering 7,000 men. Late in August, Reynolds's division joined Major General John Pope's Army of Virginia in time for the Second Battle of Manassas. Reynolds's performance, especially when compared to the rest of the Federal effort, was commendable. On the evening of the second day of the battle, when the Union left had been crushed and Pope's army was fleeing the field, Reynolds moved his brigades onto Henry House Hill for a last-ditch stand. Grabbing the flag of the Second Regiment, Reynolds waved it and shouted to his men, "Now boys, give them the steel, charge bayonets, double quick!" Reynolds's counterattack slowed the Rebel's advance and gained precious time for Pope's army to form an orderly retreat.[37]

Reynolds's gallant actions and reckless personal exposure to enemy fire did not go unnoticed. "His actions," said one of his men, "infused into the men a spirit which gave them the will to stand and fight." Pope's retreating army owed its survival largely to Reynolds's efforts and powers of inspiration. Later, Pope recognized Reynolds's contribution at the Second Battle of Manassas: "Brigadier General John F. Reynolds, Commanding the Pennsylvania Reserves, merits the highest commendation at my hands. Prompt, active, and energetic, he commanded his division with distinguished ability throughout all operations and performed his duties in all situations with zeal and fidelity."[38]

In early September 1862, Lee, unwilling to lose the offensive momentum he had gained at Manassas, decided to invade Maryland. On September 2, President Lincoln ordered McClellan to assume command of all Union forces in the East and to prepare to defend the capital. In McClellan's reorganization, Reynolds's division was assigned to Major General Joe Hooker's corps. The division had earned a reputation as a hard-fighting unit, but Reynolds never had the opportunity to share in their glory. Alarmed by Lee's invasion of Maryland and fearful that his state might be in danger, Governor Curtain issued a call for 50,000 state militia to defend Pennsylvania if attacked. Curtain demanded of President Lincoln "an active, energetic officer to command the forces in the field and one that could rally Pennsylvanians around him. It is believed that General Reynolds would be the most useful." Reynolds was relieved of command and ordered to Pennsylvania. He turned his division over to General Meade and reported to Harrisburg. Both Hooker and Reynolds felt that the Rebels had no intention of going to Harrisburg, but Curtain's political power prevailed. A disgruntled Reynolds returned to Pennsylvania, while his reserves marched to meet Lee.[39]

On September 13, Reynolds arrived at the state capital and began the task of whipping the new recruits into a fighting force. As the events at Antietam unfolded, there was little Reynolds could do. For the next two weeks, the militia would go no further south than Chambersburg, Pennsylvania. After Lee's retreat back into Virginia, the militia was disbanded, and Reynolds returned to the army, much to his relief.[40]

When Reynolds returned, he found himself temporarily in charge of the First Corps, assuming command from George Meade, who had led the corps since General Hooker was wounded at Antietam. As an old army "regular," Meade accepted the seniority system and was willing to assume his former position as division commander. Although the rivalry between Meade and Reynolds would increase as they both enjoyed military success, they were also developing a mutual respect that was rare among Federal corps commanders.[41]

In November, Reynolds was promoted to major general, and the next month, Meade also won a second star. As a corps commander, Reynolds maintained his reputation as a leader who was deeply concerned for his men's welfare and morale. He would command the First Corps to the end of his life and take as much pride in his men as they did in him.

Following Antietam, much to President Lincoln's dismay, McClellan decided to rebuild his army rather than pursue Lee. As a result, tensions between the two escalated, and on November 7, Lincoln replaced McClellan with Major General Ambrose Burnside. The removal of McClellan was a great shock to the army and, in Reynolds's view, was as "unwise, injudicious, as it was uncalled for."[42]

On November 9, Reynolds, with George Meade, Abner Doubleday, and John Gibbon, visited McClellan's headquarters for a private farewell. Senior among the group, Reynolds expressed everyone's regrets. McClellan was greatly affected by their response to his removal, almost to the point of tears. Two days later, Meade witnessed "the sincere grief of the whole army," as he termed it, on McClellan's departure.[43]

In December, Reynolds's First Corps participated in the Battle of Fredericksburg, holding the extreme Federal left and facing strongly entrenched Confederates on high ground on the south bank of the Rappahannock River. Burnside had ordered Reynolds's corps to attack the Rebel right, which was anchored by troops under Stonewall Jackson. Reynolds and other corps and division commanders agreed that the only way to carry the heights was an all-out assault with their entire force. Burnside did not concur. Instead of a concentrated, all-out assault, the attack was to be made one division at a time. Reynolds selected Meade's division to spearhead the attack. The well-positioned Confederates unleashed deadly fire, which cut Meade's division into pieces. By an almost superhuman effort, Reynolds

was able to break a portion of the enemy's line before Confederate reinforcements were able to push them back. Later in the day, Burnside
attacked other parts of the Confederate line, again with no success, and
nearly destroyed his own army beyond repair.[44]

After the debacle at Fredericksburg, "Fighting Joe" Hooker replaced
Burnside as commander of the Army of the Potomac. In May 1863 at Chancellorsville, Hooker's army was engaged in three days of intermittent fighting
in which the main body suffered another overwhelming defeat. General
Reynolds and the First Corps were not involved in the main action, being
held in reserve. On the evening of May 4, Hooker met with his corps commanders to ask their opinion on whether to retreat or risk another day's
combat. Reynolds and a majority of the corps leaders argued for the army
to renew the battle at daylight with all its strength, but Hooker decided to
withdraw during the night anyway. Reynolds bitterly asked the other corps
commanders: "What was the use of calling us together at this time of night
when he intended to retreat anyhow?"[45]

By May 6, the army had re-crossed the Rappahannock, and Reynolds was
in a bad mood. General John Gibbon recalled that Reynolds "was the
picture of woe and disgust and said plainly that we had been badly out-
generaled and whipped by half our number." The disgusted Reynolds
joined a chorus of voices urging the removal of Hooker, which finally
occurred on June 28, just three days before Gettysburg.[46]

On May 31, Reynolds took leave and traveled to Washington, where he
had a lengthy discussion with the president concerning the leadership of
the Army of the Potomac. It is believed that Lincoln offered the command
of the army to Reynolds, who declined the offer. In rejecting command of
the Army of the Potomac, Reynolds missed the chance of a lifetime.[47]

On June 28, Lincoln replaced Joe Hooker with General George Meade.
Meade was reluctant to accept the position, telling the War Department that
the army was expecting Reynolds to be appointed. Finally, he accepted, saying, "Well, I've been tried and condemned without a hearing, and I suppose I shall have to go to execution."[48]

News of the change in command was well received by officers who were
well acquainted with Meade. Elsewhere, however, there were other favor-
ites, particularly Reynolds and Sedgwick. The promotion was accepted by
most of the troops "without protest, but without enthusiasm." Facing disgrace if he failed, Meade realized that he must be successful. On the morning of June 28, a newspaperman saw Meade standing alone and lost in
thought as if "weighed down with the sense of responsibility resting on
him."[49] When Reynolds heard of Meade's promotion, he put on his best
uniform and went to his headquarters to pay his respects.

Meade was anxious to talk to Reynolds, a man he considered important
in his service and also a friend and brother. Meade expressed that he
wished the position had been given to Reynolds and that it was important

to him to have Reynolds's support. Reynolds assured Meade that the command had gone to the right man and that Meade could rely on him. Meade was greatly relieved. With that settled, the two men went on to map out a plan to bring Lee into battle.[50]

On June 30, as the situation grew more tense, General Meade ordered Reynolds to take command of the three corps forming the left wing of the Army of the Potomac. The left wing consisted of Reynolds's own First Corps, the Eleventh Corps (both of which were near Emmitsburg) and the Third Corps (which was marching toward Emmitsburg from Taneytown).[51]

Reynolds met with Major General Oliver Howard, commander of the Eleventh Corps, to plan their movement to Gettysburg. Howard admired Reynolds and remembered him in later years as an officer who governed with a steady hand, was generous and quick to recognize merit, sought to gain the confidence of his subordinates, and was foremost in battle.[52]

When Reynolds learned that Confederate forces were in the vicinity of Gettysburg, he ordered his men to move there without delay. After receiving information that the enemy was advancing on the town along the Chambersburg Pike, Reynolds galloped toward the sounds of combat with his staff and found Brigadier General John Buford's cavalry trying to slow the Rebel advance toward McPherson's Ridge. "What's the matter, John?" were Reynolds's first words. The cavalryman replied, "The devil's to pay!" and explained that the enemy threatened to overwhelm his outnumbered troops.[53]

Reynolds sent couriers to order his leading division to hurry. At the same time, he sent a message to Meade indicating that the enemy was advancing in strong force: "I fear they will get to the heights beyond town before I can. I will fight them inch by inch, and if driven into town, I will barricade the streets and hold them back as long as possible." "Good!" Meade said. "That is just like Reynolds; he will hold on to the bitter end." Meade was satisfied that Reynolds had things under control until Howard and Slocum could bring up their corps.[54]

As his men arrived, Reynolds deployed them, guiding the Second Wisconsin of the Iron Brigade to the front. Alarmed at the headway the Confederates were making, he exhorted them to hurry forward and meet the Confederates head on: "Forward men, forward for God's sake and drive those fellows out of those woods." With Reynolds leading, the Iron Brigade surged ahead. Reynolds's orderly, Sergeant Charles Veil, later wrote that "wherever the fight raged the fiercest, there the general was sure to be found, his undaunted courage always inspired the men with more energy and courage."[55]

Reynolds wanted more men. He turned in his saddle and looked anxiously toward the rear. The Iron Brigade needed help. Just then Reynolds sagged to the ground. Sergeant Veil leaped from his horse and ran over to him. Veil could find no visible wound, and there appeared to be no bleeding.

Taking hold of Reynolds's arms, he dragged him back out of the range of Confederate fire. As Veil pulled Reynolds back to the Union lines, Confederates called to him to drop the body, but he ignored their calls and kept backing off as fast as he could until he was out of range of the enemy fire.[56]

When Reynolds was examined more carefully, a bullet hole was found behind his right ear. When he was turned on his back, he gasped once, then smiled. But he never spoke and died shortly thereafter. The general's body was carried back to the nearby seminary, then away from the battle to a small stone house on the Emmitsburg road.[57]

By his action, Reynolds had protected the Federal position and enabled his men to rush forward and blunt the Confederate attack. Soon, reinforcements arrived and regrouped south of Gettysburg on Cemetery Hill. Their stand was made possible because of Reynolds's decision to fight and preserve the high ground for a later rallying point.[58]

Meade had received numerous messages during the morning but was waiting anxiously to hear from Reynolds. The first news he received was good; Reynolds's corps was holding its position. Then, at approximately 1:00 p.m., Major Riddle rode up with the bad news: Reynolds had been killed. Meade showed his sorrow and shock; he was so choked by emotion he could hardly speak. As the news spread, his men exclaimed in astonishment, "Reynolds dead? Reynolds!" The army's most dependable general had been snatched away almost before the battle had begun. "It was hard to believe and harder to bear."[59]

The final scene in this tragic event was yet to be played out. After Reynolds's death, one of his aides found a silver chain around his neck containing a Roman Catholic medal (Reynolds was not a Catholic) and a gold ring. Engraved inside the ring was the inscription, "Dear Kate." The words, as well as the fact that his West Point ring was missing from his finger, were good indications that the "confirmed old bachelor" must have had a sweetheart.[60]

On July 3, when the general's body arrived at the Philadelphia home of his married sister Jennie, the mystery was solved. A pretty, twenty-four-year-old woman arrived at the house, introduced herself as Catherine Mary Hewitt, and asked if she might view the remains. Soon the family knew that it was "Kate" Hewitt who had been John's love. Miss Hewitt said that she had met Reynolds in 1860 while serving as a governess to a San Francisco family when he was stationed at a local military post. Their friendship had developed into a romance, which Reynolds had wished to keep secret. When war began, they made a joint decision: if John survived the conflict, they would marry and honeymoon in Europe; should he die in battle, Kate had his permission to enter the convent. Without him, she said, life no longer interested her.[61]

Reynolds had never mentioned Kate in any of his letters, and the family was quite stunned when Miss Hewitt arrived at their door; however, they quickly embraced her as one of their own. They wished to make her a member of the family, but Kate kept her promise, and on July 12, she entered the convent in Emmitsburg, Maryland, only ten miles from the spot where the general had fallen. The Reynolds kept in touch with her through much of her life, but, in 1868, Kate left the order in poor health. Although the family made efforts to reestablish communication with her, Kate vanished into obscurity.[62]

John Reynolds's body arrived home in Lancaster on July 4, accompanied by his family and members of his staff. The streets were filled with people. Flags were lowered to half mast and draped with crepe as the funeral cortege moved slowly to the cemetery. The general was buried beside his mother and father. When the body was lowered into the ground, Major Riddle fell to the ground and wept.[63]

In September 1863, the Reynolds family received a request from the First Corps asking permission to raise money for a monument to be erected "as a small tribute to his memory . . . which would please the officers of the Old Corps." Reynolds was a man of honor who received many tributes, but those of the Pennsylvania Reserves and the First Corps would have undoubtedly meant the most to him.[64]

21　*George Gordon Meade*

The Cautious General

On June 28, 1863, three days before the Battle of Gettysburg, George Gordon Meade replaced Joseph Hooker as commander of the Army of the Potomac. The change in leadership did not surprise the army; after all, it was the fifth within a year. They were only surprised at the selection. "What's Meade ever done?" was the common response. Meade was just as surprised as the rest of the army.

Unlike two of his predecessors, McClellan and Hooker, Meade was completely lacking in charisma and the ability to inspire his men. Even the incompetent Burnside looked more the part of a commanding general than did Meade. Although only forty-seven, he looked considerably older, rather like a burned-out college professor. His thin, bearded face and balding head gave the impression that he was "serious, almost sad." Possessing a broad, high forehead and hawk-like nose, Meade was referred to as "a damned google-eyed old snapping turtle" by his troops. To many, this epithet would have been an insult, but it did not seem to bother Meade.[1]

George Meade was born in Cadiz, Spain, on December 31, 1815. He was one of nine children born to Richard Worsam Meade and Margaret Butler Meade. The Meades were one of the most prominent families in Philadelphia, owning a business with international interests, which often allowed them to travel abroad. Richard and his wife came from different worlds. He was Roman Catholic; Margaret was Protestant.[2]

Adversity soon came to the family fortune, and George's father died in poverty in Washington. The family was forced to return to Philadelphia, where his grandfather was a merchant. Young George spent three years in a Philadelphia elementary school and then entered a military academy at nearby Germantown. He showed aptitude for mathematics and science but wanted to study law. George reluctantly accepted an appointment to West Point in 1831 when he was unable to attend the college of his choice due to lack of money.[3]

Meade was not happy at the Academy. Slender and delicate in appearance, he freely admitted that he never wanted to be a soldier. When the nation was at peace, many young men attended West Point to get a general education rather than to serve in the army. Since the Academy was graduating more officers than were needed, many graduates resigned to become civil engineers, teachers, lawyers, or clergymen. Such was Meade's intention. He graduated nineteenth in a class of fifty-six. As a new graduate, he was bound by law to serve one year in the military. On July 1, 1835, he was named a brevet second lieutenant and assigned to Company C, Third Artillery.[4]

In 1836, after service in Florida and at the arsenal in Watertown, Massachusetts, Meade resigned from the army to pursue a career in civil engineering. Successful at first, Meade experienced the cold realities of life during the recession of 1837. It was difficult to find work as an engineer, although the regular army engineers were kept busy. Meade was hoping to marry soon; the recession could not have come at a worse time for him. Meade had been courting Margaret Sergeant, the oldest daughter of a congressman. Margaret was well educated in cultural topics and played the piano with distinction. On his twenty-fifth birthday, December 31, 1840, the two were married. In 1842, because of his new responsibilities, Meade decided to reenter the army, joining the elite Corps of Topographical Engineers.[5] During the war with Mexico, Meade served as a staff and engineering officer but not as a combat leader. He was present at Palo Alto, Resaca de la Palma, and Monterrey and was awarded a brevet of first lieutenant. After the battle at Monterrey, Meade wrote to his wife: "I wish to express to you my heartfelt gratitude that it has pleased God once more to pass me through untold dangers, and to allow me still to cling to the hope of once more being reunited to you."[6]

After the Mexican War, Meade was involved in conducting land and water surveys and constructing lighthouses along the East Coast. Although still only a lieutenant, Meade was performing advanced work. In 1856, he was promoted to captain and sent to Detroit. By now, the Meades had seven children; given the promotion and change of station, the captain moved his whole flock with him.[7]

Meade enjoyed his days in Detroit on the lakes. Unlike many of his army comrades, he was never subjected to the monotony, loneliness, and frustration of service at an isolated Western post. Although his work was going well, Meade was aware of the crisis developing in the East. As one-by-one the Southern states seceded, Meade became more concerned about the country and his family. Although he had two married sisters living in the South, Meade's allegiance was with the North. He had no difficulty choosing sides in the fight.[8]

General George G. Meade, officer of the Federal army, and other generals of the Army of the Potomac, vicinity of Washington, D.C., June 1865.

COURTESY OF THE LIBRARY OF CONGRESS

By June 1861, Meade was still in Detroit, hoping to be reassigned to the East. Meade went to Washington to see Secretary of War Simon Cameron, requesting to be assigned to one of the regiments of volunteers being formed. But by midsummer, Cameron had still not acted on Meade's request. Finally, on July 31, after appealing to Pennsylvania's Senator David Wilmot to take action, Meade was commissioned brigadier general of volunteers.[9]

Aware of his new responsibility and lack of field experience, Meade had some apprehension about his new assignment, telling his wife, "Sometimes I have a little sinking at the heart, when I reflect that perhaps I may fail at the grand scratch; but I try to console myself with the belief that I shall probably do as well as most of my neighbors."[10]

After a winter of work on the Washington defenses, he joined Major General George McClellan on the peninsula. In June 1862, Meade's brigade fought during the Battle of Seven Days at Mechanicsville, Gaines's Mill, and Glendale. At Glendale, Meade exhorted his men to continue to fight when they were hard pressed, "encouraging and cheering them by word and example." His fearlessness resulted in two wounds. The first shot hit him in the fleshy part of his forearm; the other entered his right side and exited just above his spine. Despite his wounds, Meade did not leave the field until forced to by loss of blood. As he left the field, he shouted to his men: "Fight your guns to the last, but save them if possible."[11]

Before being treated, Meade insisted on writing to his wife to ease her mind when she heard of his wounds: "My wounds are not dangerous, though they require immediate and constant attendance. I am to leave in the first boat to Old Point, and from thence home." Once Meade was home, the Philadelphia press ran an item on him: "General Meade . . . has been wounded but . . . is in good spirits. He fought with great bravery and skill, and greatly added to his reputation as a soldier."[12] On August 17, Meade rejoined his command at Falmouth, Virginia, and was gratified by cheers from each company as he rode through the camp.

August 30, at the Second Battle of Manassas, Pope's Army of Virginia was caught between Stonewall Jackson's and Longstreet's corps. His army paid dearly. Only Meade's Pennsylvania Reserves prevented a complete disaster by protecting Pope's line of retreat. After the army's defeat, morale was low. The news that McClellan was returning to command helped lift the spirits of the troops.[13]

With the return of McClellan, the Army of the Potomac and the Army of Virginia were merged and divided into six corps. Meade was subsequently given command of a division that was part of General Joseph Hooker's corps. Meade was pleased with his new assignment. "I am ready to meet the enemy," Meade wrote, "for I feel I am in the position I am entitled to."[14]

In September, Lee's Army of Northern Virginia invaded Maryland. When a copy of Lee's orders fell into McClellan's hands, the Union general knew that Lee had divided his army. Meade's division engaged a portion of the Confederate army under Major General D. H. Hill at South Mountain. A captured Confederate soldier later complimented the efforts of Meade's troops: "Your men fight like devils," he said. Later, when Lee took a stand along the Antietam Creek, Meade directed his new command flawlessly. When General Hooker was wounded in the foot, he asked Meade to take over the corps. After ammunition ran low and his men were nearly spent, Meade was forced to withdraw.

For the first time, Meade experienced a lack of public recognition and praise for his accomplishments, which caused him some pain. "I find the papers barely mention the Pennsylvania Reserves," he complained to his wife, "never mentioning my name."[15] But McClellan did notice Meade's accomplishments. After the battle at Antietam, President Lincoln visited McClellan in the field. During his visit, McClellan took the opportunity to introduce Meade to the president and to praise him openly for his good work at South Mountain and Antietam.[16]

Lincoln became impatient with McClellan when the Army of the Potomac stood idle near the village of Sharpsburg for more than a month. On November 5, he signed an order relieving him of command; in his place he appointed Major General Ambrose Burnside. Burnside's reputation with his fellow generals was not stellar. At Antietam, he had wasted several hours stubbornly hammering away at a bridge instead of ordering his men to wade across the stream. On the other hand, McClellan had been very popular with the men in the ranks, and they were saddened when he left.[17]

It did not take Burnside long to act; he immediately developed a plan to capture Richmond. Burnside hoped to catch the Confederates off guard by quickly crossing the Rappahannock and then advancing toward Richmond before Lee could stop him. Timing was important for the plan to work. Meade was critical of Burnside's plan for capturing Richmond. "True logistics were being ignored," Meade said. The war had been in progress for more than a year-and-a-half, and no one in authority seemed to know what to do. Meade began to doubt there was any chance of reaching Richmond that winter.

Any possibility of surprising Lee at Fredericksburg disappeared when the pontoon boats Burnside needed to cross the river did not arrive on time. Nevertheless, Burnside continued with his plan, crossing the river and then attacking Lee in his well-entrenched position. On December 13, Meade formed his line of 5,000 men opposite the woods and slopes held by Major General D. H. Hill's division from Jackson's corps. Against heavy enemy fire, Meade's division was the only one to break the Confederate line, but he eventually had to withdraw. The outcome of the battle might have been different had Meade's troops been properly supported. "The slightest straw almost would have kept the tide in our favor," Meade bitterly declared. Meade and his division were clearly recognized by those on the field. "General Meade was possibly the best general in the army . . . that day, and he had some of the best soldiers," a Fifth Corps veteran stated.[18] Meade's losses were heavy. Of his 5,000 troops, over 1,800, or 36 percent, were casualties. His efforts had been completely wasted.

After the Union's defeat at Fredericksburg, Burnside was replaced with Major General Joseph Hooker. Meade believed Hooker would be an improvement over Burnside. Burnside, he said, lacked the knowledge and judgment to be an army commander. As a result of Meade's outstanding performance at Fredericksburg, he was promoted to brevet major general and placed in command of the Fifth Corps. When a private in Meade's division learned that he was leaving, he wrote a letter to him expressing his feelings: "They all as a division love you as commander. They all appeared glad to hear of your promotion, but parted with you with regret. . . . They all told the same tale and that was officers and men were used alike." Meade was touched by the letter and sent it home to his wife to be placed among his cherished mementoes.[19]

Lincoln was, as usual, anxious for his army commander to attack, but Hooker was determined not to repeat Burnside's mistake of rushing into action. While giving the impression of another frontal assault on Fredericksburg, Hooker had his army cross the Rappahannock at undefended fords upstream. There they gathered at a country crossroads called Chancellorsville, ten miles west of Fredericksburg.[20]

Hooker hoped for an easy victory, since he outnumbered Lee's army by almost two to one. "Our enemy must either ungloriously [sic] fly or come out from behind his entrenchment and give us battle on our ground where certain destruction awaits him," he said. Enthusiastically, he wrote to his troops, "The rebel army is now the legitimate property of the Army of the Potomac. . . . God Almighty could not prevent [my] destroying the rebel army." Meade and the other corps commanders began to wear an anxious look; they were not as confident.[21]

The region around Chancellorsville was known as the Wilderness because it was a dense forest with tangled undergrowth and few roads. It was a perfect fighting ground for a smaller army facing a larger one. In effect, it canceled the advantage of having a larger force.

Ever daring, Lee split his army, sending Jackson with nearly two-thirds of his army on a march around Hooker's right flank. When Hooker learned that the Confederate troops were moving, he thought they were retreating, and, rather than harry them, he let them go unmolested. On the evening of May 2, while the Union soldiers were preparing their evening meal, Jackson's troops surged out of the woods behind them. Caught completely by surprise, many of the Federals abandoned their weapons and fled to the rear. The retreat, which was never orderly, turned into a rout. As nightfall approached, Jackson's advance stopped.

The next morning, Hooker tried to regroup his demoralized army. Although still outnumbering the Confederates, "Fighting Joe" had lost his nerve, and he gave up his advantage, preferring to fall back on the defensive. Meade was disgusted at Hooker's decision. "I opposed the withdrawal with all my influence," he wrote, "and I tried all I could . . . to be permitted to take my corps into action, . . . but I was overruled."[22]

Lincoln took the Chancellorsville defeat particularly hard. "My God! My God! What will the country say?" In the meantime, a group of subordinate generals sought to have Hooker removed from command, but Meade refused to join them. "I told these gentlemen I could not join in any movement against Hooker, but if the president chose to call on me officially for my opinions, I would give them." He never did. When Lincoln offered the command of the Army of the Potomac to Major General John Reynolds, who most believed to be the best qualified for the position, Reynolds declined.[23]

One month after the Battle of Chancellorsville, Lincoln had not yet decided whether to replace Hooker. Now at full strength, Lee's army needed supplies, and he decided to seek them in the North. On June 3, the Army of Northern Virginia began moving up the Rappahannock. Public alarm spread as Lee's army crossed the Potomac and moved still farther north. Lincoln urged Hooker to cut Lee's supply line, but Hooker, like McClellan, was beginning to hesitate. Leaders in Washington, as well as generals in the field, agreed that another conflict with Lee should not take place with Hooker in command. Whatever they did had to be done quickly.[24]

At 3:00 a.m. on June 28, Colonel James Hardie from the War Department arrived at General Meade's tent. Meade was awakened to receive his visitor. At first he thought he was being arrested. When told that he was now in charge of the Army of the Potomac, he tried to refuse, protesting that other generals, especially General Reynolds, were both senior and better qualified. When he was told that the assignment was not a request but an order, he accepted the reality of the situation. "Well," he said, "I've been tried and condemned without a hearing, and I suppose I shall have to go to the execution."[25]

Meade was sometimes prone to self-pity and self-criticism. He had a hair-trigger temper and, when he was upset, could be offensive and abrasive. But since the outset of the war, he had served well as a brigade, division, and then corps commander. As a commander, he recognized the importance of logistics and the ground upon which a battle was to be fought. Although not creative or aggressive, he was a very steady commander. Lee rated Meade higher than Hooker but hoped the change in command at this critical time would cause difficulty for Meade.[26]

Meade went to Hooker's headquarters to tell him of the change in command. Hooker accepted the news with grace and relief. Meade later wrote to his wife about Hooker's response: "Hooker said he was ready to turn over to me the Army of the Potomac; that he had enough of it, and almost wished he had never been born."[27]

Hooker did not leave Meade with any plans, nor even information about the position of the army. Quickly Meade improvised and moved the army toward the Susquehanna River, while shielding Washington and Baltimore from the Confederate army. In just three days, Meade's army would be engaged in the most important battle of the Civil War.

As Lee moved into Pennsylvania, his advance was almost unmolested, but his army was spread out over a wide area. This situation posed a problem for him at the moment since he had no idea of the enemy's movements. Normally, he could rely on his cavalry chief, Major General J. E. B. Stuart, for reliable information about the Union's location and strength, but Stuart was occupied elsewhere. The Battle of Gettysburg was already in its second day before Stuart joined Lee, and by that time he was of very little assistance. When Lee learned where Meade's army was, he scrambled to get his army pulled together.[28]

Meade's route to intercept Lee took him near Gettysburg, and on July 1, when a group of Confederates made their way into the Pennsylvania town in search of supplies, the Battle of Gettysburg began. What started as a skirmish eventually involved 160,000 troops.

Lee rushed troops to the scene, arriving in time to see the Union troops driven from the town. The Confederates pursued the retreating Federals up

Cemetery Hill but were unable to dislodge them before darkness set in. Some blame Confederate Lieutenant General Richard Ewell for not continuing the attack into the evening to prevent the enemy from getting the high ground.[29]

By the next morning, Meade had strengthened his position and was convinced that here was the ideal place to battle Lee. Within one day he had almost 100,000 troops in place along Cemetery Hill and Ridge. General Longstreet believed that Meade's position was nearly impregnable and argued that he be outflanked from the east, cutting him off from Washington. This flanking action would force Meade to attack, Longstreet said. But Lee was convinced of his army's invincibility and elected to stay and fight.[30]

Lee decided on the second day to pursue the offensive by applying pressure against both sides of the Union line: on the right at Culp's Hill and on the left near the Round Tops. He hoped to find a weakness that he could exploit to drive the Union forces from their good defensive position. All day the fighting was bitter, raging in places now forever known: Little Round Top, Devil's Den, the Wheat Field, and the Peach Orchard. At the end of the second day, the Confederates had failed to dislodge the Union army from its position on either flank.[31]

That evening Longstreet again tried to dissuade Lee from continuing to attack such a strong Union position. But Lee believed Meade was almost beaten; one final assault, and the enemy would crumble.

Meade summoned his corps commanders to a council of war to discuss their plans for the next day. "Should we remain and fight or should we withdraw?" Meade asked. The consensus was to stay and fight. Meade was satisfied that his generals favored holding the ground, leaving him with the decision on whether to launch a general offensive. In a dispatch to General Halleck, Meade stated, "We have suffered considerably in killed and wounded, . . . have taken a large number of prisoners. I shall remain in my present position tomorrow, but am not prepared to say, until better advised of the condition of the army, whether my operations will be of an offensive or defensive character."[32]

The morning of July 3 dawned bright. Lee was determined to strike where he thought Meade would least expect it: the center of his line. The fresh troops of Major General George Pickett's division were selected to lead the attack. Anticipating an attack by Lee, Meade was early in the saddle, riding with two of his generals from Culp's Hill to Little Round Top. Meade decided that he would make no immediate attack if Lee's assault should be repulsed. If and when he did find it advisable to attack, it would be against the Confederate right.[33]

Just after 1:00 p.m., the Confederates opened up a heavy artillery barrage against Meade's line. The Federal batteries returned the fire, but after a time they ceased. Lee incorrectly believed they had been knocked out. After two hours of firing, the Confederate guns ceased fire, and Pickett's famous charge was about to begin.[34]

Pickett spoke to his brigade commanders—Kemper, Garnett, and Armistead. "I have no orders to give you, but I advise you to head across the field as quickly as you can, for in my opinion, you are going to catch hell," he said. And catch hell they did.[35]

Without a sound, 12,000 Confederate troops moved calmly over the gently sloping open field. They came into the range of the Union artillery and then onward, until they could hear the whine of bullets. Soon they were stumbling and falling dead, screaming in anguish as they were hit. They pressed on until the line disappeared in dust and smoke. For a short time the Rebel yell could be heard, but then it died down. The survivors of the charge moved back toward the Confederate lines. The charge had been repulsed. The Union line had held, and Lee's attempt at the impossible had failed.[36]

Lee rode out to meet the survivors and accepted full responsibility for the disaster: "Upon my shoulders rests the blame," he said. Of the 12,000 Confederates who went forward, only 6,000 managed to return. Lieutenant James Whitehead of the Fifty-third Virginia Infantry described the scene of the slaughter: "The awful groans of the wounded and dying, pleading for water and help, all comes crowding into my mind. I do pray the Good Lord that I may never witness such a scene again."[37]

Meade was exultant. He had just defeated Lee and stopped the greatest threat to the North ever mounted by the Confederacy. He shouted "Hurrah!" which for him was a lot of enthusiasm.[38] Satisfied that the worst was over, Meade went off to inspect the condition of his troops. Corps officers crowded around him to offer their congratulations, and a sense of relief prevailed. The night before, Meade had slept very little; this night he had little difficulty sleeping.

On July 4, there was no fighting. The next day, Lee pulled out of his line and began to withdraw toward the Potomac. Meade, who was a naturally cautious man, did not attempt a counterattack and showed little interest in pursuing Lee.

Meade had fought the Battle of Gettysburg with great tactical skill. He placed his troops well and used his reserves effectively, fighting a completely defensive battle and launching no counterattacks. At first, Lincoln was jubilant when he learned that Lee's final attack had failed and the Confederates were retreating. But when he learned that Meade had had victory within his grasp and did not pursue the enemy, he was frustrated and depressed.[39]

Lincoln believed that, if Meade could destroy the retreating enemy, the war could end. Halleck disagreed with Lincoln on this point. Unaggressive himself, Halleck believed Meade was acting properly by cautiously following Lee and using his army to shield Washington. Nevertheless, following Lincoln's directions, Halleck directed Meade to strike the Confederates before they crossed the Potomac.[40]

General Meade received letters of congratulation from two former commanders. "You have done all that could be done," wrote McClellan, "and the Army of the Potomac has supported you nobly." Pope congratulated him with his "whole heart on the glorious victory." Meade saved the letters but believed they were "exaggerated laudation" and wanted no part of public acclaim. He thanked God, he told his wife, but if he could be relieved of this unsought position and allowed to live in peace and quiet at home, he would be happy.[41]

Now a hero, Meade sounded humble in a letter to his wife. "I see also that the papers are making a great deal too much fuss over me. I claim no extraordinary merit for the last battle, and would prefer waiting a little while to see what my career is to be before making any pretensions." But, he admitted, "it was a grand battle, and in my judgment, a most decided victory, though I did not annihilate or bag the Confederate army."[42]

In Meade's congratulatory proclamation to his army, he mentioned his expectations for the future: "The commanding General looks to the army for greater efforts to drive from our soil every vestige of the presence of the invader." Lincoln was shocked when he read it; he wanted the Confederate army destroyed. "Drive the invaders from our soil. My God! Is that all? Will our generals never get that idea out of their heads? The whole country is our soil!" the president cried out.[43]

In the ranks and in certain high places, the feeling was that Meade should have been more aggressive and not allowed Lee to escape. In a fit of frustration, Lincoln wrote a letter to him: "I do not believe you appreciate the magnitude of the misfortune involved in Lee's escape. He was within your easy grasp, and to have closed upon him would, in connection with your other late successes, have ended the war. As it is, the war will be prolonged indefinitely." Then, after more serious thought, Lincoln's good common sense prevailed, and he did not send the letter.[44]

Although Lincoln withheld the letter, he did not hesitate to let his views be known. When Meade received a telegram from Halleck that pointed out the president's disappointment in his actions, Meade offered to resign. "Having performed my duty conscientiously and to the best of my ability, the censure of the president conveyed in your dispatch . . . is in judgment so undeserved that I feel compelled most respectfully to ask to be immediately relieved from the command of the army," Meade replied. Halleck immediately sent him another message, softening his words and assuring him that Lee's escape was not sufficient cause for his removal.[45]

Halleck quickly changed from criticism to praise in his next dispatch to Meade: "Your fight at Gettysburg met with universal approbation of all military men here. You handled your troops in that battle as well, if not better, than any general has handled the army during the war. You brought all your forces into action at the right time and place, which no commander of the Army of the Potomac had done before." The letter by Halleck had a soothing affect on Meade's feelings, and he wrote a polite letter to him in response, explaining his reason for not attacking Lee before he crossed the river.[46]

After his disappointment over Meade's failure to pursue Lee aggressively died down, Lincoln defended him when some cabinet members suggested removing him from command: "What can I do with such generals as we have? Who among them is better than Meade?" Later, Lincoln said, "General Meade has my confidence as a brave and skillful officer and a true man," and he promoted him to the rank of permanent brigadier general in the regular army.[47]

As the criticism and pressure to engage Lee in an all-out battle continued, Meade moved into Virginia. He kept maneuvering, always keeping his army between the Confederates and Washington and trying to get Lee to fight on ground advantageous to the Union. Perhaps because of the criticism, Meade now began to display unnecessary caution. "In this view I am reluctant to run the risks without the positive sanction of the Government." As a result, nothing of importance was accomplished by the Army of the Potomac during the second half of 1863. The army then went into winter quarters.[48]

Because the five months after Gettysburg had not brought the Union any closer to victory, there was talk of removing Meade from command. A campaign to return Hooker to the position gained momentum. Although Congress passed a resolution praising Hooker's service, he was not returned to command the Army of the Potomac. The campaign to restore Hooker to his former position came to an end when, on March 9, 1864, Grant was appointed general-in-chief.[49] By the spring of 1864, Lincoln had found his general, one who believed, as he did, that the war would end only after the Confederate army had been destroyed. In March, when Grant took command of all the Federal armies, he decided to make his headquarters in the field with the Army of the Potomac.

Officers in the Army of the Potomac expected Grant to give most of the important assignments to officers he already knew. Grant surprised them by bringing only a few subordinates from the West, such as Phil Sheridan and Baldy Smith, allowing the existing corps and division commanders to remain in their positions. Meade believed that his presence might be an embarrassment to Grant; he offered to resign, but Grant declined to accept it.[50]

When Burnside was restored to command of his former Ninth Corps with the Army of the Potomac, an awkward situation developed. Because Burnside outranked Meade in seniority but was now only a corps commander, a special arrangement had to be developed. Grant solved the problem by giving orders to Meade regarding the movement of his army but giving separate orders to Burnside. Meade would remain subordinate to Grant, although nominally in command of the Army of the Potomac.

Meade was impressed with his new commander. "I was very pleased with Grant," he told his wife. Despite his realization that he was now being overshadowed by Grant, Meade actually seemed relieved to be rid of the responsibility. He was now, in effect, functioning as a corps commander. A magazine stated that "the Army of the Potomac was directed by Grant, commanded by Meade, and led by Hancock, Sedgwick, and Warren." Meade believed the description was accurate.[51]

During the spring of 1864, Grant began his advance against Lee in the Wilderness of Virginia, an area of dense forest and almost impenetrable thicket. On May 5, the Battle of the Wilderness began. Meade hoped the Army of the Potomac would appear at its best in the first battle under Grant's eyes. Throughout the battle, however, he could do little to direct the action. After two days of fighting in the densely wooded area, it was apparent that it would be difficult to drive Lee out of the Wilderness. The Union army had paid a high price for its efforts, suffering 18,000 casualties.

Under similar circumstances in the past, the Union generals had withdrawn to lick their wounds and wait for Lee to assume the initiative. But Grant ordered his army to move forward; he had no intention of withdrawing. "Make all preparations during the day for a night march to take position at Spotsylvania Court House," Grant ordered Meade.[52]

It was important that Union forces reach Spotsylvania before Lee's army. When the Confederates reached this key location first, Meade blamed his cavalry commander, Major General Phil Sheridan. After Meade reprimanded Sheridan, he struck back. It did not matter to him that Meade outranked him. He was not going to take blame for something he saw as Meade's fault. After stating his case, Sheridan concluded angrily, "I could whip Jeb Stuart [Lee's outstanding cavalry commander] if you would only let me." He also said he was quitting and stormed out.[53]

When Meade went to complain to Grant about Sheridan's insubordination, he repeated Sheridan's boast about defeating Stuart if given the opportunity. Grant's response was not what Meade expected: "Let him go ahead and do it."[54] In a battle of cavalry at Yellow Tavern, Sheridan defeated Stuart. Stuart was shot by a dismounted Union cavalryman and died shortly afterward. Sheridan had thus been able to make good on his boast.

Tired and battle-worn, the Army of the Potomac moved south in pursuit of Lee. At Cold Harbor, Meade was convinced that, once he received reinforcements, he would be able to break the Confederate line and open the road to Richmond. The weather during the past week had been stifling, and many of the Union troops were exhausted. The Confederates, however, were well entrenched, with log parapets along the top of the trenches, presenting a formidable line of defense. Grant ordered Meade to have his corps commanders make a reconnaissance of the enemy's position before attacking; however, they failed to do so. As a result, they had little idea of the strength of the enemy they faced. On June 2, Grant ordered an all-out attack. Many of Meade's troops had a premonition of what was to happen and sewed labels on their coats giving instructions where to send their bodies.[55]

The attack was launched at dawn. The Union regiments advanced in lines. Those in the first wave fell in heaps as Confederate rifles and artillery fired away relentlessly. Thousands fell dead or wounded in the first half hour. For a brief moment, one Union division managed to pierce the Confederate line, but there were no troops to support them.[56]

Meade sent a message to Grant asking for directions. Grant replied, "The moment it becomes certain that an assault cannot succeed, suspend the offensive; but when one does succeed, push it vigorously." When Meade received Grant's reply, he ordered another attack. Major General William Smith refused to send his corps forward, and some Union soldiers, seeing how hopeless another assault would be, fell to the ground. Finally, when Grant saw how futile additional attacks would be, he ordered Meade to call off the attack and dig in.[57]

Cold Harbor had been costly to the Army of the Potomac. Although Meade had been involved in the attack, Grant accepted the responsibility for the heavy losses, making no effort to justify his actions. From the time of the Wilderness to Cold Harbor, Union casualties exceeded 50,000 men. During the same time, Lee's casualties numbered almost 40,000. Although the Union casualties were considerably heavier, Grant was winning the battle of attrition.

By the end of June, the Army of Northern Virginia had settled in at Petersburg and was effectively dug-in around the perimeter. After Cold Harbor, Grant was reluctant to attack Confederate forces in trenches and behind earthworks. In July, a member of General Burnside's staff developed a plan to break through the Confederate defenses. It consisted of blowing a hole in the Confederate fortifications by means of an underground mine shaft filled with gunpowder. Meade and Grant were reluctant to approve the plan, but Burnside was persistent. Just hours before the caper was to take place, Meade told Burnside to change the plan. His concern was that the division selected to spearhead the advance was inexperienced, having never been in battle. The fact that it was made up of African American troops caused an additional problem. If the plan failed, Meade feared that the consequences and criticism of using these troops would fall on him. Burnside argued vigorously against a last-minute change and the use of troops not trained for this action, but Grant sided with Meade.[58]

On July 30, an attempt to carry out Burnside's plan was made. The explosion blew a large hole in the Confederate fortifications and initially caused confusion along the Confederate line, but the opportunity to exploit this advantage was bungled. Almost at once, the lack of training of these new forces became apparent. The result was a huge loss of life for Burnside's forces, as they were trapped in the crater created by the explosion. Meade had no other choice but to order Burnside's troops to withdraw. The Federal losses in this fiasco were almost 3,500 killed, wounded, and missing.[59] Although Burnside blamed Meade for the failure of the assault, Meade brushed off his "extremely insubordinate language." Later, a court of inquiry found no fault with either Burnside or Meade.

Meade's thoughts related to the war were often diverted by personal cares and were expressed in his almost daily letters to Margaret. His oldest son, Sergeant, was suffering from tuberculosis, and a sea voyage with his physician was considered. Meade took some time away from the army to visit his son in Philadelphia, only to find that Sergeant was losing his battle with the disease. He was gratified, however, by an offer from Secretary Stanton to place a government steamer at his wife's disposal should they decide to take the trip. Sergeant was not well enough to make the trip, and in February 1865, he died.[60]

For the remainder of 1864, the Union siege of Petersburg continued, day after day and month after month. Lee's plight was desperate. His men were on the verge of starving, ill-clothed, and prone to all manner of disease and infection, from pneumonia to scurvy. By March, Lee's army had dwindled to barely 28,000. Grant extended his line to the west, thinning Lee's line even more. On March 25, Lee threatened Meade's supply base at City Point but was repulsed; this attack was Lee's final stroke.[61]

On April 2, Lee's army was driven from Petersburg. In the early hours of April 3, the first Union troops entered Richmond. Finally, on April 9, Lee surrendered to Grant. After the surrender, Meade and Lee, two former West Pointers, exchanged visits. When Meade saw Lee, he removed his cap and said, "Good morning, General." Lee had not seen him since Veracruz, eighteen years earlier, and had to ask who he was. "What are you doing with all that gray in your beard?" Lee inquired. "You," Meade responded, "have to answer for most of it." Meade accepted an invitation to Lee's tent, where they discussed the long siege at Petersburg.[62]

After the war, Meade was placed in command of the Military Division of the Atlantic and the Department of the East in Philadelphia. Later, he reported to Atlanta to administer the implementation of the Reconstruction.

On October 31, 1872, Meade was taking his customary stroll with his wife when he complained of pains in his side and was put to bed with what was diagnosed as pneumonia. Four days later, his health took a turn for the worse. On November 6, 1872, George Meade died; the general was not yet fifty-seven years old. He was buried in Laurel Hill Cemetery. No military record appears on his tombstone, only a simple phrase taken from the sermon preached at his funeral: "He did his work bravely and is at rest."[63]

Perhaps the fairest summation of George Meade's career was offered by Abraham Lincoln: "Not only a brave and skillful officer, but a true man."[64]

22 *Hugh Judson Kilpatrick*

"Kill-Cavalry"

In October 1863, Judson Kilpatrick suffered an embarrassing defeat at the hands of Confederate Major General J. E. B. Stuart. His career seemed to be over. During the winter of 1864, however, he came up with a plan to redeem himself. He bragged about how he could conduct a raid on Richmond to liberate Union soldiers confined in Libby Prison.

When word of Kilpatrick's boast reached President Lincoln's office, he invited the cavalry leader to come to Washington to discuss his plan. There, Kilpatrick met with the president and Secretary of War Stanton. When he emerged from the meeting, his instructions were clear. In addition to releasing the prisoners, Kilpatrick would distribute copies of an amnesty proclamation that offered full pardon to Southern civilians under certain conditions.[1] Later it would be revealed that Kilpatrick had plans above and beyond those he had discussed with the president and secretary of war—plans that would cause controversy long after the raid. Kilpatrick is best known for this raid.

Judson Kilpatrick was an ambitious man. He possessed skill and daring and was able to cultivate influential friends. He also, however, acquired a reputation for recklessness in battle. Because of his unusually high casualty rate, caused by poor judgment, he earned the nickname "Kill-Cavalry."[2]

Kilpatrick was often less than honest. After leading raids into Confederate territory, he inflated reports of his success. His fabrications led to his rapid promotions and eventually to the command of a division. Kilpatrick had both admirers and enemies. He was either a hero or, as one Union officer put it, "a frothy braggart without brains."[3]

There were also questions about his character and moral fortitude. Although he did not smoke or gamble, activities common among Civil War soldiers, he was guilty of more disreputable activities such as thievery, adultery, and lying. In 1862, he spent three months in prison for profiteering.[4]

At times Kilpatrick demonstrated the bravery of a warrior, but on other occasions he would withdraw without a fight. At one point in his career, Major General George Meade relieved him of duty. Later, Major General William Sherman made effective use of Kilpatrick's abilities during the March to the Sea. Sherman remarked: "I know Kilpatrick is one hell of a damned fool, but I want just that sort of man to command my cavalry." Kilpatrick's performance at the end of the war earned him a promotion to the rank of major general.[5]

Kilpatrick's physical appearance was anything but attractive. He was plain and small in stature, with pale eyes and frizzy red side-whiskers. At West Point, other cadets often made him the butt of their pranks. Kilpatrick usually reacted to their teasing with good-natured repartee, though sometimes he responded with his fists. Later, to compensate for his reputation, he dressed with flair. He wore a carefully tailored uniform, high black boots, and a black felt hat that was always tilted to give the impression that he was a man of the world. A staff officer once remarked that it was difficult to look at him without chuckling.[6]

Hugh Judson Kilpatrick was born on January 14, 1836, near Deckertown, New Jersey, the second son of Simon and Julia Wickham Kilpatrick. He received a good education, and as soon as he could read, young Kilpatrick showed a strong interest in the military. He had no thoughts of being a farmer like his father. As he grew older, his dreams expanded to include politics. After gaining fame on the battlefield, he hoped to be elected governor of New Jersey and then president of the United States. Before he was twenty, Kilpatrick became involved in politics, stumping rural New Jersey for a local congressman, George Vail.[7]

When the congressman won, Vail rewarded Kilpatrick with an appointment to the U.S. Military Academy at West Point. There Kilpatrick made good grades and graduated seventeenth in a class of forty-five. During his second year at the Academy, Judson joined the Dialectic Society, playing major roles in different dramas and developing his ability as a public speaker. He was chosen to give the valedictory address for his graduating class.[8]

When talk of secession swept the country, Kilpatrick experienced difficulty with cadets from the South because of his strong pro-Union sentiments. He found himself involved in several fist fights. Despite his small size, he won more than he lost. He had a strong faith in the Union and was anxious to defend his position. He drew up a petition requesting permission for the class of 1861 to graduate earlier than scheduled so that its members could serve the nation as soon as possible. The petition was sent to the War Department and was granted.[9]

Kilpatrick married Alice Nailer of New York on the same day he graduated. Many of his classmates attended the ceremony. After a one-night

Major General Hugh Kilpatrick was an ambitious man who was able to cultivate influential friends. He also acquired a reputation for recklessness, with little regard for the safety of his men. Because of his high casualty rate and poor judgment in combat, he earned the nickname "Kill-Cavalry."

COURTESY OF THE LIBRARY OF CONGRESS

honeymoon, he left his newlywed for Washington and the war. With him he carried a silken banner bearing his wife's name.

In May 1861, he accepted a commission as second lieutenant in the First U.S. Artillery. Kilpatrick was an ambitious man and had no desire to fight in the regular army; rather, he preferred the volunteer service because he believed he would have a greater opportunity for promotion there. He asked Gouverneur Warren, his mathematics instructor at West Point, to recommend him for a post with a New York regiment. Within a short time he was commissioned captain of the Fifth New York Infantry in Duryee's Zouaves. Kilpatrick quickly molded his company into an effective fighting unit, gaining his men's confidence and respect.[10]

Kilpatrick's first assignment in the field involved scouting and foraging. He saw his first action at the Battle of Big Bethel on June 10, 1861, and had the dubious distinction of being the first regular army officer to be wounded during the war. Although the Confederates were victorious, he received praise in the Northern newspapers. During the battle, Kilpatrick displayed a knack for organization and the ability to lead and gain the confidence of his troops. His report of the engagement, however, greatly exaggerated his part in the battle. To compound the deception, he sent a copy of the report to the *New York Times*. The *Times* published the entire report. As a result of his desire for recognition, he often put his personal goals above those of his men and the army, thus incurring the dislike of his fellow officers.[11]

His performance at Big Bethel resulted in a promotion to the rank of lieutenant colonel of the Second New York Cavalry. While his command lived and trained in a camp outside of town, Kilpatrick moved into Willard's Hotel in Washington. This location made it easier for him to associate with politicians who might help his career. To help pay for the expensive room, Kilpatrick accepted bribes and used his influence to steer army contracts to certain Union sutlers.[12]

Major General George McClellan's Army of the Potomac moved into Virginia late in the spring of 1862. Kilpatrick was ordered to join Brigadier General Irvin McDowell, with the responsibility of protecting Washington from Confederate attacks. Again, Kilpatrick found ways to enhance his income. He confiscated horses from Virginia farmers for the Union army, keeping the best ones for himself and selling them in the North. He stole tobacco from plantations, selling it to the sutlers.[13]

While McClellan was active on the peninsula, Kilpatrick conducted raids throughout northern Virginia. During a raid near Falmouth Heights, he demonstrated a talent for deception and audacity. Although he had only one regiment and faced a superior Confederate force, he shouted orders to nonexistent reinforcements, giving the impression that he had a brigade of cavalry with him. When the Rebels heard these shouted commands, they were fooled into retreating across the Rappahannock River.[14]

During the summer of 1862, Kilpatrick's regiment joined Brigadier General George Bayard's cavalry brigade, a part of Major General John Pope's Army of Virginia. The aggressive Pope gave the cavalry a fighting role, encouraging Kilpatrick's raids behind enemy lines. During a raid on Beaver Dam Station on the Virginia Central Railroad, they burned the depot and captured one prisoner, a yet-unknown Confederate named John S. Mosby.[15]

Kilpatrick continued his successful raids, even making contact with Confederate Major General J. E. B. Stuart. Undaunted by what he encountered, Kilpatrick was able to slip easily into enemy territory to disrupt Confederate supply and communication lines. He had no second thoughts about ordering his men into battle, although he often remained in the background himself. This strategy resulted in large casualties, earning him the label "Kill-Cavalry."[16]

During July and August 1862, Kilpatrick's cavalry conducted successful raids on Stonewall Jackson's communication lines in the Shenandoah Valley, burning depots and destroying railroad tracks and telegraph lines. In December, Kilpatrick was promoted to colonel, and by February 1863, he was given command of a brigade.[17]

In the fall of 1862, a formal complaint was filed with the provost marshal against Kilpatrick, alleging that he had stolen a team of mules from a farmer. An investigation revealed Kilpatrick's dealings with sutlers and his sale of confiscated horses and tobacco—as well as his bribe taking. As a result, Kilpatrick was arrested and taken to the Old Capitol Prison in Washington. Sworn statements attesting to his criminal acts were taken from one of his aides and two of the regimental sutlers. "The affidavits . . . taken in the case of Colonel Kilpatrick leave little question of his guilt," Secretary of War Edwin Stanton concluded.[18]

Kilpatrick was fortunate the army needed daring cavalry leaders so badly at that time. William Whiting, the solicitor for the case, found that the evidence against Kilpatrick was made "orally and not under oath, . . . yet they render it proper to give the accused the benefit of the doubt" and recommended that the charge against him be dropped. After spending three months in prison, Kilpatrick was released on January 21, 1863. He was allowed to return to duty.[19]

Major General Joseph Hooker was now commander of the Army of the Potomac. Hooker had combined the cavalry into a single corps of 9,000 horsemen, led by Brigadier General George Stoneman. Kilpatrick was given command of the First Brigade in Brigadier General David McMurtrie Gregg's Third Division.[20]

During the Chancellorsville campaign in April 1863, Kilpatrick's brigade took part in General Stoneman's raid on the outskirts of Richmond. Although the operation as a whole was not successful, Kilpatrick's brigade acquitted itself well. With a detached force, they captured towns and destroyed lines of communication. By pushing his men hard, he penetrated to within two miles of Richmond, putting the Confederate capital into a panic. Ultimately, however, Kilpatrick had to retreat down the peninsula to avoid being captured.[21]

By June, Kilpatrick was operating under Brigadier General Alfred Pleasonton. His men had an all-out battle with Stuart's horsemen near Brandy Station with saber-to-saber fighting. Kilpatrick's brigade charged in three waves. The first two were repulsed by Confederate artillery fire, but the third regiment was able to smash into Confederate forces and scatter them. Stuart rallied his troops and finally forced Kilpatrick to retreat. After a series of charges and countercharges, Pleasonton's division retired from the field. Although Kilpatrick's name was not among the officers Pleasonton cited for gallantry, shortly thereafter, on June 14, he was promoted to brigadier general.[22]

On June 17, Kilpatrick spotted Rebel troops around Aldie, Virginia. Without bothering to determine the enemy's strength or deployment, he sent the First Massachusetts forward to attack. His recklessness caused unnecessary deaths. "Kilpatrick's standing order was 'Charge God damn 'em,' whether they were five or five thousand," a newspaper reporter wrote. The

Confederates retreated out of town, drawing Kilpatrick's men into an ambush. "My poor men were just slaughtered," Captain Charles Francis Adams of the First Massachusetts later recalled. Next, Kilpatrick sent the Second New York into the fray. Again, the casualties were high; more than a hundred of his men were killed in the crossfire. Although devastated by the carnage, Kilpatrick was determined to make one last effort to defeat the enemy. This time he sent the First Maine and personally led the charge. This attack was so ferocious that the Confederates were forced to withdraw.[23]

On June 28, 1863, General Joseph Hooker was replaced by Major General George Meade. Kilpatrick was assigned the Third Division, which contained two brigades under the newly appointed brigadier generals George Custer and Elon Farnsworth.

Kilpatrick's division arrived at Gettysburg on July 3. After Pickett's charge failed, Kilpatrick seized the opportunity to engage the enemy. He ordered Farnsworth to attack the flank of the retreating Confederates. The ground was heavily wooded and covered with large rocks and boulders. Such ground was dangerous for an all-out charge of men on horseback. When Farnsworth questioned the order, Kilpatrick accused him of being afraid to lead the attack. "I'll lead it," Farnsworth replied, "but you must take the responsibility." Farnsworth led the charge, only to be greeted with a heavy enemy barrage. In the ensuing attack, Farnsworth's brigade was shattered, and he was killed. The charge had been a disaster. As a result of Kilpatrick's foolhardiness, he lost the confidence of his men and his superiors.[24]

In his official report of the battle, Kilpatrick tried to conceal his error by blaming the infantry's failure to take advantage of the confusion Farnsworth had caused on the Confederate right. In the same report, however, he praised Farnsworth for his valor: ". . . he baptized his star in blood, and . . . for the honor of his young brigade and the glory of his corps, he yielded his noble life."[25]

After the battle, Kilpatrick tried to make amends for his failure at Gettysburg by vigorously pursuing Lee into Maryland. He captured some of Lee's wagons and did damage to his weakened forces. When he reported these engagements, Kilpatrick exaggerated the number of prisoners taken and the enemy's casualties. In his report he stated that he had "captured a brigade of infantry, two pieces of artillery, two caissons, and a large number of small arms," and claimed that he had achieved this success without help or support from other Union forces. He sent a copy of his report to the *New York Times*, where it was published.[26] When Union Brigadier General John Buford reported Kilpatrick's fight, however, the story was entirely different: "I saw two squadrons from General Kilpatrick's division gallop up the hill. . . . Their two squadrons were instantly scattered and destroyed by the fire of the rebel brigade. . . . Not a single enemy was found when the ground was examined a few hours afterward. . . . Having alarmed the enemy, he got across the ford before we could get round to his rear." When Lee saw the *New York Times* article, he was so incensed about the inaccuracy that he wrote a letter of protest to Meade. When Meade learned of the discrepancy, he asked Kilpatrick for an explanation; none was forthcoming.[27]

Until this point, few knew how Kilpatrick stretched the truth in his reports because there were few witnesses to challenge his exaggerated claims; however, at Gettysburg his fellow officers discovered he was not the heroic figure he claimed to be. They saw how he stayed in the rear, ordering his troops to carry out a suicidal attack against Lee's flank. Now they were appalled at his conduct.[28]

The closing months of 1863 were disastrous for Kilpatrick's career. In October, he again encountered J. E. B. Stuart near Buckland, Virginia. Stuart set a trap for the overeager Kilpatrick. Attacking Kilpatrick's right and left flanks, he and Major General Fitzhugh Lee forced the trapped Union troops to scatter. Kilpatrick was humiliated, and his career seemed to be ruined. At this low point, he was to receive more distressing news. In November, his wife died of influenza; two months later his son joined her.[29]

Kilpatrick was anxious to redeem himself for his loss to Stuart. In early 1864, he expressed the opinion that a raid on Richmond was possible and that he would be willing to lead it. Kilpatrick's proposal involved a force of 4,000 mounted horsemen, who would destroy railroad bridges and distribute Lincoln's amnesty proclamation during the raid. Once in Richmond, the raiders would free Union prisoners. Kilpatrick believed the prospects for success were good because the Confederates had few cavalry to defend the capital. President Lincoln was impressed by Kilpatrick's confidence and gave his approval.[30]

For his plan to work, Kilpatrick needed to surprise the Confederates On the morning of February 28, he left Stevensburg, Virginia, with 4,000 troops. Under his personal command were 3,500 troops who were to strike Richmond from the north. A detachment of 500, led by twenty-one-year-old Colonel Ulric Dahlgren, was to attack the capital from the south. Colonel Dahlgren was the son of a prominent rear admiral and had just returned to duty after having lost a leg during the Battle of Gettysburg.

The raid began as planned. Both Kilpatrick and Dahlgren met with little opposition and were able to destroy railroad lines and distribute hundreds of copies of the president's proclamation. On March 1, Kilpatrick's raiders reached the outskirts of Richmond. "We were so close that we could . . . count the spires of the churches," one of his men recalled. According to the plan, Kilpatrick was to wait for the sound of rifle fire that signaled Dahlgren's attack from the south before he moved. But Dahlgren's progress had been delayed by the high waters of the James River, which forced him to find another route. Dahlgren eventually attacked from the west, though much later than planned. Kilpatrick waited outside Richmond for two hours, but when Dahlgren still had not attacked, he retired east toward the

Chickahominy River. With snow falling, Kilpatrick crossed the river and set up camp near Mechanicsville.[31]

Despite cold and icy conditions, Kilpatrick decided to make another attempt at completing his mission. This time he sent two small detachments into the Confederate capital; one to free the prisoners and the other to kidnap President Jefferson Davis. Before his men could set off, they were attacked by a small Confederate force led by Major General Wade Hampton. Kilpatrick was unaware of the size of Hampton's force, but, as a precaution, he withdrew to the safety of the Union camp at New Kent Court House.[32]

In the meantime, Colonel Dahlgren attempted to enter Richmond, but without Kilpatrick's simultaneous attack, his efforts were thwarted. In an ambush fight, Dahlgren's detachment was cut to pieces, and he was killed. Papers were found on Dahlgren's body describing plans to burn Richmond and kill President Davis and his cabinet. Included in the papers was a portion of Dahlgren's address to his troops. Those who read them were shocked when they saw, "Jeff. Davis and Cabinet must be killed on the spot. The men must keep together and well in hand, and once in the city it must be destroyed and Jeff. Davis and the Cabinet killed."[33]

When the papers were taken to Davis, he found them amusing. "This means you, Mr. Benjamin," he said to his secretary of state. Others in Richmond, however, were not amused. General Braxton Bragg, Davis's military advisor, wanted the men who had accompanied Dahlgren on the raid to be executed and the papers published. Robert E. Lee, however, was opposed to killing the captives: "Acts in addition to intentions," he said, "are necessary to constitute crime." The captives were not killed, but the papers were published.[34]

About a month after the raid, Lee wrote a formal letter of protest to Meade about Dahlgren's intentions and asked if his instructions reflected the policy of the United States. Meade responded quickly that "neither the United States Government, myself, nor General Kilpatrick authorized, sanctioned, or approved . . . any act not . . . in accordance with the usages of war." Union leaders believed that the Rebels had made up the stories about the plans to kill Davis to arouse Confederate emotions. General Meade, on the other hand, suspected that Kilpatrick was the author of the "Dahlgren Papers." When he questioned Kilpatrick about it, Kilpatrick denied giving any such instructions to Dahlgren.[35]

Meade took the botched raid as an opportunity to demote Kilpatrick to brigade command. As a result, Kilpatrick requested to be transferred to the Western theater. On April 15, 1864, his request was granted. He was ordered to report to Major General William T. Sherman, who welcomed him.[36]

For a while, Kilpatrick was not as cocky and self-assured as he had been. Soon after joining his new division, he spearheaded the Federal drive through Tennessee and into Georgia. In a battle outside of Resaca in May,

Kilpatrick was badly wounded in the thigh. By the middle of August, he had recuperated sufficiently to be able to lead a raid against a Confederate communications center south of Atlanta, destroying miles of track. When his raiders were challenged by a Confederate cavalry unit, which threatened to surround them, Kilpatrick led a charge through the Rebels to safety.[37]

During Sherman's March to the Sea, Kilpatrick's reputation spread, and his name became infamous to Georgians. Kilpatrick's men pillaged one plantation after another. "When the main body of Kilpatrick's army came up," Catherine Whithead, a young lady whose plantation had been ravaged, wrote in her diary, "they commenced the destruction and committed every kind of depredation." Kilpatrick did not treat the slaves any better, Whithead wrote: "They took everything from the Negroes, at which I was much surprised as they professed to love them so much. They stole all their clothes and money and whatever would be at all useful to themselves." Whithead believed the plundering began with the general himself: "Even Kilpatrick asked for silver," she continued, "and when the General condescends to anything of that kind you cannot expect anything more from the men."[38]

On their destructive march, Kilpatrick confiscated horses to replace his own worn-out mounts. When his men collected about 500 more horses than they needed, he ordered the surplus killed. A farmer watched in horror as the horses were killed in his yard. "My God," he said, realizing that he could not bury so many animals. "I'll have to move." Kilpatrick's actions during the Union's march through Georgia often violated the generally accepted rules for treatment of civilians, but they were part of General Sherman's overall policy of total war.[39]

During Sherman's march, Kilpatrick's command was involved in a running war with Confederate Major General Joseph Wheeler and his cavalry. Because Wheeler was able to slow Sherman's advance, Kilpatrick was called upon to rid the area of him. In November, Kilpatrick moved his raiders north toward Augusta, hoping to draw Wheeler out. Wheeler took the bait, thinking Kilpatrick's men were the vanguard for Sherman's advance. In the meantime, Sherman was moving his army in another direction toward Savannah. When Sherman reached Savannah just before Christmas 1864, he wrote to Kilpatrick, praising his efforts: "The fact that to you, in great measure, we owe the march of four strong infantry columns . . . over 300 miles through the enemy's country . . . is honor enough for any cavalry commander."[40]

As Sherman marched through the Carolinas, he increased his efforts to make the South suffer. Kilpatrick was quick to follow his lead. At the beginning of the campaign, he issued large quantities of matches to his troops, leaving no doubt what they were to do with them. "In after years when travelers passing through South Carolina shall see chimney stacks without houses, and the country desolate," Kilpatrick said, "and shall ask 'Who did this?' some Yankee will answer, 'Kilpatrick's cavalry.'" To his foot soldiers he said, "There'll be damned little for you infantrymen to destroy after I've passed through that hellhole of secession."[41]

On April 26, General Joseph Johnston surrendered his army to General Sherman near Durham Station, North Carolina. Just before the war's end, Kilpatrick was promoted to major general of volunteers and brevet major general in the regular army.

After the war, Kilpatrick left his post to go home and campaign for one of the Republican nominees in the 1865 New Jersey gubernatorial race. When his candidate failed to get the nomination, he went to work for the opponent, Marcus Ward. During the campaign, Kilpatrick called upon one of his greatest assets: his ability as a speaker. As a reward for his efforts for the Republican Party, he was named ambassador to Chile. In South America, he met, courted, and married Louisa Valdivieso, cousin of a future president of Chile and niece of an archbishop of the Catholic Church.[42]

Kilpatrick believed his army career and rank of major general would sway people to vote for him when he ran for public office. His opponents, however, used his military record to discredit his accomplishments. Although there were times when Kilpatrick distinguished himself during the war, there were others where he exercised poor judgment. For three months during the war, he had spent time in prison for stealing horses and taking bribes. Kilpatrick's obvious exaggerations and lies in his official reports revealed to his peers and superiors that his reputation had been built on words, not deeds. During his march through the South with Sherman, his conduct had been despicable. His behavior and character became the main issue in every political race, and his opponents successfully used the issue against him.[43]

In 1869, Kilpatrick was recalled from his post in Chile. He made a run for governor of New Jersey but was unsuccessful. Still entertaining the hope of becoming president, Kilpatrick ran for a seat in the U.S. House of Representatives. He lost, but, in 1881, President James Garfield reappointed him to his old post in Chile.[44]

On July 20, 1881, while in Santiago, Kilpatrick was struck by Bright's disease, a deterioration of the kidneys. In December, just as it looked as though he would recover, Kilpatrick suffered a relapse and died. He was just forty-five years old. He was buried in the Valdivieso vaults in the Church of Sagrario in Santiago. A year later, his body was returned to the United States and reinterred at the cemetery at West Point. Classmates and men who served under him contributed money to pay for a monument to mark his grave.[45]

23 *Winfield Scott Hancock*

"Hancock the Superb"

In April 1862, General George McClellan's Army of the Potomac landed on the Virginia peninsula. Outnumbered, the Confederates at Yorktown pulled back about ten miles to Williamsburg. Earlier that spring, Major General John Magruder had built a defensive line around Williamsburg with its center bearing his name. When the Union army arrived at the Confederate line at Fort Magruder, Major General Edwin Sumner ordered an attack. One observer called it "a battle without a plan." The only redeeming aspect of the assault, aside from the bravery shown by the Union troops, was the conduct of Brigadier General Winfield Scott Hancock.[1]

Sumner ordered Hancock to prepare his brigade for an attack on the enemy's right, promising to send him reinforcements as soon as possible. After approaching within 300 yards of the Confederate works, Hancock ordered his artillery to open fire but held back his troops, waiting for reinforcements. When he inquired where the reinforcements were, Sumner ordered him to "fall back to his original position."[2]

The order disturbed Hancock because he felt this opportunity was an excellent one for engaging the enemy before they could be reinforced. He decided to hold his position for a while, protesting the order. The easy course for Hancock would have been to retire as Sumner had ordered, but professional pride dictated that he take advantage of the opportunity at hand. Six hours later, after four requests for reinforcements, Hancock still had not withdrawn.[3]

In the meantime, the Confederate troops had been reinforced. They attacked Hancock now, throwing themselves in waves against his line. As the enemy advanced, Hancock ordered his men, "Aim low, men. Aim low. Do not be in a hurry to fire until they come nearer." When the attack sputtered, Hancock ordered a counterattack: "Gentleman, charge with the bayonet." When the Confederates saw Hancock's men coming out of their shallow earthworks with bayonets, they stopped and broke for the rear.[4]

Soon after Hancock's counterattack, Union reinforcements arrived. When McClellan had learned of the situation, he immediately had recognized the opportunity to gain an advantage against the enemy and ordered reinforcements be sent to Hancock. Later, McClellan wrote, "This was one of the most brilliant engagements of the war, and General Hancock merited the highest praise." That night, the Confederates withdrew up the peninsula, and McClellan wired Washington, "Hancock was superb today." It was from this message that the general would gain the permanent nickname, "Hancock the Superb."[5]

Winfield looked the part of a general; he appeared born to command. Some believed that, had General Hancock worn citizen's clothes and been given command of a troop of men who did not know him, he still would have been obeyed at once. One of his staff members, Frank Haskell, believed the six-foot-two-inch, Second Corps commander was ". . . in many respects best looking, dignified, gentlemanly, and commanding. He was tall and well proportioned, had a ruddy complexion, brown hair, and he wore a mustache and tuft of hair upon his chin." Grant recalled him as having been "tall, well-formed, and . . . present[ing] an appearance that would attract the attention of an army as he passed." Hancock's genial personality made it easy for him to make friends. His personal courage and his presence in the thick of a fight won him the confidence of his men. No matter how heavy the fighting, the Second Corps always felt their commander had their best interest at heart.[6]

Winfield Scott Hancock was born on February 14, 1824, to Benjamin and Elizabeth Hancock in Montgomery Square near the town of Lansdale, Pennsylvania. Named after the military hero of the War of 1812, Winfield had an identical twin brother, who received the unlikely name of Hilary. When the twins were four years old, the Hancocks moved from Montgomery Square to Norristown, Pennsylvania. Winfield's father practiced law and was a deacon in the Baptist Church—he was also a lifelong Democrat. From an early age, Winfield was taught to respect and revere the law, the Almighty, and the principles and tenets of the Democratic Party.[7]

Winfield and his brother Hilary were inseparable as boys. Both boys attended the Norristown Academy and later a new public school in town. Although Winfield was a high-spirited boy, getting into a fair amount of trouble, he did well at his studies. Even as a schoolboy, he showed an interest in the military and organized a military company among his schoolmates. In 1840, Winfield entered West Point; his brother chose to study law. At this early age, Winfield committed his life to being a soldier. He would remain in the U.S. Army from the time of his admission to the Academy to the day of his death, over forty-five years later.[8]

Portrait of Major General Winfield Scott Hancock, officer of the Federal army.

As Winfield packed for his trip to West Point, his father slipped two books into his luggage and offered him some advice. One of the booklets was a copy of the Constitution, and the other, Blackstone's *Commentaries*. His father advised his son to read each of these documents at least once a year. Since he was to be an army officer, his father reasoned, he should understand the government. Winfield would always remember his father's admonition.[9]

Hancock graduated from West Point on June 30, 1844. Due to his class ranking of eighteenth out of twenty-five, Hancock had no choice in his assignment. He was designated a brevet second lieutenant in the Sixth Infantry Regiment and detailed to Indian Territory in the West, where he served two uneventful years.

When the Mexican War began in the spring of 1846, Hancock was on recruiting duty in Cincinnati. For a while, it looked as though he would be stuck in Cincinnati while his West Point classmates won glory and promotion in Mexico. When he asked to return to the Sixth Infantry Regiment, his request was denied on the basis that he was too valuable to the recruiting service. Finally, on May 31, 1847, Second Lieutenant Winfield Hancock was ordered to rejoin his regiment in Mexico.[10]

In Mexico, Hancock served under his namesake, General Winfield Scott. Though he saw limited action, he gained valuable command experience. He learned to lead by example and to take care of his men. In the decisive Battle of Churubusco, the Mexicans fought with fierce desperation, hurling back charge after charge by the Americans. During the encounter, Hancock was hit by a musket ball below the knee; the wound was minor, and he continued to advance with his platoon. Hancock fought alongside James Longstreet, George Pickett, and Lewis Armistead, men he would meet at an important moment during the Civil War. When his company commander was wounded at Churubusco, Hancock assumed command. As a result of his actions at Churubusco, Hancock won his first citation for "gallant and meritorious conduct" and a promotion to brevet first lieutenant.[11]

During the final campaign against Chapultepec and the capture of Mexico City, Hancock was sick in his tent with chills and fever and missed the fight. "I shall always be sorry that I was absent," he wrote to Hilary.[12]

After the Mexican War, Hancock was stationed in St. Louis, where he met and married Almira Russell on January 24, 1850. Almira proved to be a source of strength for her husband, and their marriage prospered through the stresses of travel, separation, and military life. A son, Russell, was born to the Hancocks in St. Louis on October 29, 1850. A second child, their daughter Ada, was born in 1857. The family remained in St. Louis until 1856, when Hancock was posted to Florida to fight the Seminole Indians.[13]

After a short tour of duty in Florida, Hancock was transferred to Fort Leavenworth, Kansas, to quiet the disorder in "Bleeding Kansas." While there, he helped prepare a military expedition that President James Buchanan was sending to put down the Mormon revolution in Utah. General Albert Sidney Johnston led the expedition late in 1857, but by the time he reached Utah, a peaceful settlement had been reached with the Mormon leader, Brigham Young.[14]

In August 1858, Hancock and the Sixth Infantry were transferred to Benicia, California. Obtaining a leave of absence, Hancock returned East to bring his family to California. At first, his wife was reluctant to make the move, but Colonel Robert E. Lee took her aside and talked to her. He told her that her "post" was by her husband's side, warning her that it would be detrimental to their marriage to live apart because they would "cease to be essential to each other." Almira took his advice and moved West with her husband. When the Hancocks reached Benicia, they found orders directing them to Los Angeles.[15]

While Hancock was at his new post, the Civil War began, and there was increased talk of secession in southern California. Although California remained in the Union, some of Hancock's colleagues and friends who were

Southerners resigned their commissions to join the Confederacy. Prior to leaving, they gathered for a party at Hancock's home. Among those leaving to join the Confederacy was Hancock's closest friend, Lewis A. Armistead. The parting of the two was very emotional, as Almira remembered:

> The most crushed of the party was Major Armistead, who, with tears which were contagious streaming down his face and hands upon Mr. Hancock's shoulders, by looking him steadily in the eyes, said, "Hancock, good-bye. You can never know what this has cost me. And I hope God will strike me dead if I am ever induced to leave my native soil." Turning to me, he placed a small satchel in my hand requesting that it should not be opened except in the event of his death, in which case, the souvenirs it contained, with the exception of a little prayer book intended for me, should be sent to his family.

On the flyleaf of the prayer book was the inscription, "Louis A. Armistead. Trust in God and fear nothing."[16]

Later that night, Armistead and the other officers who were leaving took off their blue uniforms and headed south. Armistead offered his major's uniform to Hancock. He would not accept it nor could he have used it, for later he was to jump from captain to brigadier general.[17]

As soon as Hancock heard of Fort Sumter's fall, he requested a transfer to the East. Earlier, he had proven to be a leader and a fighter and able to handle the administrative tasks of an infantry commander. Between the Mexican and Civil wars, Hancock had seriously studied the campaigns of Caesar, Napoleon, Wellington, and Frederick the Great. Hancock was as prepared as any other general to play a major role in the fight for the Union.[18]

In August, Hancock arrived in Washington, hoping to get a combat assignment. Fortunately, there were those in Washington who realized his potential. McClellan, who knew Hancock from West Point and Mexico, quickly took advantage of his availability. On September 23, Hancock was promoted to brigadier general and given the command of a brigade under Brigadier General William F. "Baldy" Smith.[19]

Hancock was unlike most regular army officers in that he liked volunteers and did his best to make them feel as important as the regular army troops. Recognizing this unique attitude, his men repaid him with their loyalty and by the way they fought. In addition, Hancock possessed all the qualities necessary to be a successful officer. He was diligent and brave but not reckless. Although he was a stern disciplinarian, he always had his troops' interest and welfare in mind. He was a master of army regulations and knew how to acquire the supplies his men needed. As a result, his troops responded to him with respect and devotion and performed well.[20]

In McClellan's Peninsula Campaign, Hancock led his brigade skillfully in a brilliant encircling movement against Williamsburg.[21] As a result, Hancock gained recognition from General McClellan who said he had been "superb." McClellan was so pleased with Hancock's brigade that he paraded each regiment before his army and personally thanked them for their part in the action at Williamsburg.[22]

Despite Hancock's individual success on the peninsula, the campaign itself was a failure. In early August 1862, McClellan received orders from Washington to withdraw his army from the peninsula and prepare it to join Major General John Pope's Army of Virginia. McClellan's Army of the Potomac was gradually being removed from his command in the process. In the meantime, with McClellan's army no longer a threat on the peninsula, Lee pounced on the hapless Pope. Pope was defeated and driven back toward Washington. President Lincoln, feeling he had no other option, reinstated McClellan as commander of the Army of the Potomac, adding to it Pope's Army of Virginia.[23]

In September, fresh from his victory on the peninsula and in northern Virginia, Lee mounted an offensive, crossing the Potomac and moving into Maryland. The result was the Battle of Antietam, the bloodiest single day of battle in American history.

At Antietam, Hancock assumed command of the First Division when Major General Israel B. Richardson was mortally wounded. His appointment received wide acclaim with the army. Francis Walker, Hancock's adjutant, noted, "An hour after Hancock rode down the line at Antietam to take up the sword that had fallen from Richardson's dying hand, every officer in his place and every man in his ranks was aware, before the sun went down, that he belonged to Hancock's division."[24]

Tactically, Antietam was a draw, but it was a strategic victory for the Union because Lee was forced to withdraw from Maryland. After the battle, the Army of the Potomac stayed at Antietam rather than pursue Lee. Lincoln tried to get McClellan to move after Lee, even going to visit him in the field. Finally, on October 26, McClellan's preparations were complete, and he began to move his army across the Potomac. By November 2, all of McClellan's army was in Virginia, but the president had lost patience. On November 7, he removed McClellan from command, replacing him with Major General Ambrose Burnside.

McClellan left his post quietly, but there was talk among the troops of marching on Washington to protest his removal from command. Although Hancock considered his friend McClellan's treatment most "ungracious and inopportune," he was careful not to express his views to the army. Hancock was opposed to the resistance to McClellan's removal, stating, "I do not sympathize in the movement going on to resist the order. 'It is useless,' I tell the gentlemen around me. 'We are serving no one man: we are serving our country.'"[25]

After the army's dispiriting loss of McClellan, Burnside moved quickly to pursue Lee. Burnside's first engagement with the enemy was at Fredericksburg in December 1862. Promoted to major general on November 29, 1862, Hancock led Richardson's old division into battle for the first time at Fredericksburg. When Hancock learned that Burnside wanted to attack the Confederates on Marye's Heights, now well entrenched with artillery, he spoke out against the foolishness of the plan. When Burnside learned of Hancock's outspoken opinion, he was angry. Burnside said he had made his plans, and all he wanted was for his generals loyally to carry them out. Hancock explained that he meant no discourtesy; however, he felt it would be difficult to take the fortified Confederate lines by a frontal attack. Burnside insisted on carrying out his plan.[26]

Hancock received his attack orders at 8:00 a.m. on December 13. The division was under heavy artillery fire as it emerged from the town of Fredericksburg. Confederate General James Longstreet was pleased with his defensive position and the placement of his artillery. He believed they were so well situated that he could "rake the ground in front as if with a fine-tooth comb."[27]

The distance from town to the stone wall at the foot of Marye's Heights was 1,700 feet. As Hancock's men advanced across the plain, they were met with heavy artillery and infantry fire from troops concealed behind the wall in rifle pits on the forward slope of the hill. As Hancock went forward with his men, a bullet cut through his overcoat grazing his abdomen; had it been a half-inch closer to his body, it would have killed him. But this event did not hamper Hancock's efforts. Back and forth he rode across the open plain, giving directions and urging his men onward. Of his five staff members, four had their horses shot from under them, and three were wounded.[28]

In the assault on Marye's Heights, Hancock's men came closer to the stone wall than did any other Union troops that day. Time after time, the attack was repulsed in this most foolhardy of attacks. Afterward, Hancock reported, "We went into action today, although we did not gain the works we sought. Out of the fifty-seven hundred men I carried into action, I have this morning in line but fourteen hundred and fifty. It was a desperate undertaking. And the army fought hard."[29]

Although the Army of the Potomac had fought hard, the Battle of Fredericksburg accomplished nothing for the Union cause. The casualties were high, costing more than 12,000 men. Burnside's failure at Fredericksburg cost him his command. On January 25, Lincoln replaced him with Major General Joseph "Fighting Joe" Hooker.

During the spring of 1863, Hooker advanced his army to Chancellorsville. Hancock later recalled how confident Hooker was of a victory over Lee: "The day before the fight, Hooker said to a general officer, 'God Almighty could not prevent me from winning a victory tomorrow.' Pray, could we expect a victory after that? Success cannot come to us through such profanity."[30]

Hooker went into battle with 130,000 men, while Lee, who had sent Longstreet with two divisions to the south side of the James River, had cut his force to 60,000 men. Never had the prospects seemed so favorable for the Army of the Potomac. Hooker was so confident that he told Lincoln he would either win a victory or be in hell. The president was less confident, cautioning Hooker to "carry plenty of water along."[31]

Despite a well-planned attack by Hooker, his men were defeated. During the battle that ensued, Hancock was struck with several shell fragments. Nevertheless, he remained on the field, continuing to direct his men. His men performed brilliantly while covering the army's retreat from the field, ensuring its safe withdrawal.[32]

Hancock was depressed by what had happened at Chancellorsville. In a letter to his wife, he wrote: "I do not know what will be the next turn of the wheel of Fortune, or what Providence has in store for the unhappy army. I have had the blues ever since I returned from the campaign." He described to his wife what he believed to be Hooker's errors in directing the army.[33] "Hooker's day is over," Hancock confided to his wife. He was concerned about who might take command of the army next; rumors were circulating that it might be he. "I have been approached again in connection with the command of the Army of the Potomac," he said. "Give yourself no uneasiness—under no circumstances would I accept the command. I do not belong to that class of generals whom the Republicans care to bolster up. I should be sacrificed."[34]

Although the Battle of Chancellorsville produced few Union heroes, Hancock's performance was considered heroic. Disgusted with Hooker's leadership, Major General Darius Couch, commander of the Second Corps asked to be relieved of his command. The thirty-nine-year-old Hancock was the obvious choice to replace Couch. On May 22, just six weeks before the Battle of Gettysburg, he was given command of the Second Corps.[35]

Hancock proved to be an outstanding corps commander. Though he took military matters seriously and was considered a strict disciplinarian on the field, Hancock was gracious, kind, and genial when off duty. He made an effort to learn and use the names of every officer in his command, a consideration often overlooked by others in the army. Those who served under him spoke of his "considerate kindness" and of his being "always sensitive of the feelings of others."[36]

Despite the numerous defeats at the hands of the Army of Northern Virginia, Hancock found that the Second Corps had a sense of pride and honor. They did not hang their heads because of defeat but were proud of their battle scars. Before the war's end, the Second Corps would experience more casualties than any other corps in the Army of the Potomac. The Second Corps welcomed Hancock as their commander. The soldiers had observed him as the leader of the First Division and believed he was a competent general. At Chancellorsville, they noticed that he had placed his regiments in the most advantageous places during the battle. He would leap from his horse, grab the first soldier at the end of the regiment's front line, physically plant him on the desired spot and then hand him the regimental colors. Then he would order the rest of the unit into line, remount, and ride off.[37]

Hooker's defeat at Chancellorsville led to another change in command of the Army of the Potomac. Just three days before the Battle of Gettysburg, Major General George Meade was appointed to the position. Meade sincerely admired Hancock because of his performances on the peninsula, Fredericksburg, and Chancellorsville. Hancock had generally been recognized as the best division commander of the Army of the Potomac.

Lee's victory at Chancellorsville gave the Confederates the confidence to go on the offensive again. When Lee advanced into Pennsylvania, Meade moved his army to meet the Confederate invaders. On July 1, 1863, the Battle of Gettysburg began when General Meade decided to concentrate his army around Gettysburg to face Lee. Initially, the battle seemed to favor the Confederates. When Major General John Reynolds was killed in the early action, Meade sent for Hancock. He needed a man on the field who could take control of the situation and restore order. When Hancock met with Meade, he pointed out that Major General Oliver O. Howard, commander of the Eleventh Corps, was senior to him and was already on the field. Showing his confidence in Hancock, Meade indicated that he wanted Hancock to take command anyway.[38]

Major General Carl Schurz of the Eleventh Corps saw Hancock when he arrived on the scene. "The appearance of General Hancock at the front was a most fortunate event. . . . It gave the troops a new inspiration. . . . His mere presence was a reinforcement, and everybody on the field felt stronger for his being there," he said. Major General Abner Doubleday, also present, agreed: "Hancock was our genius, for he at once brought order out of confusion and made such admirable disposition that he secured the ridge and held it."[39]

The impact of Hancock's presence was immediate. Reaching Cemetery Hill, he checked the retreat of a large part of two corps. He quickly turned the broken units into a defensive force that was able to hold the heights until darkness came, so that Meade could bring up fresh troops. Hancock posted parts of the First and Eleventh Corps and the first units of the approaching Twelfth Corps in strong defensive positions, with artillery commanding the ground below. He instinctively noticed the strength of this position, which would allow Meade easily to shift troops to his two wings and the center when needed. In addition, the Union held the high ground. His selection of a strong defensive position proved to be a major factor in the Northern victory.[40]

After the first day's fighting, Hancock's corps was posted in the center of the Union line. On the second day, they were engaged in heavy fighting, reinforcing different parts of the line, with Hancock personally leading some of these reinforcements.[41]

When Meade learned that Major General Daniel Sickles had been wounded, he also put Hancock in charge of Sickles's Third Corps. Hancock was now in control of all the Union forces from Cemetery Hill to Little Round Top. Hancock improvised a defense that was able to repulse the enemy throughout the late afternoon and evening.[42]

On the third day, Lee decided to attack the center of the Union line. To lead the assault, he selected Major General George Pickett's division. This infantry attack would consist of 12,000 men, preceded by a two-hour heavy artillery barrage. To the Union troops huddled along Cemetery Ridge, the barrage seemed like the end of the world. Hancock, carrying the corps flag, rode up and down the line, helping to calm his men and prepare them for the expected attack.[43] His exposure to the enemy fire was of great concern to his men. When a subordinate told him that a corps commander should not risk his life that way, Hancock replied, "There are times when a corps commander's life does not count."[44]

Finally, Pickett's division came out of their concealment in the woods and onto the open field. Garnett's brigade was on the left; Armistead's, in the center; and Kemper's, on the right. Abreast of Pickett's division on the left were the brigades of Pettigrew and Trimble. As the batteries from Little Round Top and Hancock's infantry raked the field with deadly fire, the Confederates closed ranks and continued their steady march forward. The Rebel ranks, now thinned by the murderous fire, moved up the slope toward the stone wall. By now, it was obvious that Pickett's charge against the impregnable Union position was doomed to failure. Garnett was killed as he led his men up the slope, and Kemper was critically wounded. Hancock's old friend, Lewis Armistead, placed his hat on the tip of his sword to guide his men as he led them over the wall and into the Federal guns. As Armistead stood next to the wreckage of a Union battery, he was mortally wounded by Union fire.

Hancock had been severely wounded, too, and lay not far from Armistead. Lieutenant George Benedict recalled: "My eyes were upon Hancock's striking figure when he uttered an exclamation, and I saw that he was reeling in his saddle. General Stannard bent over him as we laid him on the ground, a ragged hole an inch or more in diameter, from which blood was pouring profusely, was disclosed in the upper part of his thigh." Hancock asked to be propped up and refused to leave the field until the Confederates had been repulsed. Only later did he learn of Armistead's injury.[45]

Hancock's success at repelling Pickett's charge came with an enormous personal loss. Lewis Armistead, his best friend, lay dying on the field. Captain Henry Bingham recalled his conversation with the wounded general: "I dismounted from my horse and inquired of the prisoner his name. He replied, 'General Armistead of the Confederate army.'" When Bingham saw the seriousness of Armistead's wound, he asked if there was anything of value in his possession that needed to be taken care of. "Tell General Hancock for me," Armistead said, "that I have done him and done all an injustice which I shall regret or repent the longest day I live." Bingham then took Armistead's spurs, pocketbook, watch, chain, and seal and gave them to Hancock.[46] Bingham had Armistead taken to the Eleventh Union Army Corps field hospital, the home of George Spangler. Armistead lived less than two days, dying at the Spangler home on July 5.[47]

Before Hancock was taken from the field, he sent a message to General Meade: "Tell General Meade that the troops under my command have repulsed the enemy's assault and that we have gained a great victory. The enemy is now flying in all directions in my front." When Meade learned of Hancock's wound, he removed his hat and said, "Say to General Hancock that I regret exceedingly that he is wounded, and that I thank him for the Country and for myself for the service he rendered today."[48]

Meantime, Hancock was placed in an ambulance and attended by Dr. Alexander N. Dougherty. The surgeon removed a minie ball that had entered his groin, carrying with it pieces of wood and a bent iron nail. Although weakened by loss of blood, Hancock dictated another message to Meade: "I have never seen a more formidable attack and if the Sixth and Fifth Corps have pressed up, the enemy will be destroyed. The enemy must be short of ammunition, as I was shot with a tenpenny nail. I did not leave the field till the victory was entirely secured and the enemy was no longer in sight." The message was delivered to Meade, but he elected not to follow Hancock's advice.[49]

Rarely in history has a subordinate general had the opportunity to influence the outcome of an important battle and to shape the destiny of a nation. Hancock did so at Gettysburg. Only once during the three days did Meade reject Hancock's advice—when he wanted a prompt Union counterattack after repulsing Pickett's assault.[50]

Hancock stayed at his father's house in Norristown, Pennsylvania, while he recovered from his wound. Not until the spring of 1864 would Hancock return to duty in the Wilderness of Virginia. Even then, his wound had not completely healed. The Wilderness was a vast tangle of forest where the roads were narrow and dark. In this environment, Hancock found he could not employ the maneuvers he had used at Gettysburg.[51] Grant hoped to get through the underbrush and fight in the open, but Lee had no intention of giving up the advantage of fighting in the Wilderness.

During Hancock's operations in the Wilderness and the assault on the "mule shoe" salient (an outward projection of the Confederate line) at Spotsylvania, his corps captured 3,000 men from Lieutenant General Richard Ewell's corps, including most of the famed Stonewall Brigade. Lee responded by building a line across the base of the salient, and the battle continued, hand-to-hand at the "bloody angle" (named for the bloody fighting that took place there).[52]

Despite his losses, Grant continued to pursue Lee. At Cold Harbor, he ordered a costly frontal assault against Lee's formidable position, with the brunt of the attack falling on Hancock's Second Corps. On the night of June 2 before the attack, the troops were in position. It rained that night, settling the dust and cooling the air. Before daylight, Hancock formed his columns. When his troops saw the fortifications they were being asked to attack, they wrote their names on pieces of paper and pinned the slips to their blouses so that their bodies might be identified.[53]

The Federal forces surged forward with "great gallantry," only to be slaughtered by the thousands. Eventually, Confederate commanders ordered their men to cease firing to allow Federal officers on the field to surrender their troops rather than risk further damage. When they did not respond, the Confederates opened fire, and the slaughter continued.[54]

Confederate Brigadier General E. McIver Law described the carnage: "I had seen the dreadful carnage in front of Marye's Hill at Fredericksburg, and on the 'old railroad cut,' which Jackson's men held at Second Manassas; but I had seen nothing to exceed this. It was not war; it was murder."[55]

Thousands of Union soldiers lay dead and wounded within rifle range of the Confederate works. Others, unhurt, lay still on the battlefield, unwilling to risk running back for fear of Confederate sharpshooters. "It was almost impossible to move and live, the lifting of a head or hand being a signal for volleys of musketry," one survivor recalled. Some of those wishing to surrender were shot by their Union comrades behind them before they reached the Confederate lines.[56]

Because Grant delayed in sending a flag of truce to Lee requesting an armistice for removing the dead and wounded, the Federal wounded lay unattended on the field for five days. By the time he did request an armistice, most of the wounded were dead. Hancock expressed great concern about Grant's blunder because of the large number of his wounded troops left on the field to die.[57] Hancock's corps lost over 3,500 men at Cold Harbor, including over fifty of its best officers. The Second Corps had been cut to pieces and would never completely recover.

Grant continued to pursue Lee, finally pinning him down at Petersburg in June 1864. While the siege of Petersburg dragged on, Grant sent Hancock to destroy a stretch of the Weldon Railroad, three miles south of Ream's Station. It was here that Hancock's magnificent career as a commander would suffer a setback. The Second Corps that Hancock had relied on so heavily at Gettysburg was no longer the same corps. His veterans were exhausted, and the replacements included draftees or bounty men who had been paid to join the army in place of another. When they were attacked, the Second Corps did something they had never done before—they turned and ran.[58]

Hancock tried his best to stem the rout. Exposing himself recklessly, he joined the battle, personally leading, cursing, and trying to get his men to fill the hole in his line. Hancock had seen his troops fail before, but never had he been mortified by seeing them driven from the field and his lines and guns taken; never before had his Second Corps failed to respond.[59]

Shortly after the Battle of Ream's Station, Hancock began suffering from his Gettysburg wound, forcing him to relinquish his command. In his parting remarks to his beloved corps, Hancock said: "Soldiers of the Second Corps, I desire in parting with you to express the regret I feel at the necessity for our separation. The story of the Second Corps will live in history, and to its officers and men will be ascribed the honor of having served their country with unsurpassed fidelity and courage."[60]

In November 1864, Hancock was assigned commander of the Washington garrison with the responsibility of recruiting a corps of veterans. His efforts met with little success. One of Hancock's most difficult tasks during this time occurred after President Lincoln's assassination. One of those convicted in the conspiracy was a woman named Mary Surratt, mother of one of the other conspirators. Along with three others, she was sentenced to death. Although responsible for carrying out the sentence, Hancock was opposed to the execution of Mrs. Surratt and believed it was a miscarriage of justice. He was so hopeful of a last-minute reprieve for her that he stationed relay couriers between the White House and the site of the execution; but the reprieve never came, and Mrs. Surratt was hanged. In his remarks to the presiding judge, he expressed his feelings about the situation: "I have been in many a battle and have seen death, and mixed with it disaster and victory. I have been in a living hell of fire, and shell and grapeshot, and, by God, I'd sooner be there ten thousand times over than to give the order this day for the execution of that poor woman. But I am a soldier, sworn to obey, and obey I must."[61]

In April 1866, Congress passed a resolution acknowledging Hancock's great service at Gettysburg. Appointed to the permanent rank of major general, he was sent West and assigned to command the Department of Missouri. At once, he was faced with an explosive problem with the Cheyenne, who were threatening both settlers and military units in the area. Hancock organized an expedition force and marched to Fort Larned, Kansas. Rather than attack the Indians when he had the opportunity, Hancock tried to negotiate with them. When he exercised restraint rather than force, the Indians took advantage of him and fled their village. Later, Hancock was criticized for what was believed laxness, and the subsequent Indian outbreak of 1867 was blamed on him. In modern times, however, whereas other army officers are criticized for their inhumane treatment of Native Americans, Hancock is perceived as having held an enlightened perspective.[62]

In August 1867, President Andrew Johnson ordered Hancock to the command of the Fifth Military District, which included Texas and Louisiana. Reconstruction was in a state of chaos when he took over. Hancock's first act was to issue his famous General Order Number 40, which was a reaffirmation of the Bill of Rights. It insisted that civilian authorities properly execute the law; guaranteed freedom of speech and of the press, trial by jury, and the right of habeas corpus; and guaranteed the preservation of personal and property rights. It was intended to heal and rebuild the nation.[63]

While Hancock's proclamation was a breath of fresh air for the South, it provoked great controversy in the North. Radical Republicans in Washington were infuriated by it and severely criticized him. Although Hancock governed magnanimously, radicals in Congress brought pressure on Grant to overrule many of his pronouncements. When Hancock asked to be reassigned, the president assigned him to the Department of the Atlantic under George Meade. When Meade died, Hancock became the senior major general of the army, a position he held until his death.[64]

In 1880, Hancock was nominated as the Democratic presidential candidate. In a close election, he was defeated by a fellow Union general, James A. Garfield. Allegations were made that the Republicans had committed fraud, but Hancock put an end to these claims. He silenced his supporters by saying, "The campaign is over and the true Christian spirit is to forgive and forget." For the next hundred years, the former Confederate states formed a consistent, dependable political base for the Democratic Party.[65]

After the election, Hancock continued his command of the Division of the East. Near the end of his life, he endured one personal tragedy after another. He outlived his only son and saw the death of his teenaged daughter. Because of his generosity in helping his old comrades from the Second Corps, he was nearly penniless when he died. On February 7, 1886, at the age of sixty-one, Hancock died of diabetic complications at his home in New York. He was buried in Montgomery Cemetery in Norristown.[66]

Hancock's death was met with a great outpouring of grief, especially from the former members of his beloved Second Corps. Of the many eulogies presented at his funeral, the one that seemed to express the true feelings of the men went thus: "One felt safe when near him." To the end, Hancock bore the title of "the superb."[67]

24 Epilogue

The Death of a President

General Lee surrendered to Grant on April 9, 1865. Lincoln was happy when he received the additional news that General Sherman was about to negotiate the surrender of General Johnston's army in North Carolina. The Confederate government was in flight after the fall of Richmond just five days earlier. In planning for the peace, Lincoln had said that he did not want to hang or kill the Confederate leaders, "even the worst of them." "Enough lives have been sacrificed; we must extinguish our resentment if we expect harmony and union," he added.[1]

In Lincoln's first inaugural address, he had said: "The Union of the States is perpetual. No State upon its own mere motion can lawfully get out of the Union." Later, he said: "The country has placed me in the helm of the ship; I'll try to steer her through." And steer her through he did, despite harsh criticism from the press and even from members of the cabinet. Adding to his burden was the infighting and incompetence of some of his generals.

The course of events during the first three years of the war forced Lincoln to be an active president and commander-in-chief. He was thus closely involved in the development of Union strategy. With inspirational leadership, he led the country through these years of suffering.

At the beginning of the war, Lincoln was flooded with requests for commissions from would-be generals and their political supporters. He used military patronage to unite the North. Democrats such as Nathaniel Banks, John A. McClernand, Benjamin Butler, and Daniel Sickles were given command positions, thus saddling the army with some incompetents. Lincoln, however, saw their appointments as good investments in national cohesion.[2]

While Lincoln was learning the elements of military science during the early months of the war, he relied heavily on Major General George McClellan. From the Peninsula Campaign to Antietam, Lincoln made every effort to make the partnership work. Lincoln was willing to humble himself to get McClellan to fight. He endured humiliations, but he failed in the end.[3] Lincoln's replacement for McClellan, Ambrose Burnside, proved to be no better.

In the West, Lincoln faced some of the same problems. Just before he removed McClellan, Lincoln replaced General Don Carlos Buell who, like McClellan, had the "slows." In Buell's place the president appointed William Rosecrans, who was reputed to be what Lincoln was looking for: a fighting general.[4]

By the spring of 1863, Lincoln was desperate for a major Union victory. Despite doubts, Lincoln turned to "Fighting Joe" Hooker. Lincoln told the general that he had been given command of the Army of the Potomac not because of, but in spite of, Hooker's comments about the nation needing "a Dictator." "Only those generals who gain success can set up dictators. What I ask of you is military success, and I will risk the dictatorship."[5]

Lincoln urged Hooker to attack Lee. In doing so, he failed Hooker. The Wilderness was a poor place to attack; the advantage Hooker enjoyed with the size of his army was lost when he had difficulty coordinating the movement of his troops. Before he could go on the offensive, Lee did. The result was a devastating defeat for the Union army. When Lincoln received the news, his response was, "My God, my God, what will the country say! What will the country say!"[6]

Burnside and Hooker were not Lincoln's only problems in 1863. He also had trouble with two of his political generals, Butler and Frémont, who wanted new assignments. Lincoln had used the political generals earlier in the war to unify the North. Now he would not give them new positions unless they could demonstrate real ability.[7]

When Lee came north in June of 1863, Lincoln was jubilant. He saw this as an opportunity to destroy Lee's army once and for all. After Meade's victory at Gettysburg, the North was exultant; however, Lincoln was disappointed when Meade did not follow up his victory.[8]

Lincoln got more good news on July 5 when he learned that General Grant had captured Vicksburg. Lincoln had been beset by demands to remove Grant. The president had refused to yield to the pressure. "I rather like the man," he said. "I think I'll try him a little longer." With the fall of Vicksburg, Lincoln felt vindicated.

By mid-October, Lincoln decided to change the command system in the West. All departments and armies in the West were placed under the command of Grant. Grant immediately replaced Rosecrans with General George Thomas.

While Lincoln had been occupied with Western problems, Meade had remained inactive. When Lincoln learned that Meade's primary objective was the capture of Richmond and not the destruction of Lee's army, he decided it was time to bring Grant away from the West. William T. Sherman was selected to replace Grant.

Lincoln's strategy for winning the war was to fight the enemy on two fronts. Grant would pursue Lee in an attempt to destroy the Army of Northern Virginia, while Sherman attempted to eliminate Joseph Johnston's army in the West.

On May 4, the Army of the Potomac crossed the Rapidan. Grant outnumbered Lee two-to-one. In that month, Grant suffered terrible losses. As the casualties continued to swell, Lincoln was pressed to replace Grant. A few days after Grant's costly attack at Cold Harbor, Lincoln told Grant: "I have just read your dispatch. . . . You will succeed. God bless you all." Despite the large protest from the public, Lincoln refused to give up on Grant.[9]

Lincoln and Grant worked well together. The commander-in-chief, however, demonstrated who was in charge. He told Grant where to go and what to do. Together, they moved toward victory at last. As the end of the war came in sight, Lincoln pushed for a policy of unconditional surrender.[10]

From the start of the war, Lincoln was resolved in his desire to preserve the Union. As a politician, he was able to build coalitions among warring political factions. Despite having no military experience, he developed a strategy for fighting the war and appointed and replaced generals as he saw fit. Had it not been for Lincoln's active management of military affairs and constant prodding of his commanders, the outcome of the war might have been different. Lincoln was the glue that held the Union together. Now that the four-year nightmare was finally over, Lincoln was ready to reunite the country and establish a lasting peace.

In his plan for Reconstruction, there would be no punishment or retribution when the Southern armies surrendered. Men and officers were to take paroles, surrender their arms, and go home. There were to be no bloodbaths of vengeance against the Confederate leaders, Lincoln had said. The country was to be restored—"one nation, indivisible, with liberty and justice for all." This was Lincoln's dream. But there was one more senseless act to follow; one that would destroy all Lincoln's dreams and hopes for the future.

April 14, 1865, was the last full day of Lincoln's life. In the morning, the president met with his cabinet and General Grant. In their discussion, Lincoln again stated that he had no intention of taking part in the hanging or killing of Confederate leaders. The best course was to allow them to leave the country, he said. "Enough lives have been sacrificed; we must extinguish our resentments if we expect harmony and union."[11]

After the meeting, Lincoln invited Grant and his wife to attend the theater that night with himself and Mrs. Lincoln. Grant accepted the invitation but later had to cancel because of a change in plans. In their place, Lincoln invited a popular young couple, Major Henry Rathbone and Miss Clara Harris, daughter of New York Senator Ira Harris. The rest of the day was busy yet pleasant.

Lincoln's bodyguard, John Parker, was waiting at Ford's Theater when the Lincolns and their guests arrived. The play was underway when the party entered the presidential box. As the orchestra struck up "Hail to the Chief," Lincoln bowed to the audience and sat down in his rocker to enjoy the rest of the play. After seeing Lincoln to his box, Parker wandered away to watch the performance, leaving the president completely unprotected.

On the stage, an actor was delivering a humorous soliloquy: "Well I guess I know enough to turn you inside out, old gal—you sock-dologizing old man-trap. Heh, Heh, Heh." This amused the audience, as the assassin, John Wilkes Booth, knew it would. Amid the laughter, Booth pushed open the door to Lincoln's box and fired a single shot to the back of the president's head; Lincoln fell forward in his chair. Major Rathbone jumped to his feet and tried to hold the assailant, but Booth stabbed him and broke free. To the amazement of the theatergoers, Booth leaped to the stage ten feet below the box. One of his spurs caught in the flag draped below the box, which caused him to land off balance and break his leg. Jumping to his feet, Booth shouted, "Sic semper tyrannus!" (thus always to tyrants), the motto of the Commonwealth of Virginia. He then limped across the stage and out the back door. Two weeks later, troops caught up with Booth in a barn in Virginia, where they shot and killed him.[12]

The wounded Lincoln was carried to a small bedroom in a house across the street. Doctors present agreed that the wound was fatal, and someone was sent to notify Secretary of War Edwin Stanton of the tragedy. When he arrived, Stanton took charge of the situation, interrogating eyewitnesses and gathering information.[13]

At 7:22 a.m. on April 15, Lincoln breathed his last breath. With tears streaming down his face, Stanton pronounced his epitaph, "Now he belongs to the ages."[14]

Lincoln's death transformed him from a controversial, unpopular politician into a martyred hero. His body lay in state under the dome of the capitol while thousands filed past the open coffin. On April 21, a nine-car funeral train set out with the bodies of Abraham and Willie Lincoln, the president's son, for their home in Springfield. On May 4, Lincoln was buried in Oak Ridge Cemetery.

Lincoln served his country well during the Civil War. The nation still suffers from the tragedy of his assassination just when his leadership had brought the war to a glorious and successful conclusion. Had he lived beyond the war and had the opportunity to implement his more conciliatory Reconstruction plan, the years of pain suffered by the South might have been reduced.

Notes

CHAPTER 1. The Making of a President

1. G. Boritt, ed., *Lincoln's Generals* (New York: Oxford University Press, 1994), xiv.
2. Boritt, *Lincoln's Generals*, 105–106.
3. T. Williams, *Lincoln and His Generals* (New York: Alfred Knopf, 1952), 1.
4. R. Morris, "Editorial," *America's Civil War* 13 (July 2000): 6.
5. H. Mitgang, *The Fiery Trial: A Life of Lincoln* (New York: The Viking Press, 1974), 20.
6. D. Donald, *Lincoln* (New York: Simon & Schuster, 1995), 24.
7. B. Chadwick, *The Two American Presidents: A Dual Biography of Abraham Lincoln and Jefferson Davis* (Secaucus, NJ: Carol Publishing Group, 1999), 26–27.
8. Chadwick, *Two American Presidents*, 27.
9. Ibid.
10. M. Burlingame, *The Inner World of Abraham Lincoln* (Urbana: University of Illinois Press, 1994), 38–39.
11. Ibid., 40–41.
12. Chadwick, *Two American Presidents*, 28.
13. Ibid., 31.
14. Ibid., 32–33.
15. Donald, *Lincoln*, 46.
16. Chadwick, *Two American Presidents*, 34–35.
17. Donald, *Lincoln*, 52–53.
18. Chadwick, *Two American Presidents*, 38.
19. Ibid., 39–40.
20. Donald, *Lincoln*, 85.
21. Ibid., 86–87.
22. Ibid., 87–88.
23. Ibid., 90–93.
24. Ibid., 94.
25. Chadwick, *Two American Presidents*, 43.
26. S. Lorant, *Lincoln* (New York: Bonanza Books, 1979), 194–195.
27. Mitgang, *The Fiery Trial*, 30–31.
28. S. Lorant, *The Life of Abraham Lincoln* (New York: Bantam Books, Inc., 1976), 50.
29. Mitgang, *The Fiery Trial*, 30–31.
30. Ibid., 31–32.
31. Ibid., 32–35.

32. Lorant, *The Life of Abraham Lincoln*, 65.

33. C. Strozier, *Lincoln's Quest for Union* (New York: Basic Books, Inc., Publishers, 1982), 208–210.

34. S. Oats, *Abraham Lincoln: The Man behind the Myths* (New York: Harper & Row, Publishers Inc., 1984), 40.

35. Oats, *Abraham Lincoln*, 40–41.

36. Strozier, *Lincoln's Quest*, 210–211.

37. Ibid., 217.

38. Ibid., 219.

39. A. Marrin, *Commander in Chief: Abraham Lincoln and the Civil War* (New York: Dutton Children's Books, 1997), 55–57.

40. Mitgang, *The Fiery Trial*, 35–36.

41. Marrin, *Commander in Chief*, 57.

42. R. Freedman, *Lincoln: A Photobiography* (New York: Clarion Books, 1987), 55.

43. Marrin, *Commander in Chief*, 60–61.

44. Freedman, *Lincoln, a Photobiography*, 56.

45. Ibid., 57, 59.

46. Ibid., 59.

47. Ibid., 60.

48. R. Bruns, *Abraham Lincoln* (New York: Chelsea House Publishers, 1986), 70.

49. J. Stevenson, "Personality," *America's Civil War* 7 (November 1994): 93.

50. Bruns, *Abraham Lincoln*, 70.

51. Marrin, *Commander in Chief*, 70.

52. Freedman, *Lincoln, a Photobiography*, 61.

53. Marrin, *Commander in Chief*, 71.

54. Bruns, *Abraham Lincoln*, 74.

CHAPTER 2. **Abraham Lincoln: Commander-in-Chief**

1. Mitgang, *The Fiery Trial*, 73–74.

2. J. McPherson, "Tried by War," *Civil War Times Illustrated* 34 (November/December 1995): 68.

3. P. Paludan, *The Presidency of Abraham Lincoln* (Lawrence: University Press of Kansas, 1994), 24.

4. Ibid., 24–25.

5. Ibid., 25.

6. Ibid., 25–26.

7. Lorant, *The Life of Abraham Lincoln*, 119.

8. Ibid., 137.

9. Ibid., 139.

10. McPherson, "Tried by War," 69.

11. Lorant, *The Life of Abraham Lincoln*, 140.

12. Williams, *Lincoln and His Generals*, 8.

13. Ibid., 8–9.

14. Chadwick, *Two American Presidents*, 179.

15. Donald, *Lincoln*, 262–267.

16. J. McPherson, *Abraham Lincoln and the Second American Revolution* (New York: Oxford University Press, 1990), 114–115.

17. McPherson, "Tried by War," 69.

18. R. Farrell, "Lincoln Takes Charge," *Civil War Times Illustrated* 39 (February 2001): 30.

19. P. Kunhardt et al., *Lincoln* (New York: Alfred A. Knopf, 1992), 54.

20. McPherson, *Lincoln and the Revolution*, 77.

21. Chadwick, *Two American Presidents*, 184.

22. Ibid., 183.

23. W. Garrison, *The Lincoln No One Knows* (Nashville: Rutledge Hill Press, 1993), 125.

24. McPherson, "Tried by War," 68.

25. E. Rofuse, "Lincoln Takes Charge," *Civil War Times Illustrated* 39 (February 2001): 27.

26. Neely, *The Last Best Hope of Earth* (Cambridge: Harvard University Press, 1993), 77.

27. Donald, *Lincoln*, 329.
28. W. Jones, *After the Thunder* (Dallas: Taylor Publishing Co., 2000), 231.
29. Lorant, *The Life of Abraham Lincoln*, 151.
30. Ibid., 153.
31. Jones, *After the Thunder*, 231.
32. Ibid., 232.
33. Lorant, *The Life of Abraham Lincoln*, 154.
34. Neely, *Last Best Hope of Earth*, 67.
35. Ibid., 64.
36. D. Riggs, "Commander in Chief: Abe Lincoln," *America's Civil War* 13 (July 2000): 35.
37. Ibid., 35.
38. Ibid.
39. Donald, *Lincoln*, 361.
40. Williams, *Lincoln and His Generals*, 156.
41. McPherson, "Tried by War," 71.
42. Ibid., 72.
43. Ibid., 71–72.
44. Donald, *Lincoln*, 384–385.
45. Neely, *Last Best Hope of Earth*, 76.
46. Bruns, *Abraham Lincoln*, 91.
47. Chadwick, *Two American Presidents*, 278.
48. Bruns, *Abraham Lincoln*, 91.
49. Ibid., 98.
50. Ibid.
51. W. Davis, *Lincoln's Men* (New York: Touchstone, 1999), 92.
52. Ibid., 93.
53. Ibid., 94.
54. Williams, *Lincoln and His Generals*, 174–175.
55. Donald, *Lincoln*, 390, 395.
56. Ibid., 398–399.
57. Ibid., 411.
58. Bruns, *Abraham Lincoln*, 100.
59. Lorant, *The Life of Abraham Lincoln*, 169.
60. McPherson, "Tried by War," 72.
61. Marrin, *Commander in Chief*, 132.
62. Ibid., 132–133.
63. Chadwick, *Two American Presidents*, 183.
64. Marrin, *Commander in Chief*, 136–137.
65. Ibid., 137–138.
66. Riggs, "Commander in Chief," 38.
67. E. Nichols, *Toward Gettysburg* (New York: The Pennsylvania State University Press, 1958), 184.
68. Donald, *Lincoln*, 144.
69. Nichols, *Toward Gettysburg*, 191.
70. McPherson, "Tried by War," 72–73.
71. Riggs, "Commander in Chief," 36.
72. Williams, *Lincoln and His Generals*, 228.
73. Ibid., 228–229.
74. Riggs, "Commander in Chief," 36.
75. Marrin, *Commander in Chief*, 138–139.
76. Chadwick, *Two American Presidents*, 303–304.
77. Riggs, "Commander in Chief," 39.
78. Donald, *Lincoln*, 447.
79. Ibid., 490.
80. Freedman, *Lincoln, a Photobiography*, 98.
81. Chadwick, *Two American Presidents*, 304.
82. Marrin, *Commander in Chief*, 145–146.
83. Ibid., 147–148.
84. Chadwick, *Two American Presidents*, 316.
85. Ibid., 305.

86. Ibid., 306.
87. Riggs, "Commander in Chief," 40.
88. Ibid., 40.
89. Donald, *Lincoln*, 489–490.
90. Ibid., 491–492.
91. Ibid., 497.
92. Ibid., 498–499.
93. McPherson, "Tried by War," 75.
94. Chadwick, *Two American Presidents*, 382.
95. Marrin, *Commander in Chief*, 161.
96. Chadwick, *Two American Presidents*, 383.
97. Ibid., 383–384.
98. Ibid., 385.
99. Ibid., 387–388.
100. Marrin, *Commander in Chief*, 171.
101. Ibid.
102. J. Glatthaar, *The March to the Sea and Beyond* (New York: New York University Press, 1985), 4–5.
103. Marrin, *Commander in Chief*, 173–174.
104. Ibid., 175.
105. Williams, *Lincoln and His Generals*, 346–347.
106. Ibid., 348.
107. Marrin, *Commander in Chief*, 177–178.
108. Freedman, *Lincoln, a Photobiography*, 112–113.
109. Marrin, *Commander in Chief*, 187.
110. Ibid., 188.
111. Jones, *After the Thunder*, 17.
112. Marrin, *Commander in Chief*, 192.
113. Jones, *After the Thunder*, 12.
114. W. Jones, *Behind Enemy Lines* (Dallas: Taylor Publishing Co., 2001), 86.

CHAPTER 3.   Winfield Scott: "Old Fuss and Feathers"

1. A. Castel, "Winfield Scott: Part I," *American History Illustrated* 16 (June 1981): 10.
2. Ibid., 10–11.
3. M. Grimsley, "Overthrown," *Civil War Times Illustrated* 19 (July 1980): 20.
4. Ibid.
5. T. Johnson, *Winfield Scott* (Lawrence: University Press of Kansas, 1998), 8.
6. Ibid., 8–9.
7. Ibid., 9.
8. Castel, "Scott: Part I," 12.
9. Johnson, *Winfield Scott*, 10–11.
10. Castel, "Scott: Part I," 12.
11. Ibid.
12. Ibid.
13. Johnson, *Winfield Scott*, 27.
14. Castel, "Scott: Part I," 15.
15. R. Winders, *Polk's Army* (College Station: Texas A&M University Press, 1997), 26.
16. Castel, "Scott: Part I," 16.
17. Ibid., 16–17.
18. Johnson, *Winfield Scott*, 72.
19. Ibid., 72–73.
20. Ibid., 73–74.
21. Ibid., 77.
22. Ibid., 106.
23. Ibid., 116.
24. Winders, *Polk's Army*, 29.

25. Johnson, *Winfield Scott*, 125.

26. Winders, *Polk's Army*, 27.

27. Castel, "Scott: Part I," 17.

28. A. Castel, "Winfield Scott: Part II," *American History Illustrated* 16 (July 1981): 20.

29. Castel, "Scott: Part II," 21–22.

30. Ibid., 23.

31. Ibid., 24.

32. M. Coit and the Editors of Life, *The Sweep Westward* (New York: Time Inc., 1963), 112.

33. Castel, "Scott: Part II," 26.

34. J. Eisenhower, *So Far from God: The U.S. War with Mexico, 1846–1848* (New York: Random House, 1989), xxv.

35. Eisenhower, *Far from God*, xxv.

36. Castel, "Scott: Part II," 27–28.

37. J. Taylor, "Compassion Is Always Due to an Enraged Imbecile," *American History Illustrated* 10 (February 1976): 18.

38. Ibid., 20.

39. Johnson, *Winfield Scott*, 220.

40. Ibid., 222.

41. Ibid., 222–223.

42. Ibid., 224.

43. Ibid., 226.

44. Ibid., 224.

45. Ibid., 225.

46. W. Davis and the Editors of Time-Life Books, *First Blood: Fort Sumter to Bull Run* (Alexandria: Time-Life Books, Inc., 1983), 27.

47. Ibid., 27–28.

48. Ibid., 28.

49. Johnson, *Winfield Scott*, 226.

50. Castel, "Scott: Part II," 28.

51. Johnson, *Winfield Scott*, 228.

52. J. McPherson, *Battle Cry of Freedom: The Civil War Era* (New York: Oxford University Press, 1988), 359.

53. Grimsley, "Overthrown," 25.

54. Ibid.

55. Ibid.

56. McPherson, *Battle Cry*, 360.

57. Johnson, *Winfield Scott*, 232.

58. McPherson, *Battle Cry*, 360.

59. Castel, "Scott: Part II," 29.

60. Johnson, *Winfield Scott*, 234–237.

61. Castel, "Scott: Part II," 29.

CHAPTER 4.   Irvin McDowell: Hard Luck General

1. E. Longacre, "Fortune's Fool," *Civil War Times Illustrated* 18 (May 1979): 20.

2. Ibid.

3. Ibid., 20, 22.

4. Ibid., 22.

5. Ibid.

6. Davis et al., *First Blood*, 110.

7. Longacre, "Fortune's Fool," 22.

8. W. Davis, *Battle at Bull Run* (Baton Rouge: Louisiana State University Press, 1977), 10–11.

9. Williams, *Lincoln and His Generals*, 17.

10. W. Davis et al., *Civil War Journal: The Battles* (Nashville: Rutledge Hill Press, 1998), 71.

11. Ibid.

12. Davis et al., *First Blood*, 110.

13. Williams, *Lincoln and His Generals*, 19.

14. Longacre, "Fortune's Fool," 24.

15. Davis et al., *First Blood*, 110–111.

16. S. Foote, *The Civil War, A Narrative: Fort Sumter to Perryville* (New York: Random House, 1958), 71.

17. Longacre, "Fortune's Fool," 25.

18. Davis et al., *Battles*, 81.

19. Longacre, "Fortune's Fool," 25–26.

20. Williams, *Lincoln and His Generals*, 20–21.

21. Longacre, "Fortune's Fool," 26.

22. Davis, *Battle at Bull Run*, 252.

23. Ibid., 253–254.

24. Longacre, "Fortune's Fool," 26.

25. Ibid., 26–27.

26. Ibid., 28.

27. Ibid.

28. Ibid., 28–29.

29. F. Wilshin, *Manassas* (Washington: National Park Service, 1953), 21.

30. Longacre, "Fortune's Fool," 29.

31. Ibid.

32. Ibid., 30.

33. Ibid.

34. Ibid., 31.

35. Ibid., 30.

36. E. Warner, *Generals in Blue: Lives of the Union Commanders* (Baton Rouge: Louisiana State University Press, 1964), 379–380.

37. S. Sears, *Controversies & Commanders: Dispatches from the Army of the Potomac* (Boston: Houghton Mifflin Company, 1999), 58–59.

38. Longacre, "Fortune's Fool," 31.

39. Ibid., 20.

CHAPTER 5.   Benjamin F. Butler: "The Beast"

1. F. Klein, "Butler at Bermuda Hundred," *Civil War Times Illustrated* 6 (November 1967): 6.

2. G. Patterson, "The Beast of New Orleans," *Civil War Times Illustrated* 32 (May/June 1993): 29.

3. C. Hearn, *When the Devil Came Down to Dixie* (Baton Rouge: Louisiana State University Press, 1997), 7.

4. Ibid.

5. Ibid., 8.

6. D. Nolan, *Benjamin Franklin Butler: The Damndest Yankee* (Novato, CA: Presidio Press, 1991), 9.

7. Patterson, "Beast of New Orleans," 30.

8. Nolan, *Damndest Yankee*, 17–18.

9. Hearn, *Devil Came to Dixie*, 12.

10. Ibid., 16–17.

11. Ibid., 13.

12. Patterson, "Beast of New Orleans," 30.

13. Nolan, *Damndest Yankee*, 38.

14. Patterson, "Beast of New Orleans," 30.

15. Ibid., 31.

16. Ibid.

17. L. Baldwin, "First Blood in Baltimore," *America's Civil War* 8 (November 1995): 36.

18. Hearn, *Devil Came to Dixie*, 29.

19. Nolan, *Damndest Yankee*, 101–102.

20. Patterson, "Beast of New Orleans," 31.

21. K. King, "Bold, but Not Too Bold," *America's Civil War* 6 (March 1993): 49.

22. Nolan, *Damndest Yankee*, 110–112.

23. Patterson, "Beast of New Orleans," 32.

24. Ibid.
25. D. Nellis, "'The Damned Rascal': Benjamin Butler in New Orleans," *Civil War Times Illustrated* 12 (October 1973): 4.
26. E. Longacre, *Army of Amateurs: General Benjamin F. Butler and the Army of the James, 1863–1865* (Mechanicsburg, PA: Stackpole Books, 1997), 1.
27. Longacre, *Army of Amateurs*, 1–2.
28. Patterson, "Beast of New Orleans," 32.
29. Ibid., 32–33.
30. D. Smith, "The Beast of New Orleans," *Civil War Times Illustrated* 8 (October 1969): 15.
31. Nolan, *Damndest Yankee*, 159.
32. Ibid., 160.
33. Ibid.
34. Patterson, "Beast of New Orleans," 33.
35. Ibid.
36. Nellis, "Damned Rascal," 8–9.
37. Smith, "Beast of New Orleans," 12.
38. Ibid., 14.
39. Nolan, *Damndest Yankee*, 197–198.
40. Ibid., 223.
41. Patterson, "Beast of New Orleans," 33, 62.
42. Smith, "Beast of New Orleans," 17–18.
43. Hearn, *Devil Came to Dixie*, 3.
44. Ibid., 4.
45. Patterson, "Beast of New Orleans," 62.
46. Nolan, *Damndest Yankee*, 223.
47. Smith, "Beast of New Orleans," 20.
48. Hearn, *Devil Came to Dixie*, 227.
49. Ibid., 227–228.
50. Patterson, "Beast of New Orleans," 62.
51. Longacre, *Army of Amateurs*, 30–31.
52. Patterson, "Beast of New Orleans," 63.
53. Klein, "Butler at Bermuda Hundred," 47.
54. Patterson, "Beast of New Orleans," 64.
55. Ibid.
56. Ibid.
57. Hearn, *Devil Came to Dixie*, 235.
58. Ibid., 236.
59. Patterson, "Beast of New Orleans," 64.
60. Hearn, *Devil Came to Dixie*, 236–237.
61. Ibid., 237.
62. Ibid., 237–238.
63. Ibid., 238.
64. Ibid., 238–239.
65. Patterson, "Beast of New Orleans," 66.
66. Nolan, *Damndest Yankee*, 340.
67. Ibid., 341–342.
68. Ibid., 344.
69. Longacre, *Army of Amateurs*, 5–6.
70. Ibid., 6.

CHAPTER 6.   George B. McClellan: The General with the "Slows"

1. W. Davis et al., *Civil War Journal: The Leaders* (Nashville: Rutledge Hill Press, 1997), 108.
2. S. Sears, *George B. McClellan: The Young Napoleon* (New York: Ticknor & Fields, 1988), 2–3.
3. Ibid., 4.
4. J. Waugh, *The Class of 1846* (New York: Warner Books, Inc., 1994), 13–14.
5. Sears, *Young Napoleon*, 12.
6. Ibid.

7. Waugh, *Class of 1846*, 66.

8. Ibid., 73.

9. Ibid., 74–75.

10. Davis et al., *Civil War Journal: The Leaders*, 109–110.

11. Sears, *Young Napoleon*, 24.

12. Ibid., 42.

13. Ibid.

14. Ibid., 43–44.

15. Davis et al., *Civil War Journal: The Leaders*, 111.

16. Sears, *Young Napoleon*, 51.

17. Ibid., 60–61.

18. J. Robertson, *General A. P. Hill: The Story of a Confederate Warrior* (New York: Random House, 1987), 27–28.

19. Ibid., 28–29.

20. W. Hassler, *A. P. Hill: Lee's Forgotten General* (Chapel Hill: The University of North Carolina Press, 1957), 22.

21. Sears, *Young Napoleon*, 62–63.

22. Ibid., 64.

23. Ibid., 66–67.

24. Davis et al., *Civil War Journal: The Leaders*, 112.

25. Ibid., 113.

26. Williams, *Lincoln and His Generals*, 24–25.

27. Ibid., 25.

28. T. Rowland, *George B. McClellan and Civil War History* (Kent: The Kent State University Press, 1998), 54.

29. Ibid., 50.

30. R. Reeder, *The Northern Generals* (New York: Duell, Sloan & Pearce, 1964), 20.

31. Davis et al., *Civil War Journal: The Leaders*, 113.

32. B. Catton, *Mr. Lincoln's Army* (New York: Doubleday & Company, 1951), 68.

33. Davis et al., *Civil War Journal: The Leaders*, 115–116.

34. Ibid., 118.

35. Ibid.

36. Reeder, *The Northern Generals*, 21.

37. Davis et al., *Civil War Journal: The Leaders*, 121–122.

38. Rowland, *McClellan and Civil War*, 49.

39. S. Sears, "McClellan vs. Lee: The Seven-Day Trial," *Military Quarterly* 1 (Autumn 1988): 10.

40. Davis et al., *Civil War Journal: The Leaders*, 121–123.

41. S. Sears, *To the Gates of Richmond: The Peninsula Campaign* (New York: Ticknor & Fields, 1992), 347.

42. Ibid.

43. Davis et al., *Civil War Journal: The Leaders*, 124.

44. S. Sears, "Lincoln and McClellan," *Lincoln's Generals*, ed. G. Boritt (New York: Oxford University Press, 1994), 40.

45. R. Luthin, *The Real Abraham Lincoln* (Englewood Cliffs: Prentice Hall, 1960), 329.

46. A. Castel, "George McClellan: 'Little Mac,'" *Civil War Times Illustrated* 13 (May 1974): 9.

47. Ibid., 9–10.

48. Ibid., 10.

49. Ibid.

50. Ibid.

51. Ibid.

52. J. Stokesbury, *A Short History of the Civil War* (New York: William Morrow & Company, Inc., 1995), 118.

53. Sears, "Lincoln and McClellan," 43.

54. Rowland, *McClellan and Civil War*, 232.

55. Sears, *Young Napoleon*, 339.

56. Ibid., 341.

57. Ibid., 341–343.

58. Ibid., 344.

59. Ibid., 348.

60. Ibid.

61. Ibid., 349–350.

62. Ibid., 354.

63. Ibid., 363–364.

64. J. McPherson, *Ordeal by Fire* (New York: Alfred A. Knopf, 1982), 441.

65. Ibid.

66. Sears, *Young Napoleon*, 366–367.

67. Ibid., 361.

68. Ibid., 361–362.

69. Ibid., 363.

70. Luthin, *Real Abraham Lincoln*, 553.

71. J. G. Randall and D. Donald, *The Civil War and Reconstruction* (Lexington: D. C. Heath & Company, 1969), 478–479.

72. Stokesbury, *A Short History*, 280.

73. Davis et al., *Civil War Journal: The Leaders*, 130.

74. Ibid., 386.

75. Ibid., 391.

76. Ibid., 395.

77. Ibid., 400–401.

78. Ibid., 401.

79. Ibid.

80. B. Sell, *Leaders of the North and South* (New York: Michael Friedman Publishing Group, Inc., 1996), 38.

CHAPTER 7. Don Carlos Buell: "The McClellan of the West"

1. R. Morris, "At Perryville, Don Carlos Buell Won a Battlefield Victory, but Lost a Political War," *America's Civil War* 8 (September 1995): 6.

2. S. Engle, *Don Carlos Buell: Most Promising of All* (Chapel Hill: The University of North Carolina Press, 1999), xiii.

3. Ibid., 3.

4. Ibid., 4.

5. Ibid., 6.

6. Ibid., 7.

7. Ibid., 17–18.

8. Ibid., 20–21.

9. Ibid., 23–25.

10. Ibid., 26–28.

11. Ibid., 34.

12. Ibid., 40–42.

13. Ibid., 48.

14. Ibid., 65–66.

15. Ibid., 70.

16. Ibid., 71.

17. Williams, *Lincoln and His Generals*, 44.

18. Foote, *The Civil War*, 145.

19. Williams, *Lincoln and His Generals*, 44.

20. Engle, *Don Carlos Buell*, 90–95.

21. Williams, *Lincoln and His Generals*, 45–46.

22. Foote, *The Civil War*, 146.

23. Ibid., 146.

24. Engle, *Don Carlos Buell*, 140–141.

25. Foote, *The Civil War*, 156.

26. Williams, *Lincoln and His Generals*, 56–57.

27. Engle, *Don Carlos Buell*, 172–177.

28. Ibid., 185.

29. Ibid., 193–204.

30. Ibid., 205–208.

31. Foote, *The Civil War*, 343.

32. Ibid., 346–348.

33. Engle, *Don Carlos Buell*, 235.

34. Ibid., 236–237.

35. Ibid., 237–238.

36. Ibid., 242.

37. Ibid., 245.

38. J. Street and the Editors of Time-Life Books, *The Struggle for Tennessee: Tupelo to Stones River* (Alexandria: Time-Life Books, 1985), 15.

39. Engle, *Don Carlos Buell*, 267–268.

40. Street et al., *Struggle for Tennessee*, 17.

41. Ibid.

42. J. McDonough, *War in Kentucky: From Shiloh to Perryville* (Knoxville: The University of Tennessee Press, 1994), 48.

43. Engle, *Don Carlos Buell*, 281.

44. Ibid., 287–288.

45. Ibid., 294.

46. Ibid., 300.

47. Ibid., 304–305.

48. McDonough, *War in Kentucky*, 224.

49. Ibid.

50. K. Czech, "Reviews," *America's Civil War* 8 (September 1995): 64.

51. Street, *Struggle for Tennessee*, 67.

52. Engle, *Don Carlos Buell*, 310.

53. Street, *Struggle for Tennessee*, 80.

54. Ibid.

55. Warner, *Generals in Blue*, 52.

56. Engle, *Don Carlos Buell*, 337.

57. Ibid., 343–344.

CHAPTER 8.   William S. Rosecrans: "Old Rosy"

1. W. Lamers, *The Edge of Glory: A Biography of General William S. Rosecrans, U.S.A.* (Baton Rouge: Louisiana State University Press, 1961), 3.

2. E. Longacre, "A General Vanquished in the West," *Civil War Times Illustrated* 24 (October 1985): 16.

3. Ibid.

4. Ibid.

5. Lamers, *Edge of Glory*, 6.

6. Ibid., 9–11.

7. Ibid., 10–11.

8. Ibid., 12.

9. Ibid., 13–15.

10. Longacre, "Vanquished in the West," 16, 18.

11. Ibid., 18.

12. Lamers, *Edge of Glory*, 17–18.

13. Longacre, "Vanquished in the West," 18.

14. Lamers, *Edge of Glory*, 34–38.

15. Longacre, "Vanquished in the West," 18–19.

16. Lamers, *Edge of Glory*, 78–80.

17. Longacre, "Vanquished in the West," 19.

18. T. Winchel, "A Fierce Little Fight in Mississippi," *Civil War Times Illustrated* 33 (July/ August 1994): 54.

19. Ibid., 55–59.

20. Longacre, "Vanquished in the West," 44.

21. Lamers, *Edge of Glory*, 122–123.

22. Ibid., 123.

23. Longacre, "Vanquished in the West," 44.

24. Ibid.

25. Lamers, *Edge of Glory*, 174–176.

26. Longacre, "Vanquished in the West," 44.

27. Lamers, *Edge of Glory*, 183.

28. Williams, *Lincoln and His Generals*, 205.

29. Lamers, *Edge of Glory*, 201.

30. S. Woodworth, *Six Armies in Tennessee: The Chickamauga and Chattanooga Campaign* (Lincoln: University of Nebraska Press, 1998), 3.

31. Williams, *Lincoln and His Generals*, 206.

32. Lamers, *Edge of Glory*, 245.

33. Ibid., 247.

34. Longacre, "Vanquished in the West," 45.

35. Ibid.

36. Lamers, *Edge of Glory*, 268–269.

37. Longacre, "Vanquished in the West," 45.

38. E. Dupuy and T. Dupuy, *The Compact History of the Civil War* (New York: MJF Books, 1993), 264–265.

39. Warner, *Generals in Blue*, 411.

40. Williams, *Lincoln and His Generals*, 277–278.

41. W. Davis et al., *The Battles*, 405.

42. Ibid., 404–405.

43. Ibid., 405–406.

44. Ibid., 405.

45. J. Taylor, "'With More Sorrow Than I Can Tell,'" *Civil War Times Illustrated* 20 (April 1981), 24.

46. Williams, *Lincoln and His Generals*, 284.

47. P. Cozzens, *This Terrible Sound: The Battle of Chickamauga* (Urbana: University of Illinois Press, 1992), 528.

48. Ibid., 528.

49. Lamers, *Edge of Glory*, 396.

50. Longacre, "Vanquished in the West," 47.

51. Lamers, *Edge of Glory*, 401–402.

52. Ibid., 403.

53. Ibid., 433.

54. Ibid., 437–438.

55. Longacre, "Vanquished in the West," 47.

56. Lamers, *Edge of Glory*, 440–441.

57. Longacre, "Vanquished in the West," 47.

58. Lamers, *Edge of Glory*, 442–443.

59. Ibid., 443.

60. Ibid., 443–444.

61. Ibid., 446.

62. Ibid., 449.

CHAPTER 9.   John Pope: The "Miscreant"

1. W. Greene, *The Second Battle of Manassas* (Conshochocken, PA: Eastern National, 1995), 1.

2. J. Hennessy, "The Second Battle of Manassas: Lee Suppresses the 'Miscreant' Pope," *Blue & Gray* 9 (August 1992): 11.

3. Ibid., 1.

4. J. Wert, "Returning to the Killing Ground," *America's Civil War* 4 (July 1991): 18.

5. Ibid., 18.

6. J. Hennessy, *Return to Bull Run* (New York: Simon & Schuster, 1993), 13.

7. J. Cullen, "Five Cent Pope," *Civil War Times Illustrated* 19 (April 1980): 4.

8. P. Cozzens, *General John Pope: A Life for the Nation* (Urbana: University of Illinois Press, 2000), 1, 9.

9. Ibid., 7–8.

10. Ibid., 8–9.
11. Ibid., 9.
12. Ibid., 10–11.
13. Ibid., 13.
14. Cullen, "Five Cent Pope," 6.
15. Cozzens, *General John Pope*, 25–27.
16. Ibid., 28.
17. Ibid.
18. Ibid., 30–31.
19. Cullen, "Five Cent Pope," 6.
20. Williams, *Lincoln and His Generals*, 117.
21. Ibid., 118.
22. Cullen, "Five Cent Pope," 8.
23. Ibid.
24. Williams, *Lincoln and His Generals*, 119.
25. Cullen, "Five Cent Pope," 8.
26. Hennessy, "Second Battle," 11.
27. Wert, "The Killing Ground," 20.
28. Williams, *Lincoln and His Generals*, 119–120.
29. Cullen, "Five Cent Pope," 9.
30. Ibid., 9.
31. Ibid., 44.
32. Wert, "The Killing Ground," 20.
33. Cullen, "Five Cent Pope," 45.
34. Ibid.
35. Williams, *Lincoln and His Generals*, 156–157.
36. Greene, *Second Battle of Manassas*, 37.
37. Wert, "The Killing Ground," 25.
38. Cozzens, *General John Pope*, 198–199.
39. Williams, *Lincoln and His Generals*, 159–160.
40. Cozzens, *General John Pope*, 200.
41. Cullen, "Five Cent Pope," 47.
42. Ibid.
43. Cozzens, *General John Pope*, 338–339.
44. Ibid., 340.

CHAPTER 10.   John A. McClernand: The Congressman General

1. R. Kiper, *Major General John Alexander McClernand: Politician in Uniform* (Kent: The Kent State University Press, 1999), xi.
2. Ibid., 1.
3. E. Longacre, "Congressman Becomes General: General John A. McClernand," *Civil War Times Illustrated* 21 (November, 1982): 31.
4. Kiper, *Politician in Uniform*, 4.
5. Ibid., 6.
6. Longacre, "Congressman Becomes General," 31.
7. Kiper, *Politician in Uniform*, 8.
8. Ibid., 11.
9. Ibid., 13.
10. Ibid., 17–18.
11. Longacre, "Congressman Becomes General," 31–32.
12. Kiper, *Politician in Uniform*, 21.
13. Longacre, "Congressman Becomes General," 32.
14. Ibid., 32.
15. Ibid., 34.
16. Ibid.
17. Ibid.
18. Ibid.

19. Ibid.

20. Kiper, *Politician in Uniform*, 89.

21. Longacre, "Congressman Becomes General," 35.

22. Ibid.

23. E. Miers, *The Web of Victory: Grant at Vicksburg* (Baton Rouge: Louisiana State University Press, 1984), 30.

24. D. Nevin and the Editors of Time-Life Books, *The Road to Shiloh: Early Battles in the West* (Alexandria: Time-Life Books, 1983), 119.

25. Mier, *The Web of Victory*, 30–31.

26. J. Korn and Editors of Time-Life Books, *War on the Mississippi: Grant's Vicksburg Campaign* (Alexandria: Time-Life Books, 1985), 56.

27. Longacre, "Congressman Becomes General," 36.

28. Williams, *Lincoln and His Generals*, 190–191.

29. Longacre, "Congressman Becomes General," 36.

30. G. Perret, *Ulysses S. Grant: Soldier and President* (New York: Random House, 1997), 241.

31. Longacre, "Congressman Becomes General," 37.

32. Ibid., 38.

33. Kiper, *Politician in Uniform*, 265.

34. Ibid., 266.

35. Longacre, "Congressman Becomes General," 39.

36. Korn, *War on the Mississippi*, 147.

37. Ibid.

38. M. Fellman, *Citizen Sherman* (New York: Random House, 1995), 320.

39. Korn, *War on the Mississippi*, 147–148.

40. Kiper, *Politician in Uniform*, 273.

41. Williams, *Lincoln and His Generals*, 228–229.

42. Longacre, "Congressman Becomes General," 39.

43. Kiper, *Politician in Uniform*, 293.

44. Ibid., 293–295.

45. Ibid., 296.

46. Longacre, "Congressman Becomes General," 39.

47. Kiper, *Politician in Uniform*, 302.

CHAPTER 11. Henry Wagner Halleck: "Old Brains"

1. S. Ambrose, *Halleck: Lincoln's Chief-of-Staff* (Baton Rouge: Louisiana State University Press, 1962), 142.

2. Ibid.

3. Ibid., 143.

4. Ibid., 3.

5. Ibid., 6.

6. B. McGinty, "Old Brains in the New West," *American History Illustrated* 13 (May 1978): 12–13.

7. Ibid., 13.

8. Ibid., 15.

9. Ibid., 17–18.

10. Ibid., 11.

11. Nevin et al., *The Road to Shiloh*, 58–59.

12. Ambrose, *Halleck*, 14–15.

13. Williams, *Lincoln and His Generals*, 50–51.

14. Ibid., 56–57.

15. Ambrose, *Halleck*, 34.

16. Ibid., 42.

17. Ibid.

18. Williams, *Lincoln and His Generals*, 82–83.

19. Nevin et al., *The Road to Shiloh*, 157.

20. Williams, *Lincoln and His Generals*, 68.

21. Ibid., 132–133.

22. Ambrose, *Halleck*, 61–62.
23. R. Weigley, *A Great Civil War: A Military and Political History, 1861–1865* (Bloomington: Indiana University Press, 2000), 136.
24. Ibid.
25. Williams, *Lincoln and His Generals*, 146.
26. Ibid., 147–148.
27. Catton, *Mr. Lincoln's Army*, 202–203.
28. Weigley, *A Great Civil War*, 143–144.
29. Ambrose, *Halleck*, 65.
30. Williams, *Lincoln and His Generals*, 133–134.
31. Ambrose, *Halleck*, 86.
32. Engle, *Don Carlos Buell*, 319.
33. Ibid., 320.
34. Ambrose, *Halleck*, 92.
35. Ibid., 93.
36. Ibid.
37. Williams, *Lincoln and His Generals*, 193–194.
38. Ibid., 197.
39. Ambrose, *Halleck*, 97–98.
40. Ibid., 101–102.
41. Ibid., 116.
42. Williams, *Lincoln and His Generals*, 208–209.
43. McPherson, *Battle Cry*, 639.
44. Ibid., 641.
45. Ibid., 642–645.
46. Ambrose, *Halleck*, 133.
47. Williams, *Lincoln and His Generals*, 257–261.
48. Ambrose, *Halleck*, 142–143.
49. Williams, *Lincoln and His Generals*, 270–271.
50. Ibid., 283.
51. R.Wooster, *The Civil War 100* (Secaucus, NJ: Carol Publishing Company, 1998), 78.
52. Ambrose, *Halleck*, 163.
53. Ibid., 168–170.
54. Weigley, *A Great Civil War*, 371–372.
55. B. Simpson, *Ulysses S. Grant: Triumph Over Adversity, 1822–1865* (Boston: Houghton Mifflin Company, 2000), 398.
56. McGinty, "Old Brains," 18.

CHAPTER 12. **Ambrose E. Burnside: Reluctant Commander**

1. J. Cullen, "The Battle of Fredericksburg," *American History Illustrated* 13 (June 1978): 4.
2. W. Marvel, *Burnside* (Chapel Hill: University of North Carolina, 1991), 1–2.
3. Cullen, "The Battle of Fredericksburg," 4.
4. Ibid.
5. Marvel, *Burnside*, 3.
6. Ibid.
7. Ibid., 3–5.
8. E. Stackpole, *The Fredericksburg Campaign* (Harrisburg: Stackpole Books, 1991), 58.
9. Marvel, *Burnside*, 10.
10. Ibid., 10–11.
11. Ibid., 13.
12. Ibid., 13–14.
13. Ibid., 18.
14. Ibid., 19–20.
15. Davis et al., *The Battles*, 75.
16. Ibid.
17. Ibid.
18. Ibid., 76–78.

19. Ibid., 79.

20. Ibid., 83.

21. Marvel, *Burnside*, 28.

22. Ibid., 28–29.

23. E. Thomas, "The Lost Confederates of Roanoke," *Civil War Times Illustrated* 15 (May 1976): 10–11.

24. J. Luvaas, "Burnside's Roanoke Expedition," *Civil War Times Illustrated* 7 (December 1968): 47.

25. Marvel, *Burnside*, 99–100.

26. G. Skoch, "Burnside's Geography Class," *Civil War Times Illustrated* 33 (January/February 1995): 35–36.

27. Williams, *Lincoln and His Generals*, 162.

28. R. Bailey and the Editors of Time-Life Books, *The Bloodiest Day: The Battle of Antietam* (Alexandria: Time-Life Books, 1984), 15.

29. Williams, *Lincoln and His Generals*, 163–164.

30. Ibid., 165.

31. Bailey, *The Bloodiest Day*, 120.

32. Ibid., 122.

33. Davis et al., *The Battles*, 161–162.

34. Ibid., 163.

35. Marvel, *Burnside*, 148.

36. Davis et al., *The Battles*, 173.

37. Williams, *Lincoln and His Generals*, 178.

38. Davis et al., *The Battles*, 174–175.

39. Ibid., 175.

40. Ibid., 176.

41. Ibid., 177.

42. Stackpole, *The Fredericksburg Campaign*, 127.

43. Davis et al., *The Battles*, 177.

44. Ibid., 176–177.

45. Ibid., 179, 181.

46. Ibid., 182–183.

47. H. Hattaway, *Shades of Blue and Gray* (Columbia: University of Missouri Press, 1997), 108–109.

48. Ibid., 109.

49. Davis et al., *The Battles*, 187.

50. Ibid., 190.

51. Hattaway, *Shades of Blue and Gray*, 110.

52. Cullen, "The Battle of Fredericksburg," 46.

53. Davis et al., *The Battles*, 191.

54. J. Stevens, *1863: The Rebirth of a Nation* (New York: Bantam Books, 1999), 77.

55. T. Rice, "Wading to Glory," *Civil War Times Illustrated* 20 (May 1981): 19.

56. Stevens, *Rebirth of a Nation*, 77–78.

57. Ibid., 79–80.

58. Rice, "Wading to Glory," 24–25.

59. Williams, *Lincoln and His Generals*, 204.

60. Marvel, *Burnside*, 216–217.

61. Ibid., 231.

62. Ibid., 234–237.

63. M. Haskew, "Icy Assault Routed," *America's Civil War* 4 (May 1991): 25.

64. Williams, *Lincoln and His Generals*, 280–281.

65. Ibid., 281.

66. Skoch, "Burnside's Geography Class," 39.

67. Ibid., 40.

68. Ibid., 40–41.

69. Marvel, *Burnside*, 408–410.

70. Ibid., 417.

71. Ibid., 422–423.

72. Ibid., 424–425.

73. Ibid., 425.

CHAPTER 13.   Ulysses S. Grant: "Unconditional Surrender Grant"

1. Simpson, *Triumph over Adversities*, 115.
2. Ibid., 116.
3. Ibid., 117.
4. Ibid.
5. Ibid.
6. A. McFall, "Grant's Early War Days," *America's Civil War* 7 (November 1994): 34.
7. Davis et al., *Civil War Journal: The Leaders*, 183.
8. Jones, *After the Thunder*, 75.
9. Davis et al., *Civil War Journal: The Leaders*, 184.
10. M. Grimsley, "Ulysses S. Grant," *Civil War Times Illustrated* 28 (January/February 1990): 21–22.
11. Jones, *After the Thunder*, 76.
12. Ibid.
13. Ibid.
14. Editors of American Heritage, *The American Heritage Pictorial History of the Presidents* (Great Neck, NJ: American Heritage), 456.
15. Grimsley, "Ulysses S. Grant," 22.
16. Ibid., 22–26.
17. G. Perret, *Soldier and President*, 39–40.
18. Ibid., 43.
19. Ibid., 51.
20. Grimsley, "Ulysses S. Grant," 24.
21. Editors of American Heritage, *History of the Presidents*, 451.
22. Ibid., 458.
23. Perret, *Soldier and President*, 107–198.
24. Jones, *After the Thunder*, 79.
25. Ibid.
26. Grimsley, "Ulysses S. Grant," 21.
27. Jones, *After the Thunder*, 79.
28. Perret, *Soldier and President*, 208–209.
29. Sell, *Leaders of the North and South*, 26.
30. Simpson, *Triumph over Adversities*, 170–171.
31. Ibid., 215.
32. Jones, *After the Thunder*, 80.
33. Sell, *Leaders of the North and South*, 26–28.
34. Perret, *Soldier and President*, 306.
35. Ibid., 312.
36. Sell, *Leaders of the North and South*, 28.
37. Davis et al., *Civil War Journal: The Leaders*, 199.
38. Ibid., 199–200.
39. Simpson, *Triumph over Adversities*, 341.
40. Ibid., 342.
41. Davis et al., *Civil War Journal: The Leaders*, 200–201.
42. Perret, *Soldier and President*, 358.
43. Ibid.
44. C. Dowdey, *Lee* (New York: Bonanza Books, 1965), 268.
45. J. Korn and the Editors of Time-Life Books, *Pursuit to Appomattox: The Last Battle* (Alexandria: Time-Life Books, 1987), 134.
46. W. McFeely, *Grant* (New York: W. W. Norton, 1981), 217.
47. Jones, *After the Thunder*, 24.
48. Ibid., 83.
49. R. Wilson, "Meeting at the McLean House," *American History Illustrated* 22 (September 1987): 48.
50. Korn et al., *Pursuit to Appomattox*, 108.
51. Jones, *After the Thunder*, 83.
52. Ibid.
53. Perret, *Soldier and President*, 360.

54. McFeely, *Grant*, 216.
55. Grimsley, "Ulysses S. Grant," 47–48.
56. Ibid., 48.
57. W. Nye, "Grant: Genius of Fortune's Child," *Civil War Times Illustrated* 4 (June 1965): 8.
58. Ibid.
59. Ibid.
60. Grimsley, "Ulysses S. Grant," 48.
61. Editors of American Heritage, *History of the Presidents*, 459.
62. Perret, *Soldier and President*, 368.
63. Davis et al., *Civil War Journal: The Leaders*, 202.
64. Grimsley, "Ulysses S. Grant," 61.
65. Ibid., 61–62.
66. Perret, *Soldier and President*, 377–378.
67. Ibid., 381.
68. Ibid., 412.
69. Jones, *After the Thunder*, 88.
70. Grimsley, "Ulysses S. Grant," 63.
71. L. Frost. *U. S. Grant Album* (New York: Bonanza Books, 1966), 160.
72. T. H. Williams et al., *The Union Restored* (New York: Time Inc., 1963), 154.
73. Jones, *After the Thunder*, 89.
74. Ibid.
75. Editors of American Heritage, *History of the Presidents*, 466.
76. Jones, *After the Thunder*, 90.
77. L. Poggiali, "The Death of U. S. Grant and the Cottage on Mount McGregor," *Blue & Gray* 10 (February 1993): 61.
78. Ibid.
79. Davis et al., *Civil War Journal: The Leaders*, 207.
80. Editors of American Heritage, *History of the Presidents*, 466.

CHAPTER 14.   Daniel E. Sickles: A Man of Controversy

1. C. Cooney, "The General's Badge of Honor," *American History Illustrated* 20 (April 1985): 16.
2. E. Longacre, "Damnable Dan Sickles," *Civil War Times Illustrated* 23 (May 1984): 16.
3. Ibid., 16–17.
4. W. A. Swanberg, *Sickles the Incredible: A Biography of Daniel Edgar Sickles* (Gettysburg: Stan Clark Military Books, 1956), 77.
5. Ibid., 77–78.
6. Ibid., 78–79.
7. Ibid., 79.
8. Ibid., 80–81.
9. Davis et al., *The Leaders*, 262.
10. Swanberg, *Sickles the Incredible*, 83.
11. T. Balderston, "The Sad, Shattered Life of Teresa Sickles," *American History Illustrated* 17 (September 1982): 41.
12. Ibid.
13. Davis et al., *The Leaders*, 256.
14. Balderston, "Life of Teresa Sickles," 41.
15. Davis et al., *Civil War Journal: The Leaders*, 256.
16. Ibid., 256–257.
17. Ibid., 257.
18. Ibid.
19. Balderston, "Life of Teresa Sickles," 43.
20. Swanberg, *Sickles the Incredible*, 50–51.
21. Balderston, "Life of Teresa Sickles," 43.
22. Davis et al., *Civil War Journal: The Leaders*, 258.
23. Ibid., 258–259.
24. Swanberg, *Sickles the Incredible*, 56.
25. Balderston, "Life of Teresa Sickles," 44.

26. Davis et al., *Civil War Journal: The Leaders*, 259.
27. Ibid., 259.
28. Ibid., 260.
29. Ibid.
30. Balderston, "Life of Teresa Sickles," 45.
31. Ibid.
32. Davis et al., *Civil War Journal: The Leaders*, 260.
33. Swanberg, *Sickles the Incredible*, 106.
34. M. Chesnut, *A Diary from Dixie* (New Haven: Yale University, 1981), 247.
35. Swanberg, *Sickles the Incredible*, 109.
36. Longacre, "Damnable Dan Sickles," 18.
37. Swanberg, *Sickles the Incredible*, 110.
38. Longacre, "Damnable Dan Sickles," 18–19.
39. Ibid., 19.
40. Davis et al., *Civil War Journal: The Leaders*, 265.
41. Ibid., 265–266.
42. Longacre, "Damnable Dan Sickles," 19.
43. Ibid.
44. Swanberg, *Sickles the Incredible*, 158–159.
45. Longacre, "Damnable Dan Sickles," 19.
46. Ibid., 20.
47. Ibid.
48. Ibid.
49. G. Rice, "Devil Dan Sickles' Deadly Salients," *America's Civil War* 11 (November 1998): 41–42.
50. Davis et al., *Civil War Journal: The Leaders*, 267–268.
51. Longacre, "Damnable Dan Sickles," 22.
52. Davis et al., *Civil War Journal: The Leaders*, 268–269.
53. Rice, "Deadly Salients," 43.
54. G. Kross, "To Die Like Soldiers," *Blue & Gray* 15 (Campaign 1998): 6–7.
55. Rice, "Deadly Salients," 43.
56. Longacre, "Damnable Dan Sickles," 24.
57. Davis et al., *Civil War Journal: The Leaders*, 269.
58. Ibid., 270–271.
59. Longacre, "Damnable Dan Sickles," 24.
60. Davis et al., *Civil War Journal: The Leaders*, 271.
61. Ibid., 272.
62. Longacre, "Damnable Dan Sickles," 25.
63. Ibid.
64. Ibid.
65. F. Cleaves, *Meade of Gettysburg* (Norman: University of Oklahoma Press, 1960), 214–215.
66. Ibid., 216.
67. Ibid., 216–217.
68. Longacre, "Damnable Dan Sickles," 25.
69. Davis et al., *Civil War Journal: The Leaders*, 272.
70. Longacre, "Damnable Dan Sickles," 17.
71. Ibid., 25.
72. Swanberg, *Sickles the Incredible*, 384–385.
73. W. Piston, *Lee's Tarnished Lieutenant* (Athens: The University of Georgia Press, 1987), 160–161.
74. Davis et al., *Civil War Journal: The Leaders*, 274.
75. Ibid.
76. Ibid.
77. Cooney, "Badge of Honor," 17.

CHAPTER 15.   William Tecumseh Sherman: Advocate of Total War

1. Korn et al., *Pursuit to Appomattox*, 157–158.
2. J. Marszalek, *Sherman: A Soldier's Passion for Order* (New York: Vintage Books, 1993), 2–4.

3. Ibid., 4–5.

4. Ibid., 6.

5. Ibid., 6–9.

6. Ibid., 9–10.

7. Ibid., 15.

8. Ibid., 17.

9. A. Castel, "The Life of a Rising Son, Part I: The Failure," *Civil War Times Illustrated* 18 (July 1979): 4.

10. Marszalek, *Sherman*, 22–23.

11. Ibid., 23.

12. Fellman, *Citizen Sherman*, 9–10.

13. Castel, "Rising Son, Part I," 4–6.

14. Ibid., 6.

15. Ibid., 7.

16. L. Lewis, *Sherman: Fighting Prophet* (New York: Harcourt, Brace & World, 1958), 1.

17. Ibid., 1–2.

18. Castel, "Rising Son, Part I," 7.

19. Ibid., 7, 42.

20. Ibid., 42.

21. Ibid.

22. Ibid., 43.

23. Ibid., 44.

24. Ibid., 45.

25. Ibid.

26. Fellman, *Citizen Sherman*, 102.

27. Castel, "Rising Son, Part I," 46.

28. A. Castel, "The Life of a Rising Son, Part II: The Subordinate," *Civil War Times Illustrated* 18 (August 1979): 15.

29. Ibid.

30. Ibid., 16.

31. Ibid., 20.

32. B. Sell, *Leaders of the North and South* (New York: Michael Friedman Publishing Group, Inc., 1996), 35.

33. Fellman, *Citizen Sherman*, 199–200.

34. Castel, "Rising Son, Part II," 21.

35. A. Castel, "The Life of a Rising Son, Part III: The Conqueror," *Civil War Times Illustrated* 18 (October 1979): 10.

36. Ibid.

37. Ibid., 13.

38. Davis et al., *Civil War Journal: The Leaders*, 355.

39. Ibid.

40. Ibid., 352.

41. Ibid., 353.

42. Ibid., 358–360.

43. E. Miers, *The General Who Marched to Hell* (New York: Collier Books, 1951), 266–267.

44. O. Dunphy, "March to the Sea," *America's Civil War* 3 (July 1990): 49.

45. M. Grimsley, *The Hard Hand of War* (New York: Cambridge University Press, 1995), 199.

46. Marszalek, *Sherman*, 312–313.

47. Grimsley, *Hard Hand of War*, 200.

48. C. Roland, *The American Iliad* (Lexington: University Press of Kentucky, 1991), 242.

49. Lewis, *Fighting Prophet*, 493.

50. Davis et al., *Civil War Journal: The Leaders*, 362–363.

51. Ibid., 363.

52. J. McDonough and J. Jones, *War So Terrible* (New York: W. W. Norton, 1987), 323–324.

53. Ibid., 324.

54. Marszalek, *Sherman*, 344–345.

55. Castel, "Rising Son, Part III," 19.

56. T. Fleming, "The Big Parade," *Civil War Chronicles* (Summer 1991): 60.

57. Ibid., 62.

58. Ibid., 63–64.
59. Ibid., 64.
60. O. Eisenschimal, "Sherman: Hero or War Criminal?" *Civil War Times Illustrated* 2 (January 1964): 35.
61. Marszalek, *Sherman*, 358.
62. Ibid., 361.
63. Ibid., 361–362.
64. Ibid., 362.
65. Ibid., 259–260.
66. Ibid., 261.
67. Ibid., 363.
68. Ibid., 422.
69. Ibid., 424–425.
70. C. Royster, *The Destructive War* (New York: Alfred A. Knopf, 1991), 375–376.
71. B. Davis, *Sherman's March* (New York: Random House, 1980), 290–300.
72. Ibid.
73. Marszalek, *Sherman*, 484–488.
74. Ibid., 331.
75. Ibid., 331–332.
76. Ibid., 332.

CHAPTER 16.   John Sedgwick: "Uncle John"

1. H. Round, "'Uncle John' Sedgwick," *Civil War Times Illustrated* 5 (December 1966): 3.
2. Ibid., 13.
3. Ibid., 14.
4. Ibid.
5. A. Hemingway, "Travel," *America's Civil War* 8 (March 1995): 70.
6. Ibid.
7. Round, "'Uncle John' Sedgwick," 14.
8. R. Winslow, *General John Sedgwick* (Novato, CA: Presidio Press, 1982), 2.
9. Ibid.
10. Ibid.
11. Ibid.
12. Ibid., 5.
13. Round, "'Uncle John' Sedgwick," 16.
14. L. Tagg, *The Generals of Gettysburg* (Mason City, IA: Savas Publishing Company, 1998), 104.
15. Winslow, *General John Sedgwick*, 28–29.
16. Ibid., 38.
17. Ibid., 39–40.
18. Jones, *After the Thunder*, 232–233.
19. Winslow, *General John Sedgwick*, 40.
20. Bailey et al., *The Bloodiest Day*, 86–87.
21. Ibid., 87–88.
22. Winslow, *General John Sedgwick*, 46–47.
23. Ibid., 47.
24. Ibid., 48.
25. Tagg, *The Generals of Gettysburg*, 104.
26. Winslow, *General John Sedgwick*, 52.
27. Ibid., 54–55.
28. Ibid., 55–58.
29. Round, "'Uncle John' Sedgwick," 17–18.
30. Winslow, *General John Sedgwick*, 58–59.
31. Tagg, *The Generals of Gettysburg*, 104.
32. E. Stackpole, *Chancellorsville: Lee's Greatest Battle* (Harrisburg: Stackpole Books, 1958), 96.
33. Winslow, *General John Sedgwick*, 62.
34. Tagg, *The Generals of Gettysburg*, 104.

35. W. Goolrick and the Editors of Time-Life Books, *Rebels Resurgent: Fredericksburg to Chancellorsville* (Alexandria: Time-Life Books, 1985), 154–156.

36. Ibid., 159–160.

37. Winslow, *General John Sedgwick*, 87–88.

38. Tagg, *The Generals of Gettysburg*, 105.

39. Ibid., 104–105.

40. Winslow, *General John Sedgwick*, 95.

41. Ibid., 96.

42. Round, "'Uncle John' Sedgwick," 19.

43. Ibid.

44. Winslow, *General John Sedgwick*, 110.

45. Ibid., 111–112.

46. Winslow, *General John Sedgwick*, 113.

47. Ibid., 113.

48. Ibid., 124–125.

49. Ibid., 133–134.

50. Ibid., 134.

51. Ibid., 138.

52. Ibid., 140–141.

53. Ibid., 143–144.

54. Ibid., 144–145.

55. Ibid., 145.

56. Ibid., 149.

57. Round, "'Uncle John' Sedgwick," 21.

58. Winslow, *General John Sedgwick*, 163.

59. Ibid., 165.

60. Ibid., 166.

61. Ibid., 172.

62. G. Jaynes and the Editors of Time-Life Books, *The Killing Ground: Wilderness to Cold Harbor* (Alexandria: Time-Life Books, 1986), 88.

63. Ibid.

64. Winslow, *General John Sedgwick*, 175.

65. Ibid., 178.

66. Ibid.

CHAPTER 17. Joseph Hooker: "Fighting Joe"

1. W. Hebert, *Fighting Joe Hooker* (Indianapolis: The Bobbs-Merrill Company, 1944), 7.

2. Ibid., 8.

3. Stackpole, *Lee's Greatest Battle*, 6–7.

4. Herbert, *Fighting Joe Hooker*, 17.

5. Ibid., 18.

6. Ibid., 19.

7. Ibid., 20.

8. Ibid., 20–21.

9. Ibid., 21.

10. Ibid., 22.

11. E. Furgurson, *Chancellorsville 1863: The Souls of the Brave* (New York: Vintage Books, 1993), 20–21.

12. Hebert, *Fighting Joe Hooker*, 25.

13. Ibid., 27.

14. Furgurson, *Chancellorsville 1863*, 22.

15. Hebert, *Fighting Joe Hooker*, 33.

16. Furgurson, *Chancellorsville 1863*, 23.

17. Hebert, *Fighting Joe Hooker*, 38.

18. Furgurson, *Chancellorsville 1863*, 23.

19. W. Hassler, *Commanders of the Army of the Potomac* (Baton Rouge: Louisiana State University Press, 1962), 130.

20. Furgurson, *Chancellorsville 1863*, 24.
21. Ibid.
22. Hebert, *Fighting Joe Hooker*, 49.
23. W. Hassler, "Fighting Joe Hooker," *Civil War Times Illustrated* 14 (August 1975): 6.
24. Ibid.
25. Ibid.
26. Furgurson, *Chancellorsville 1863*, 25.
27. Editors of Time-Life Books, *1863: Turning Point of the Civil War* (Alexandria: Time-Life Books, 1998), 18.
28. Hassler, "Fighting Joe Hooker," 6–8.
29. Ibid., 8.
30. Hebert, *Fighting Joe Hooker*, 114–115.
31. Wooster, *The Civil War 100*, 25.
32. Hebert, *Fighting Joe Hooker*, 117–118.
33. Ibid., 118.
34. Ibid., 128–130.
35. Hassler, "Fighting Joe Hooker," 9.
36. Hebert, *Fighting Joe Hooker*, 144–145.
37. Ibid., 147.
38. Hassler, "Fighting Joe Hooker," 9, 36.
39. Editors of Time-Life Books, *Turning Point*, 14.
40. Hassler, "Fighting Joe Hooker," 36.
41. Editors of Time-Life Books, *Turning Point*, 14.
42. Ibid.
43. Ibid., 15.
44. Ibid.
45. Ibid., 23.
46. Hassler, "Fighting Joe Hooker," 41.
47. Sears, *Controversies & Commanders*, 169.
48. Editors of Time-Life Books, *Turning Point*, 36.
49. Ibid.
50. Hassler, "Fighting Joe Hooker," 41–42.
51. Editors of Time-Life, *Turning Point*, 65.
52. Ibid.
53. Hassler, "Fighting Joe Hooker," 42.
54. Hebert, *Fighting Joe Hooker*, 239–240.
55. Hassler, "Fighting Joe Hooker," 42–43.
56. Ibid., 43.
57. Ibid., 44.
58. Woodworth, *Six Armies in Tennessee*, 185–188.
59. Hassler, "Fighting Joe Hooker," 44.
60. Hebert, *Fighting Joe Hooker*, 273.
61. Ibid., 203.
62. Hassler, "Fighting Joe Hooker," 46.
63. Hebert, *Fighting Joe Hooker*, 285.
64. Ibid.
65. Ibid., 286.
66. Ibid., 287.
67. Hassler, "Fighting Joe Hooker," 46.
68. Ibid.
69. Hebert, *Fighting Joe Hooker*, 293–294.
70. Ibid., 295–296.

CHAPTER 18.   George H. Thomas: "The Rock of Chickamauga"

1. F. Cleaves, *Rock of Chickamauga* (Norman: University of Oklahoma Press, 1948), 65.
2. Ibid., 67.
3. Ibid., 4–8.

4. Ibid., 9.

5. Ibid., 14–15.

6. F. Downey, "From Chapultepec to Lookout Mountain," *Civil War Times* 2 (August/ September 1960): 5.

7. Ibid.

8. Cleaves, *Rock of Chickamauga*, 28.

9. Ibid., 43.

10. Ibid., 45.

11. Ibid., 48–49.

12. Ibid., 50–51.

13. Ibid., 54–60.

14. Ibid., 76.

15. Ibid., 89–90.

16. Ibid., 92–94.

17. G. Tucker, "George H. Thomas," *Civil War Times Illustrated* 5 (April 1966): 32.

18. Cleaves, *Rock of Chickamauga*, 105.

19. Ibid.

20. Ibid., 107.

21. Ibid., 112–113.

22. Engle, *Don Carlos Buell*, 305–310.

23. Cleaves, *Rock of Chickamauga*, 117–118.

24. Ibid., 118–119.

25. Ibid., 119.

26. Ibid., 120–121.

27. Hattaway, *Shades of Blue and Gray*, 104.

28. Cleaves, *Rock of Chickamauga*, 131–132.

29. Ibid., 136.

30. Editors of Time-Life Books, *Turning Point*, 209–210.

31. Ibid., 210.

32. J. Korn and the Editors of Time-Life Books, *The Fight for Chattanooga: Chickamauga to Missionary Ridge* (Alexandria: Time-Life Books, 1985), 34–35.

33. Ibid., 35–36.

34. Davis et al., *The Battles*, 404–405.

35. Editors of Time-Life Books, *Turning Point*, 222–223.

36. Ibid., 223.

37. Ibid., 246.

38. Ibid., 246.

39. Cleaves, *Rock of Chickamauga*, 176.

40. Editors of Time-Life Books, *Turning Point*, 246.

41. Davis et al., *The Battles*, 405–407.

42. Cozzens, *This Terrible Sound*, 523.

43. Cleaves, *Rock of Chickamauga*, 179–180.

44. Editors of Time-Life Books, *Turning Point*, 262.

45. Ibid., 262–263.

46. Cleaves, *Rock of Chickamauga*, 209.

47. C. Anders, *Fighting Confederates* (New York: Dorset Press, 1968), 95.

48. Davis et al., *The Battles*, 437–438.

49. Ibid., 440–442.

50. Ibid., 446–447.

51. Cleaves, *Rock of Chickamauga*, 257.

52. Ibid., 257–258.

53. Ibid., 259.

54. Davis et al., *The Battles*, 451.

55. Cleaves, *Rock of Chickamauga*, 268.

56. Ibid., 273.

57. Ibid., 273–274.

58. Ibid., 297.

59. Ibid., 259.

60. Ibid., 306–307.

CHAPTER 19.   **Philip Sheridan: Worth His Weight in Gold**

1. E. Stackpole, "Sheridan's Ride—As It Really Happened," *Civil War Times* 3 (October 1961): 12.
2. Ibid.
3. Ibid., 12–13.
4. T. Lewis and the Editors of Time-Life Books, *The Shenandoah in Flames* (Alexandria: Time-Life Books, 1987), 152–153.
5. Ibid., 153–154.
6. R. Morris, *Sheridan, The Life and Wars of General Phil Sheridan* (New York: Vintage Press, 1992), 1.
7. Ibid., 10–11.
8. T. Lewis, *The Guns of Cedar Creek* (New York: Harper & Row, 1988), 35–36.
9. Ibid., 36.
10. Morris, *Sheridan*, 13–14.
11. Ibid., 14–15.
12. Ibid., 17.
13. Lewis, *Guns of Cedar Creek*, 38.
14. Ibid., 38–39.
15. Ibid., 39.
16. Ibid., 39–40.
17. Morris, *Sheridan*, 39–40.
18. P. Sheridan, *The Personal Memoirs of P. H. Sheridan* (New York: De Capo Press, 1992), 65–66.
19. R. O'Connor, *Sheridan: The Inevitable* (Indianapolis: Bobbs Merrill, 1953), 56–60.
20. Sheridan, *Personal Memoirs*, 75–77.
21. Ibid., 84.
22. R. Weigley, "Philip Sheridan: A Personal Profile," *Civil War Times Illustrated* 7 (July 1968): 8.
23. Lewis, *Guns of Cedar Creek*, 43.
24. Ibid., 44.
25. Street et al., *Struggle for Tennessee*, 58.
26. Ibid., 80–81.
27. Ibid., 124.
28. Lewis, *Guns of Cedar Creek*, 46–47.
29. Morris, *Sheridan*, 152.
30. Davis et al., *The Leaders*, 338.
31. G. Perret, *Soldier and President*, 314–315.
32. Ibid., 316.
33. Ibid.
34. Ibid.
35. Davis et al., *The Leaders*, 340.
36. Morris, *Sheridan*, 183.
37. Davis et al., *The Leaders*, 340.
38. Morris, *Sheridan*, 184.
39. Davis et al., *The Leaders*, 341–342.
40. Lewis, *Shenandoah in Flames*, 153.
41. B. Catton, *American Heritage New History of the Civil War* (New York: Viking, 1996), 499.
42. Davis et al., *The Leaders*, 342.
43. Ibid., 344.
44. Morris, *Sheridan*, 258.
45. Ibid., 269.
46. O'Connor, *Sheridan, the Inevitable*, 294–296.
47. Morris, *Sheridan*, 300.
48. O'Connor, *Sheridan, the Inevitable*, 299.
49. Ibid., 301–302.
50. Ibid., 306–307.
51. Morris, *Sheridan*, 327–328.
52. O'Connor, *Sheridan, the Inevitable*, 312–314.

53. Ibid., 314–315.
54. Morris, *Sheridan*, 348–349.
55. O'Connor, *Sheridan, the Inevitable*, 333–334.
56. Ibid., 337.
57. Ibid., 339–340.
58. Ibid., 341.
59. Ibid., 349.
60. Lewis, *Guns of Cedar Creek*, 305.
61. O'Connor, *Sheridan: The Inevitable*, 356–357.

CHAPTER 20.   John F. Reynolds: Man of Honor

1. Tagg, *The Generals of Gettysburg*, 9.
2. Ibid.
3. E. Longacre, "John F. Reynolds, General," *Civil War Times Illustrated* 11 (August 1972): 35.
4. Ibid.
5. M. Riley, *"For God's Sake, Forward," John F. Reynolds, USA* (Gettysburg, PA: Farnsworth House Military Impressions, 1995), 3.
6. Longacre, "John F. Reynolds, General," 36.
7. Riley, *"For God's Sake, Forward,"* 7.
8. Nichols, *Toward Gettysburg*, 4–7.
9. Ibid., 8–9.
10. Riley, *"For God's Sake, Forward,"* 7–8.
11. Ibid., 8.
12. Nichols, *Toward Gettysburg*, 13.
13. Longacre, "John F. Reynolds, General," 36.
14. Riley, *"For God's Sake, Forward,"* 16.
15. Ibid.
16. Ibid.
17. Ibid., 18.
18. Ibid., 18–19.
19. Ibid., 20.
20. Ibid., 20–21.
21. Ibid., 21.
22. Nichols, *Toward Gettysburg*, 70.
23. Ibid., 71.
24. Riley, *"For God's Sake, Forward,"* 21–22.
25. Nichols, *Toward Gettysburg*, 73.
26. Ibid., 75.
27. Riley, *"For God's Sake, Forward,"* 22.
28. Longacre, "John F. Reynolds, General," 36.
29. Riley, *"For God's Sake, Forward,"* 23.
30. Longacre, "John F. Reynolds, General," 38.
31. Ibid.
32. Ibid.
33. Nichols, *Toward Gettysburg*, 97.
34. Ibid., 98–99.
35. Ibid., 99.
36. Longacre, "John F. Reynolds, General," 39.
37. Nichols, *Toward Gettysburg*, 115.
38. Longacre, "John F. Reynolds, General," 39.
39. Ibid.
40. Riley, *"For God's Sake, Forward,"* 34.
41. Ibid.
42. Ibid., 34–35.
43. Cleaves, *Meade of Gettysburg*, 85.
44. Longacre, "John F. Reynolds, General," 40.
45. Ibid.

46. Tagg, *The Generals of Gettysburg*, 11.
47. Riley, "*For God's Sake, Forward,*" 42.
48. Ibid., 45.
49. Cleaves, *Meade of Gettysburg*, 128–129.
50. Ibid., 45.
51. H. Pfanz, *Gettysburg—Culp's Hill and Cemetery Hill* (Chapel Hill: University of North Carolina Press, 1993), 14.
52. Ibid., 16.
53. Longacre, "John F. Reynolds, General," 41–42.
54. Cleaves, *Meade of Gettysburg*, 135.
55. Riley, "*For God's Sake, Forward,*" 51.
56. R. Hoffsommer, "Sergeant Charles Veil's Memoir on the Death of Reynolds," *Civil War Times Illustrated* 21 (June 1982): 23.
57. Nichols, *Toward Gettysburg*, 206.
58. Longacre, "John F. Reynolds, General," 42.
59. Cleaves, *Meade of Gettysburg*, 135.
60. Longacre, "John F. Reynolds, General," 43.
61. Ibid.
62. Ibid.
63. Ibid., 54.
64. Ibid.

CHAPTER 21.   George Gordon Meade: The Cautious General

1. Tagg, *The Generals of Gettysburg*, 1.
2. Cleaves, *Meade of Gettysburg*, 3.
3. J. Cullen, "George Gordon Meade," *Civil War Times Illustrated* 14 (May 1975): 6–7.
4. Cleaves, *Meade of Gettysburg*, 11–12.
5. Ibid., 16–18.
6. Ibid., 36.
7. Ibid., 49.
8. Ibid., 52.
9. Ibid., 53–54.
10. Cullen, "George Gordon Meade," 7.
11. Tagg, *The Generals of Gettysburg*, 2.
12. Cleaves, *Meade of Gettysburg*, 69.
13. Cullen, "George Gordon Meade," 8.
14. Ibid.
15. Ibid.
16. Cleaves, *Meade of Gettysburg*, 81.
17. Ibid., 84–85.
18. Cullen, "George Gordon Meade," 8.
19. Cleaves, *Meade of Gettysburg*, 97.
20. P. Batty and P. Parish, *The Divided Union* (Topsfield, MA: Salem House Publishers, 1987), 128.
21. Cleaves, *Meade of Gettysburg*, 106.
22. Cullen, "George Gordon Meade," 8.
23. Ibid.
24. Cleaves, *Meade of Gettysburg*, 120–121.
25. C. Clark and the Editors of Time-Life Books, *Gettysburg: The Confederate High Tide* (Alexandria: Time-Life Books, 1985), 34.
26. Hattaway, *Shades of Blue and Gray*, 142–143.
27. Clark et al., *The Confederate High Tide*, 35.
28. Batty and Parish, *The Divided Union*, 133.
29. Davis et al., *The Battles*, 253.
30. Batty and Parish, *The Divided Union*, 133–134.
31. Davis et al., *The Battles*, 254–258.
32. Cleaves, *Meade of Gettysburg*, 136–137.
33. Ibid., 157.

34. Batty and Parish, *The Divided Union*, 136.
35. Davis et al., *The Battles*, 267.
36. D. Freeman, *Lee of Virginia* (New York: Charles Scribner's Sons, 1958), 133–134.
37. Davis et al., *The Battles*, 277.
38. Ibid., 278.
39. Williams, *Lincoln and His Generals*, 263.
40. Ibid., 266.
41. Cleaves, *Meade of Gettysburg*, 172.
42. Cullen, "George Gordon Meade," 41.
43. Ibid.
44. Cleaves, *Meade of Gettysburg*, 185.
45. Ibid., 186.
46. Cullen, "George Gordon Meade," 42.
47. Ibid., 44.
48. Ibid., 44–45.
49. Hebert, *Fighting Joe Hooker*, 269–270.
50. Perret, *Soldier & President*, 303–304.
51. Cullen, "George Gordon Meade," 45.
52. Perret, *Soldier & President*, 313–314.
53. Ibid., 316.
54. Ibid.
55. Ibid., 329.
56. Ibid., 330.
57. Ibid., 331.
58. W. Davis and the Editors of Time-Life Books, *Death in the Trenches: Grant at Petersburg* (Alexandria: Time-Life Books, 1986), 74.
59. Cleaves, *Meade of Gettysburg*, 278–282.
60. Ibid., 292, 303.
61. Ibid., 334.
62. Ibid., 334.
63. Ibid., 349–351.
64. Ibid., 69.

CHAPTER 22.   **Hugh Judson Kilpatrick: "Kill-Cavalry"**

1. V. Jones, "The Kilpatrick-Dahlgren Raid: Boldly Planned . . . Timidly Executed," *Civil War Times Illustrated* 4 (April 1965): 13–14.
2. E. Thomas, "The Kilpatrick-Dahlgren Raid—Part I," *Civil War Times Illustrated* 16 (February 1978): 4.
3. E. Longacre, "Judson Kilpatrick," *Civil War Times Illustrated* 10 (April 1971): 25.
4. Ibid.
5. S. Martin, *Kill-Cavalry: The Life of Union General Hugh Judson Kilpatrick* (Mechanicsburg, PA: Stackpole Books, 2000), 193.
6. Longacre, "Judson Kilpatrick," 25.
7. Martin, *Life of General Kilpatrick*, 15–16.
8. Longacre, "Judson Kilpatrick," 25.
9. Ibid.
10. Ibid., 25–26.
11. Martin, *Life of General Kilpatrick*, 27–29.
12. S. Martin, "Kill-Cavalry," *Civil War Times Illustrated* 38 (February 2000): 25.
13. Ibid.
14. Longacre, "Judson Kilpatrick," 26.
15. Martin, "Kill-Cavalry," 26.
16. Martin, *Life of General Kilpatrick*, 58.
17. Longacre, "Judson Kilpatrick," 26.
18. Martin, *Life of General Kilpatrick*, 57.
19. Ibid., 7.
20. Martin, "Kill-Cavalry," 27.

21. Longacre, "Judson Kilpatrick," 26.
22. Martin, "Kill-Cavalry," 28.
23. Ibid.
24. Ibid., 28–29.
25. Longacre, "Judson Kilpatrick," 29.
26. Ibid.
27. Martin, *Life of General Kilpatrick*, 125.
28. Ibid., 126.
29. Martin, "Kill-Cavalry," 30.
30. R. Suhr, "The Kilpatrick-Dahlgren Raid on Richmond," *Military Heritage* 1 (June 2000): 50.
31. Martin, "Kill-Cavalry," 30.
32. Ibid.
33. E. Thomas, "The Kilpatrick-Dahlgren Raid—Part II," *Civil War Times Illustrated* 17 (April 1978): 31.
34. Martin, *Life of General Kilpatrick*, 169–170.
35. Ibid., 171.
36. Martin, "Kill-Cavalry," 30.
37. Longacre, "Judson Kilpatrick," 30–31.
38. A. Lee, "Tangling with 'Kilcavalry,'" *Civil War Times Illustrated* 37 (June 1998): 67–68.
39. Martin, *Life of General Kilpatrick*, 197.
40. Longacre, "Judson Kilpatrick," 32.
41. Ibid., 23.
42. Martin, "Kill-Cavalry," 59.
43. Martin, *Life of General Kilpatrick*, 234–235.
44. Martin, "Kill-Cavalry," 59.
45. Martin, *Life of General Kilpatrick*, 262–263.

CHAPTER 23.   Winfield Scott Hancock: "Hancock the Superb"

1. D. Jordan, *Winfield Scott Hancock: A Soldier's Life* (Bloomington: Indiana University Press, 1996), 43.
2. Ibid.
3. G. Faeder, "Superb Was the Day," *America's Civil War* 3 (March 1991): 51.
4. G. Tucker, *Hancock the Superb* (Dayton: Morningside Bookshop, 1980), 87.
5. Faeder, "Superb Was the Day," 52.
6. Tagg, *The Generals of Gettysburg*, 33.
7. Jordan, *A Soldier's Life*, 5–6.
8. Ibid., 6–7.
9. G. Tucker, "Winfield S. Hancock: A Personal Profile," *Civil War Times Illustrated* 7 (August 1968): 5–6.
10. Jordan, *A Soldier's Life*, 14.
11. Tucker, *Hancock*, 41.
12. Jordan, *A Soldier's Life*, 16.
13. Davis et al., *The Leaders*, 235.
14. Jordan, *A Soldier's Life*, 25–26.
15. Ibid., 26–27.
16. Davis et al., *The Leaders*, 236–237.
17. Tucker, "Winfield S. Hancock," 7.
18. T. Shulman, "To Be Held at All Hazards," *Civil War Times Illustrated* 32 (September/ October 1993): 47.
19. Davis et al., *The Leaders*, 237.
20. Ibid., 238.
21. Ibid.
22. Tucker, *Hancock*, 89.
23. Jordan, *A Soldier's Life*, 49–50.
24. Davis et al., *The Leaders*, 240.
25. Jordan, *A Soldier's Life*, 56.
26. Ibid., 61.
27. Tucker, *Hancock*, 105–106.

28. Ibid., 106–107.
29. Davis et al., *The Leaders*, 241.
30. Ibid., 242.
31. Tucker, *Hancock*, 118.
32. Tagg, *The Generals of Gettysburg*, 34.
33. Jordan, *A Soldier's Life*, 75.
34. Tucker, *Hancock*, 124.
35. Tagg, *The Generals of Gettysburg*, 34.
36. Jordan, *A Soldier's Life*, 58.
37. Tagg, *The Generals of Gettysburg*, 34.
38. Davis et al., *The Leaders*, 245.
39. Tagg, *The Generals of Gettysburg*, 34.
40. Tucker, "Winfield S. Hancock," 9.
41. Davis et al., *The Leaders*, 246.
42. Tagg, *The Generals of Gettysburg*, 35.
43. Davis et al., *The Leaders*, 246.
44. Tucker, *Hancock*, 151.
45. Davis et al., *The Leaders*, 247–248.
46. W. Motts, *"Trust in God and Fear Nothing": General Lewis A. Armistead, CSA* (Gettysburg: Farnsworth House Military Impressions, 1994), 46.
47. J. T. Wert, *Gettysburg: Day Three* (New York: Simon & Schuster, 2001), 247.
48. Ibid., 246.
49. Ibid., 247–248.
50. Tucker, "Winfield S. Hancock," 9.
51. B. Trinque, "Battle Fought on Paper," *America's Civil War* 6 (May 1993): 32.
52. E. Furgurson, *Not War but Murder: Cold Harbor 1864* (New York: Alfred A. Knopf, 2000), 19–20.
53. Tucker, *Hancock*, 223.
54. Furgurson, *Not War but Murder*, 154.
55. Tucker, "Winfield S. Hancock," 10.
56. Furgurson, *Not War but Murder*, 154.
57. Tucker, *Hancock*, 230–231.
58. Davis et al., *The Leaders*, 248–249.
59. Tucker, *Hancock*, 254–255.
60. Davis et al., *The Leaders*, 249–250.
61. Tucker, "Winfield S. Hancock," 10.
62. Ibid., 45.
63. Ibid., 47.
64. Ibid.
65. Davis et al., *The Leaders*, 252.
66. Warner, *Generals in Blue*, 204.
67. Davis et al., *The Leaders*, 252.

CHAPTER 24.   Epilogue: The Death of a President

1. Jones, *Behind Enemy Lines*, 86.
2. Williams, *Lincoln and His Generals*, 8–9.
3. Boritt, ed., *Lincoln's Generals*, xv.
4. Williams, *Lincoln and His Generals*, 184.
5. Ibid., 210.
6. Ibid., 238.
7. Ibid., 214.
8. Boritt, ed., *Lincoln's Generals*, xviii.
9. L. Longford, *Abraham Lincoln* (New York: G. P. Putnam's Sons, 1975), 185.
10. Boritt, ed., *Lincoln's Generals*, xxi.
11. R. Fowler, *The Assassination of Abraham Lincoln* (Yorktown: Eastern Acorn Press, 1987), 7.
12. Jones, *Behind Enemy Lines*, 80.
13. Marrin, *Commander in Chief*, 218–219.
14. Jones, *Behind Enemy Lines*, 81.

Bibliography

Ambrose, Stephen E. *Halleck: Lincoln's Chief-of-Staff.* Baton Rouge: Louisiana State University, 1962.

Anders, Curt. *Fighting Confederates.* New York: Dorset Press, 1968.

Bailey, Ronald H., and the Editors of Time-Life Books. *The Bloodiest Day: The Battle of Antietam.* Alexandria: Time-Life Books, 1984.

Balderston, Thomas. "The Sad, Shattered Life of Teresa Sickles." *American History Illustrated* 17, no. 5 (September 1982): 41–45.

Baldwin, Leo. "First Blood in Baltimore." *America's Civil War* 8, no. 2 (November 1995): 36.

Batty, Peter, and Peter Parish. *The Divided Union.* Topsfield, MA: Salem House Publishers, 1987.

Boritt, Gabor S. *Lincoln's Generals.* New York: Oxford University Press, 1994.

Bruns, Roger. *Abraham Lincoln.* New York: Chelsea House Publishers, 1986.

Burlingame, Michael. *The Inner World of Abraham Lincoln.* Urbana: University of Illinois Press, 1994.

Castel, Albert. "George B. McClellan: 'Little Mac.'" *Civil War Times Illustrated* 13, no. 2 (May 1974): 9–10.

———. "The Life of a Rising Son, Part I: The Failure." *Civil War Times Illustrated* 18, no. 4 (July 1979): 4–7; 42–46.

———. "The Life of a Rising Son, Part II: The Subordinate." *Civil War Times Illustrated* 18, no. 5 (August 1979): 15–21.

———. "The Life of a Rising Son, Part III: The Conqueror." *Civil War Times Illustrated* 18, no. 6 (October 1979): 10–13, 19.

———. "Winfield Scott, Part I." *American History Illustrated* 16, no. 3 (June 1981): 10–17.

———. "Winfield Scott, Part II." *American History Illustrated* 16, no. 4 (July 1981): 20–28.

Catton, Bruce. *Mr. Lincoln's Army.* New York: Doubleday & Company, Inc., 1951.

———. *American Heritage New History of the Civil War.* New York: Viking, 1996.

Chadwick, Bruce. *The Two American Presidents: A Dual Biography of Abraham Lincoln and Jefferson Davis.* Secaucus, NJ: Carol Publishing Group, 1999.

Chesnut, Mary. *A Diary from Dixie.* New Haven: Yale University, 1981.

Clark, Champ, and the Editors of Time-Life Books. *Gettysburg: The Confederate High Tide.* Alexandria: Time-Life Books, 1985.

Cleaves, Freeman. *Rock of Chickamauga.* Norman: University of Oklahoma Press, 1948.

———. *Meade of Gettysburg.* Norman: University of Oklahoma Press, 1960.

Coit, Margaret, and the Editors of Life. *The Sweep Westward.* New York: Time Inc., 1963.

Cooney, Charles. "The General's Badge of Honor." *American History Illustrated* 20, no. 2 (April 1985): 16.

Cozzens, Peter. *This Terrible Sound: The Battle of Chickamauga.* Urbana: University of Illinois Press, 1992.

———. *General John Pope: A Life for the Nation.* Urbana: University of Illinois Press, 2000.

Cullen, Joseph. "George Gordon Meade." *Civil War Times Illustrated* 14, no. 2 (May 1975): 6–8, 41–45.

———. "The Battle of Fredericksburg." *American History Illustrated* 13, no. 3 (June 1978): 4, 46.

———. "Five Cent Pope." *Civil War Times Illustrated* 19, no. 1 (April 1980): 4–9, 44–47.

Czech, Kenneth. "Reviews." *America's Civil War* (September 1995).

Davis, Burke. *Sherman's March.* New York: Random House, 1980.

Davis, William C. *Battle at Bull Run.* Baton Rouge: Louisiana State University Press, 1977.

———. *Lincoln's Men.* New York: Touchstone, 1999.

Davis, William, et al. *Civil War Journal: The Leaders.* Nashville: Rutledge Hill Press, 1997.

———. *Civil War Journal: The Battles.* Nashville: Rutledge Hill Press, 1998.

Davis, William, and the Editors of Time-Life Books. *First Blood: Fort Sumter to Bull Run.* Alexandria: Time-Life Books, 1983.

———. *Death in the Trenches: Grant at Petersburg.* Alexandria: Time-Life Books, 1986.

Donald, David H. *Lincoln.* New York: Simon & Schuster, 1995.

Dowdey, Clifford. *Lee.* New York: Bonanza Books, 1965.

Downey, Fairfax. "From Chapultepec to Lookout Mountain." *Civil War Times* 2, no. 5 (August/September 1960): 5.

Dunphy, Owen. "March to the Sea." *America's Civil War* 3, no. 2 (July 1990): 49.

Dupuy, Ernest, and Trevor Dupuy. *The Compact History of the Civil War.* New York: MJF Books, 1993.

Editors of American Heritage. *The American Heritage Pictorial History of the Presidents.* Great Neck, NJ: American Heritage.

Editors of Time-Life Books. *1863: Turning Point of the Civil War.* Alexandria: Time-Life Books, 1998.

Eisenhower, John. *So Far from God: The U. S. War with Mexico, 1846–1848.* New York: Random House, 1989.

Eisenschimal, Otto. "Sherman: Hero or War Criminal." *Civil War Times Illustrated* 2, no. 9 (January 1964): 35.

Engle, Stephen. *Don Carlos Buell: Most Promising of All.* Chapel Hill: The University of North Carolina Press, 1999.

Faeder, Gustav. "Superb Was the Day." *America's Civil War* 3, no. 6 (March 1991): 51–52.

Farrell, Rick. "Lincoln Takes Charge." *Civil War Times Illustrated* (February 2001).

Fellman, Michael. *Citizen Sherman.* New York: Random House, 1995.

Fleming, Thomas. "The Big Parade." *Civil War Chronicles* (Summer 1991).

Foote, Shelby. *The Civil War, A Narrative: Fort Sumter to Perryville.* New York: Random House, 1958.

Fowler, Robert. *The Assassination of Abraham Lincoln.* Yorktown: Eastern Acorn Press, 1987.

Freedman, Russell. *Lincoln: a Photobiography.* New York: Clarion Books, 1987.

Freeman, Douglas Southall. *Lee of Virginia.* New York: Charles Scribner's Sons, 1958.

Frost, Lawrence A. *U. S. Grant Album.* New York: Bonanza Books, 1966.

Furgurson, Ernest B. *Chancellorsville 1863: The Souls of the Brave.* New York: Vintage Books, 1993.

———. *Not War But Murder: Cold Harbor 1864.* New York: Alfred A. Knopf, 2000.

Garrison, Webb. *The Lincoln No One Knows.* Nashville: Rutledge Hill Press, 1993.

Glatthaar, Joseph. *The March to the Sea and Beyond.* New York: University Press, 1985.

Goolrick, William K., and the Editors of Time-Life Books. *Rebels Resurgent: Fredericksburg to Chancellorsville.* Alexandria: Time-Life Books, 1985.

Greene, Wilson. *The Second Battle of Manassas.* Conshohocken, PA: Eastern National, 1995.

Grimsley, Mark. "Overthrown." *Civil War Times Illustrated* 19, no. 7 (November 1980): 20, 25.

———. "Ulysses S. Grant." *Civil War Times Illustrated* 28, no. 7 (January/February 1990): 21–26, 47–48, 61–63.

———. *The Hard Hand of War.* New York: Cambridge University Press, 1995.

Haskew, Michael. "Icy Assault Routed." *America's Civil War* 4 (May 1991).

Hassler, Warren Jr. *Commanders of the Army of the Potomac.* Baton Rouge: Louisiana State University Press, 1962.

———. "Fighting Joe Hooker." *Civil War Times Illustrated* 14 (August 1975): 6.

Hassler, William. *A. P. Hill: Lee's Forgotten General.* Chapel Hill: The University of North Carolina Press, 1957.

Hattaway, Herman. *Shades of Blue and Gray.* Columbia: University of Missouri Press, 1997.

Hearn, Chester. *When the Devil Came Down to Dixie.* Baton Rouge: Louisiana State University Press, 1997.

Hebert, Walter H. *Fighting Joe Hooker.* Indianapolis: The Bobbs-Merrill Company, 1944.

Hemingway, Al. "Travel." *America's Civil War* 8, no. 1 (March 1995): 70.

Hennessy, John J. "The Second Battle of Manassas: Lee Suppresses the 'Miscreant' Pope." *Blue & Gray* 9, no. 6 (August 1992): 1, 11.

———. *Return to Bull Run.* New York: Simon & Schuster, 1993.

Hoffsommer, Robert, ed. "Sergeant Charles Veil's Memoir on the Death of Reynolds." *Civil War Times Illustrated* 21, no. 4 (June 1982): 23.

Jaynes, Gregory, and the Editors of Time-Life Books. *The Killing Ground: Wilderness to Cold Harbor.* Alexandria: Time-Life Books, 1986.

Johnson, Timothy. *Winfield Scott.* Lawrence: University Press of Kansas, 1998.

Jones, Virgil. "The Kilpatrick-Dahlgren Raid: Boldly Planned . . . Timidly Executed." *Civil War Times Illustrated* 4, no. 1 (April 1965): 13–14.

Jones, Wilmer L. *After the Thunder: Fourteen Men Who Shaped Post-Civil War America.* Dallas: Taylor Publishing Company, 2000.

————. *Behind Enemy Lines: Civil War Spies, Raiders, and Guerrillas*. Dallas: Taylor Publishing Company, 2001.

Jordan, David M. *Winfield Scott Hancock: A Soldier's Life*. Bloomington: Indiana University Press, 1996.

King, Kendall. "Bold, But Not Too Bold." *America's Civil War* 6, no. 1 (March 1993): 49.

Kiper, Richard L. *Major General John Alexander McClernand: Politician in Uniform*. Kent: The Kent State University Press, 1999.

Klein, Frederic. "Butler at Bermuda Hundred." *Civil War Times Illustrated* 6, no. 7 (November 1967): 6, 47.

Korn, Jerry, and the Editors of Time-Life Books. *The Fight For Chattanooga: Chickamauga to Missionary Ridge*. Alexandria: Time-Life Books, 1985.

————. *War on the Mississippi: Grant's Vicksburg Campaign*. Alexandria: Time-Life Books, 1985.

————. *Pursuit to Appomattox: The Last Battle*. Alexandria: Time-Life Books, 1987.

Kross, Gary. "To Die Like Soldiers." *Blue & Gray* 15, no. 5 (Campaign, 1998): 6–7.

Kunhardt, Philip, et al. *Lincoln*. New York: Alfred A. Knopf, 1992.

Lamers, William M. *The Edge of Glory, A Biography of General William S. Rosecrans, U.S.A.* Baton Rouge: Louisiana State University Press, 1961.

Lee, Angela. "Tangling With 'Kilpatrick.'" *Civil War Times Illustrated* 37, no. 3 (June 1998): 67–68.

Lewis, Lloyd. *Sherman: Fighting Prophet*. New York: Harcourt, Brace & World, 1958.

Lewis, Thomas A., and the Editors of Time-Life Books. *The Shenandoah in Flames: The Valley Campaign of 1864*. Alexandria: Time-Life Books, 1987.

————. *The Guns of Cedar Creek*. New York: Harper & Row, 1988.

Longacre, Edward G. "Judson Kilpatrick." *Civil War Times Illustrated* 10, no. 1 (April 1971): 25–33.

————. "John F. Reynolds, General." *Civil War Times Illustrated* 11, no. 5 (August 1972): 35–43, 54.

————. "Fortune's Fool." *Civil War Times Illustrated* 18, no. 2 (May 1979): 20–31.

————. "Congressman Becomes General: General John A. McClernand." *Civil War Times Illustrated* 21, no. 7 (November 1982): 31–39.

————. "Damnable Dan Sickles." *Civil War Times Illustrated* 23 (May 1984): 16.

————. "A General Vanquished in the West." *Civil War Times Illustrated* 24, no. 6 (October 1985): 16–19, 44–47.

————. *Army of Amateurs: General Benjamin F. Butler and the Army of the James, 1863–1865*. Mechanicsburg, PA: Stackpole Books, 1997.

Longford, Lord. *Abraham Lincoln*. New York: G. P. Putnam's Sons, 1975.

Lorant, Stefan. *The Life of Abraham Lincoln*. New York: Bantam Books, Inc., 1976.

————. *Lincoln*. New York: Bonanza Books, 1979.

Luthin, Reinhard H. *The Real Abraham Lincoln*. Englewood Cliffs: Prentice-Hall, Inc., 1960.

Luvaas, Jay. "Burnside's Roanoke Expedition." *Civil War Times Illustrated* 7, no. 8 (December 1968): 47.

Marrin, Albert. *Commander in Chief: Abraham Lincoln and the Civil War*. New York: Dutton Children's Books, 1997.

Marszalek, John F. *Sherman: A Soldier's Passion for Order*. New York: Vintage Books, 1993.

Martin, Samuel J. "Kill-Cavalry." *Civil War Times Illustrated* 38, no. 7 (February 2000): 25–30, 59.

———. *Kill-Cavalry: The Life of Union General Hugh Judson Kilpatrick.* Mechanicsburg, PA: Stackpole Books, 2000.

Marvel, William. *Burnside.* Chapel Hill: University of North Carolina Press, 1991.

McDonough, James L. *War in Kentucky: From Shiloh to Perryville.* Knoxville: The University of Tennessee Press, 1994.

McDonough, James L., and James Jones. *War So Terrible.* New York: W. W. Norton & Company, 1987.

McFall, Arthur. "Grant's Early War Days." *America's Civil War* 7, no. 5 (November 1994): 34.

McFeely, William S. *Grant.* New York: W. W. Norton, 1981.

McGinty, Brian. "Old Brains in the New West." *American History Illustrated* 13, no. 2 (May 1978): 11–18.

McPherson, James M. *Ordeal by Fire.* New York: Alfred A. Knopf, 1982.

———. *Battle Cry of Freedom: The Civil War Era.* New York: Oxford University Press, 1988.

———. *Abraham Lincoln and the Second American Revolution.* New York: Oxford University Press, 1990.

———. "Tried by War." *Civil War Times Illustrated* 34, no. 5 (November/December 1995): 68–75.

Miers, Earl S. *The General Who Marched to Hell.* New York: Collier Books, 1951.

———. *The Web of Victory: Grant at Vicksburg.* Baton Rouge: Louisiana State University Press, 1984.

Mitgang, Herbert. *The Fiery Trial: A Life of Lincoln.* New York: The Viking Press, 1974.

Morris, Roy Jr. *Sheridan: The Life and Wars of General Phil Sheridan.* New York: Vintage Press, 1992

———. "At Perryville, Don Carlos Buell Won a Battlefield Victory, but Lost a Political War." *America's Civil War* 8, no. 4 (September 1995): 6.

———. "Editorial." *America's Civil War* 13, no. 3 (July 2000): 6.

Motts, Wayne E. *"Trust In God and Fear Nothing": General Lewis A. Armistead, CSA.* Gettysburg: Farnsworth House Military Impression, 1994.

Neely, Mark E. *The Last Best Hope of Earth.* Cambridge: Harvard University Press, 1993.

Nellis, David. "'The Damned Rascal:' Benjamin Butler in New Orleans." *Civil War Times Illustrated* 12, no. 6 (October 1973): 4, 8–9.

Nevin, David, and the Editors of Time-Life Books. *The Road to Shiloh: Early Battles in the West.* Alexandria: Time-Life Books, 1983.

Nichols, Edward. *Toward Gettysburg.* New York: The Pennsylvania State University Press, 1958.

Nolan, Dick. *Benjamin Franklin Butler: The Damndest Yankee.* Novato, CA: Presidio Press, 1991.

Nye, Wilbur. "Grant: Genius or Fortune's Child." *Civil War Times Illustrated* 4, no. 3 (June 1965): 8.

Oats, Stephen B. *Abraham Lincoln: The Man behind the Myths.* New York: Harper & Row, Publishers, Inc., 1984.

O'Connor, Richard. *Sheridan: The Inevitable.* Indianapolis: Bobbs Merrill, 1953.

Paludan, Phillip. *The Presidency of Abraham Lincoln.* Lawrence: University Press of Kansas, 1994.

Patterson, Gerald. "The Beast of New Orleans." *Civil War Times Illustrated* 32, no. 2 (May/June 1993): 29–33, 62–66.

Perret, Geoffrey. *Ulysses S. Grant: Soldier and President.* New York: Random House, 1997.

Pfanz, Harry. *Gettysburg—Culp's Hill and Cemetery Hill.* Chapel Hill: University of North Carolina Press, 1993.

Piston, William G. *Lee's Tarnished Lieutenant.* Athens: The University of Georgia Press, 1987.

Poggiali, Leonard. "The Death of U. S. Grant and the Cottage on Mount McGregor." *Blue & Gray* 10, no. 3 (February 1993): 61.

Randall, J. G., and David Donald. *The Civil War and Reconstruction.* Lexington: D. C. Heath & Company, 1969.

Reeder, Red. *The Northern Generals.* New York: Duell, Sloan & Pearce, 1964.

Rice, Gary. "Devil Dan Sickles' Deadly Salients." *America's Civil War* 11, no. 5 (November 1998): 41–43.

Rice, Thomas. "Wading to Glory." *Civil War Times Illustrated* 20, no. 2 (May 1981): 19: 24–25.

Riggs, Derold. "Commander in Chief: Abe Lincoln." *America's Civil War* 13, no. 3 (July 2000): 35–40.

Riley, Michael. *"For God's Sake, Forward," John F. Reynolds, USA.* Gettysburg, PA: Farnsworth House Military Impressions, 1995.

Robertson, James I. *General A. P. Hill: The Story of a Confederate Warrior.* New York: Random House, 1987.

Rofuse, Ethan. "Lincoln Takes Charge." *Civil War Times Illustrated* 39, no. 7 (February 2001): 27.

Roland, Charles. *The American Iliad.* Lexington: University Press of Kentucky, 1991.

Round, Herold. "'Uncle John' Sedgwick." *Civil War Times Illustrated* 5, no. 8 (December 1966): 3, 13–14, 17–19.

Rowland, Thomas J. *George B. McClellan and Civil War History.* Kent: The Kent State University Press, 1998.

Royster, Charles. *The Destructive War.* New York: Alfred A. Knopf, 1991.

Sears, Stephen W. *George B. McClellan, The Young Napoleon.* New York: Ticknor & Fields, 1988.

———. "McClellan vs. Lee: The Seven-Day Trial." *Military Quarterly* 1, no. 1 (Autumn 1988): 11–12.

———. *To the Gates of Richmond: The Peninsula Campaign.* New York: Ticknor & Fields, 1992.

———. "Lincoln and McClellan." In *Lincoln's Generals*, edited by Gabor S. Boritt (New York: Oxford University Press, 1994), 40.

———. *Controversies & Commanders: Dispatches from the Army of the Potomac.* Boston: Houghton Mifflin Company, 1999.

Sell, Bill. *Leaders of the North and South.* New York: Michael Friedman Publishing Group, Inc., 1996.

Sheridan, Philip H. *The Personal Memoirs of P. H. Sheridan.* New York: De Capo Press, 1992.

Shulman, Terry. "To Be Held at All Hazards." *Civil War Times Illustrated* 32, no. 4 (September/October 1993): 47.

Simpson, Brooks D. *Ulysses S. Grants: Triumph Over Adversities, 1862–1865.* Boston: Houghton Mifflin Company, 2000.

Skoch, George. "Burnside's Geography Class." *Civil War Times Illustrated* 33, no. 6 (January/February 1995): 35–36; 39–41.

Smith, David. "The Beast of New Orleans." *Civil War Times Illustrated* 8, no. 6 (October 1969): 12–20.

Smith, Robert. "Impossible Campaign Attempted." *Military History* 10, no. 1 (April, 1993): 34–35.

Stackpole, Edward J. *Chancellorsville: Lee's Greatest Battle*. Harrisburg: Stackpole Books, 1958.

———. "Sheridan's Ride—As It Really Happened." *Civil War Times* 3, no. 6 (October 1961): 12–13.

———. *The Fredericksburg Campaign*. Harrisburg: Stackpole Books, 1991.

Stevens, Joseph E. *1863: The Rebirth of a Nation*. New York: Bantam Books, 1999.

Stevenson, James. "Personality." *America's Civil War* 7, no. 5 (November 1994): 93.

Stokesbury, James L. *A Short History of the Civil War*. New York: William Morrow & Company, Inc., 1995.

Street, James Jr., and the Editors of Time-Life Books. *The Struggle For Tennessee: Tupelo to Stones River*. Alexandria: Time-Life Books, 1985.

Strozier, Charles. *Lincoln's Quest for Union*. New York: Basic Books, Inc., Publishers, 1982.

Suhr, Robert. "The Kilpatrick-Dahlgren Raid on Richmond." *Military Heritage* 1, no. 6 (June 2000): 50.

Swanberg, W. A. *Sickles: The Incredible*. Gettysburg: Stan Clark Military Books, 1956.

Tagg, Larry. *The Generals of Gettysburg*. Mason City, IA: Savas Publishing Company, 1998.

Taylor, John. "Compassion Is Always Due to an Enraged Imbecile." *American History Illustrated* 10, no. 10 (February 1976): 18–20.

———. "With More Sorrow Than I Can Tell." *Civil War Times Illustrated* 20, no. 1 (April 1981): 24.

Thomas, Emory M. "The Lost Confederate of Roanoke." *Civil War Times Illustrated* 15, no. 2 (May 1976): 10–11.

———. "The Kilpatrick-Dahlgren Raid—Part I." *Civil War Times Illustrated* 16, no. 10 (February 1978): 4.

———. "The Kilpatrick-Dahlgren Raid—Part II." *Civil War Times Illustrated* 17, no. 1 (April 1978): 31.

Trinque, Bruce. "Battle Fought on Paper." *America's Civil War* 6, no. 2 (May 1993): 32.

Tucker, Glenn. "George H. Thomas." *Civil War Times Illustrated* 5, no. 1 (April 1966): 32.

———. "Winfield S. Hancock: A Personal Profile." *Civil War Times Illustrated* 7, no. 5 (August 1968): 5–10, 45–47.

———. *Hancock the Superb*. Dayton: Morningside Bookshop, 1980.

Warner, Ezra J. *Generals in Blue: Lives of the Union Commanders*. Baton Rouge: Louisiana State University Press, 1964.

Waugh, John C. *The Class of 1846*. New York: Warner Books, Inc., 1994.

Weigley, Russell. "Philip Sheridan: A Personal Profile." *Civil War Times Illustrated* 7, no. 4 (July 1968): 8.

———. *A Great Civil War: A Military and Political History, 1861–1865*. Bloomington: Indiana University Press, 2000.

Wert, Jeffry T. "Returning to the Killing Ground." *America's Civil War* 4, no. 2 (July, 1991): 18, 25.

———. *Gettysburg, Day Three*. New York: Simon & Schuster, 2001.

Williams, T. Harry. *Lincoln and His Generals*. New York: Alfred Knopf, 1952.

Williams, T. Harry, et al. *The Union Restored*. New York: Time Inc., 1963.

Wilshin, Francis. *Manassas*. Washington: National Park Service, 1953.

Wilson, Ronald. "Meeting at the McLean House." *American History Illustrated* 22, no. 5 (September 1987): 48.

Winchel, Terrence. "A Fierce Little Fight in Mississippi." *Civil War Times Illustrated* 33, no. 3 (July/August 1994): 54–59.

Winders, Richard. *Polk's Army*. College Station: Texas A&M University Press, 1997.

Winslow, Richard Elliott III. *General John Sedgwick*. Novato, CA: Presidio Press, 1982.

Woodworth, Steven E. *Six Armies in Tennessee: The Chickamauga and Chattanooga Campaigns*. Lincoln: University of Nebraska Press, 1998.

Wooster, Robert. *The Civil War 100*. Secaucus, NJ: Carol Publishing Company, 1998.

Index

About the Author

WILMER L. JONES is an independent researcher who has spent the past 45 years studying the Civil War. He is the author of *After the Thunder: Fourteen Men Who Shaped Post–Civil War America* and *Behind Enemy Lines: Civil War Spies, Raiders, and Guerrillas.*